KT-432-482

STEP-BY-STEP COOK BOOK

First published in the United Kingdom in 2007 by
Collins & Brown
10 Southcombe Street
London
W14 0RA

An imprint of Anova Books Company Ltd

Text copyright © National Magazine Company Limited and
Collins & Brown 2007
Photography copyright © Collins & Brown 2007

The moral right of the author has been asserted.

All rights reserved. No part of this publication may be reproduced, stored in a retrieval system, or transmitted in any form or by any means electronic, mechanical, photocopying, recording or otherwise, without the prior written permission of the copyright owner.

The expression *Good Housekeeping* used in the title of the book is the trademark of the National Magazine Company and The Hearst Corporation, registered in the United Kingdom and USA, and other principal countries of the world, and is the absolute property of the National Magazine Company and The Hearst Corporation. The use of this trademark other than with the express permission of The National Magazine Company and The Hearst Corporation is strictly prohibited.

Commissioning Editor: Susannah Blake
Design Manager: Gemma Wilson
Production Manager: Morna McPherson
Editorial Assistant: Tom Stainer
Photographers: Nicky Dowey (recipes) and Craig Robertson (steps)
Home Economists: Mari Mererid Williams and Lucy McKelvie (recipes) and Stella Sargeson (steps)
Assistant Home Economists: Siobhan Boyle and Joanna Lee
Stylist: Susannah Blake
Copy-editor: Jan Cutler
Proofreaders: Barbara Dixon and Anne Johnson
Designer: Ben Cracknell Studios I Ruth Rudd
Nutritional analysis: Clare Emery
Indexer: Hilary Bird

ISBN 978-1-84340-413-2

A CIP catalogue for this book is available from the British Library.

9 8 7 6 5 4 3 2 1

Reproduction by Spectrum Colour Ltd, UK
Printed and bound by CT Printing Ltd., China

This book can be ordered direct from the publisher.
Contact the marketing department, but try your bookshop first.

www.anovabooks.com

Notes

- Both metric and imperial measures are given for the recipes. Follow either set of measures, not a mixture of both, as they are not interchangeable.
- All spoon measures are level. 1 tsp = 5ml spoon; 1 tbsp = 15ml spoon.
- Ovens and grills must be preheated to the specified temperature.
- Use sea salt and freshly ground black pepper unless otherwise suggested.
- Fresh herbs should be used unless dried herbs are specified in a recipe.
- Medium eggs should be used except where otherwise specified. Free-range eggs are recommended.

Dietary guidelines

- Note that certain recipes contain raw or lightly cooked eggs. The young, elderly pregnant women and anyone with immune-deficiency disease should avoid these because of the slight risk of salmonella.
- Note that some recipes contain alcohol. Check the ingredient list before serving to children.

STEP-BY-STEP COOK BOOK

COLLINS & BROWN

Contents

Foreword 9

Kitchen Equipment 10
Basic equipment and utensils 10
Pots, pans and bakeware 13
Electrical equipment 15

Sauces 16
Savoury sauces 18
Fruit sauces 22
Mayonnaise and flavoured butters 23
Salsas 24
Salad dressings 25
Sweet sauces 26
Decorative effects 30

Stocks and Soups 32
Making stock 34
Making soups 36
Simple garnishes 39
The recipes 40

Eggs 50
Basic egg preparation 52
Cooking with eggs 53
Making omelettes 56
Making soufflés 57
Making meringues 58
Making batters 61
The recipes 62

Fish and Shellfish 74
Preparing round fish 76
Preparing flat fish 77
Cooking fish 78
Preparing prawns 83
Preparing crabs 84
Preparing lobsters 85
Preparing mussels and clams 86
Preparing scallops and oysters 87
Preparing squid and cuttlefish 88
Preparing octopus 89
The recipes 90

Poultry and Game Birds 106
Preparing poultry 108
Cooking poultry 112
The recipes 118

Meat and Game 134
Preparing beef 136
Preparing lamb 140
Preparing pork 143
Preparing and cooking ham 146
Preparing hare and rabbit 147
Cooking meat and game 148
Roasting and carving 150
The recipes 152

Vegetables 168
Preparing onions and shallots 170
Preparing garlic and leeks 171
Preparing shoots, stems and corn 172
Preparing peas, beans and pods 174
Mushrooms 175
Preparing vegetable fruits 176
Preparing cabbage and broccoli 180
Preparing roots and tubers 181
Cooking vegetables 183
The recipes 190

Fruit and Nuts **204**
Preparing orchard fruits 206
Preparing citrus fruits 207
Preparing stone fruits 208
Preparing berries and currants 209
Preparing exotic fruits 210
Preparing other fruits 211
Cooking fruit 214
Making smoothies and purées 217
Preparing nuts 218
Preparing chestnuts 220
Preparing coconut 221
The recipes 222

Rice, Grains and Pulses **234**
Cooking rice 236
Making risotto 237
Making paella 238
Making sushi 239
Cooking other grains 240
Cooking polenta 242
Using beans and lentils 243
The recipes 244

Pasta and Noodles **258**
Making fresh pasta 260
Cooking pasta 262
Cooking Asian-style noodles 263
The recipes 264

Pastry **276**
Making pastry 278
Using pastry 280
Using choux 282
Using filo 283
The recipes 284

Sweet and Savoury Breads **298**
Bread basics 300
Shaping loaves 301
Using a bread machine 302
Making classic breads 303
Making pizza and focaccia 306
Cooking with bread 308
The recipes 310

Cakes, Cookies, Biscuits and Traybakes **320**
Lining tins 322
Making cakes 324
Making roulades 327
Making cupcakes and muffins 328
Making cheesecakes 329
Filling and topping cakes 330
Making biscuits 332
Decorating and filling biscuits 338
The recipes 340

Chocolate **354**
Using chocolate 356
The recipes 360

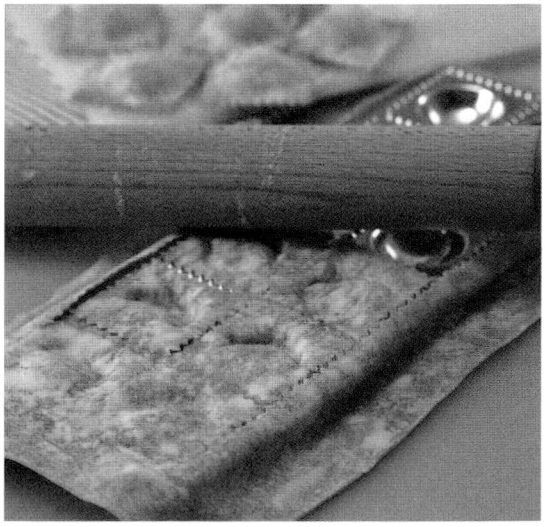

Sugar 370
Working with sugar 372
The recipes 376

Ice creams, Sorbets and Iced Desserts 386
Making ice cream 388
Layering, shaping and rippling 389
Making parfaits 390
Making sorbet 391
The recipes 392

Preserves 402
Preparing jars 404
Potting preserves 405
Making jams 406
Making marmalade 407
Making jellies 408
Making fruit curds and cheeses 409
Making bottled fruits 410
Making pickles 411
Making chutneys 412
Making refrigerator preserves 413
Making relishes 414
Making sauces 415
The recipes 416

Herbs, Spices and Flavourings 426
Using herbs 428
Using spices 429
Making flavoured vinegars 430
Making flavoured sugar and salt 431

Freezing and Drying 432
Freezing stocks, sauces and stews 434
Freezing fruit 435
Freezing vegetables 436
Freezing meat, poultry and fish 437
Drying fruit, vegetables and herbs 438

Microwaves 440
Using a microwave 442
Cooking in the microwave 443

Useful Information 446
Health and nutrition 446
Food storage and hygiene 448
Glossary of cookery terms 450

Index 454

Foreword

I always say I learned to cook twice – first while watching my mum rustling up supper or more extravagant dishes in our kitchen at home and second when I went to train at cookery school. Both I count with equal value. The home kitchen was important as that was where most of the mistakes were made! And the school training was invaluable as I learned all the elementary rules of cooking.

In this book we've put together a winning combination of both. We start with the basics in each chapter, teaching you the step-by-step way to prepare and cook lots of different ingredients. The second part of the chapter puts those techniques into practice with gorgeous recipes, all of which have been rigorously tested in the Good Housekeeping Institute so they're guaranteed to work the first time you make them.

Since the Good Housekeeping Institute was set up in 1924, there's been a significant change in women's role in society with more of us going out to work than ever before. But knowing how to cook is still just as important as it was then. We hope you enjoy this book, learn from it and use it for many years to come.

Emma

Emma Marsden
Cookery Editor

Basic equipment and utensils

Chopping boards

These kitchen essentials come in two materials: wood and some type of plastic (usually polypropylene).

Having a range of sizes will give you more chopping options, with small boards for chopping or slicing small quantities. For most people, three boards should suffice, in sizes of: 15–23cm (6–9in), 20.5–30.5cm (8–12in) and 25.5–35.5cm (10–14in).

Wood Wooden boards are best made from a single plank of wood rather than several pieces glued together, as the joins may harbour bacteria. Some modern wooden boards nowadays are dishwasher-safe, although many of them are not. You should try to check beforehand if this is important to you.

Polypropylene These boards can be bought in colour-coded sets so that you can have separate boards for meat, fish, and fruit and vegetables. They are suitable for washing in the dishwasher.

Knives

Good knives are essential and there are three cardinal rules to follow when buying knives.

- Buy knives singly, rather than in a set: the different sizes chosen to represent one manufacturer's knife set might not suit you.
- Try them out before buying – you need to hold the knife to see if it feels comfortable and balanced in your hand.
- Don't try to save money: knives are an investment, and good blades never come cheap.

At the very minimum, there are five basic types of knife, which will set you up you for most tasks:

- A small paring knife.
- A carving knife suitable for filleting, slicing and boning.
- A large 'cook's' knife for general chopping and slicing.
- A bread knife with serrated edge.
- A utility knife.

Sharp blades

Keep your knives sharp or they will be difficult – and probably dangerous – to use. There are several types of sharpener available: the traditional steel or whetstone is adequate for most home cooks, but the best ones have a diamond coating that is particularly hard-wearing. Remember that, as a general rule to go by, it is best to sharpen knives little but often.

Scales

Accurate measurement is essential when following most recipes, particularly baking. Usually used to measure dry ingredients, the most accurate scale is the electronic type, capable of weighing up to 2kg (4½lb) or 5kg (11lb) in increments of 1–5g. Buy one with a flat platform on which you can put your own bowl or measuring jug and always remember to set the scale to zero before adding the ingredients.

Measuring jugs

These can be plastic or glass, and are available in sizes ranging from 500ml (18fl oz) to 2 litres (3½ pints), or even 3 litres (5¼ pints). Have two – a large one and a small one – marked with both metric and imperial.

Measuring cups

Commonly used in the US, these are used for measuring both liquid and dry ingredients. Cups are bought in sets of ¼, ⅓, ½ and 1 cups. A standard 1 cup measure is equivalent to about 250ml (9fl oz).

Measuring spoons

Useful for the smallest units, accurate spoon measurements go up to 15ml (1 tbsp). These may be in plastic or metal, and often come in sets attached together on a ring.

Mixing bowls

For small quantities, the bowls you use for soup, cereals and so on will suffice. However, when mixing larger quantities, such as cake or bread mixtures, you will need at least two large bowls, including one very large one with a diameter of up to 38cm (15in).

Stainless steel bowls work best when you are using a hand whisk, or when you need to place the bowl into a larger bowl filled with iced water for chilling down or to place it over simmering water.

Easy slicing

- A mandolin offers the easiest way of making uniform, thin slices or shreds (see page 182). French metal ones are the best but also pricey.
- Smaller mandolins, which usually have a plastic frame holding the blades, are less versatile but also cheaper.
- A mezzaluna – a curved board and knife – is good for chopping herbs.

Plastic or glass bowls are best if you need to use them in the microwave.

Steel bowls with a rubber foot will keep their grip on the worksurface.

Bowls with gently tapered sides – much wider at the rim than at the base – will be useful for mixing dough and can also be used as salad bowls.

Spoons

For general mixing, the cheap and sturdy wooden spoon still can't be beaten, but equivalents made from thermoplastic materials are heatproof and may suit you better. The spoon should be stiff, so that it can cope with thick foods such as polenta and dough.

A large metal spoon for folding ingredients together and a slotted spoon for skimming and lifting ingredients out of liquids are also invaluable items to have.

Spatulas

You should have at least three: one metal for use in ordinary pans and one acrylic (to withstand high temperatures), and one suitable for non-stick pans.

Metal spatulas should be sturdy enough to lift heavy foods, such as a joint that you are browning before braising it.

Tongs

Most cooks will recommend that you buy at least one pair of tongs. You are bound to find them invaluable and, if this is your first ever pair, you will wonder how you managed without them in the kitchen up until now.

The all-metal ones with scalloped edges on the gripping heads are particularly good. They can be used for lifting food in and out of pans and for turning – which is especially useful for frying because spitting fat can be dangerous.

Other extras

- Fine sieve
- Colander
- Steamer
- Bulb baster (metal is best)
- Apple corer
- Vegetable peeler
- Wire whisks
- Pastry brush
- Rolling pin
- Graters: fine and coarse
- Poultry shears (or sturdy kitchen scissors)
- Digital instant-read thermometer

Pots, pans and bakeware

There is a huge variety of cooking vessels available, made from different materials. The main choices are:

- Stainless steel (with an inner core of another metal to improve heat conduction).
- Cast iron (plain or enamelled).
- Aluminium (usually anodised for stick-resistance and lower reactivity with food).

Frying pans

The most practical choices are aluminium or stainless steel with a non-stick coating. A range of sizes is useful: 20.5cm (8in), 24–25.5cm (9½–10in) and 30cm (11½in).

Look for pans with a thick base, for even and efficient heating. Non-stick coatings reduce oil and fat usage, but must be used with non-metal utensils to prevent scratches, and shouldn't be allowed to get very hot when empty.

Cast iron pans

These may be enamelled or plain. Although heavy for their size, they are favoured by some cooks for their slow, steady conduction of heat – and some can be used in the oven.

Sauté pans

Consider buying one of these; its straight sides make it better than a frying pan for braising on the hob.

Pans

For most purposes, especially for general all-purpose pans and stockpots, stainless steel is best. You need at least three sizes of pan: small (about 16cm/6¼in in diameter), medium (about 24cm/9½in in diameter), and one large pan for making stock and pasta. Non-stick properties are generally less important in pans, but can be useful when making sauces or egg-based dishes. Anodised aluminium, which is stick-resistant, is another good choice for smaller pans.

Your hob

This is probably the most useful item in your kitchen, and if you were to count the number of times you use it every day, you would probably be amazed. Most pans are designed for use on conventional gas or electric hobs. If you have an induction or halogen hob, however, you will always need to ensure that any cookware you purchase will be compatible with it.

Casseroles

Cast iron is the material of choice for a flameproof casserole. It conducts heat slowly and steadily, and its thick walls and bases protect the food from high oven heat.

These casseroles are enamelled and must be treated with care. Although expensive, if treated well, they will last for decades. It's worth having at least two, one for small dishes and one larger one. The oval-shaped dishes are best for larger casseroles.

Bakeware

As well as being thin enough to conduct heat quickly and efficiently, bakeware should be sturdy enough not to warp. Most bakeware is made from aluminium, and it may have enamel or non-stick coatings.

Roasting tins Enamelled steel is excellent, and many have non-stick coatings, which make cleaning easier. It's worth having several sizes:

- A small one for just a few pieces of meat or vegetables.
- A medium-size tin for chickens and small joints.
- A very large one for turkeys or cooking for a crowd.

Baking trays Shallower than a roasting tin, these are good for cooking potatoes and vegetables that don't produce a lot of liquid during cooking.

Cake tins Available in many shapes and sizes, tins may be single-piece, loose-based or spring-form.

Loaf tins Available in various sizes, one of the most useful is probably a 900g (2lb) tin.

Pie tins and muffin tins You should have both single-piece tins and loose-based tins for flans and pies.

Baking dishes Usually ceramic or Pyrex, you should have them in several sizes, ranging from 15–23cm (6–9in) to 25.5–35.5cm (10–14in).

Silicone

A newer material for muffin pans and other bakeware is flexible, oven-safe silicone. It is safe to touch straight from the oven, is inherently non-stick and is also flexible – making it a lot easier to remove muffins and other bakes from their pans than it used to be.

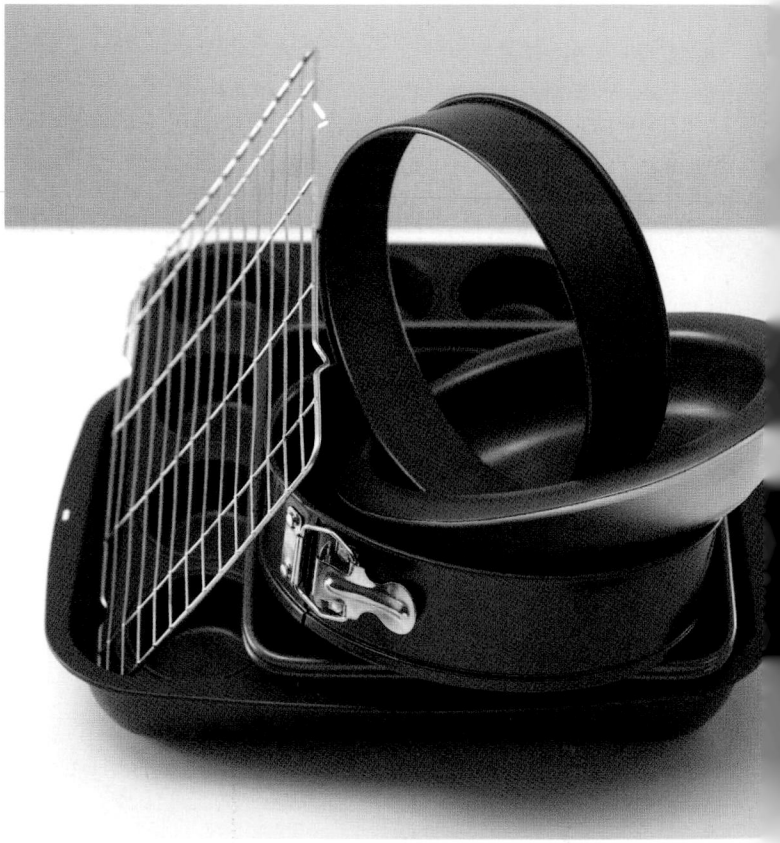

Electrical equipment

Electrical equipment

For quick preparation, a food processor is extremely useful. When it comes to all electrical kitchen appliances, however, the amount of space you have is a consideration.

Food processor For certain tasks, such as making breadcrumbs or pastry or for chopping large quantities of onions or nuts, food processors are unbeatable. Most come with a number of attachments – dough hooks, graters, slicers – which are well worth having even if only for occasional use.

Blenders These are less versatile than food processors, but unmatched for certain tasks, such as puréeing fruit, vegetables and soups, and for making smoothies.

The traditional jug blender is great but some cooks prefer a 'stick' blender, which can be used directly in a pan, bowl or jug.

Freestanding mixers Some cooks don't see the need for electric mixers whereas others swear by them. They may well be a good investment if you do a lot of baking, but decide first whether you have space in your kitchen. They take up a lot, and are big and heavy to store until needed.

Electric hand mixers Useful for creaming together butter and sugar in baking and for making meringues. They don't take up a lot of space and can be packed away easily.

Bread machines Kneading bread by hand takes very little time and effort but bread machines are useful for making and baking bread if you have limited time. Doughs can also be prepared by the machine and then shaped and baked in the oven.

Ice cream makers Even if you make ice cream only a few times a year, a good machine will save lots of time and produce better results. The type with two freezing tubs enables you to make two flavours at once, or a larger quantity of a single flavour.

Get the best

To make sure that you stay up to date at all times and that you always get the very best that a modern cook can have, it's a good idea to check out the latest equipment that has been tried and tested on your behalf by the Good Housekeeping Institute on their website: www.goodhousekeeping.co.uk

1 SAUCES, DRESSINGS AND ACCOMPANIMENTS

The addition of rich gravies and sauces can transform both savoury and sweet dishes – from the simplest drizzle of balsamic dressing over a salad, a spoonful of refreshing salsa served with grilled fish or chicken, a dollop of creamy mayonnaise for dunking chips into or fresh pesto tossed with pasta to lashings of custard poured over fruit pies or crumbles or a swirl of raspberry coulis or chocolate sauce with ice cream. This chapter is packed with recipes and easy-to-follow techniques for all the classic sauces and accompaniments you will ever want to make. There's essential advice plus variations and troubleshooting tips on saving a split or curdled sauce, and handy hints on freezing and ideas for creating stunning decorative effects for special meals.

Savoury sauces

Sauces and gravies add the finishing touch to many dishes, adding moisture to roast meats or a smooth texture and contrasting flavour that complements grilled meats, fish and vegetables.

White wine gravy

Perfect served with roast chicken. To serve eight, you will need 4 tbsp plain flour, 500ml (18fl oz) chicken stock, 150ml (¼ pint) dry white wine, 2 tbsp redcurrant jelly, salt and ground black pepper.

1 When the chicken is cooked, skim the fat from the juices in the roasting tin. In a bowl, mix 3 tbsp of the juices with the flour to make a paste.

2 Pour the chicken stock, white wine and redcurrant jelly into the roasting tin and scrape the residue from the base of the tin using a wooden spoon.

3 Return the roasting tin to the heat and whisk in the flour mixture. Simmer gently for 5–10 minutes, then season to taste with salt and pepper and pour into a jug to serve.

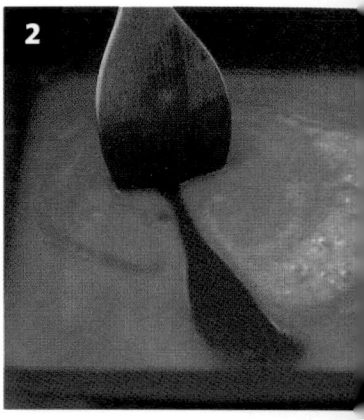

Rich red wine gravy

This rich gravy goes well with roasted chicken or meat such as beef. To serve eight, you will need 4 tbsp plain flour, 300ml (½ pint) red wine, 1.1 litres (2 pints) chicken or beef stock, salt and ground black pepper.

1 When the roast is cooked, strain the juices from the roasting tin into a bowl and skim off any fat, reserving 3 tbsp of the fat.

2 Return the fat to the tin and whisk in the flour. Cook over a medium heat until the flour browns. Remove from the heat, stir in wine or port until smooth. Bubble for 2–3 minutes.

3 Stir in the chicken or meat juices and the stock, then bubble for 10–15 minutes until reduced by half and the gravy is smooth. Skim off any fat and season.

Shallot and mushroom sauce

To serve six, you will need 375g (13oz) shallots, peeled, 1 tbsp olive oil, 300ml (½ pint) red wine, 225g (8oz) quartered button mushrooms, 1 halved celery stick, 4 thyme sprigs, 40g (1½oz) butter, 1 tsp sugar, 15g (½oz) flour.

1 Chop 2 shallots and fry in the oil until golden. Add the wine and bubble to reduce to 2 tbsp.

2 Add the mushrooms and cook for 3 minutes. Add 600ml (1 pint) water, the celery and thyme; simmer for 20 minutes. Heat 25g (1oz) butter in another pan, add the whole shallots and sugar, cover and cook gently for 20 minutes. Remove the thyme and celery, pour sauce over the shallots and reduce by half. Blend remaining butter and flour, whisk into the sauce and simmer for 1–2 minutes. Season.

Bread sauce

To serve eight, you will need 1 quartered onion, 4 cloves, 2 bay leaves, 450ml (¾ pint) milk, 175g (6oz) fresh breadcrumbs, 50g (2oz) butter, 200ml (7fl oz) crème fraîche, salt and ground black pepper.

1 Stud each onion quarter with a clove, then put in a pan with 1 bay leaf and the milk. Gently heat on the lowest setting for 15 minutes.

2 Remove the pan from the heat and discard the onion quarters, cloves and bay leaf.

3 Stir the breadcrumbs, butter and crème fraîche into the milk. Season with salt and black pepper and serve garnished with a bay leaf.

4 Alternatively, store in the refrigerator for up to two days.

Béchamel sauce

For 300ml (½ pint) sauce, you will need 1 slice of onion, 6 black peppercorns, 1 bay leaf, 1 blade of mace, 300ml (½ pint) semi-skimmed milk, 15g (½oz) butter, 15g (½oz) plain flour, a pinch of freshly grated nutmeg, salt and ground black pepper.

1 Put the onion, peppercorns, bay leaf, mace and milk in a pan. Bring almost to the boil, then remove from the heat, cover, and leave to infuse for 20 minutes. Strain.

2 Melt the butter in a pan over a low heat. Add the flour and cook, stirring, for 1 minute; do not colour.

3 Remove from the heat and slowly pour in the milk, whisking. Season with salt, pepper and nutmeg.

4 Return to the heat and cook, stirring, until the sauce is thickened and smooth. Simmer for 12 minutes.

Variations

- **Simple white sauce** Omit the seasonings except salt and pepper.
- **Thick binding sauce** Increase the butter and flour to 25g (1oz) each.
- **Cheese sauce** Stir in 50g (2oz) grated Cheddar or Gruyère cheese and a pinch of powdered mustard.
- **Parsley sauce** Stir in 2 tbsp finely chopped parsley.
- **Onion sauce** At step 4, stir in a large, finely diced, sautéed onion.

Hollandaise sauce

To serve six, you will need 4 tbsp white wine vinegar, a blade of mace, 1 slice of onion, 1 bay leaf, 6 black peppercorns, 3 medium egg yolks, 150g (5oz) unsalted butter, a little lemon juice, salt and white pepper.

1 Put the vinegar, mace, onion, bay leaf and peppercorns in a pan. Bring to the boil and reduce to 1 tbsp. Cut the butter into ten pieces.

2 Put the egg yolks in a heatproof bowl with one piece of butter and a pinch of salt. Beat, then strain in the vinegar mixture. Place over a pan of hot water, making sure it doesn't touch the water. Whisk for 3 minutes until pale and starting to thicken.

3 Add a piece of butter and beat until absorbed. Repeat with the remaining pieces of butter. Season and add lemon juice to taste. Serve.

Perfect results

- Make sure the sauce doesn't get too hot during cooking; if in doubt, dip the base of the bowl in very cold water for a couple of seconds.
- Beat in each piece of butter completely before adding the next.
- If the sauce begins to curdle, add an ice cube, then beat again.

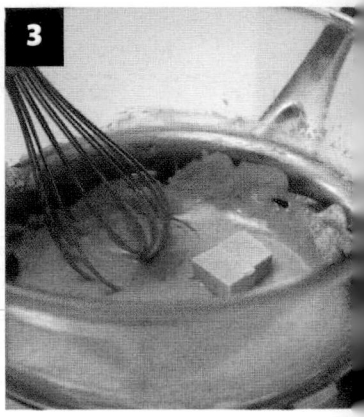

Béarnaise sauce

To serve four to six, you will need 4 tbsp white wine vinegar, 2 finely chopped shallots, a few sprigs of fresh tarragon, 6 black peppercorns, 2 medium egg yolks, 75g (3oz) unsalted butter at room temperature, 2 tsp freshly chopped parsley or chervil (optional), salt and white pepper.

1 Put the vinegar, shallots, tarragon and peppercorns in a pan. Bring to the boil and reduce to 1 tbsp.

2 Cut the butter into ten pieces. Put the egg yolks in a heatproof bowl with one piece of butter and a pinch of salt. Beat, then strain in the vinegar. Place over a pan of hot water. Whisk for 3–4 minutes until pale and starting to thicken.

3 Add a piece of butter and beat in until completely absorbed. Repeat with the remaining butter. Season with salt and pepper to taste. Stir in the herbs, if using. Serve.

Simple tomato sauce

To serve eight, you will need 2 chopped Spanish onions, 4 tbsp olive oil, 2 crushed garlic cloves, 2 × 400g cans chopped plum tomatoes, 2 tbsp torn basil leaves, salt and ground black pepper.

1 Gently fry the onions in the oil for 10 minutes. Add the garlic and cook for a further 10 minutes, stirring occasionally, until very soft.

2 Add the tomatoes and season. Bring to the boil and simmer gently for 30 minutes or until the sauce is thick and pulpy. Add the basil and check the seasoning.

Pesto

Use on pasta or in salad dressings, mixed into crème fraîche for dips, or spread on toasted ciabatta and topped with cheese and tomato. To serve four, you will need 50g (2oz) fresh basil leaves, roughly torn, 1–2 garlic cloves, 25g (1oz) pinenuts, 6 tbsp extra virgin olive oil, 2 tbsp freshly grated Parmesan, salt and ground black pepper, lemon juice to taste (optional).

1 Put the basil leaves in a food processor with the garlic, pinenuts and 2 tbsp olive oil. Process to a fairly smooth paste.

2 Gradually add the remaining oil and season with salt and pepper.

3 Transfer to a bowl and stir in the Parmesan. Check the seasoning and add a squeeze of lemon juice if you like. Store in the refrigerator for up to three days, cover with a thin layer of olive oil and seal tightly.

Variations

- **Coriander pesto** Use fresh coriander instead of basil and add 1 deseeded and finely chopped chilli with the garlic. Omit the cheese.
- **Rocket pesto** Replace the basil with rocket leaves and add 1 tbsp freshly chopped parsley.
- **Sun-dried tomato pesto** Replace half the basil with 50g (2oz) sun-dried tomatoes, drained of oil and roughly chopped. Blend.

Fruit sauces

Tart fruit sauces complement meat well. They are traditionally served with poultry, game and fatty meats such as pork, duck and goose, which are suited to the astringency of fruit sauces.

Cranberry sauce

To serve eight, you will need 225g (8oz) fresh cranberries, grated zest and juice of 1 orange, 4 tbsp fine-shred marmalade, 125g (4oz) light muscovado sugar, 50ml (2fl oz) port.

1 Put all the ingredients in a pan.

2 Bring to the boil and simmer for 5–10 minutes, stirring occasionally, until thick. Store in the refrigerator.

Apple sauce

This is the perfect accompaniment for roast pork or goose.

To serve eight, you will need about 450g (1lb) cooking apples (such as Bramleys), 2 tbsp sugar (or to taste), 25g (1oz) butter.

1 Peel, core and slice the apples and put them in a pan with 2–3 tbsp water.

2 Cover and cook gently for about 10 minutes, stirring occasionally, until soft and reduced to a pulp.

3 Beat the pulp with a wooden spoon until smooth, then pass it through a sieve if you want a very smooth sauce. Stir in sugar to taste and then the butter. Serve warm.

Variations

- Apple sauce can be seasoned with a little cinnamon, nutmeg or mace.
- You can use dessert apples instead of cooking apples. Granny Smiths and Cox's Orange Pippin would both be good choices.
- Sweeten the sauce with honey instead of sugar if you wish.

Freezing tip

Both these fruit sauces can be frozen for up to one month. Follow the instructions on page 434 for freezing sauces.

Mayonnaise and flavoured butters

The simplest of accompaniments, mayonnaise goes well with salads, poached fish and poultry, while a slice of flavoured butter makes a delicious topping for grilled meats, fish and vegetables.

Mayonnaise

For 250ml (9fl oz), you will need 2 large egg yolks, 1 tsp English mustard, 200ml (7fl oz) sunflower oil, 100ml (3½fl oz) virgin olive oil, 1 tsp white wine vinegar or lemon juice, salt and ground black pepper.

1 Put the egg yolks in a 900ml (1½ pint) bowl. Stir in the mustard, 1 tsp salt and plenty of black pepper.

2 Combine the oils and add 1 tsp to the egg yolks. Whisk thoroughly, then add another 1 tsp and whisk until thickened. Continue adding about half the oil, 1 tbsp at a time. Whisk in the vinegar or lemon juice, then add the oil in a thin, steady stream until the mayonnaise is thick.

3 Check the seasoning, adding more vinegar or lemon juice if necessary. Cover and keep in the refrigerator for up to four days.

Cook's tips

Sometimes mayonnaise splits or curdles but it's easy to fix:

- Add a splash of cold water (about 1 tbsp) and stir in with a spoon. Continue with the recipe.
- If this doesn't work, put another egg yolk into a clean bowl and gradually whisk in the curdled mixture 1 tbsp at a time.

Flavoured butter

Allow 25g (1oz) soft unsalted butter per serving.

1 Beat in the flavourings (see Variations). Turn out on to clingfilm, shape into a log, and wrap tightly. Chill in the refrigerator for at least 1 hour. (Or freeze for up to 1 month.)

2 Slice the log into pieces, about 5mm (¼in) thick and serve.

Variations

For 125g (4oz) unsalted butter:

- **Anchovy butter** 6 mashed anchovy fillets.
- **Herb butter** 2 tbsp finely chopped herbs, a squeeze of lemon juice.
- **Garlic butter** 1 crushed garlic clove, 2 tsp finely chopped fresh parsley.

Salsas

Finely chopped fresh herbs and raw ingredients make salsas a tasty addition to meat and fish. They are quick to make and have a refreshing flavour, and you can create endless variations.

Avocado salsa

Particularly good with fish and Mexican-style dishes.
To serve four to six, you will need 3 large ripe tomatoes, 1 large red pepper, 2 small red chillies, 1 red onion, finely chopped, 4 tbsp freshly chopped coriander, 2 tbsp chopped parsley, 2 ripe avocados, salt and ground black pepper.

1 Quarter, deseed and dice the tomatoes. Core, deseed and finely chop the pepper. Then halve, deseed and finely chop the chillies and combine with the tomatoes, peppers, onion and herbs.

2 Halve, stone, peel and dice the avocados. Add to the salsa and season well with salt and pepper. Toss well and serve within about 10 minutes. (Cut avocado flesh will discolour if left for longer than this.)

About salsas

The word *salsa* means different things in various languages, but all have the following in common:

- They are a type of relish, containing mostly raw ingredients, for serving alongside a meat or fish dish.
- They are highly flavoured, so you only need a little for each serving.
- They always contain at least one form of acid, to give them 'bite'.

Salsa verde

This piquant sauce is good for grilled fish and meat.
To serve four, you will need a small handful of parsley, about 40g (1½oz) 6 tbsp fresh white breadcrumbs, 5 tbsp extra virgin olive oil, 1 tsp capers, 1 gherkin, 2 tbsp lemon juice, 1 tbsp chopped chives.

1 Put all the ingredients in a food processor. Process until combined.

2 Transfer to a bowl, check the seasoning and adjust as necessary.

Salad dressings

Whether you prefer your dressing tart and piquant or rich and creamy, always dress and toss your salad just before serving, and avoid overdressing – instead simply aim to coat the leaves well.

Balsamic dressing

To serve four, you will need 2 tbsp balsamic vinegar, 4 tbsp extra virgin olive oil, salt and ground black pepper.

1 Whisk the vinegar and oil in a small bowl. Season with salt and pepper to taste.

2 If not using immediately, whisk briefly before drizzling over salad.

Cook's tips

- Add 1 tsp cold water to the dressing to help it to emulsify easily.
- To get a really good emulsion, shake the dressing vigorously in a screw-topped jar.

French dressing

To make 100ml (3½fl oz), you will need 1 tsp Dijon mustard, a pinch of sugar, 1 tbsp red or white wine vinegar, 6 tbsp extra virgin olive oil, salt and ground black pepper.

1 Put the mustard, sugar and vinegar in a small bowl, and season with salt and pepper. Whisk thoroughly until well combined, then gradually whisk in the oil until thoroughly combined.

Variations

- **Herb dressing** Use half the mustard, replace the vinegar with lemon juice, and add 2 tbsp chopped herbs, such as parsley, chervil and chives.
- **Garlic dressing** Add 1 garlic clove, crushed, to the dressing at step 2.

Blue cheese dressing

To serve four, you will need 50g (2oz) Roquefort cheese, 2 tbsp low-fat yogurt, 1 tbsp white wine vinegar, 5 tbsp extra virgin olive oil.

1 Crumble the cheese into a food processor with the yogurt, vinegar and olive oil.

2 Whiz for 1 minute until thoroughly combined. Season to taste.

Sweet sauces

Sweet sauces can transform simple sweet dishes and desserts such as home-made ice cream, stewed or poached fruit and soufflés into decadent desserts and luscious puddings with very little effort.

Vanilla custard

Perfect as an accompaniment to hot desserts, such as crumbles, cobblers and pies, a simple vanilla custard can be served hot or cold.
To serve eight, you will need 600ml (1 pint) full-fat milk, 1 vanilla pod or 1 tbsp vanilla extract, 6 large egg yolks, 2 tbsp golden caster sugar, 2 tbsp cornflour.

1 Put the milk in a pan. Split the vanilla pod and scrape the seeds into the pan, then drop in the pod. If using vanilla extract, pour it in. Bring to the boil, then turn off the heat and leave to cool for 5 minutes.

2 Put the egg yolks, sugar and cornflour in a bowl and whisk to blend. Remove the vanilla pod from the milk and gradually whisk the warm milk into the egg mixture.

3 Rinse out the pan. Pour the custard back in and heat gently, whisking constantly, for 2–3 minutes. The mixture should thicken enough to coat the back of a wooden spoon in a thin layer. Remove the pan from the heat.

4 If you are not serving the custard immediately, pour it into a jug. Cover the surface with a round of wet greaseproof paper to keep a skin from forming, then cover with clingfilm and chill. To serve hot, reheat very gently.

Perfect custard

- To avoid curdling, don't let the custard overheat during cooking.
- To control the heat better, use a double boiler instead of a pan.
- If you want a much thinner consistency, omit the cornflour.
- Custard may be made up to four hours in advance. Cover and chill until needed.

Chocolate sauce

Simple to make and delicious drizzled over ice cream or a bowl of fresh berries.
To serve four, you will need 75g (3oz) good-quality dark chocolate, 140ml (4½ fl oz) double cream.

1 Put the chocolate in a small heatproof bowl over a pan of gently simmering water. Pour the cream over the top.

2 Leave the chocolate to stand over the heat for about 10 minutes until completely melted – don't stir while it is melting. Once melted, stir the chocolate and cream together until smooth, then serve immediately.

Melting chocolate

- However tempting, be sure to leave the chocolate alone while it is melting: stirring will make it thicken into a sticky mess (see page 356).
- The heat should be at its lowest setting.
- Make sure the base of the bowl is not touching the water.

Variations

- Use a mint-flavoured chocolate instead of plain.
- Add a shot of espresso to the chocolate and cream while they are melting.
- Pour a slug of orange-flavoured liqueur into the chocolate and cream while they are melting.

Butterscotch sauce

To serve eight, you will need 50g (2oz) butter, 50g (2oz) golden caster sugar, 75g (3oz) light muscovado sugar, 150g (5oz) golden syrup, 125ml (4fl oz) double cream, a few drops vanilla, juice of ½ lemon.

1 Heat the butter, sugars and syrup gently, stirring, until melted. Cook for 5 minutes, then remove from heat.

2 Stir in cream, vanilla and lemon, stir over a low heat for 1–2 minutes.

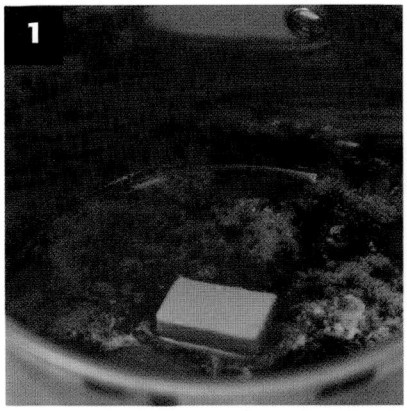

Rum sabayon

This mousse-like sauce is good served with cakes and puddings. (You can also make it with sweet wine or liqueur.)
To serve eight, you will need 75g (3oz) golden caster sugar, 3 medium egg yolks, 140ml (4½fl oz) double cream, 2 tbsp dark rum, the zest of 1 lemon, 2 tbsp lemon juice.

1 Put the sugar in a pan with 100ml (3½fl oz) water. Heat over a low heat until the sugar dissolves, then boil for 7–8 minutes until syrupy.

2 Beat the egg yolks in a bowl until they are thick and pale. Whisking constantly, gradually drizzle in the syrup. Whisk until cool.

3 Whip the cream until stiff, then add the rum, lemon zest and juice. Fold into the egg mixture. Cover and chill until needed.

Perfect sabayon

- Don't let the syrup colour while you're boiling it.
- Add the syrup very gradually to the eggs, if they get too hot, they will curdle.

Rum mascarpone

This sauce is great with baked fruit. To serve six, you will need 250g (9oz) well-chilled mascarpone, 2–3 tbsp light muscovado sugar, 2–3 tbsp dark rum.

1 Spoon the mascarpone into a bowl and stir in the sugar.

2 Add the rum. Cover and set aside in a cool place.

Brandy butter

To serve eight to ten, you will need 125g (4oz) unsalted butter, 125g (4oz) light muscovado sugar, sieved, 6 tbsp brandy.

1 Put the butter in a bowl and beat until very soft. Gradually beat in the sugar until very light and fluffy.

2 Beat in the brandy, a spoonful at a time. Chill for at least 3 hours.

Raspberry coulis

This simple fruit purée is great with ice cream and meringues.
To serve four to six, you will need 225g (8oz) raspberries, 2 tbsp Kirsch or framboise eau de vie, icing sugar, to taste.

1 Put the raspberries in a blender or food processor with the Kirsch or eau de vie. Whiz until they are completely puréed.

2 Transfer the purée to a fine sieve, and press and scrape it through the sieve until nothing is left but the dry pips.

3 Sweeten with icing sugar to taste and chill until needed.

Variations

- Use different soft fruits and liqueurs. For example, try crème de cassis with blackcurrants or amaretto with apricots.
- Make a cooked sauce by simmering fruit half-covered in water with half its weight of sugar. When soft, sieve and sharpen with lemon juice. If you wish, you can thicken it with cornflour, about 1 tsp per 300ml (½ pint) sauce.

Decorative effects

Sauces don't just have to be served as a simple accompaniment to sweet and savoury dishes, they can be used to stunning effect too – drizzled, dripped, trailed and piped to give a truly professional finish.

Teardrops and hearts

1 Put a few spoonfuls of sauce on the serving plate and tip it so that the sauce spreads out in an even layer.

2 Drop small blobs of the second sauce 2.5–5cm (1–2in) from the rim of the plates, to form a circle.

3 Using a small knife, or a skewer, draw the tip knife through the 'blobs' of sauce to form a tail.

Feathering

1 Put a few spoonfuls of the base sauce on your serving plates and tip the plates so that the sauce spreads out in an even layer.

2 Working quickly but carefully, apply concentric circles of decorative sauce to the base.

3 Take a small knife, or a skewer, and run it through the sauces from the edge of the plate to the centre of the circles. Turn the plate and repeat until you have a symmetrical pattern of feather shapes.

Perfect decorations

- For maximum effect, use two sauces of contrasting colour – one as a base and one as decoration. Good examples would be custard (as a base) with fruit coulis, chocolate sauce or butterscotch sauce (as decoration).
- To make your life easier before a dinner party, decorate the plates ahead of time and then refrigerate them until needed.
- Applying the decorative sauce is easiest with a fine-nozzled piping bag (for thicker sauces) or a plastic squeeze-bottle (like those used for sauces in fish and chip shops) for thinner sauces.

Drizzling

An easy and attractive decoration, this can be done with either one or two sauces.

1 Using a plastic bottle or a small spoon, scatter fine 'ribbons' of sauce, in a pattern of roughly parallel lines, all over the plate.

2 If using a second sauce of a contrasting colour, scatter the ribbons at an angle to the first.

3 Alternatively, use one sauce as a base sauce to cover the plate and drizzle the other sauce over the top.

4 Rather than drizzling the sauce on the plate, sauces can also look attractive drizzled over dishes such as ice cream and desserts.

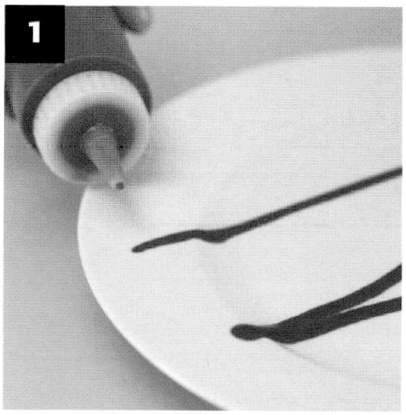

Coloured sauces

Choose two sauces that contrast well together. Spoon the first sauce over half the plate. Spoon the second sauce over the other half and tip the plate in one direction and then another so that the sauces gently flow against each other in a softened shape.

Piping

1 Pipe a wavy border on the plate with the darker sauce, then spoon a thinner pale sauce or cream into the centre and tip the plate to allow it fill up the border.

2 Alternatively, pipe a decorative pattern such as a spiral around a dessert or main course to give a stunning effect.

Rippling

Spoon the base sauce on to the plate, then spoon a contrasting sauce in a circle over the top. Using a knife or skewer, gently stir the circle of sauce so that it ripples into the base sauce.

STOCKS AND SOUPS

A truly sensational soup is usually dependent on using a really good, well-flavoured stock. This chapter guides you through all the basics of making the four essential stocks – vegetable, meat, chicken and fish – and includes hints and tips on degreasing, storing, freezing and getting the best results every time. The illustrated step-by-step techniques then go on to demonstrate the basics of soup-making from blending, puréeing and thickening to making simple garnishes before moving on to the delicious soups in the recipe section. With a great selection to choose from, try your hand at making chilled Gazpacho with tortilla chips, creamy Pea and watercress soup, light Spring vegetable broth, Asian-style Hot and sour soup or chunky Spinach and rice soup.

Making stock

Good stock can mark the difference between a good dish and a great one. It gives depth of flavour to many dishes. There are four main types of stock: vegetable, meat, chicken and fish.

Vegetable stock

For 1.2 litres (2 pints), you will need 225g (8oz) each onions, celery, leeks and carrots, chopped, 2 bay leaves, a few thyme sprigs, 1 small bunch parsley, 10 black peppercorns, ½ tsp salt.

1 Put all the ingredients in a pan and pour in 1.7 litres (3 pints) cold water. Bring slowly to the boil and skim the surface. Partially cover and simmer for 30 minutes. Adjust the seasoning. Strain the stock through a fine sieve and leave to cool.

Meat stock

For 900ml (1½ pints), you will need 450g (1lb) each meat bones and stewing meat, 1 onion, 2 celery sticks and 1 large carrot, sliced, 1 bouquet garni (2 bay leaves, a few thyme sprigs and a small bunch parsley), 1 tsp black peppercorns, ½ tsp salt

1 Preheat the oven to 220°C (200°C fan oven) gas 7. Put the meat and bones in a roasting tin and roast for 30–40 minutes, turning now and again, until they are well browned.

2 Put the bones in a large pan with the remaining ingredients and add 2 litres (3½ pints) cold water. Bring slowly to the boil and skim the surface. Partially cover and simmer for 4–5 hours. Adjust the seasoning. Strain through a muslin-lined sieve and cool quickly. Degrease (see opposite) before using.

Chicken stock

For 1.2 litres (2 pints), you will need 1.6kg (3½lb) chicken bones, 225g (8oz) each onions and celery, sliced, 150g (5oz) choped leeks, 1 bouquet garni (2 bay leaves, a few thyme sprigs and a small bunch parsley), 1 tsp black peppercorns, ½ tsp salt.

1 Put all the ingredients in a large pan with 3 litres (5¼ pints) cold water.

2 Bring slowly to the boil and skim the surface. Partially cover the pan and simmer gently for 2 hours. Adjust the seasoning if necessary.

3 Strain the stock through a muslin-lined sieve into a bowl and cool quickly. Degrease (see opposite) before using.

What makes a good stock?

Most stocks are made by cooking bones or fish trimmings with vegetables. Vegetables and herbs add flavour to any stock. Use onions, leeks, carrots and celery but avoid strongly flavoured vegetables such as cabbage and turnip, or those that disintegrate, such as potatoes. If you plan to make your own stock:

- Ask your butcher or fishmonger for bones and trimmings. They can be frozen for up to six months until you have enough to make stock.
- Stock can be stored in the refrigerator for three days or frozen for up to four months (see page 434), so it is worth making a large quantity.
- If you have made a lot of stock for freezing, reduce it after cooking so that it takes up less freezer space. First degrease it (see opposite), then put it in a clean pan and simmer at medium heat until it's reduced by about three-quarters. Leave to cool completely before storing.

Fish stock

For 900ml (1½ pints), you will need 900g (2lb) fish bones and trimmings, washed, 2 carrots, 1 onion and 2 celery sticks, sliced, 1 bouquet garni (2 bay leaves, a few thyme sprigs, and a small bunch parsley), 6 white peppercorns, ½ tsp salt.

1 Put all the ingredients in a large pan with 900ml (1½ pints) cold water. Bring slowly to the boil and skim the surface.

2 Partially cover the pan and simmer gently for 30 minutes. Adjust the seasoning if necessary.

3 Strain through a muslin-lined sieve into a bowl and cool quickly. Fish stock tends not to have much fat in it and so does not usually need to be degreased. However, if it does seem to be fatty, you will need to remove this by degreasing it (see technique below).

Variation

Court bouillon is an enriched fish stock that is perfect for poaching fish (see page 78). Simply add 150ml (¼ pint) dry white wine and 3 tbsp white wine vinegar to the fish stock recipe at step 1.

Degreasing stock

Meat and poultry stock needs to be degreased. (Vegetable stock does not.) You can mop the fat from the surface using kitchen paper, but the following methods are easier and more effective. There are three main methods that you can use: ladling, pouring and chilling.

1 Ladling While the stock is warm, place a ladle on the surface. Press down to allow the fat floating on the surface to trickle over the edge until the ladle is full. Discard the fat, then repeat until all the fat has been removed.

2 Pouring For this you need a degreasing jug or a double-pouring gravy boat, which has the spout at the base of the vessel. When you fill the jug or gravy boat with a fatty liquid, the fat rises. When you pour, the stock comes out while the fat stays behind in the jug.

3 Chilling This technique works best with stock made from meat, whose fat solidifies when cold. Put the stock in the refrigerator until the fat becomes solid, then remove the pieces of fat using a slotted spoon.

Cook's tips

- To get a clearer liquid when making fish, meat or poultry stock, strain the cooked stock through four layers of muslin in a sieve.
- If you want to keep stock for more than three days, transfer to a pan and reboil gently for five minutes to make it safe for further storage. Cool and put in a clean bowl then chill for a further three days.
- When making meat or chicken stock, make sure there is a good ratio of meat to bones. The more meat you use, the more flavour.

Making soups

Soups are nutritious and full of flavour, and can be light for a first course or substantial for a main course, containing pulses, vegetables, meat, chicken or fish. A basic soup is simple to make.

Puréeing soups

1 Using a jug blender Allow the soup to cool, then fill the jug about half full, making sure that there is more liquid than solids. Cover the lid with a teatowel and hold it on tightly. Blend until smooth, then add more solids and blend again until all the soup is smooth. (If you have a lot of soup, transfer each batch to a clean pan.)

2 Using a stick blender Allow the soup to cool. Stick the blender deep down into the soup, switch it on, and keep it moving so that all the soup is puréed.

3 Using a mouli The mouli-légumes is a traditional favourite of chefs, who require a perfectly uniform texture in their soups. It makes a fine purée although it takes longer than using a blender. Fit the fine plate to the mouli-légumes and set it over a bowl with a teatowel underneath to keep it from moving on the table. Fill the bowl of the mouli about halfway, putting in more solids than liquid. Work in batches if you have a particuarly large quantity of soup. When the solids are puréed, repeat with the liquid.

4 Using a sieve If you don't have a blender or mouli-légumes, you can purée soup by pushing it through a sieve, although this will take a much longer time.

Simple vegetable soup

You can use almost any mixture of vegetables to make soup.
To make a basic soup for four, fry 1 or 2 finely chopped onions in 2 tbsp oil or 1 tbsp oil and 25g (1oz) butter, and add 1 or 2 crushed garlic cloves if you like. Add 450g (1lb) chopped mixed vegetables, such as leeks, potatoes, celery, fennel, canned tomatoes and parsnip (these can be chopped finely or cut into larger dice for a chunky soup). Add 1.1 litres (2 pints) home-made stock. Bring to the boil and simmer for 20–30 minutes until the vegetables are tender. Leave chunky or blend until smooth if you prefer.

Chunky soups

1 Cut up the vegetables into bite-sized pieces. Heat oil or butter in the soup pan and cook the onions and garlic until soft and lightly coloured.

2 Add the remaining ingredients, putting in the vegetables that need the longest cooking first. Pour in some stock and bring to the boil.

3 Simmer gently until all the ingredients are tender. If too much liquid cooks away, just add more.

4 If any ingredients need brief cooking, add them at the very end. Using something starchy in the soup will thicken the broth, or you can use any of the techniques on page 38.

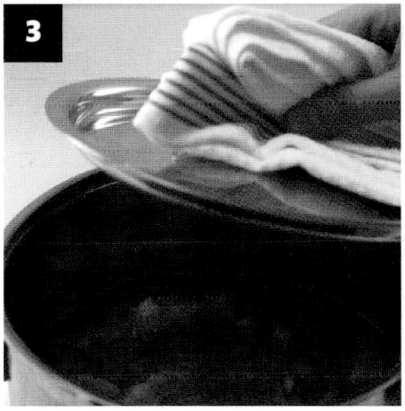

Partially puréed soups

1 For a smooth yet chunky soup, purée one-third to half of it, then stir back into the soup.

2 Alternatively, chop the vegetables, but set aside a few choice pieces. While the soup is cooking, steam or boil these pieces until just tender and refresh in cold water. Just before serving, cut into smaller pieces and add to the soup.

Thickening soups

You can thicken soup before serving to give it a smoother texture and more richness.

1 Cornflour Because cornflour is maize flour stripped of everything except the purest starch, it requires little cooking. Measure the cornflour into a bowl – you will need 1–2 tbsp cornflour per 1 litre (1¾ pints) soup. Add about double the volume of cold water and whisk until the cornflour is completely dissolved. Stir into the soup and heat briefly. (Potato starch can be used in the same way as cornflour.)

2 Egg and cream Cream adds texture and richness, but to thicken a soup, egg yolks and cream work better. Remove the soup from the heat. Using one yolk per 4 tbsp double or whipping cream, whisk them together in a bowl. Add a little of the hot soup – not too much, or the egg will curdle. Whisk well, add more soup, and whisk again. When you have a cupful of liquid, pour it back into the soup. You can turn on the heat again, but don't let the soup simmer or the egg yolk will curdle.

3 Breadcrumbs Add fresh or dry breadcrumbs to the soup during cooking, a handful at a time. Cook for 20 minutes or so, then add more if you need to. Purée the soup if you want a smooth texture. (A handful of cooked rice or mashed potato works in the same way, but make sure they cook for a long time until tender.)

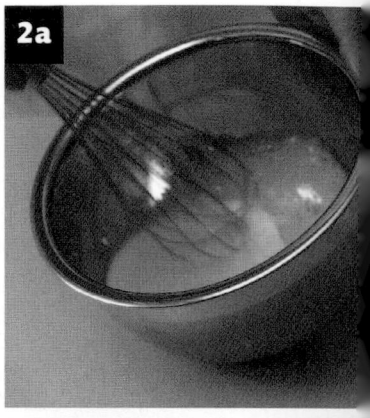

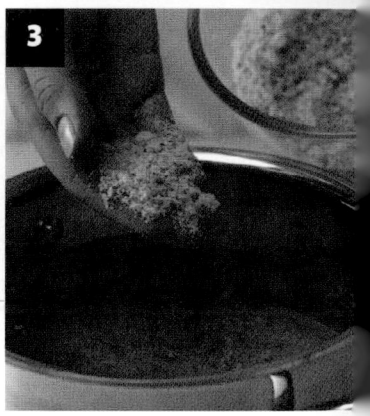

4 Beurre manié This butter and flour paste is useful for thickening soups and sauces. Using equal parts of butter and flour – you will need 1–2 tbsp of each for a soup – cream the butter in a bowl with a wooden spoon and then mix in the flour thoroughly to make a smooth paste. Add to the soup gradually in small pieces, stirring well with each addition. Add only as much as you need to get the desired consistency. (You can store any left over beurre manié in a sealed container for up to three days in the refrigerator or freeze for up to six months.)

Simple garnishes

A garnish can make a huge difference to the presentation of a soup. It might be as simple as a sprinkling of herbs, a drizzle of cream, or some quickly cooked croûtons scattered over the top.

Toasted croûtons

1 Cut the crusts off sliced white bread, then cut into dice 1–2cm (½–¾in) square. Put the bread on a baking sheet and drizzle lightly with oil, then toss well with your hands.

2 Spread the bread dice in a single layer and bake at 200°C (180°C fan oven) mark 6 for 8–10 minutes until lightly browned.

Fried croûtons

Croûtons fried in a generous amount of oil will crispen all over.

1 Cut the crusts off sliced white bread, then cut into dice 1–2cm (½–¾in) square.

2 Heat the oil medium-hot in a frying pan. Fry in a single layer, stirring constantly, until brown all over. Drain on kitchen paper.

Fresh herbs

A simple sprinkling of fresh herbs makes a delicious garnish for soups. Fresh herb flowers can also make a pretty and unusual garnish.

1 Chop the herbs just before serving, and choose a herb that complements that flavour of soup – for example, basil with tomato, chives with creamy soups, or coriander with Asian-style soups.

Cream

Cream and other dairy products such as yogurt and crème fraîche can also make a simple garnish, drizzled or spooned on to soup just before serving. They also add body and texture so use sparingly if the soup already includes cream.

Gazpacho with Tortilla Chips

SERVES 8

900g (2lb) ripe tomatoes
4 garlic cloves
50g (2oz) fresh white breadcrumbs
6 tbsp extra-virgin olive oil
juice of 1½ small limes
1 red chilli, deseeded and chopped
2 cucumbers, deseeded and chopped
2 bunches spring onions, chopped
1 red pepper, deseeded and chopped
600ml (1 pint) tomato juice
6 tbsp freshly chopped coriander
salt and ground black pepper
175g bag tortilla chips to serve

To garnish

1 large avocado
juice of ½ small lime
140ml (4½fl oz) soured cream
a few fresh coriander sprigs

PREPARATION TIME 25–30 minutes, plus 2 hours or overnight chilling

PER SERVING

181 calories
13g fat (of which 2g saturates)
14g carbohydrate
0.6g salt

TECHNIQUES

see also making breadcrumbs (page 308)

Cook's tip

Don't be tempted to make the garnish too far in advance. The delicate pale green flesh of avocado discolours when exposed to air so is best prepared shortly before serving.

1 Score a cross in the skin at the base of each tomato, then put into a bowl. Pour over enough boiling water to cover them, leave for 30 seconds, then transfer to a bowl of cold water. Peel, discarding the skins, then cut into quarters. Discard the seeds.

2 Put all the gazpacho ingredients into a large bowl and mix well, then whiz together in batches in a food processor until smooth, and transfer to a bowl or jug. Season generously with salt and pepper and stir the soup well. Cover and chill for at least 2 hours or overnight.

3 Just before serving, peel and roughly dice the avocado, then toss in lime juice to coat. Serve the soup garnished with soured cream, the avocado, a sprinkling of black pepper and coriander. Serve the tortilla chips separately.

Vichyssoise with Spinach Cream

SERVES 4–6

1kg (2¼lb) trimmed leeks, chopped
50g (2oz) butter
350g (12oz) onions, roughly chopped
1.1 litres (2 pints) vegetable stock
140ml (4½fl oz) double cream
225g (8oz) potatoes, sliced
salt and ground black pepper
cooked peeled prawns and fresh basil sprigs to garnish

For the spinach cream

15g (½oz) butter
125g (4oz) spinach leaves
zest of 1 lemon
140ml (4½fl oz) double cream

PREPARATION TIME 20 minutes, plus minimum 6 hours chilling
COOKING TIME 40 minutes

PER SERVING

610 calories per serving for 4
54g fat (of which 33g saturates)
25g carbohydrate
1g salt
407 calories per serving for 6
36g fat (of which 22g saturates)
17g carbohydrate
0.6g salt

TECHNIQUES

see also peeling prawns (page 83)

Get ahead

Complete the recipe to the end of step 3, cool, cover and chill overnight.
To use Complete the recipe.

1 Rinse the leeks in cold water, drain and set aside. Melt the butter in a large heavy-based pan and add the onions and leeks. Cook, stirring, for 10 minutes. Add the stock, cream and potatoes. Bring to the boil, cover and simmer for 30–40 minutes until the vegetables are tender.

2 Cool slightly, then process in batches until smooth (see page 36). Pass through a fine sieve if you like, then season generously with salt and pepper. Chill for 6 hours or overnight.

3 Meanwhile, to make the spinach cream, heat the butter in a pan, add the spinach and lemon zest. Cook, stirring, for 5 minutes. Add the cream and bubble for 1–2 minutes. Whiz in a blender or food processor until smooth. Season, then chill.

4 Ladle the soup into chilled bowls and spoon in the spinach cream. Garnish with prawns and basil, sprinkle with black pepper and serve.

Pea and Watercress Soup

SERVES 8
75g (3oz) butter
175g (6oz) watercress
10–12 spring onions
700g (1lb 9oz) baking potatoes, peeled and roughly chopped
225g (8oz) frozen petits pois
1.7 litres (3 pints) hot vegetable stock
140ml (4½fl oz) double cream
salt and ground black pepper

PREPARATION TIME 20 minutes
COOKING TIME 30–35 minutes

PER SERVING
206 calories
12g fat (of which 7g saturates)
20g carbohydrate
0.4g salt

TECHNIQUES
see also making stock (page 34)

1 Melt the butter in a large pan, then add the watercress and spring onions, snipping them into rough pieces with scissors as you drop them into the pan. Cook gently over a low heat for 10 minutes.

2 Add the potatoes to the pan with the peas and most of the vegetable stock. Cover, bring to the boil, then simmer gently for 20–25 minutes until the potatoes are very tender.

3 Pour in the cream, then season to taste with salt and pepper.

4 Purée the soup in the pan with a hand-held blender, or leave to cool, then purée in a liquidiser. Add a little extra stock if the soup is too thick.

5 Warm the soup through to serve – but don't boil it or the cream will split.

Cook's tip

A hand-held blender with a metal stem is perfect for making soups, as there's no need to wait for the soup to cool before blending. The mixture can be puréed in the pan, too, which saves washing-up time.

Herb and Lemon Soup

SERVES 6

1.7 litres (3 pints) chicken stock
140g (4½oz) orzo or other soup pasta
3 medium eggs
juice of 1 large lemon
2 tbsp finely chopped chives
2 tbsp finely chopped chervil
salt and ground black pepper
lemon wedges to serve

PREPARATION TIME 10 minutes
COOKING TIME 15–20 minutes

PER SERVING

120 calories
3g fat (of which 1g saturates)
18g carbohydrate
0.4g salt

TECHNIQUES

see also making stock (page 34)

1 Bring the stock to the boil in a large pan. Add the pasta and cook for 5 minutes, or according to the pack instructions.

2 Beat the eggs in a bowl until frothy, then add the lemon juice and 1 tbsp cold water. Slowly stir in two ladlefuls of the hot stock. Return the mixture to the pan, then warm through over a very low heat for 2–3 minutes.

3 Add the herbs and seasoning. Serve in soup bowls, with lemon wedges.

Cook's tip

Once you have added the eggs, don't boil the soup or the eggs will curdle.

Spring Vegetable Broth

SERVES 4

1 tbsp olive oil
4 shallots, chopped
1 fennel bulb, chopped
1 leek, chopped
5 small carrots, chopped
1.1 litres (2 pints) hot fresh chicken stock
2 courgettes, chopped
1 bunch asparagus, chopped
2 × 400g cans cannellini beans, drained and rinsed
50g (2oz) Gruyère or Parmesan cheese shavings to serve

PREPARATION TIME 20 minutes
COOKING TIME about 20 minutes

PER SERVING

264 calories
6g fat (of which 3g saturates)
35g carbohydrate
2.4g salt

TECHNIQUES

see also preparing vegetables (pages 170–182), making chicken stock (page 34)

1 Heat the oil in a large pan. Add the shallots, fennel, leek and carrots, and fry for 5 minutes or until they start to soften.

2 Add the stock, cover and bring to the boil. Add the courgettes, asparagus and beans, then simmer for 5–6 minutes until the vegetables are tender. Ladle into bowls and sprinkle with a little cheese.

Variation

This broth is also good with a tablespoon of pesto added to each bowl and served with chunks of crusty bread.

Hot and Sour Soup

SERVES 4

1 tbsp vegetable oil
2 turkey breasts, about 300g (11oz), or the same quantity of tofu, cut into strips
5cm (2in) piece fresh root ginger, peeled and grated
4 spring onions, finely sliced
1–2 tbsp Thai red curry paste
75g (3oz) long-grain wild rice
1.1 litres (2 pints) hot weak chicken or vegetable stock or boiling water
200g (7oz) mangetouts, sliced
juice of 1 lime
4 tbsp roughly chopped coriander to garnish

PREPARATION TIME 20 minutes
COOKING TIME 30–35 minutes

PER SERVING

255 calories
10g fat (of which 1g saturates)
19g carbohydrate
0.7g salt

TECHNIQUES

see also making stock (page 34), preparing fresh spices (page 429)

1 Heat the oil in a deep pan. Add the turkey or tofu and cook over a medium heat for 5 minutes or until browned. Add the ginger and spring onions and cook for a further 2–3 minutes. Stir in the curry paste and cook for 1–2 minutes to warm the spices.

2 Add the rice and stir to coat in the curry paste. Pour the hot stock or boiling water into the pan. Stir once, then bring to the boil. Lower the heat and leave to simmer, covered, for 20 minutes.

3 Add the mangetouts and cook for a further 5 minutes or until the rice is cooked. Just before serving, squeeze in the lime juice and stir to mix. Ladle into bowls and sprinkle with the coriander.

Parsnip Soup with Cheese Crisps

SERVES 8

40g (1½oz) butter
150g (5oz) onion, roughly chopped
225g (8oz) floury potatoes, such as King Edward's, peeled and chopped
400g (14oz) parsnips, peeled and chopped
4 tsp paprika, plus extra to dust
1.1 litres (2 pints) vegetable stock
450ml (¾ pint) milk
4 tbsp double cream
65g (2½oz) sliced chorizo sausage, cut into fine strips
salt and ground black pepper

For the Parmesan crisps

1 large parsnip, about 75g (3oz), peeled
vegetable oil, to fry
3 tbsp freshly grated Parmesan

PREPARATION TIME 30 minutes
COOKING TIME 1 hour

PER SERVING

111 calories
81g fat (of which 35g saturates)
72g carbohydrate
3g salt

TECHNIQUES

see also making stock (page 34), making vegetable crisps (page 186)

Freezing tip

Prepare to the end of step 2, then cool, pack and freeze.
To use Thaw the soup overnight at cool room temperature. Then complete the recipe.

1 Melt the butter in a large heavy-based pan. Add the onion and cook over a gentle heat for 5 minutes. Add the potatoes, parsnips and paprika. Mix well and cook gently, stirring occasionally, for 15 minutes or until the vegetables begin to soften. Add the stock, milk and cream, and season. Bring to the boil and simmer for about 25 minutes or until the vegetables are very soft. Add 50g (2oz) chorizo. Allow the soup to cool a little, then whiz in a blender or food processor until smooth. The soup can be thinned with additional stock or milk, if you like. Check the seasoning and put back in the pan.

2 Using a swivel vegetable peeler, peel off long, wide strips of parsnip until there is nothing left to peel. Pour the oil into a large pan or deep-sided frying pan to a depth of 2.5cm (1in) and heat to a medium temperature. Fry the parsnip strips in batches until light golden and crisp. Drain on kitchen paper and sprinkle lightly with salt. Arrange the strips in six piles on a baking sheet, then sprinkle with half the Parmesan and the remaining chorizo. Cook the Parmesan crisps at 200°C (180°C fan oven) mark 6 for 3–5 minutes until the cheese just begins to melt.

3 Reheat the soup. Serve topped with the Parmesan Crisps, sprinkled with the remaining Parmesan and dusted with paprika.

Cauliflower Soup

SERVES 6

2 × 400ml cans coconut milk
750ml (1¼ pints) vegetable stock
4 garlic cloves, finely chopped
5cm (2in) piece fresh root ginger, peeled and finely chopped
4 lemongrass stalks, roughly chopped
4 kaffir lime leaves, shredded (optional)
4 red chillies
2 tbsp groundnut oil
2 tsp sesame oil
1 large onion, thinly sliced
2 tsp ground turmeric
2 tsp sugar
900g (2lb) cauliflower florets
2 tbsp lime juice
2 tbsp light soy sauce
4 spring onions, shredded
4 tbsp freshly chopped coriander
salt and ground black pepper

PREPARATION TIME 25 minutes
COOKING TIME 40 minutes

PER SERVING
113 calories
5g fat (of which 1g saturates)
15g carbohydrate
1.4g salt

TECHNIQUES
see also preparing fresh spices (page 429)

Cook's tip

If you want to make your own coconut milk using freshly grated coconut flesh rather than buying it canned, check out the technique on page 221.

1 Put the coconut milk and stock into a pan. Add the garlic and ginger with the lemongrass, lime leaves and chillies. Bring to the boil, cover and simmer for 15 minutes. Strain and keep the liquid to one side.

2 Heat the oils together in a clean pan. Add the onion, turmeric and sugar, and fry gently for 5 minutes. Add the cauliflower to the pan and stir-fry for 5 minutes or until lightly golden.

3 Add the reserved liquid, the lime juice and soy sauce. Bring to the boil, then cover and simmer for 10–15 minutes until the cauliflower is tender. Season with salt and pepper, then add the spring onions to the soup with the coriander, and serve.

Spinach and Rice Soup

SERVES 4

4 tbsp extra-virgin olive oil
1 onion, finely chopped
2 garlic cloves, crushed
2 tsp freshly chopped thyme or a large pinch of dried thyme
2 tsp freshly chopped rosemary or a large pinch of dried rosemary
zest of ½ lemon
2 tsp ground coriander
¼ tsp cayenne pepper
125g (4oz) arborio rice
1.1 litres (2 pints) vegetable stock
225g (8oz) fresh or frozen and thawed spinach, shredded
4 tbsp pesto sauce
salt and ground black pepper
extra-virgin olive oil and freshly grated Parmesan to serve

PREPARATION TIME 10 minutes
COOKING TIME 25–30 minutes

PER SERVING

335 calories
20g fat (of which 4g saturates)
29g carbohydrate
0.7g salt

TECHNIQUES

see also preparing vegetables (pages 170–182), chopping herbs (page 428), making stock (page 34)

Cook's tip

You can buy good-quality pesto from the supermarket, but it's easy to make yourself from fresh basil leaves, garlic, pinenuts, olive oil and Parmesan. Check out the technique on page 21.

1 Heat half the oil in a pan. Add the onion, garlic, herbs, lemon zest and spices, then fry gently for 5 minutes.

2 Add the remaining oil with the rice and cook, stirring, for 1 minute. Add the stock, bring to the boil and simmer gently for 20 minutes or until the rice is tender.

3 Stir the spinach into the soup with the pesto sauce. Cook for 2 minutes, then season to taste with salt and pepper.

4 Serve drizzled with a little oil and topped with Parmesan.

Squash, Lentil and Prawn Soup

SERVES 6–8

75g (3oz) butter
75g (3oz) each carrots, onions, celery and leeks, roughly chopped
2 garlic cloves, crushed
175g (6oz) Puy lentils
900ml (1½ pints) fish stock
200ml (7fl oz) vermouth
140ml (4½fl oz) double cream
2 fresh thyme sprigs
2 bay leaves
6–8 small squashes, each weighing about 700g (1lb 9oz)
18–24 large raw prawns, peeled and deveined
salt and ground black pepper
chopped chives to garnish

PREPARATION TIME 20 minutes
COOKING TIME 55 minutes

PER SERVING

388 calories per serving for 6
24g fat (of which 15g saturates)
21g carbohydrate
0.7g salt
291 calories per serving for 8
18g fat (of which 11g saturates)
16g carbohydrate
0.6g salt

TECHNIQUES

see also preparing prawns (page 83)

Freezing tip

Complete the soup to the end of step 2, then cool quickly, pack and freeze.
To use Thaw the soup overnight at cool room temperature, then complete the recipe.

1 Heat 50g (2oz) butter in a large pan and cook the vegetables, stirring occasionally, for 5 minutes. Add the garlic and cook for 1 minute. Stir in the lentils, stock and 150ml (¼ pint) vermouth with the cream, herbs and seasoning. Add 300ml (½ pint) water. Bring to the boil, cover and simmer for 40–45 minutes until the vegetables are tender. Discard the herbs.

2 Meanwhile, preheat the oven to 200°C (180°C fan oven) mark 6. Trim the bases of the squashes so that they are flat, and cut the tops off at the stalk end. Scoop out the seeds. Put the squashes in a roasting tin and cook for 40 minutes or until tender. Scoop out some of the flesh and add to the soup. Cool slightly, then process the mixture in batches in a food processor until smooth. Pass through a fine sieve, if you like, and adjust the seasoning. If the soup is too thick, dilute with stock or water, put back into the wiped-out pan and keep warm.

3 Put the prawns in a pan with the remaining butter and vermouth, and simmer for 2–3 minutes until the prawns turn pink. Strain the prawn liquid into the soup. Ladle into bowls or the hollowed-out squashes, add the prawns and garnish with the chives.

3

EGGS

Eggs are a wonderfully versatile ingredient that can be enjoyed on their own – cooked simply – or used in literally hundreds of different ways. In this chapter, you can learn all the basics from simple boiling, poaching and frying through to more complex techniques such as making omelettes, pancakes, soufflés and meringues. Once you've mastered the basics, try the delicious recipes such as Mixed mushroom frittata, Twice-baked soufflés, Cinnamon pancakes filled with fruit compote and sweet, nutty Hazelnut meringue cake.

Basic egg preparation

There are only three essentials to basic egg preparation: cracking, separating and whisking – and once you have mastered these simple techniques you will be able to cook eggs in lots of different ways.

Separating

You'll need to separate eggs for making a sauce such as mayonnaise, a soufflé, meringue, or some cakes. It's easy, but it requires some care.

1 Crack the egg more carefully than usual: right in the middle to make a break between the two halves that is just wide enough to get your thumbnail into.

2 Holding the egg over a bowl with the large end pointing down, carefully lift off the small half. Some of the white will drip and slide into the bowl while the yolk sits in the large end of the shell.

3 Carefully slide the yolk into the smaller end, then back into the large end to allow the remaining white to drop into the bowl. Take care not to break the yolk; even a speck can stop the whites from whisking up.

Cook's tip

If you're separating more than one egg, break each one into an individual cup. Separating them individually means that if you break one yolk, you won't spoil the whole batch. Keeping the whites yolk-free is particularly important for techniques such as whisking.

Whisking

1 Use an electric or hand whisk. Make sure that there is no trace of yolk in the whites and that the whisk and bowl are clean and dry. At a low speed, use the whisk in a small area of the whites until it starts to become foamy.

2 Increase the speed and work the whisk through the whites until glossy and soft rounded peaks form. Do not over-whisk as the foam will become dry and grainy.

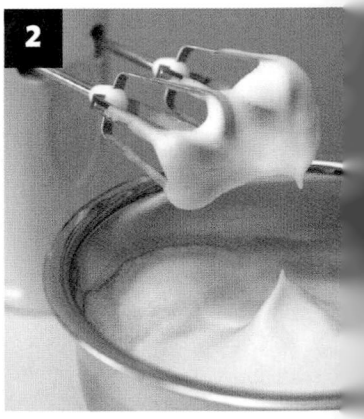

Cooking with eggs

There are numerous ways to cook with eggs - from the simplest techniques such as boiling, poaching and scrambling to more complex techniques such as making omelettes, soufflés and meringues.

Boiling: method 1

1 Bring a small pan of water to the boil. Once the water is boiling, add a medium egg. For a soft-boiled egg, cook for 6 minutes; for a salad egg, cook for 8 minutes; and for a hard-boiled egg, cook for 10 minutes.

2 Remove the egg from the water with a slotted spoon and serve.

Boiling: method 2

1 Put a medium egg in a small pan and cover with cold water. Put on a lid and bring to the boil. When the water begins to boil, remove the lid and cook for 2 minutes for a soft-boiled egg, 5 minutes for a salad egg, and 7 minutes for a hard-boiled egg.

2 Remove the egg from the water with a slotted spoon and serve.

Perfect boiled eggs

There are two ways to boil an egg, starting in boiling water or starting in cold water. Both work well as long as you follow certain rules:

- The egg must be at room temperature.
- For both methods, cover the eggs with water, plus 2.5cm (1in) or so extra.
- If starting in boiling water, use an egg pick - if you like, to pierce the broad end of the shell. This allows air in the pocket at the base of the egg to escape and avoids cracking.
- Gently lower in the eggs using a long spoon to avoid cracking them.
- Cook at a simmer rather than a rolling boil.

Coddling

A variation of soft-boiled eggs, coddled eggs are very soft and have tender whites. They are particularly good for using when the eggs are going to be cooked again after peeling, such as in a pie or for recipes such as Scotch eggs.

1 Using a slotted spoon, gently lower the whole eggs into a pan of simmering water, then remove the pan from the heat.

2 Leave the eggs to stand in the water for 4–5 minutes, where they will cook gently with the residual heat of the water.

Poaching

1 Heat about 8cm (3¼in) of lightly salted water in a shallow frying pan to a bare simmer. Crack a very fresh egg into a cup, then slip it into the water. (The whites in a fresh egg are firmer and will form a 'nest' for the yolk while older egg whites are watery and spread out in the pan.)

2 Cook for 3–4 minutes until the white is barely set. Remove with a slotted spoon and drain on kitchen paper.

Scrambling

1 Allow 2 eggs per person. In a bowl, beat the eggs well but lightly with a fork and season with salt and ground black pepper.

2 Melt a knob of butter in a small heavy-based pan over a low heat – use a heat diffuser if necessary. (Using a non-stick pan minimises the amount of butter you need to use.)

3 Pour in the eggs, and start stirring immediately, using a wooden spoon or a flat-headed spatula to break up the lumps as they form. Keep the eggs moving about as much as possible during cooking.

4 As the eggs start to set, scrape the bottom of the pan to keep the egg from overcooking, and break up any larger lumps that may form. Your aim is to have a smooth mixture with no noticeable lumps.

5 Scrambled eggs may be well cooked and quite firm, or very 'loose' and runny; this is a matter of taste. They will continue to cook even when taken off the heat, so remove them from the pan when they are still a little softer than you want to serve them.

Frying

1 Heat a good knob of butter or a little oil over a medium-high heat. Break the egg into a shallow bowl, then slide gently into the pan.

2 Cook for 2–3 minutes, gently shaking the pan to slosh the butter or oil over the egg white. Adjust the heat so that the egg doesn't become too brown underneath while the yolk remains cool. For a firm yolk, carefully turn the egg over and cook for a few seconds more.

Baking

You can crack eggs into individual dishes or into a large shallow pan and bake them. They may be cooked on their own, or baked with meat or vegetable accompaniments.

1 Generously smear individual baking dish(es) or one large baking dish with butter.

2 Put in any accompaniments, if using (see box on Variations and accompaniments, right). If using vegetable-based accompaniments, use the back of a spoon to make a hollow or hollows in which to break the egg or eggs. Carefully crack the egg or eggs into the hollows.

3 Bake for 8–10 minutes at 200°C (180°C fan oven) mark 6, or 15–18 minutes at 180°C (160°C fan oven) mark 4, until the whites are just set; the yolks should still be quite runny.

Variations and accompaniments

- Eggs are delicious baked on a simple bed of sautéed vegetables (such as ratatouille), lightly browned diced potatoes with onions, and well-cooked spinach.
- Accompaniments must be fully cooked before they are transferred to the dish and the raw eggs put on top.
- Other simple additions include chopped fresh herbs or a few shreds of crisp bacon.
- If liked, drizzle a small spoonful of cream and a good grinding of black pepper on top of the eggs before baking.

Making omelettes

There are numerous different types of omelette – from the classic folded omelette made from simple beaten eggs to thick omelettes such as Spanish tortilla and Italian frittata.

Classic omelette

1 To make an omelette for one person, heat a heavy-based 18cm (7in) frying pan or omelette pan. Using a fork, beat 2 eggs and season.

2 Add 15g (½oz) butter to the pan and let it sizzle for a few moments without browning, then pour in the eggs and stir a few times with a fork.

3 As the omelette begins to stick at the sides, lift it up and allow the uncooked egg run into the gap.

4 When the omelette is nearly set and the underneath is brown, loosen the edges and give the pan a sharp shake to slide the omelette across.

5 Add a filling (such as grated cheese or fried mushrooms), if you like, and fold the far side of the omelette towards you. Tilt the pan to slide the omelette on to the plate and serve.

Perfect omelettes

- Don't add butter until the pan is already hot, otherwise it will brown too much.
- Beat the eggs lightly.
- Use a high heat.

Potato and chorizo tortilla

To serve four, you will need 6 tbsp olive oil, 450g (1lb) very thinly sliced potatoes, 225g (8oz) thinly sliced onions, 2 chopped garlic cloves, 50g (2oz) chorizo, cut into strips, 6 large eggs, salt and ground black pepper.

1 Heat the oil in an 18cm (7in) non-stick frying pan. Add the potatoes, onion and garlic, and stir to coat. Cover. Cook gently for 15 minutes, stirring occasionally, until the potato is soft. Season with salt.

2 Add the chorizo to the pan. Beat the eggs and season with salt and ground black pepper, then pour into the pan and cook for about 5 minutes until the edges are beginning to brown and the egg looks about three-quarters set.

3 Put the tortilla under a preheated grill and quickly brown the top. Remove from the heat and leave to cool. Loosen the edges of the tortilla and serve cut into wedges.

Making soufflés

Light fluffy soufflés made with whisked egg whites folded into a richly flavoured egg custard may be sweet or savoury. For a perfect rise, use a traditional straight-sided soufflé dish.

Cheese soufflé

To serve four, you will need 25g (1oz) butter, plus extra to grease, 1 tbsp freshly grated Parmesan, 200ml (7fl oz) milk, 6 black peppercorns, a few onion and carrot slices, 1 bay leaf, 2 tbsp plain flour, 2 tsp Dijon mustard, large pinch of cayenne pepper, 4 large eggs, separated, plus 1 egg white, 75g (3oz) mature Cheddar cheese, finely grated, salt and ground black pepper.

1 Butter four ramekins. Coat the bottom and sides with Parmesan. Put the milk, peppercorns, onion, carrot and bay leaf in a pan. Bring to the boil, remove from the heat, cover and leave for 30 minutes. Strain. Preheat the oven to 180°C (160°C fan oven) mark 4.

2 Melt the butter in a pan. Stir in the flour and mustard. Add salt, pepper and cayenne, and cook for 1 minute, stirring. Take off the heat and stir in the milk. Slowly bring to the boil and cook, stirring, until thick. Cool slightly, then beat in the egg yolks, one at a time. Stir in all but 1 tbsp of the cheese.

3 Whisk the egg whites until they stand in soft peaks.

4 Mix a large spoonful of egg white into the sauce, then gently fold in the remaining egg whites.

5 Spoon into the dish(es). Sprinkle with the reserved cheese. Stand the dishes on a baking sheet. Cook for 20 minutes or until golden brown, risen and just firm to the touch. Serve.

Perfect soufflés

- Run a knife around the inside of the dish before baking to help achieve the classic 'hat' effect.
- To prepare ahead, prepare to the end of step 2 and leave to stand for several hours before baking.
- Ensure you have a well-flavoured and well-seasoned sauce because the egg white will dilute the flavour.
- When you fold the sauce and egg whites together, work very gently to avoid knocking the air out of the egg whites.

Making meringues

Sweet and simple to make, meringues have just two ingredients, egg whites and sugar, and they have a lovely freshness that's often lacking in store-bought ones. Stored carefully, they will keep well.

Simple meringues

For 12 meringues, you will need 3 medium egg whites, 175g (6oz) caster sugar.

1 Preheat the oven to 170°C (150°C fan oven) mark 3. Cover a baking sheet with baking parchment. Put the egg whites into a large clean bowl.

2 Whisk them until soft peaks form. Add a spoonful of sugar and whisk until glossy.

3 Keep adding the sugar a spoonful at a time, whisking thoroughly after each addition until you have used half the sugar. The mixture should be thick and glossy.

4 Sprinkle the remaining sugar over the mixture and then gently fold in using a metal spoon.

5 Hold a dessertspoon in each hand and pick up a spoonful of mixture in one spoon, then scrape the other one against it to lift the mixture off. Repeat the process a few times, to form a rough oval shape. Using the empty spoon, push the oval on to the baking sheet; hold it just over the sheet so that it doesn't drop from a great height. Continue this process with the remaining mixture to make 12 meringues.

6 Put the meringues in the oven and bake for 15 minutes, then turn the oven off and leave them in the oven to dry out overnight.

Variations

- For a richer flavour, add 1 tsp vanilla extract or 50g (2oz) ground almonds or toasted hazelnuts.
- You can add a tiny amount of food colouring to make them a pale pink, lilac, and so on.
- Shape the meringues using a pastry bag instead of dessertspoons, if you like.
- Poaching the meringues keeps them soft throughout, perfect for serving on a pool of custard to make Floating Islands. To poach meringues, form them into ovals using two soup spoons and poach in a pan of simmering water for about 3 minutes.

Perfect meringues

- Baking meringues is best done in the evening, or whenever you know you won't be needing your oven for a good few hours, as they must be left to dry in the turned-off oven for several hours.
- Get a pan of water simmering gently before you start making your meringues, and line a large baking sheet with greaseproof paper or a silicone baking mat.
- Make sure your mixing bowl is spotlessly clean, as the tiniest trace of grease can keep the whites from whisking up properly. Also, check that your electric whisk is absolutely clean.
- If using a free-standing mixer with a whisk attachment, rather than a handheld whisk, put the bowl of the mixer over the pan of simmering water. Dry it off and return it to the mixer stand.
- Don't rush the whisking process. If the egg whites are not beaten long enough, they won't hold their shape when baked.

Pavlova

This meringue variation has a chewy texture from the addition of vinegar and cornflour, which soften it, eliminating the crunchiness of ordinary meringue.

You will need 4 medium egg whites, 225g (8oz) golden caster sugar, 1 tbsp cornflour, 1 tbsp vanilla extract, 2 tsp white wine vinegar.

1 Preheat the oven to 130°C (110°C fan oven) mark ½. Take a large sheet of baking parchment and a large baking sheet. Draw a 20.5cm (8in) circle on the paper, then turn the paper over and place it on the baking sheet.

2 In a clean grease-free bowl, beat the egg whites until stiff peaks form.

3 Add the sugar, 1 tbsp at a time, until the mixture is stiff and glossy. Mix together the cornflour, vanilla and vinegar in a small bowl and sprinkle over the meringue mixture. Whisk for another minute.

4 Put a little dab of meringue under each corner of the parchment, to secure it to the baking sheet. Using a metal spoon, make a continuous ring of meringue inside the edge of the marked circle. Fill the empty circle with meringue, then flatten it out as evenly as possible with a palette knife or spatula.

5 Bake until it's firm about the edges and slightly soft in the centre (about 1¼ hours). Leave to cool.

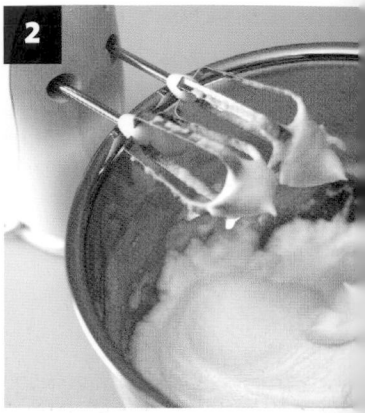

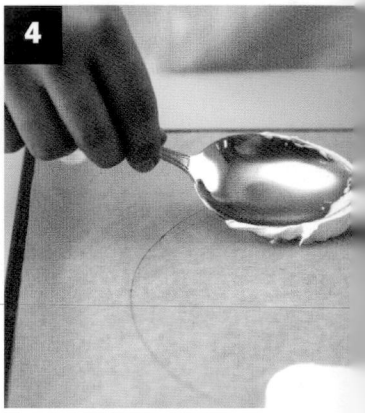

Pavlova toppings

1 Whip 280ml (9½fl oz) double cream until it gently holds its shape and spread it over the cooked, cooled pavlova.

2 Top with fresh seasonal fruits. In summer, berries such as strawberries, raspberries and blueberries make an excellent choice. You can also try chopped mango and whole redcurrants or sliced kiwi fruit and halved white seedless grapes.

Making batters

Batters can serve a number of purposes, and are remarkably versatile for something so simple. All you need to remember when working with them is to mix quickly and lightly.

Pancakes

To make eight pancakes, you will need 125g (4oz) plain flour, a pinch of salt, 1 medium egg, 300ml (½ pint) milk, oil and butter to fry.

1 Sift the flour and salt, make a well in the middle and whisk in the egg. Work in the milk, then leave to stand for 20 minutes. Heat a pan and coat lightly with fat. Coat thinly with batter.

2 Cook for 1½–2 minutes until golden, carefully turning once.

Drop scones

For 15–18 pancakes, you will need 125g (4oz) self-raising flour, 2 tbsp caster sugar, 1 medium egg, beaten, 150ml (¼ pint) milk, a little vegetable oil to grease.

1 Mix the flour and sugar in a bowl. Make a well in the centre and mix in the egg and a little milk to achieve the consistency of thick cream.

2 Oil a griddle or heavy frying pan and heat it until medium-hot. Drop some of the batter in small rounds on to the griddle or pan, and cook at a steady heat until bubbles rise to the surface (2–3 minutes).

3 Turn and cook for another 2–3 minutes, then remove to a clean teatowel. Cover with another teatowel to keep them moist, and continue cooking the scones until you have used all the batter.

Piperade

SERVES 4

2 tbsp olive oil
1 medium onion, finely chopped
1 garlic clove, finely chopped
1 red pepper, deseeded and chopped
375g (13oz) tomatoes, peeled, deseeded and chopped
pinch of cayenne pepper
8 large eggs
salt and ground black pepper
freshly chopped flat-leafed parsley to garnish

PREPARATION TIME 20 minutes
COOKING TIME 20 minutes

PER SERVING
232 calories
17g fat (of which 4g saturates)
7g carbohydrate
0.4g salt

TECHNIQUES
see also preparing vegetables (pages 170–182)

1 Heat the oil in a heavy-based frying pan. Add the onion and garlic, and cook gently for 5 minutes. Add the red pepper and cook for 10 minutes or until softened.

2 Add the tomatoes, increase the heat and cook until they are reduced to a thick pulp. Season well with cayenne pepper, salt and pepper.

3 Lightly whisk the eggs and add to the frying pan. Using a wooden spoon, stir gently until they've just begun to set but are still creamy. Garnish with parsley and serve immediately.

Cook's tip

For a substantial brunch, serve the piperade with chunks of crusty baguette.

Creamy Baked Eggs

SERVES 4
butter to grease
4 sun-dried tomatoes
4 medium eggs
4 tbsp double cream
salt and ground black pepper

PREPARATION TIME 5 minutes
COOKING TIME 15–18 minutes

PER SERVING
161 calories
14g fat (of which 7g saturates)
3g carbohydrate
0.2g salt

TECHNIQUES
see also baking eggs (page 55)

1 Preheat the oven to 180°C (160°C fan oven) mark 4. Grease four individual ramekins.

2 Put 1 tomato in each ramekin and season with salt and pepper. Carefully break an egg on top of each, then drizzle 1 tbsp cream over each egg.

3 Bake for 15–18 minutes – the eggs will continue to cook once they have been taken out of the oven.

4 Leave to stand for 2 minutes before serving.

Mixed Mushroom Frittata

SERVES 4
1 tbsp olive oil
300g (11oz) mixed mushrooms, sliced
2 tbsp freshly chopped thyme
zest and juice of ½ lemon
50g (2oz) watercress, chopped
6 medium eggs, beaten
salt and ground black pepper

PREPARATION TIME 15 minutes
COOKING TIME 15–20 minutes

PER SERVING
149 calories
12g fat (of which 3g saturates)
0g carbohydrate
0.3g salt

TECHNIQUES
see also preparing mushrooms (page 175)

1 Heat the oil in a large deep frying pan over a medium heat. Add the mushrooms and thyme, and stir-fry for 4–5 minutes until starting to soften and brown. Stir in the lemon zest and juice, then bubble for 1 minute. Lower the heat.

2 Preheat the grill. Add the watercress to the beaten eggs, season with salt and pepper and pour into the pan. Cook on the hob for 7–8 minutes until the sides and base are firm but the centre is still a little soft.

3 Transfer to the grill and cook for 4–5 minutes until just set. Cut into wedges to serve.

Cook's tip

This frittata tastes especially good served with chunks of stoneground, wholegrain bread and a crisp green salad.

Warm Lentil and Egg Salad

SERVES 4

1 tbsp olive oil
1 onion, 1 carrot and 1 celery stick, finely chopped
2 red peppers, deseeded and roughly chopped
200g (7oz) flat mushrooms, sliced
200g (7oz) lentils, rinsed and drained
600ml (1 pint) hot vegetable stock
4 medium eggs
100g (3½oz) spinach
2 tbsp good-quality balsamic vinegar
ground black pepper

PREPARATION TIME 20 minutes
COOKING TIME 35–40 minutes

PER SERVING

300 calories
10g fat (of which 2g saturates)
33g carbohydrate
0.3g salt

TECHNIQUES

see also preparing vegetables (pages 170–182), cooking lentils (page 243)

1 Heat the oil in a large pan. Add the onion, carrot and celery, and cook for 5 minutes. Add the peppers and mushrooms. Cover and cook for a further 5 minutes. Stir in the lentils and stock. Bring to the boil and simmer, covered, for 25–30 minutes.

2 Meanwhile, bring a large pan of water to the boil. Break the eggs into the water and cook for 3–4 minutes. Lift them out with a slotted spoon, drain on kitchen paper and keep warm.

3 A couple of minutes before the end of the lentil cooking time, add the spinach and cook until wilted. Stir in the vinegar. Spoon on to four plates or bowls and top each with a poached egg. Season with pepper and serve.

Cook's tip

For the best flavour, use a really good quality vegetable stock or try making your own fresh stock (page 34).

Salmon and Asparagus Pie

SERVES 6–8

275g (10oz) plain flour, plus extra to dust
200g (7oz) chilled butter, cubed
1 large egg, beaten, plus 1 large egg, beaten, to glaze

For the filling

2 large eggs and 2 large yolks, beaten
200ml (7fl oz) crème fraîche
3 tbsp freshly chopped dill
25g (1oz) butter
200g (7oz) button mushrooms, sliced
150g (5oz) thick asparagus tips
450g (1lb) fresh salmon fillet, cut into wide strips, 11.5cm (4½in) long
salt and ground black pepper

PREPARATION TIME 40 minutes, plus 1½ hours chilling and cooling
COOKING TIME 1 hour 10 minutes

PER SERVING

782 calories per serving for 6
59g fat (of which 32g saturates)
37g carbohydrate
0.8g salt
587 calories per serving for 8
45g fat (of which 24g saturates)
28g carbohydrate
0.6g salt

TECHNIQUES

see also making pastry (page 278)

Cook's tips

- To check the pie is cooked, insert a skewer in the centre for 30 seconds – it should feel hot when you pull it out.
- Cool the pie in the tin for 1 hour to serve warm, or 3 hours to serve at room temperature.

1 Whiz the flour, butter and salt in a food processor until they resemble breadcrumbs. Add one egg and 2 tbsp cold water and pulse until the mixture just comes together. Knead lightly. Cut off one-third, wrap both pieces and chill for 30 minutes.

2 Preheat the oven to 200°C (180°C fan oven) mark 6. Roll out the larger piece to a 28cm (11in) round. Use to line a 20.5cm (8in), 5cm (2in) deep, loose-based tin and prick the base with a fork. Line with greaseproof paper and baking beans and put on a baking sheet. Bake for 25 minutes. Remove paper and beans, brush the pastry with beaten egg and cook for 5–10 minutes until the pastry is almost cooked. Cool.

3 To make the filling, combine the whole eggs, crème fraîche and dill and season. Melt the butter and fry the mushrooms for 1–2 minutes. Season and cool. Add the asparagus to boiling water, return to the boil, then drain. Refresh in iced water. Arrange half the fish in the pie case. Arrange the vegetables on top. Finish with fish and pour over the crème fraîche mixture to within 1cm (½in) of the top. Brush the rim with beaten egg. Cut the remaining pastry into a 25.5cm (10in) round, place on top and seal the edges. Brush with egg. Make a steam hole. Put the baking tray in the oven to heat. Bake the pie on the tray for 40 minutes or until golden and the filling is cooked. Cool in the tin.

Twice-baked Soufflés

SERVES 8

25g (1oz) ground almonds
50g (2oz) butter, plus extra to grease
250g (9oz) cauliflower florets
150ml (¼ pint) milk
40g (1½oz) plain flour
75g (3oz) Cheddar cheese, finely grated
75g (3oz) Emmenthal cheese, finely grated
3 large eggs, separated
285ml (9½fl oz) double cream
1 tbsp grainy mustard
salt and ground black pepper
rocket leaves and cherry tomatoes to serve
olive oil and balsamic vinegar to drizzle

PREPARATION TIME 20 minutes
COOKING TIME 1¼ hours

PER SERVING
385 calories
35g fat (of which 20g saturates)
7g carbohydrate
0.7g salt

TECHNIQUES
see also preparing cauliflower (page 180), separating eggs (page 52)

Freezing tip

Prepare the recipe to the end of step 3, then wrap separately and freeze.
To use Complete the recipe. Cook the soufflés from frozen at 200°C (180°C fan oven) mark 6 for 25–30 minutes until golden.

1 Preheat the oven to 180°C (160°C fan oven) mark 4. Cook the almonds under a grill, turning until lightly toasted. Grease and baseline eight 150ml (¼ pint) ramekins with greaseproof paper. Dust with the almonds.

2 Cook the cauliflower in salted boiling water for 5–10 minutes until tender. Drain, plunge into iced water and drain again, then blend with the milk for 2–3 minutes until smooth. Melt the butter in a pan, add the flour and mix to a smooth paste. Stir in the cauliflower purée and bring to the boil. Cool a little, then beat in the cheeses and egg yolks. Season.

3 Whisk the whites to a soft peak and fold in. Spoon the mixture into the ramekins, put into a roasting tin and fill halfway up the sides with hot water. Cook for 20–25 minutes until firm to the touch. Turn off the oven. Remove from the roasting tin and cool completely. Run a knife around the edge of the soufflés and turn out on to a baking sheet.

4 Preheat the oven to 200°C (180°C fan oven) mark 6. Pour the cream into a wide pan, bring to the boil and bubble until syrupy and reduced by one-third. Add the mustard and season. Spoon a little cream over the soufflés and bake for 15–20 minutes until golden. Serve with rocket leaves and cherry tomatoes drizzled with olive oil and balsamic vinegar.

Savoury Pudding

SERVES 6

150–175g (5–6oz) thickly sliced white bread (such as sourdough), crusts left on
65g (2½oz) butter, softened
Dijon mustard
200g (7oz) sliced ham, very roughly chopped
140g (4½oz) mature Cheddar cheese, grated
575ml (19½fl oz) full-fat milk
5 large eggs, beaten
pinch of freshly grated nutmeg
2 tbsp freshly chopped herbs, such as parsley, marjoram or thyme
salt and ground black pepper

PREPARATION TIME 15 minutes, plus 15 minutes soaking
COOKING TIME 1¼ hours

PER SERVING
411 calories
28g fat (of which 15g saturates)
17g carbohydrate
2.2g salt

1 Spread the bread generously with butter and sparingly with mustard. Put half the slices in the base of a 2 litre (3½ pint) ovenproof dish. Top with the ham and half the cheese, then with the remaining bread, butter side up. Whisk together the milk, eggs, nutmeg and plenty of salt and pepper. Stir in the herbs, then slowly pour the mixture over the bread. Scatter the remaining cheese on top and leave to soak for 15 minutes. Meanwhile, preheat the oven to 180°C (160°C fan oven) mark 4.

2 Put the dish in a roasting tin and fill halfway up the sides with hand-hot water, then cook for 1–1¼ hours until puffed up, golden brown and just set to the centre.

Cinnamon Pancakes

SERVES 6
140g (4½oz) plain flour
½ tsp ground cinnamon
1 medium egg
300ml (½ pint) skimmed milk
olive oil to fry
fruit compote or sugar to serve

PREPARATION TIME 5 minutes
COOKING TIME 20 minutes

PER SERVING
148 calories
6g fat (of which 1g saturates)
21g carbohydrate
0.1g salt

TECHNIQUES
see also making pancakes (page 61), stewing fruit (page 214), pan-frying fruit (page 215), baking fruit (page 216)

1 In a large bowl, whisk together the flour, cinnamon, egg and milk to make a smooth batter. Leave to stand for 20 minutes.

2 Heat 1 tsp oil in a heavy-based frying pan over a medium heat. Pour in a ladleful of batter and tilt the pan to coat the base with an even layer. Cook for 1 minute or until golden. Flip over and cook for 1 minute. Repeat with the remaining batter, adding more oil if necessary, to make six pancakes. Serve filled with a fruit compote or a sprinkling of sugar.

Cook's tip

The secret to making pancakes is to ensure the pan is really hot before you start. The first one is always rubbery as a tyre, so don't worry – just try again with a fresh ladleful of batter.

Baked Orange Custard

SERVES 6
zest of 1 orange
450ml (¾ pint) milk
140ml (4½fl oz) double cream
75g (3oz) clear honey (see Cook's tips)
2 large eggs, plus 4 large yolks
25g (1oz) caster sugar
slivers of orange zest to decorate

PREPARATION TIME 10 minutes, plus 30 minutes infusing and 15 minutes cooling
COOKING TIME 50 minutes or 1 hour 10 minutes, plus minimum 6 hours chilling

PER SERVING
294 calories
21g fat (of which 11g saturates)
18g carbohydrate
0.2g salt

TECHNIQUES
see also zesting citrus fruits (page 207), separating eggs (page 52)

1 Put the orange zest, milk and cream in a pan, then bring to the boil. Set aside for 30 minutes to infuse.

2 Preheat the oven to 150°C (130°C fan oven) mark 2. Put a 1.7 litre (3 pint) soufflé dish or six 150ml (¼ pint) coffee cups or ramekins in the oven to warm through. Bring the honey to the boil in a small heavy-based pan. Bubble for 2–3 minutes until it begins to caramelise (see Cook's tips). Pour the caramel into the warmed dish, cups or ramekins and rotate to coat the base. Set aside to cool and harden.

3 Put the eggs, yolks and sugar into a bowl, and beat together until smooth. Add the infused milk mixture, stir until well combined, then strain into the dish(es).

4 Put the dish, cups or ramekins in a roasting tin, adding enough hot water to come halfway up the side(s). Bake for 1 hour 10 minutes for the soufflé dish or 45–50 minutes for the coffee cups or ramekins until just set in the middle (see Cook's tips). Cool and chill for at least 6 hours or overnight. Decorate with orange zest.

Cook's tips

- Look for a mild flower honey such as lavender or orange blossom; strong honeys will be overpowering.
- The honey needs to be cooked to a golden-brown caramel – any darker and it will become bitter.
- The custard may still be wobbly after cooking, but don't worry – it will firm up on cooling and chilling.

Mango Gratin with Sabayon

SERVES 6

3 large ripe mangoes
5 medium egg yolks
6 tbsp golden caster sugar
300ml (½ pint) champagne or sparkling wine
6 tbsp dark muscovado sugar to sprinkle
langues de chat biscuits to serve

PREPARATION TIME 5 minutes
COOKING TIME 10 minutes, plus optional 10 minutes resting

PER SERVING
249 calories
5g fat (of which 1g saturates)
45g carbohydrate
0g salt

TECHNIQUES
see also preparing mangoes (page 210), separating eggs (page 52)

1 Slice the mangoes and arrange in six serving glasses. Whisk the egg yolks and sugar in a large bowl over a pan of simmering water until the mixture is thick and falls in soft ribbon shapes. Add the champagne or sparkling wine and continue to whisk until the mixture is thick and foamy again. Remove from the heat.

2 Spoon the sabayon over the mangoes, sprinkle each with dark muscovado sugar, then blow-torch the top to caramelise or leave for 10 minutes to go fudgey. Serve with biscuits.

Finishing touches

Make your own crisp dessert macaroons to serve with this fruity gratin. Try rolled vanilla biscuits (page 333) or melted ginger biscuits (page 315).

Baked Raspberry Meringue Pie

SERVES 8
8 trifle sponges
450g (1lb) raspberries, lightly crushed
2–3 tbsp raspberry liqueur
3 medium egg whites
150g (5oz) golden caster sugar

PREPARATION TIME 15 minutes
COOKING TIME 8 minutes

PER SERVING
176 calories
2g fat (of which 1g saturates)
37g carbohydrate
0.1g salt

TECHNIQUES
see also separating eggs (page 52), preparing berries (page 209)

1 Preheat the oven to 230°C (210°C fan oven) mark 8. Put the trifle sponges in the bottom of a 2 litre (3½ pint) ovenproof dish. Spread the raspberries on top and drizzle over the raspberry liqueur.

2 Whisk the egg whites in a clean grease-free bowl until stiff peaks form. Gradually whisk in the sugar until the mixture is smooth and glossy. Spoon the meringue mixture over the raspberries and bake for 6–8 minutes until golden.

Cook's tip

If you don't have any raspberry liqueur, you can use another fruit-based liqueur such as Grand Marnier instead.

Toasted Hazelnut Meringue Cake

SERVES 8
oil to grease
175g (6oz) skinned hazelnuts, toasted
3 large egg whites
175g (6oz) golden caster sugar
250g carton mascarpone cheese
285ml (9½fl oz) double cream
3 tbsp Baileys Irish Cream liqueur, plus extra to serve
140g (4½oz) frozen raspberries
340g jar redcurrant jelly

PREPARATION TIME 10 minutes, plus cooling
COOKING TIME about 30 minutes

PER SERVING
598 calories
38g fat (of which 16g saturates)
57g carbohydrate
0.1g salt

TECHNIQUES
see also toasting nuts (page 218), separating eggs (page 52)

1 Preheat the oven to 190°C (170°C fan oven) mark 5. Lightly oil two 18cm (7in) sandwich tins and baseline with baking parchment. Whiz the hazelnuts in a food processor until finely chopped.

2 Put the egg whites into a clean grease-free bowl and whisk until stiff peaks form. Whisk in the sugar, a spoonful at a time. Fold in half the nuts using a metal spoon. Divide the mixture between the tins and spread evenly. Bake in the middle of the oven for about 30 minutes, then leave to cool in the tins for 30 minutes.

3 To make the filling, put the mascarpone cheese in a bowl. Beat in the cream and liqueur until smooth. Put the raspberries and redcurrant jelly into a pan and heat gently until the jelly has melted. Sieve, then cool.

4 Use a palette knife to loosen the edges of the meringues, then turn out on to a wire rack. Peel off the baking parchment and discard. Put a large sheet of baking parchment on a board and sit one meringue on top, flat side down. Spread a third of the mascarpone mixture over the meringue, then drizzle with raspberry purée. Top with the other meringue, then cover the whole cake with the rest of the mascarpone mixture. Sprinkle with the remaining hazelnuts. Carefully put the cake on to a serving plate and drizzle with more liqueur, if you like.

Freezing tip

Freezing the meringue makes it slightly softer but no less tasty. Make the cake up to the end of step 4 but don't put on serving plate or drizzle with more liqueur. Using the paper, lift the cake into the freezer, then freeze until solid. Once solid, freeze in a sturdy container for up to one month.
To use Thaw overnight in the refrigerator, then complete the recipe.

4 FISH AND SHELLFISH

Healthy and delicious, but often intimidating for the home cook, this chapter takes the mystery out of preparing and cooking fish and shellfish. There are clearly illustrated, easy-to-follow step-by-step instructions for all the basic techniques – from preparing and cooking fish, peeling and butterflying prawns and cooking and removing the meat from crab and lobsters to cleaning and cooking mussels and clams, opening scallops and oysters, and cleaning and preparing squid, cuttlefish and octopus. The comprehensive recipe collection builds on these skills with delicious recipes such as Seafood and lime kebabs, Crab cakes with mayonnaise, Tuna with coriander rice, Stir-fried prawns with cabbage, Fish and chips, Smoked fish pie and Thai shellfish curry.

Preparing round fish

Round fish include all those fish with a round body such as cod, herring, mackerel and trout. Most fishmongers will prepare them for you but it is very simple to clean, bone and fillet them yourself.

Cleaning and boning

1 Cut off the fins with scissors. Using the blunt edge of a knife, scrape the fish from tail to head and rinse off the loose scales. (The scaled fish should feel smooth.)

2 Insert a sharp knife at the hole towards the rear of the stomach and slit the skin up to the gills. Ease out the entrails. Use scissors to snip out anything that remains. With the knife, cut along the vein under the backbone. Wash the cavity under running water.

3 Working from the belly side of the fish, cut along one side of the backbone, then remove as many fine bones as possible and separate the backbone from the flesh.

4 Turn the fish over and repeat on the other side of the backbone. Carefully snip the backbone with scissors, then remove.

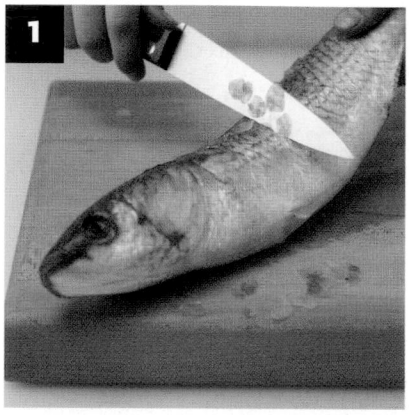

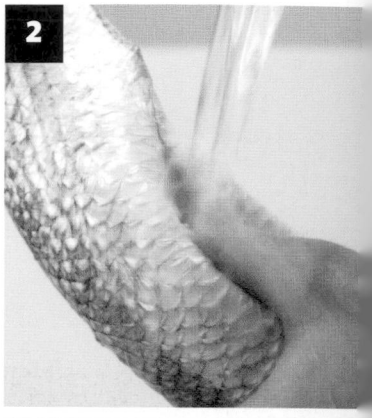

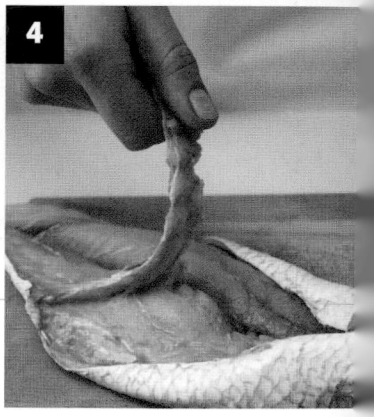

Filleting

1 Using a very sharp knife, cut through the flesh down to the backbone just behind the head.

2 Working from the head end, insert the knife between the flesh and the ribs on the back of the fish.

3 Holding the knife flat on the ribs, cut all the way down to the tail until the flesh is completely detached along the full length of the fish.

4 Lift the detached portion of flesh and, with the knife again placed flat on the ribs, cut until the flesh is detached from the bones and remove the fillet.

5 Turn the fish over and repeat on the other side, again working from head to tail, to remove the second fillet from the fish.

Cook's tip

Some cooks find it easier to remove the second fillet by keeping the fish with the un-boned side down and working the knife under the ribs on both back and belly side of the fillet.

Preparing flat fish

These techniques are suitable for flat-shaped fish such as turbot, plaice and sole. Flat fish is often used filleted for recipes and sometimes rolled around a stuffing. For this, it also needs to be skinned.

Cleaning and skinning

1 To gut, slit open the skin just behind the head of the fish where the stomach sac begins. Work your fingers in and pull the entrails out, then snip out the remainder with scissors.

2 Thick-skinned fish, such as sole, can be skinned by hand. Make a nick right down to the backbone where the body meets the tail. Work your fingers under the skin until you have lifted enough to get a grip on.

3 Holding the tail in one hand, pull on the flap in the direction of the head. The skin should come away in a single sheet.

4 Thinner-skinned fish can be filleted first, then skinned using a knife. Put the fillet on a board with the skin down and the tail towards you. Make a nick in the tail flesh, just deep enough to cut through to the skin, and lift the little flap of flesh with the knife.

5 Hold the knife on the skin at a very shallow angle, almost parallel to the work surface, and work it between flesh and skin to remove the skin in a single piece.

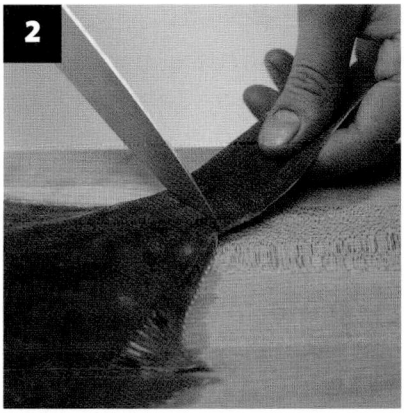

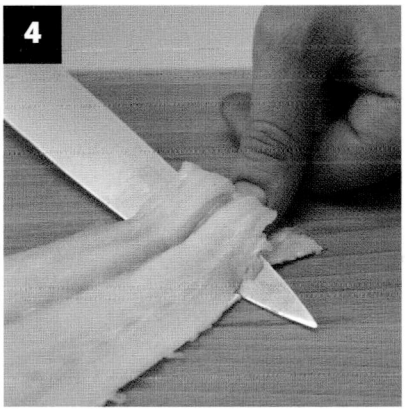

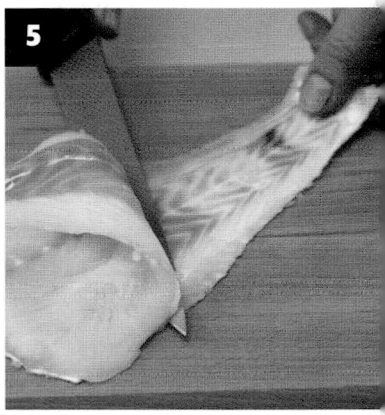

Filleting

1 Insert a sharp knife between the flesh and ribs on one side of the backbone. Holding the knife nearly parallel to the backbone, cut between the backbone and the flesh until detached. Turn the fish round and repeat on the other side.

2 Turn the fish over and repeat on the other side. Smaller fish may only provide two fillets.

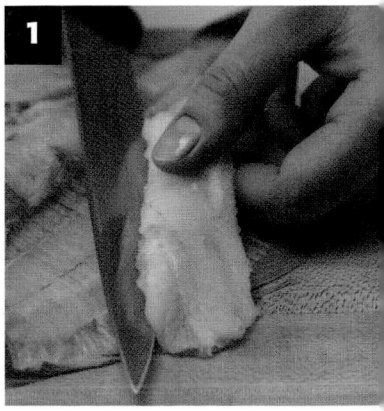

Cooking fish

Fish is wonderfully versatile and can be cooked in many ways – from the simplest steaming and poaching to quick stir-frying, crispy deep-frying and delicious roasting, baking and braising.

Steaming

A large traditional bamboo steamer is usually suitable for steaming small fish or pieces of fish, but a wok fitted with a bamboo, wood or metal trivet is often useful for steaming larger whole fish.

1 Put the fish on a lightly oiled heatproof plate that will hold it comfortably and will fit comfortably inside the steamer.

2 Season the fish with salt and ground black pepper or marinate (see box below).

3 Bring the water in the steamer to the boil over a medium heat. Put the fish in its plate in the steamer, put the lid on tightly and cook until the fish is just cooked through. Allow about 10 minutes of cooking per 2.5cm (1in) thickness.

Poaching

Fish can be poached whole or in pieces. If you're cooking a large fish such as salmon, you will need a salmon poacher. Smaller fish or pieces can be cooked in a large frying pan or in a roasting dish.

1 Put the fish in the pan and add enough poaching liquid (see page 35) to just cover it.

2 Bring it to the boil, then turn the heat right down so that the liquid is just simmering. The fish will need about 10 minutes of cooking per 2.5cm (1in) thickness.

3 Remove the fish carefully to a serving platter and allow it to drain well. Pour off the water before saucing and serving.

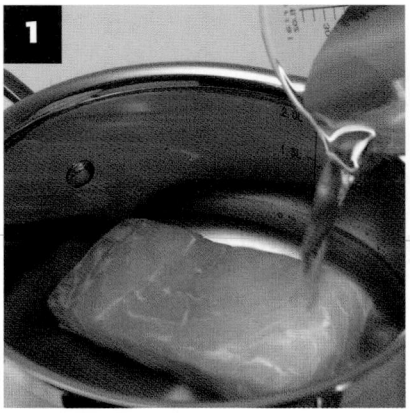

Marinades

- Because fish is already tender, marinades are used for flavour and not to tenderise. Therefore, fish only requires to be marinated briefly – about 10 minutes is usually enough.
- If you are cooking whole fish, slash the skin diagonally on both sides so that the marinade can penetrate the flesh underneath it. While cooking, spoon the marinade over the fish to get the most flavour.
- The simplest marinades are best: try combining vegetable oil, soy sauce and garlic, or extra-virgin olive oil, lemon juice and chopped shallots.

Pan-frying whole fish

1 Put in enough oil to fill the pan to a depth of about 5mm (¼in). Put the pan over a medium-high heat. Dust small whole fish with flour, then slip them carefully into the hot oil.

2 When they are lightly browned and looking crisp underneath, turn them using two spatulas. Cook until the second side is brown and the flesh just cooked through.

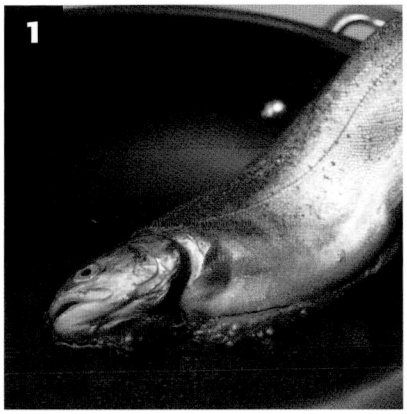

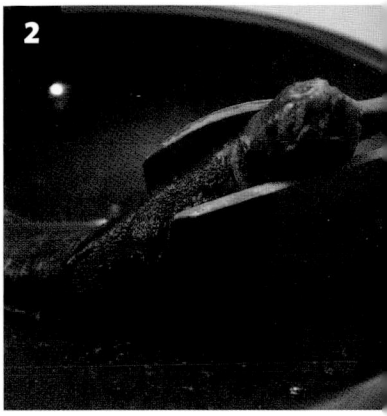

Pan-frying fillets or steaks

1 Put in enough oil to fill the pan to a depth of about 3mm (⅛in) and heat over a medium-high heat. Add the fish to the pan. If you like, you can dust the fish with flour first.

2 Cook for a few minutes, then lift, using tongs, to check the colour underneath. If it is brown, turn the fish over completely and fry until cooked through.

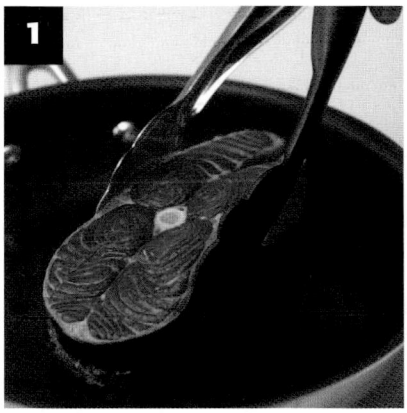

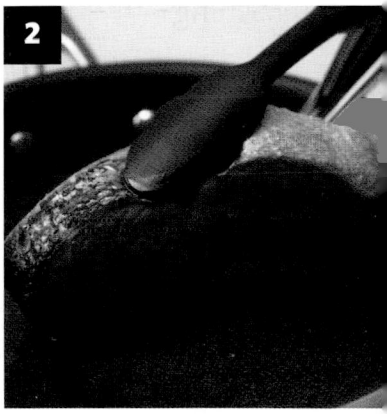

Searing

1 Put in enough oil (or a mixture of oil and clarified butter) to fill the pan to a depth of about 3mm (⅛in). Add the fish to the pan and fry.

2 Fry firm-fleshed fish such as tuna and salmon, or shellfish such as scallops, over very high heat so that it cooks quickly – or stays undercooked in the middle while browning deeply on the outside.

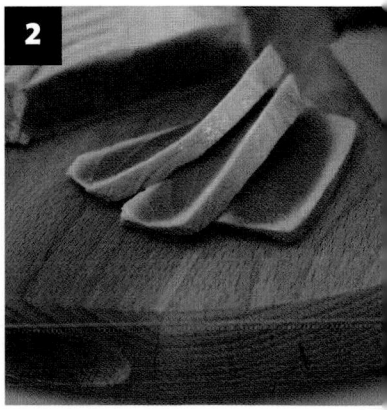

Stir-frying

Choose a firm fish such as monkfish as more delicate fish will break up.

1 Cut into bite-sized pieces. Heat a wok or large pan until very hot.

2 Add oil to coat. Add the fish and toss over a high heat for 2 minutes until just cooked. Remove to a bowl. Cook vegetables and flavourings. Return the fish to heat through.

Deep-frying

1 Prepare the fish for frying (either small whole fish or fish pieces) and chill. Prepare the seasoned flour, batter or coating. Heat vegetable oil in a deep-fryer to 180°C (test by frying a small cube of bread; it should brown in 40 seconds). Start battering or coating your fish.

2 Carefully lower the fish into the oil, taking care not to splash. Don't put too many pieces of fish into the pan at once (if you do, the temperature drops and the fish takes longer to cook and becomes greasy).

3 As the fish becomes golden and crisp, remove it with a slotted spoon and drain on kitchen paper. Serve immediately or keep warm in the oven until everything is cooked.

Coatings and batters

Flour, egg and breadcrumbs For a light coating, roll the food in flour seasoned with salt and pepper. For a crunchy coating, dip the floured food in beaten egg, then coat with dry breadcrumbs.

Coating batter You will need 125g (4oz) plain flour, sifted, pinch of salt, 1 medium egg, 150ml (¼ pint) milk. Mix the flour, salt, egg and enough milk for a stiff batter that will coat the back of a spoon; beat until smooth. Dip the food into the batter, drain slightly, then put into the hot fat.

Tempura batter For this delicate batter, you will need 125g (4oz) plain flour, 125g (4oz) cornflour, pinch of salt, 1 medium egg yolk, 300ml (½ pint) sparkling water. Lightly whisk the ingredients (the batter should be lumpy). Deep-fry at 170°C (a cube of bread should brown in 40 seconds).

Roasting

Good for firm fish, such as salmon and cod, at least 4cm (1½in) thick.

1 Preheat the oven to 190°C (170°C fan oven) mark 5. Arrange the fish on an oiled baking sheet.

2 Whisk together 2 parts olive oil to 1 part lemon juice. Brush over the fish. Roast for 10 minutes per 2.5cm (1in) thickness of fish until cooked.

Baking

This method is suitable for cooking whole fish and larger pieces of fish. Cooking times will vary according to the weight and thickness of fish. To bake a whole salmon for six to eight, you will need 2.5kg (5½lb) salmon, filleted, 1 bulb fennel, cored and sliced, 2 tbsp extra-virgin olive oil, 1 lemon, thinly sliced, a few sprigs of dill, 4 tbsp dry white wine, black pepper.

1 Cook the fennel gently in half the olive oil for about 10 minutes until softened, then set aside to cool. Meanwhile, preheat the oven to 190°C (170°C fan oven) mark 5.

2 Using tweezers, remove any remaining pin-bones from the salmon. Lay one fillet in a roasting dish, skin side down. Lay the lemon slices on top with the fennel, dill and a grinding of black pepper and spoon over the wine. Lay the other fillet on top, skin side up.

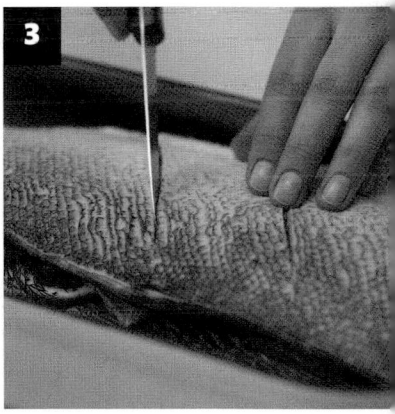

3 Score the skin every 5cm (2in) with a sharp knife. Brush with the remaining oil and scrunch pieces of foil against the fleshy parts of the fish, leaving the skin exposed.

4 Bake the fish for 30–40 minutes until the skin is opaque and the flesh firm to the touch. To test if it is cooked, slip a knife into the scored fish – it should be opaque.

5 Serve hot or cold with minted new potatoes and mayonnaise.

Braising

This is a good method when you want a fairly hearty dish that has its own sauce.

To serve four, you will need 1 tbsp oil, 15g (½oz) butter, 1 onion, chopped, 2 garlic cloves, crushed, 2 tbsp each freshly chopped parsley and thyme, 400g can chopped tomatoes, 1 large, flat fish, such as turbot or sole, about 900g (2lb).

1 Put the oil and butter in a large frying pan and cook the onion and garlic until soft.

2 Add the herbs and tomatoes to the pan, and cook until the tomatoes are fairly thick.

3 Lay the fish over the vegetables and spoon the tomatoes over it. Cook for another 5–10 minutes until the fish is just cooked through.

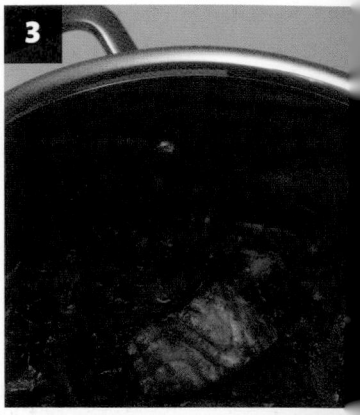

Perfect braised fish

- Choose thick, fairly firm-fleshed fish if you are cooking it in pieces – cod, haddock, monkfish, hake and whiting are all good choices. Shellfish, squid and cuttlefish are also suitable.
- You can choose a variety of vegetables to cook in braised dishes. Make sure that all the other ingredients are cooked and their flavours well developed before you add the fish.
- Once you add the fish to the pan, don't move it about too much as the flesh can easily break up. Be careful when removing it from the pan.

Grilling

Suitable for thick cuts such as fillets and steaks; small to medium whole fish such as sardines and mackerel; and flat fish on the bone such as plaice. Leave the skin on fillets.

1 Brush the outside of the fish with oil or marinate (see page 78).

2 Set the grill to high and cook until the fish starts to turn golden, then turn carefully. Allow 4–5 minutes for fillets and 10–15 minutes for thick steaks, cutlets and whole fish.

Preparing prawns

Full of flavour and perhaps at their best served simply, raw prawns are delicious served boiled, steamed, stir-fried, grilled and used in soup. They can be cooked in or out of their shells.

Peeling and butterflying

1 To shell prawns, pull off the head and put to one side. Using pointed scissors, cut through the soft shell on the belly side.

2 Prise the shell off, leaving the tail attached. (Add to the head; it can be used later for making stock.)

3 Using a small sharp knife, make a shallow cut along the length of the back of the prawn. Using the point of the knife, carefully remove and discard the black vein (the intestinal tract) that runs along the back of the prawn.

4 To 'butterfly' the prawn, cut halfway through the flesh lengthways from the head end to the base of the tail, and open up the prawn.

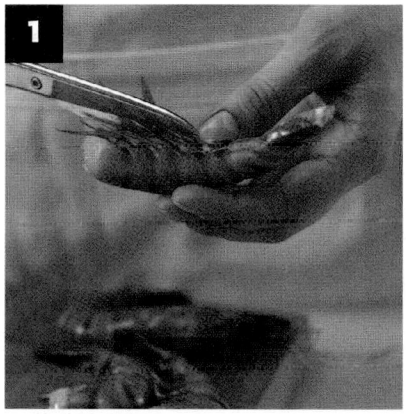

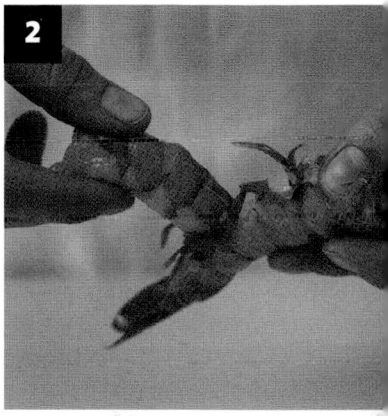

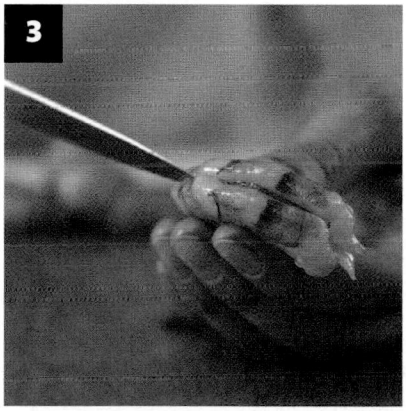

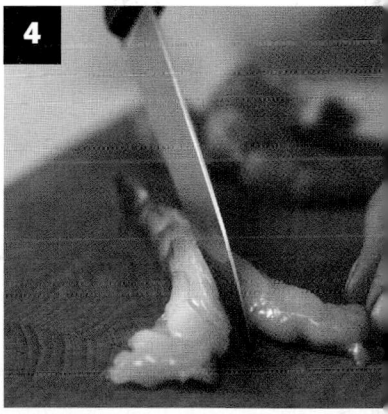

Langoustines and crayfish

- Related to the prawn, langoustines and crayfish can be shelled in the same way as prawns. To extract the meat from langoustine claws, pull off the small pincer from the claws, then work with small scissors to cut open the main section all the way along its length. Split open and carefully pull out the flesh in a single piece. To extract the meat from large crayfish claws, crack them open using a hammer or lobster cracker, then remove the meat.
- Also known as scampi, langoustines are at their best when just boiled or steamed, and then eaten from the shells. They can also be used in a shellfish soup.
- Crayfish are sold either live or cooked. To cook, boil in court bouillon for 5–10 minutes. Remove from the stock and cool. Eat crayfish from the shell or in a soup.

Preparing crabs

The amazing taste of fresh crab makes this one of the favourite shellfish and it is also reasonably priced. Avoid frozen crab, as the flesh is watery, and prepare your own for the best flavour.

Preparing and cooking

1 Live crabs must be humanely killed before cooking. Put the crab on a board, with the belly facing up. Take a large chef's knife and plunge it straight down into the crab's head, right between or just below the eyes.

2 Put the crab in a pan of boiling water and cook for 5 minutes per 450g (1lb). Alternatively, steam for 8 minutes per 450g (1lb).

3 To serve whole, simply set on the table with crackers and crab picks for diners to use themselves.

4 To remove the cooked meat for a recipe, put the crab on a board, with the belly facing up. Twist off the legs and claws. Lift off and discard the 'apron' (tail) – long and pointed in a male, short and broad in a female.

5 Pull the body out of the shell and remove and discard the feathery gills and grey stomach sac. Cut the body into pieces and pick out the meat using your fingers and a crab pick or small knife. Scrape the brown meat from the shell, keeping it separate from the white meat. If there is roe in a female, keep that separate, too.

6 Crack the claws with the back of a large knife, and pull out the meat in a single piece or in large chunks.

7 Cut through the shells of the legs with scissors, then cut through the opposite side. Pull off the shell halves to expose the meat and remove.

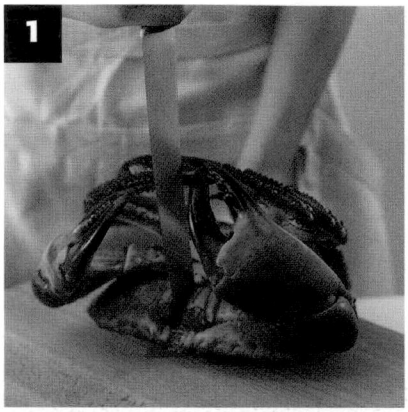

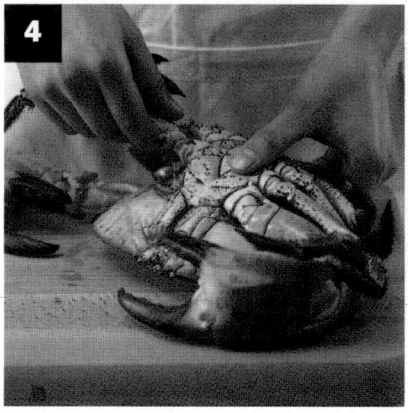

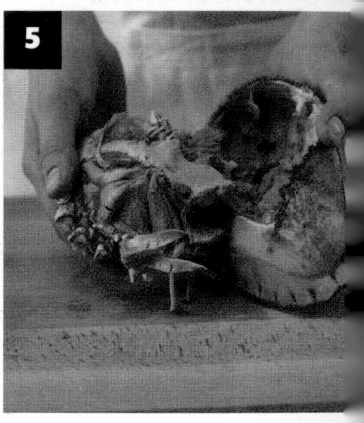

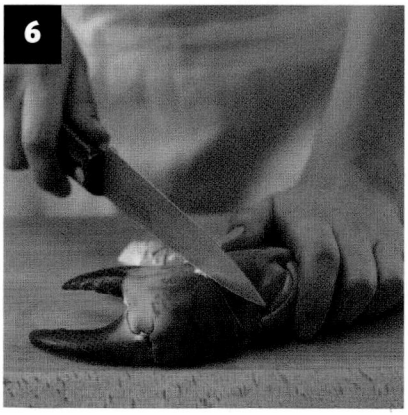

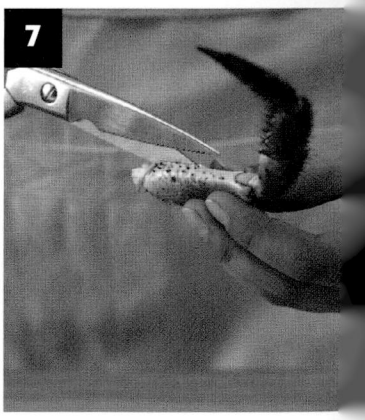

Preparing lobsters

The king of the crustaceans, lobster has a wonderfully sweet flavour and is excellent served simply: cold with a salad and mayonnaise or a sauce, or hot with butter.

Preparing and cooking

1 To kill a lobster humanely before grilling, boiling or baking, put it on a chopping board and hold the body firmly. Take a large chef's knife and plunge it straight down into the lobster's head, right between or just below the eyes. (It is inhumane to simply plunge it into boiling water or to put it into cold water and then bring it up to the boil.)

2 To cook the lobster whole, put it into a pot of boiling water and cook for 15–20 minutes.

3 If you are going to split the raw lobster for grilling or baking, cut the freshly killed lobster right through the head, then cut all the way down the length of the tail to split it in two.

4 Remove the head sac, which lies just behind the eyes, and discard. If you wish, you can remove the black coral (tomalley) and the green intestine, which lie inside the back of the shell just behind the head sac, or they may be left in place for cooking.

5 If you want the tail meat in one piece, split the head to where the tail begins, then use scissors to cut through the soft shell of the belly, down to the tail.

6 Pull the tail meat out with your fingers. Clean the head as in step 3. Cut off the claws and spiny legs. Crack the claws with a hammer or lobster cracker and remove the meat. Save the shells to make stock.

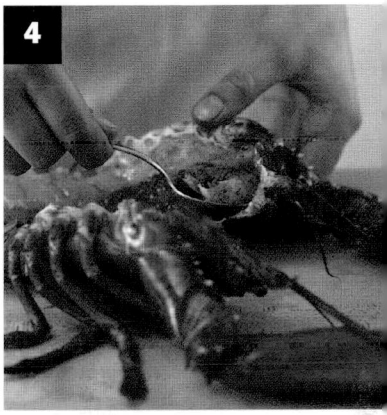

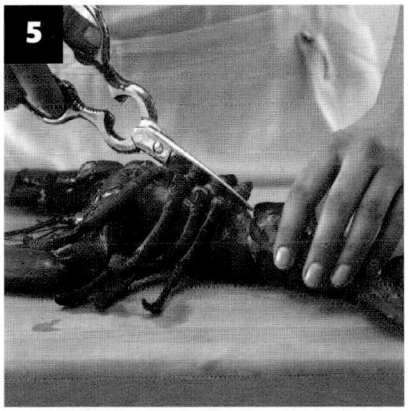

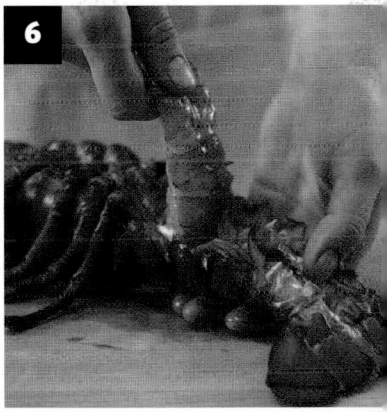

Buying shellfish

Shellfish should be as fresh as possible and should have a mild, fresh smell of the sea.

- Live lobsters are dark blue in colour and turn bright pink when cooked. When buying a live lobster, choose one with all its claws and legs intact.
- The common brown crab is most often found in fishmongers, but there are many varieties. When buying live crabs, look for a really lively one and make sure all its legs are intact.
- Prawns are sold ready-cooked and raw. Try to buy fresh ones when you can as they have the best taste and texture.
- When choosing molluscs, choose those with tightly closed, undamaged shells. Mussels, clams, scallops and oysters sold fresh are still alive and an open shell may indicate the shellfish is far from fresh. Tap the shell – it should close. If not, discard it.

Preparing mussels and clams

Two of the most popular shellfish, mussels and clams take moments to cook. Careful preparation is important, so give yourself enough time to get the shellfish ready.

Cooking mussels

1 Scrape off the fibres attached to the shells (beards). If the mussels are very clean, give them a quick rinse under the cold tap. If they are very sandy, scrub them with a stiff brush.

2 If the shells have sizeable barnacles on them, it's best (though not essential) to remove them. Rap them sharply with a metal spoon or the back of a washing-up brush, then scrape off.

3 Discard any open mussels that don't shut when sharply tapped; this means they are dead and could be dangerous to eat.

4 In a large heavy-based pan, fry 2 finely chopped shallots and a generous handful of parsley in 25g (1oz) butter for about 2 minutes until soft. Pour in 1cm (½in) dry white wine.

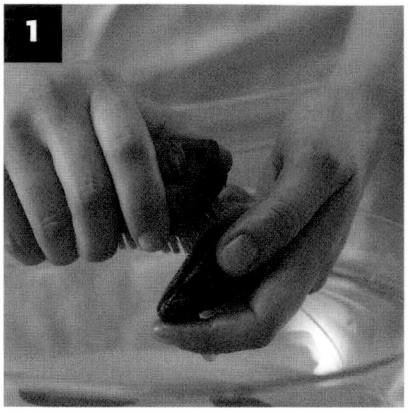

5 Add the mussels to the pan and cover tightly with a lid. Steam for 5–10 minutes until the shells open. Immediately take the pan away from the heat.

6 Using a slotted spoon, remove the mussels from the pan and discard any that haven't opened, then boil the cooking liquid rapidly to reduce. Pour over the mussels and serve immediately.

Cooking clams

Small clams are usually used as an ingredient; larger clams can be eaten raw in the shell.

1 To cook, rinse or lightly scrub the clams. Place in a large bowl of cold salted water (2 tbsp salt per 1 litre/ 1¾ pints water). Leave to stand for a few hours to allow the clams to open and release any sand and grit.

2 Cook as for mussels, then use according to the recipe.

Preparing scallops and oysters

Both of these delicately flavoured shellfish are contained within shells that can be a little tricky to open. Ask your fishmonger to prepare them if you prefer. The fish themselves have a marvellous taste.

Opening scallops

Scallops can be eaten raw, either seasoned or marinated in citrus juice with seasonings (see page 78). They take very little cooking, usually between 5 and 10 minutes.

1 Hold the scallop with the flat half of the shell facing up. Firmly ease a very sharp small knife between the shells at a point close to the hinge.

2 Keeping the knife angled towards the flat shell, cut all along the shell surface until the two shells can be separated easily. Cut along the bottom of the rounded shell to release its contents. Cut loose the meat and the grey/orange coral and discard everything else.

3 Now rinse off any grit, cut the coral from the round meat, and cut the little scrap of muscle from the edge of the meat.

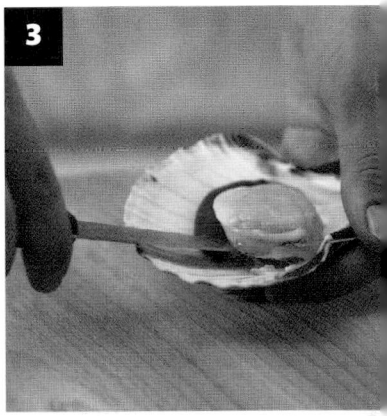

Cooking scallops

- Gently poach the white meat in wine for 5 minutes, then add the coral and simmer for 5 minutes.
- Sauté until crisp on the outside.
- Sear briefly on each side in a very hot pan until the surface browns and the inside remains tender.
- Thread on to skewers and grill.
- Bake in the shell with a sauce.

Opening oysters

Oysters can be fried, poached and grilled, or eaten straight from the shell with red wine vinegar flavoured with shallots, or just with lemon juice.

1 Hold the oyster in one hand with the flat half of the shell facing up, using a towel to protect your hand. Insert an oyster knife in the hinge and twist.

2 When the upper shell comes off, scrape off any shell and cut under the oyster to release it from the shell.

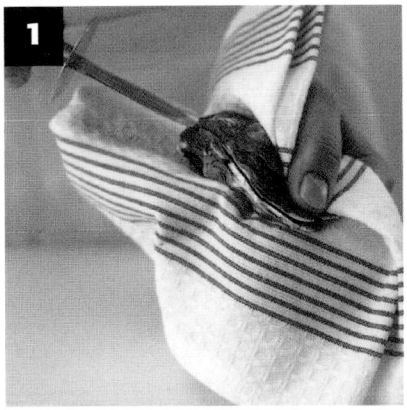

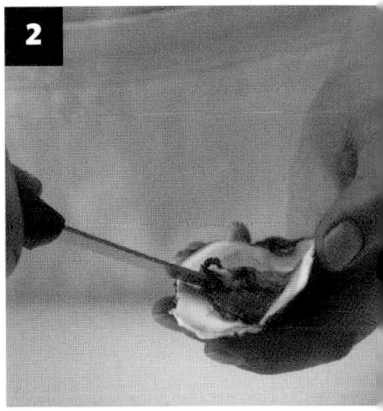

Preparing squid and cuttlefish

Sliced into rings or left whole and stuffed, squid is a popular, flavourful and easily available fish. The less common cuttlefish also has a good flavour and is especially good in stews.

Cleaning and preparing

1 If you want to save the ink for using in a dish, position the head over a bowl and cut open the ink sac so that the ink can drain into it. Set aside.

2 Cut off the tentacles just behind the 'beak'.

3 Pull out the beak and clean the tentacles well, getting off as many of the plastic-like rings from the suckers as you can.

4 Reach inside the body and pull out the internal organs, including the plastic-like 'pen' (in squid) or cuttle bone (in cuttlefish).

5 Scrape and pull off the loose, slippery skin covering the body. Rinse the body thoroughly to remove all internal organs, sand and other debris.

6 Detach the wings and set aside, then cut up the tentacles and body as required in your recipe. Generally speaking, the longer the squid or cuttlefish is going to be cooked, the larger the pieces should be.

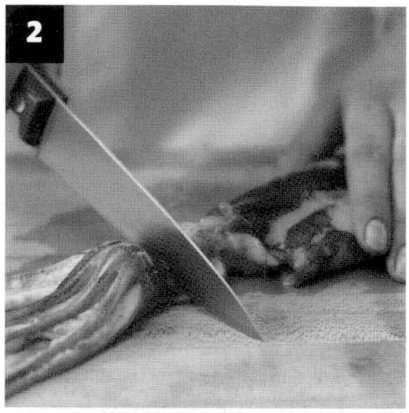

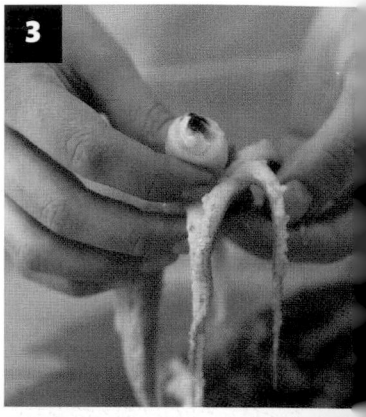

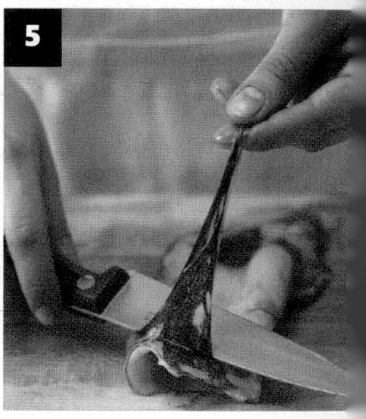

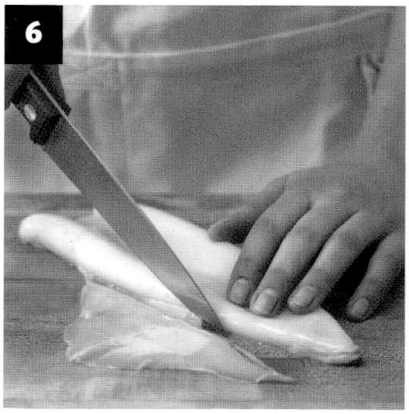

Cook's tip

Small squid are the sweetest and are generally best if cooked for a very short time: fried with a flour or batter coating, stir-fried, grilled or barbecued. Smaller cuttlefish can be treated in the same way. Larger cuttlefish and very large squid can be stewed.

Preparing octopus

Small octopus can be cooked briefly like squid, but mostly they should be cooked slowly for a long time to make them tender. Cooking in red wine helps to tenderise large octopus.

Cleaning and preparing

1 Cut off the tentacles just behind the 'beak' (mouth).

2 Pull out the beak and clean the tentacles well, getting off as many of the plastic-like rings from the suckers as you can.

3 Turn the body inside out to expose the sac containing the internal organs. Pull out the sac and rub, scrape and pull off the loose, slippery skin covering the body. Rinse the body thoroughly to remove all internal organs, sand and other debris.

4 Cut up the tentacles and body as required in your recipe.

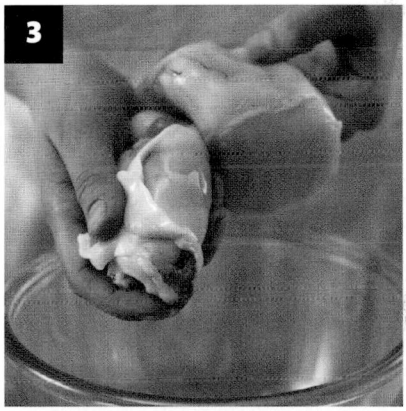

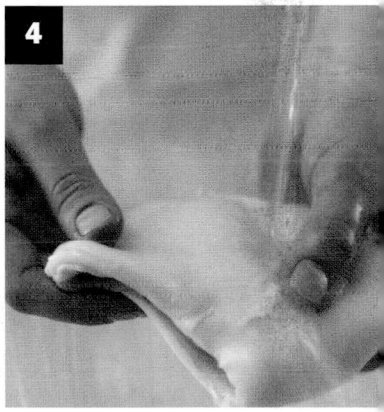

How to buy the best fish

For the best results, fish should be as fresh as possible. It's often hard to tell in the supermarket how fresh a piece of fish is but there are some key signs to look for. A really fresh fish will have:

- An even covering of scales with no patches and no damage to the fins.
- Bright and clear eyes and bright red gills.
- Flesh that feels firm rather than soft and spongy.
- Individual fillets should be moist, shiny and plump.

Smoked Salmon Parcels

SERVES 6

6 large scallops or 12 small queen scallops with corals attached, about 225g (8oz) total weight
1 large ripe avocado
1 garlic clove, crushed
4 small spring onions, finely chopped
1 green chilli, deseeded and chopped
1 tbsp grapeseed oil
zest and juice of 1 lime, plus extra to squeeze
6 large slices of smoked salmon, about 300g (11oz) total weight and 23cm (9in) in length
salt and ground black pepper
rocket leaves and lime wedges to garnish

For the coriander dressing

25g (1oz) fresh coriander sprigs
1 small garlic clove, crushed
50ml (2fl oz) grapeseed oil
1 tbsp lime juice
pinch of caster sugar

PREPARATION TIME 40 minutes
COOKING TIME 6 minutes

PER SERVING

219 calories
13g fat (of which 2g saturates)
3g carbohydrate
2.5g salt

TECHNIQUES

see also opening scallops (page 87), preparing vegetables (pages 170–182), zesting citrus fruits (page 207), making salad dressings (page 25)

1 To make the coriander dressing, put all the ingredients in a blender and process until smooth. Set aside.

2 To make the parcels, remove any tough membrane from the scallops and season with salt and pepper. Put in a steamer and cook for about 5 minutes or until the flesh is just white. Alternatively, put the scallops on a heatproof plate, cover with another plate and steam over a pan of simmering water for about 3 minutes on each side. Drain and set on kitchen paper to cool.

3 Put the avocado, garlic, spring onions, chilli, oil and lime zest and juice in a bowl. Mash the avocado with a fork, then mix together and season.

4 Lay the salmon slices on a worksurface, put a large scallop or two small ones on each slice and spoon the avocado mixture on top. Roll the salmon around the filling.

5 To serve, put the parcels on serving plates and squeeze a little lime juice over each. Drizzle with the coriander dressing, garnish with rocket leaves and sprinkle with pepper.

Seafood and Lime Kebabs

SERVES 4

225g (8oz) peeled raw king prawns, deveined
550g (1¼lb) monkfish fillet, cut into 2.5cm (1in) cubes
juice of ½ lime
1 garlic clove, crushed
2 tbsp chilli oil
2 tbsp teriyaki sauce
2 limes and 1 lemon, each cut into 8 wedges
finely chopped and deseeded green chilli, spring onion curls and flat-leafed parsley to garnish
deep-fried noodles to serve (see Cook's tip)

PREPARATION TIME 25 minutes, plus 1 hour marinating
COOKING TIME 6 minutes

PER SERVING
363 calories
10g fat (of which 2g saturates)
34g carbohydrate
0.8g salt

TECHNIQUES
see also preparing prawns (page 83), preparing chillies (page 177)

1 Put the king prawns and monkfish in a bowl. Combine the lime juice, garlic, chilli oil and teriyaki sauce and pour over the top. Stir well to coat and leave in a cool place for up to 1 hour. Meanwhile, if using wooden skewers soak eight in water for 30 minutes.

2 Remove the seafood from the marinade and thread on to the skewers interspersed with lime and lemon wedges.

3 Heat a griddle or grill. Grill the kebabs for 3 minutes, turning once during cooking and brushing with the marinade. Garnish with green chilli, spring onions and parsley, and serve with deep-fried noodles.

Cook's tip

To make the deep-fried noodles, soak 175g (6oz) egg noodles in boiling water for 10 minutes, drain and dry well. Deep-fry in batches until golden.

Quick Salmon Mousse

SERVES 6

225g (8oz) skinless salmon fillet, roughly chopped
2 small fennel bulbs, thinly sliced
2 small avocados, sliced
1 courgette, pared into strips with a potato peeler
6–8 tbsp vinaigrette dressing
250g (9oz) ricotta or other soft cheese
2 tbsp freshly chopped chives
juice of ½ lemon
100g bag mixed salad leaves
6 slices toasted walnut bread
6 slices smoked salmon
salt and ground black pepper
lemon wedges to garnish

PREPARATION TIME 20 minutes, plus cooling

PER SERVING
468 calories
28g fat (of which 8g saturates)
19g carbohydrate
3.2g salt

TECHNIQUES
see also preparing vegetables (pages 170–182, making salad dressings (page 25)

1 Put the salmon fillet into a bowl and pour over enough boiling water to cover. Cover with clingfilm and leave to cool.

2 Put the fennel, avocado and courgette into a shallow dish and spoon over the vinaigrette dressing.

3 Drain the salmon and mash into the cheese with half the chives and the lemon juice. Season well with salt and pepper.

4 Arrange the fennel, avocado and courgette on six plates with the salad leaves. Put a slice of bread on to each plate, then top with a mound of the salmon mix and a fold of smoked salmon. Garnish with lemon wedges, sprinkle with the remaining chives and serve immediately.

Crab Cakes with Mayonnaise

SERVES 4

1 tbsp sunflower oil
3 spring onions, finely sliced
2 garlic cloves, crushed
1 red chilli, deseeded and chopped
350g (12oz) crabmeat
2 tsp tomato ketchup
4 tbsp mayonnaise
1 tsp Worcestershire sauce
50g (2oz) fresh white breadcrumbs
vegetable oil to fry
salt and ground black pepper
spring onion curls, crushed, sliced red chilli and lime wedges to garnish

For the chilli mayonnaise

2 tbsp sweet chilli sauce
1 tbsp freshly chopped coriander
zest and juice of 1 lime
5 tbsp mayonnaise

For the coating

50g (2oz) seasoned flour
1 large egg, beaten
125g (4oz) fresh white breadcrumbs

PREPARATION TIME 30 minutes, plus 1½ hours chilling
COOKING TIME 15 minutes

PER SERVING

620 calories
37g fat (of which 5g saturates)
50g carbohydrate
3.2g salt

TECHNIQUES

see also preparing vegetables (pages 170–182), preparing crab (page 84), making breadcrumbs (page 308), making mayonnaise (page 23)

1 To make the chilli mayonnaise, combine the ingredients in a bowl. Season with salt and pepper, cover and chill. Set aside. (This can be made a day in advance.)

2 To make the crab cakes, heat the sunflower oil in a pan, add the spring onions and cook, stirring, for 3 minutes. Remove from the heat and stir in the garlic and chilli. Transfer to a large bowl and cool. Add the crabmeat, ketchup, mayonnaise, Worcestershire sauce and breadcrumbs, and stir until well combined. Season.

3 Using your hands, shape the mixture into 12 cakes, and put on a baking sheet. Cover and chill for at least 1 hour.

4 To make the coating, dip the cakes into the seasoned flour, then the beaten egg and breadcrumbs. Put back on the baking sheet and chill for 30 minutes.

5 Heat 2.5cm (1in) vegetable oil in a pan. Fry the cakes in batches for 2–3 minutes on each side until golden. Remove the cakes from the pan and drain on kitchen paper. Season, garnish with the spring onion curls, chilli and lime wedges, and serve with the chilli mayonnaise.

Tuna with Coriander Rice

SERVES 4

250g (9oz) basmati rice
8 × 125g (4oz) tuna steaks
5cm (2in) piece fresh root ginger, peeled and grated
1 tbsp olive oil
100ml (3½fl oz) orange juice
300g (11oz) pak choi, roughly chopped
a small handful of freshly chopped coriander
ground black pepper
lime wedges to garnish

PREPARATION TIME 10 minutes
COOKING TIME about 10 minutes

PER SERVING

609 calories
15g fat (of which 4g saturates)
51g carbohydrate
0.6g salt

TECHNIQUES

see also cooking rice (page 236), preparing fresh spices (page 429), searing fish (page 79)

1 Cook the rice according to the pack instructions.

2 Meanwhile, put the tuna steaks in a shallow dish. Add the ginger, oil and orange juice, and season well with pepper. Turn the tuna over to coat.

3 Heat a non-stick frying pan until really hot. Add four tuna steaks and half the marinade. Cook for 1–2 minutes on each side until just cooked. Repeat with the remaining tuna and marinade. Remove the fish from the pan and keep warm.

4 Add the pak choi to the frying pan and cook for 1–2 minutes until wilted. When the rice is cooked, drain and stir the coriander through. Serve the tuna with the pak choi, rice and pan juices, and garnish with lime wedges.

Cook's tip

Basmati rice should be washed before cooking to remove excess starch and to give really light, fluffy results. Check out the technique for rinsing rice on page 236.

Dill Salmon

SERVES 4
4 tbsp Dijon mustard-flavoured mayonnaise
4 tbsp finely chopped fresh dill
4 tbsp clear honey
1 tbsp lemon juice
4 thick skinless salmon fillets, about 150g (5oz) each
tomato salad to serve

PREPARATION TIME 2 minutes
COOKING TIME 5–7 minutes

PER SERVING
422 calories
28g fat (of which 5g saturates)
12g carbohydrate
0.4g salt

TECHNIQUES
see also making mayonnaise (page 23), chopping herbs (page 428), skinning fish (page 77), grilling fish (page 82)

1 Preheat the grill to high. Put the mayonnaise into a bowl with the dill, honey and lemon juice. Mix together.

2 Put the salmon fillets on to a baking sheet and spread the mayonnaise mixture over the top. Grill for 5–7 minutes, depending on the thickness, until just cooked. Serve with tomato salad.

Cook's tip

There's no need to turn the salmon over halfway through – just remember to keep a close eye on it and lower the heat if necessary, so that the honey in the sauce doesn't burn.

Simple Smoked Haddock

SERVES 4
25g (1oz) unsalted butter
1 tbsp olive oil
1 garlic clove, thinly sliced
4 thick smoked haddock or cod fillets, about 175g (6oz) each
a small handful of freshly chopped parsley (optional)
finely grated zest of 1 small lemon, plus lemon wedges to serve

PREPARATION TIME 10 minutes
COOKING TIME about 10 minutes

PER SERVING
217 calories
9g fat (of which 4g saturates)
1g carbohydrate
3.4g salt

TECHNIQUES
see also preparing garlic (page 171), chopping herbs (page 428), pan-frying fish (page 79)

1 Heat the butter, oil and garlic in a large non-stick pan until the mixture starts to foam and sizzle. Put the fish into the pan, skin side down, and fry over a high heat for 10 minutes – this will give a golden crust underneath the fish.

2 Turn the fish over and scatter the parsley, if using, and lemon zest over it, then fry for a further 30 seconds. Put each cooked fillet on to a plate and spoon over some of the buttery juices. Serve with the lemon wedges.

Cook's tip

Smoked fish is quite salty so always taste the sauce before seasoning with any extra salt.

Stir-fried Prawns with Cabbage

SERVES 4

225g (8oz) pak choi or Chinese mustard cabbage
2 tbsp vegetable oil
2 garlic cloves, thinly sliced
1 lemongrass stalk, cut in half and bruised
2 kaffir lime leaves, finely torn
1 small red onion, thinly sliced
1 hot red chilli, deseeded and sliced
4cm (1½in) piece fresh root ginger, peeled and cut into long thin shreds
1 tbsp coriander seeds, lightly crushed
450g (1lb) large peeled raw prawns, deveined
175g (6oz) mangetouts, halved
2 tbsp Thai fish sauce (nam pla)
juice of 1 lime, or to taste
fried deseeded and sliced red chilli to garnish

PREPARATION TIME 30 minutes
COOKING TIME 6 minutes

PER SERVING
193 calories
8g fat (of which 1g saturates)
7g carbohydrate
1.4g salt

TECHNIQUES
see also preparing prawns (page 83)

Cook's tip

Thai fish sauce is a salty condiment with a distinctive, pungent aroma that is used in Thai and South-east Asian cooking. You can buy it in most large supermarkets and Asian food stores.

1 Tear the pak choi or cabbage leaves into manageable-sized pieces. Heat the oil in a wok or large frying pan. Add the garlic, lemongrass, lime leaves, onion, chilli, ginger and coriander seeds, and stir-fry for 2 minutes.

2 Add the prawns, mangetouts and pak choi or cabbage, and stir-fry until the vegetables are cooked but still crisp and the prawns are pink and opaque, about 2–3 minutes.

3 Add the fish sauce and lime juice, and heat through for 1 minute. Discard the lemongrass. Garnish with fried red chilli and serve immediately while the vegetables are crisp.

Foil-baked Fish

SERVES 4

1 small butternut squash, peeled and cut into small cubes
½ red onion, finely sliced
2 garlic cloves, finely chopped
1 tbsp dill, roughly chopped, plus extra to garnish
1 tbsp olive oil
4 thick haddock or salmon fillets, about 150g (5oz) each
125g (4oz) spinach
salt and ground black pepper

PREPARATION TIME 20 minutes
COOKING TIME 20 minutes

PER SERVING
186 calories
4g fat (of which 1g saturates)
6g carbohydrate
0.4g salt

TECHNIQUES
see also preparing vegetables (pages 170–182)

1 Preheat the oven to 220°C (200°C fan) mark 7. Cut out four 40.5cm (16in) squares of foil.

2 Put the squash in a bowl. Add the onion, garlic, dill and oil, and toss to coat. Season well with salt and pepper. Divide the vegetable mixture equally among the four squares of foil.

3 Top each pile of vegetables with a piece of fish. Season again, then bring the foil together and crimp the edges so that the fish and vegetables are completely enclosed. Put the parcels on a baking tray and roast for 15 minutes or until the fish is cooked through and the squash is just tender.

4 Carefully open each of the foil parcels and add the spinach. Close again and roast for a further 5 minutes or until the spinach has wilted. Garnish with dill and serve.

Cook's tip

Serve with a wedge of lemon to squeeze over the fish, and boiled new potatoes.

Oven-poached Cod with Herbs

SERVES 4

10 spring onions, sliced
2 garlic cloves, crushed
6 tbsp shredded fresh mint
6 tbsp freshly chopped flat-leafed parsley
juice of ½ lemon
150ml (¼ pint) fish, chicken or vegetable stock
4 cod fillets, about 200g (7oz) each
salt and ground black pepper
lemon wedges to garnish
mashed potato to serve

PREPARATION TIME 10 minutes
COOKING TIME 10 minutes

PER SERVING

177 calories
2g fat (of which trace saturates)
2g carbohydrate
0.6g salt

TECHNIQUES

see also preparing vegetables (pages 170–182), chopping herbs (page 428), making stock (page 34), mashing potatoes (page 184)

1 Preheat the oven to 230°C (210°C fan oven) mark 8. Combine the spring onions (putting some of the green part to one side), garlic, mint, parsley, lemon juice and stock in an ovenproof dish that can hold the cod in a single layer.

2 Put the cod on the herb and garlic mixture, and turn to moisten. Season with salt and pepper, and roast for 8–10 minutes.

3 Sprinkle with the reserved spring onion, garnish with lemon wedges and serve with mashed potato.

Mussel and Potato Stew

SERVES 4

25g (1oz) butter
200g pack rindless back bacon rashers, cut into strips
700g (1lb 9oz) white potatoes, cut into large chunks
198g can sweetcorn kernels, drained
1kg (2¼lb) mussels, tapped, and open or damaged ones discarded
140ml (4½fl oz) single cream
1 tbsp freshly chopped parsley
salt and ground black pepper

PREPARATION TIME 15 minutes
COOKING TIME 15 minutes

PER SERVING

472 calories
23g fat (of which 11g saturates)
42g carbohydrate
2.8g salt

TECHNIQUES

see also preparing mussels (page 86)

1 Melt the butter in a large pan, add the bacon and cook, stirring, until the strips separate. Add the potatoes and 150ml (¼ pint) water and season lightly with salt and pepper. Cover with a tight-fitting lid and cook for 10 minutes or until the potatoes are almost tender.

2 Add the sweetcorn and mussels to the pan, cover, bring to the boil and simmer for 2–3 minutes until the mussels open. Discard any mussels that don't open. Add the cream and chopped parsley, and serve.

Cook's tip

To make sure mussels are safe to eat, check them carefully before cooking for cracks and split shells. Discard these, and any that do not close when sharply tapped. Any mussels that remain closed after cooking should also be discarded.

Fish and Chips

SERVES 4

900g (2lb) Desirée potatoes, peeled
2–3 tbsp olive oil
sea salt flakes
sunflower oil to deep-fry
2 × 128g packs batter mix
1 tsp baking powder
¼ tsp salt
330ml bottle of lager
4 plaice fillets, about 225g (8oz) each, skin on, trimmed and cut in half
plain flour to dust
2 garlic cloves, crushed
8 tbsp mayonnaise
1 tsp lemon juice
salt and ground black pepper
lemon wedges and chives to garnish

PREPARATION TIME 30 minutes
COOKING TIME 40–50 minutes

PER SERVING

1185 calories
79g fat (of which 18g saturates)
73g carbohydrate
3.2g salt

TECHNIQUES

see also coatings and batters (page 80), making mayonnaise (page 23), deep-frying fish (page 80), making potato chips (page 186)

1 Preheat the oven to 240°C (220°C fan oven) mark 9. Cut the potatoes into chips. Put them in a pan of boiling salted water, cover and bring to the boil. Boil for 2 minutes, drain well, then turn on to kitchen paper to remove the excess moisture. Tip into a large non-stick roasting tin, toss with the olive oil and season with sea salt. Roast for 40–50 minutes until golden and cooked, turning from time to time.

2 Half-fill a deep-fat fryer with sunflower oil and heat to 190°C. Put the batter mix into a bowl with the baking powder and salt, and gradually whisk in the lager. Season the plaice and lightly dust with plain flour. Dip two of the fillets into the batter and deep-fry in the hot oil until golden. Keep hot in the oven while you deep-fry the remaining plaice fillets.

3 Mix the garlic, mayonnaise and lemon juice together in a bowl and season well. Serve the garlic mayonnaise with the plaice and chips, garnished with lemon wedges and chives.

Smoked Fish Pie

SERVES 4

700g (1½lb) floury potatoes, such as Maris Piper, peeled and chopped
25g (1oz) butter
1 tbsp plain flour
½ onion, finely sliced
75ml (3fl oz) double cream
150ml (¼ pint) hot vegetable stock
a splash of white wine (optional)
15g (½oz) freshly grated Parmesan
2 tsp Dijon mustard
350g (12oz) undyed skinless smoked haddock, roughly chopped
140g (4½oz) frozen peas
salt and ground black pepper

PREPARATION TIME 15 minutes
COOKING TIME 30–40 minutes

PER SERVING
340 calories
18g fat (of which 11g saturates)
23g carbohydrate
2.2g salt

TECHNIQUES
see also mashing potatoes (page 184), making stock (page 34), skinning fish (page 77)

1 Put the potatoes into a pan of cold salted water and bring to the boil. Simmer for 15–20 minutes until tender. Drain well, tip back into the pan, then mash with 15g (½oz) butter. Season with salt and pepper.

2 Preheat the oven to 220°C (200°C fan) mark 7. Heat the remaining butter in a large pan, add the flour and onion, and cook for 10 minutes or until the onion is soft and golden. Add the cream, stock, wine (if using), Parmesan and mustard. Stir everything together and season.

3 Add the fish and peas, and turn off the heat. Stir the mixture carefully.

4 Put the fish mixture into a 2.3 litre (4 pint) ovenproof dish. Cover with the mash, then cook in the oven for 15–20 minutes until the fish is cooked through.

Freezing tip

Prepare the fish mixture to step 3, then put into a freezerproof container, cool and freeze for up to one month.
To use Thaw and continue with the recipe.

Peppered Mackerel

SERVES 4

4 tsp whole mixed peppercorns
4 mackerel, gutted, about 250g (9oz) each
1 tbsp sunflower oil
200ml (7fl oz) full-fat crème fraîche
lemon wedges to garnish
asparagus and sugarsnap peas to serve

PREPARATION TIME 10 minutes
COOKING TIME 15 minutes

PER SERVING
764 calories
63g fat (of which 22g saturates)
1g carbohydrate
0.4g salt

TECHNIQUES
see also preparing round fish (page 76)

1 Lightly crush 2 tsp peppercorns using a pestle and mortar. Sprinkle one side of each mackerel with half the crushed peppercorns.

2 Heat the oil in a frying pan. Add the fish, peppered side down, and cook for 5–7 minutes over a medium-high heat. Sprinkle the mackerel with the remaining crushed peppercorns, turn the fish over and continue to fry for 5–7 minutes until cooked (see Cook's tips). Remove and keep warm.

3 Wipe out the pan, add the crème fraîche and bring to the boil. Stir in the remaining peppercorns. (If the sauce becomes too thick, add some boiling water.)

4 Spoon the sauce over the mackerel, garnish with lemon wedges and serve with asparagus.

Cook's tips

- If the mackerel are large, make three shallow slashes on either side of the fish.
- To test whether the fish is cooked, prise the flesh from the backbone with a knife; it should be opaque and come away easily.

Thai Green Shellfish Curry

SERVES 6

1 tbsp vegetable oil
1 pack fresh Thai herbs (containing 1 lemongrass stalk, 2 Thai chillies, coriander leaves, 2 lime leaves), all chopped
1–2 tbsp green Thai curry paste
400ml can coconut milk
450ml (¾ pint) vegetable stock
375g (13oz) queen scallops with corals
250g (9oz) raw tiger prawns, peeled with tails on
salt and ground black pepper
coriander leaves to garnish
jasmine rice to serve

PREPARATION TIME 5 minutes
COOKING TIME 15 minutes

PER SERVING
156 calories
5g fat (of which 1g saturates)
6g carbohydrate
0.8g salt

TECHNIQUES
see also making coconut milk (page 221), making vegetable stock (page 34), opening scallops (page 87), preparing prawns (page 83)

1 Heat the oil in a wok and fry the Thai herbs for 30 seconds. Add the curry paste and fry for 1 minute.

2 Add the coconut milk and stock, and bring to the boil. Simmer for 5–10 minutes until reduced a little. Season well with salt and pepper.

3 Add the scallops and tiger prawns, bring to the boil and simmer gently for 2–3 minutes until cooked. Spoon into bowls of Thai jasmine rice and garnish with coriander.

Cook's tip

Jasmine rice is also known as Thai fragrant rice and has a distinctive taste and texture. It is traditionally served with Thai food and is available in supermarkets and Asian stores.

Spanish Fish Stew

SERVES 4

350g (12oz) small salad potatoes, halved
175g (6oz) chorizo sausage, skinned and roughly chopped
350g jar roasted peppers in olive oil, drained and chopped, oil reserved
1 garlic clove, crushed
2 small red onions, cut into thick wedges
175ml (6fl oz) dry white wine
300g (11oz) passata
25g (1oz) pitted black olives
450g (1lb) chunky white fish such as cod and haddock, cut into large cubes
salt and ground black pepper

PREPARATION TIME 20 minutes
COOKING TIME 1 hour 10 minutes

PER SERVING
463 calories
22g fat (of which 6g saturates)
32g carbohydrate
1.8g salt

TECHNIQUES
see also preparing vegetables (pages 170–182)

1 Preheat the oven to 170°C (150°C fan oven) mark 3. Put the potatoes, chorizo, roasted peppers, garlic, onions, wine and passata into a large flameproof casserole with 2 tbsp of the oil from the peppers. Season with salt and pepper.

2 Bring to the boil over a medium heat, cover with a tight-fitting lid, then cook in the oven for 45 minutes.

3 Add the olives and fish and put back in the oven for 15 minutes or until the fish is opaque and completely cooked through.

Cook's tip

Passata is a useful storecupboard ingredient from the Italian kitchen, which is used in sauces and stews. It is made from ripe tomatoes that have been puréed and sieved to make a very smooth sauce.

POULTRY AND GAME BIRDS

Chicken is a real staple of the family kitchen and the other poultry and game birds make a popular treat too – whether it's a festive roast turkey or goose, or a delicious recipe with duck or guinea fowl. This chapter guides you through the basic preparation techniques from cleaning, trussing and spatchcocking to boning, jointing and cutting escalopes. The cooking section demonstrates all the techniques from roasting, carving and stuffing to frying, grilling, pot-roasting, steaming and marinating before building on the basics with the comprehensive recipe collection. Try delicious Sticky chicken thighs, Stuffed chicken breasts, Chicken with white wine and capers, Barbecued marinated poussins, Turkey and broccoli stir-fry, Crispy duck salad or Goose with roasted apples.

Preparing poultry

Chicken and other poultry and game birds may be bought whole for roasting or in pieces ready for cooking. It is often cheaper to buy a whole bird, then joint it yourself for cooking as required.

Cleaning and trussing

1 Before stuffing a bird for roasting, clean it thoroughly. Put the bird in the sink and pull out any loose fat with your fingers. Then run cold water through the cavity and dry the bird well using kitchen paper.

2 It is not necessary to truss poultry before roasting it but it gives the bird a neater shape for serving at the table. Cut the wishbone out by pulling back the flap of skin at the neck end and locating the tip of the bone with a small sharp knife. Run the knife along the inside of the bone on both sides, then on the outside. Take care not to cut deep into the breast meat. Use poultry shears or sharp-pointed scissors to snip the tip of the bone from the breastbone, and pull the bone away from the breast. Snip the two ends or pull them out by hand.

3 Pull off any loose fat from the neck or cavity. Put the wing tips under the breast and fold the neck flap on to the back of the bird. Thread a trussing needle and use it to secure the neck flap.

4 Push a metal skewer through the legs, at the joint between thigh and drumstick. Twist some string around both ends of the skewer and pull firmly to tighten.

5 Turn the bird over. Bring the string over the ends of the drumsticks, pull tight and tie to secure the legs in place.

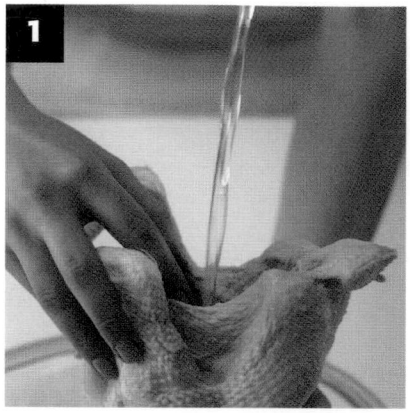

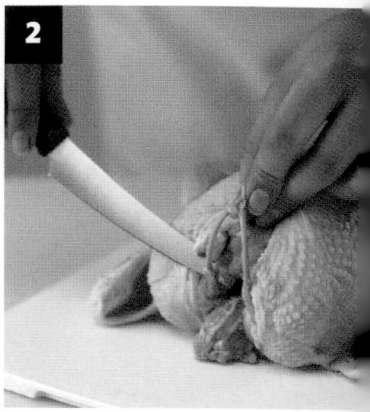

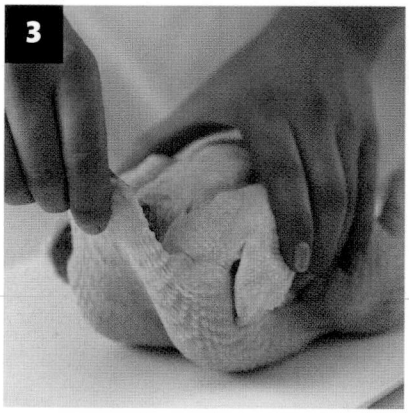

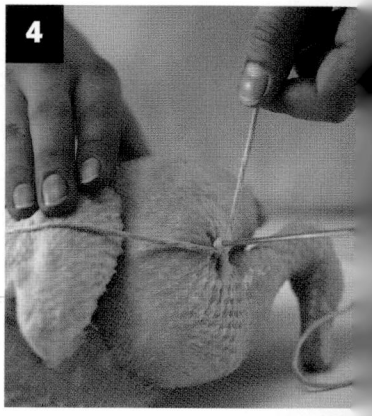

Hygiene

Raw poultry and meat contain harmful bacteria that can spread easily to anything they touch.

- Always wash your hands, kitchen surfaces, chopping boards, knives and equipment before and after handling poultry or meat.
- Don't let raw poultry or meat touch other foods.
- Always cover raw poultry and meat and store in the bottom of the refrigerator, where it can't touch or drip on to other foods.

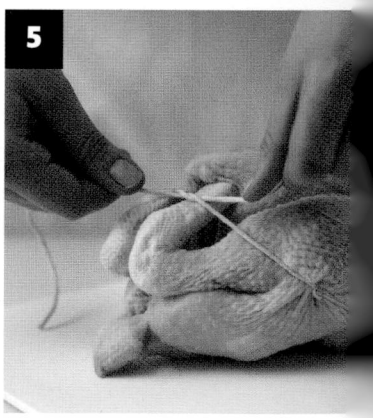

Spatchcocking

A technique to flatten smaller poultry and guinea fowl for grilling.

1 Hold the bird on a board, breast down. Cut through one side of the backbone with poultry shears. Repeat on other side and remove.

2 Turn bird over, press down until you hear breastbone crack. Thread skewers through legs and breasts.

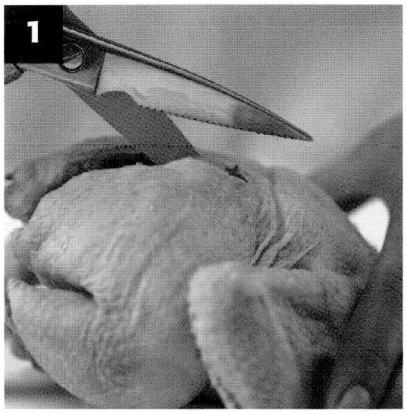

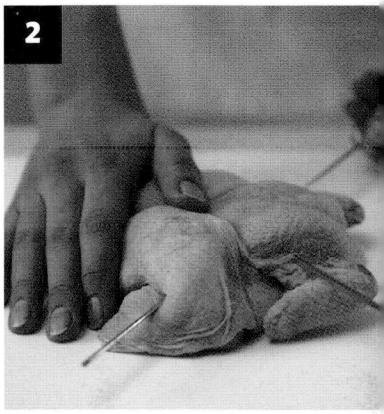

Boning

Boned poultry, stuffed and roasted, makes an attractive dish.

1 Using a meat knife with a curved blade, remove the wishbone (see step 2, page 108) and the first two sections of the wings.

2 Lay the chicken breast side down, with the back facing up, and cut down to the backbone along the whole length of the bird. Pulling skin and flesh away as you go, work a sharp knife between the flesh and bone down one side of the bird. Always cut in, towards the bone.

3 You will soon reach the joints connecting the thigh and wing to the body. Cut through both joints, taking care not to cut through the skin. Do not pierce the skin; it will be the casing for your cooked dish. Continue cutting down between the breast meat and ribcage, again taking care to cut towards the bone.

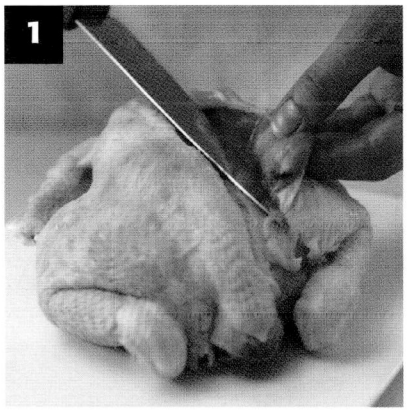

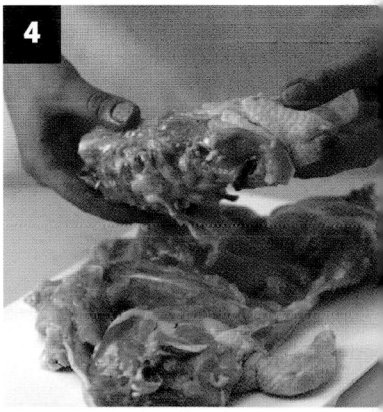

4 When you reach the tip of the breastbone, turn the bird around and repeat on the other side. Cut through the soft cartilage along the length of the breastbone to remove the boned flesh in a single piece.

5 To remove the wings and legs, cut the tendons at the end of the bones and then use a small chopping knife to scrape off the flesh along the full length of the bone. Pull out the bone. Do this twice with the legs to remove the thigh and drumstick.

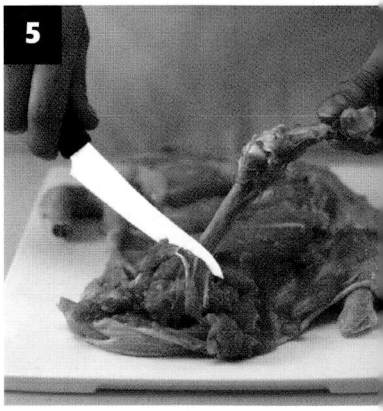

Jointing

You can buy pieces of chicken in the supermarket or butcher, but it is more economical to joint the bird yourself. Use the wing tips and bones to make stock (see page 34).

1 Using a sharp meat knife with a curved blade, cut out the wishbone and remove the wings in a single piece. Remove the wing tips.

2 With the tail pointing towards you and breast side up, pull one leg away and cut through the skin between leg and breast. Pull the leg down until you crack the joint between the thigh bone and ribcage.

3 Cut through that joint, then cut through the remaining leg meat. Repeat on the other side.

4 To remove the breast without any bone, make a cut along the length of the breastbone. Gently teasing the flesh away from the ribs with the knife, work the blade down between the flesh and ribs of one breast and cut it off neatly. (Always cut in, towards the bone.) Repeat on the other side.

5 To remove the breast with the bone in, make a cut along the full length of the breastbone.

6 Using poultry shears, cut through the breastbone, then cut through the ribcage following the outline of the breast meat. Repeat on the other side. Trim off any flaps of skin or fat.

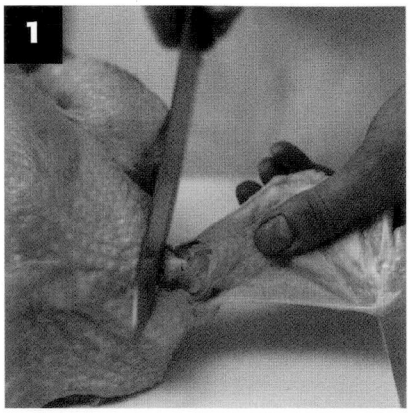

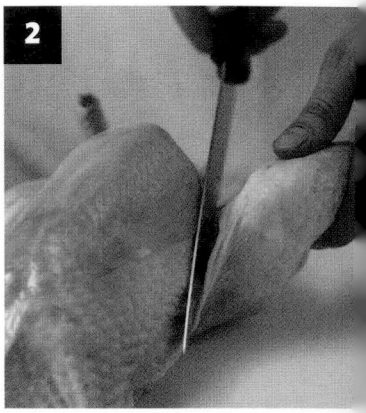

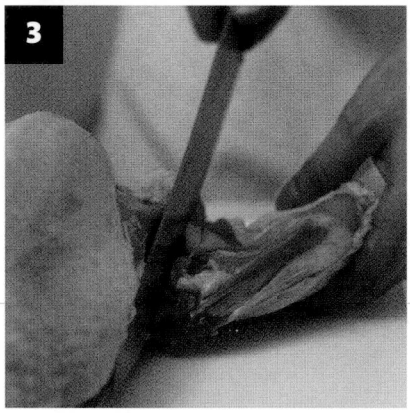

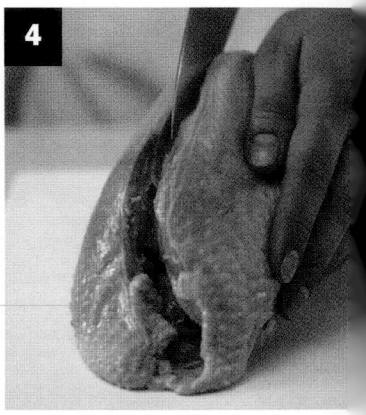

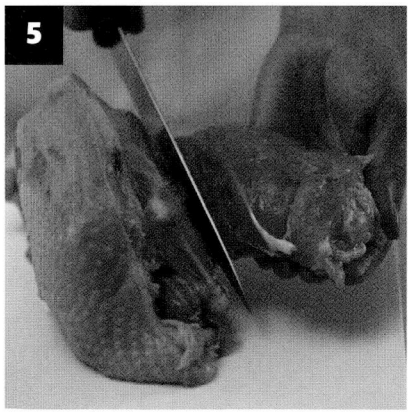

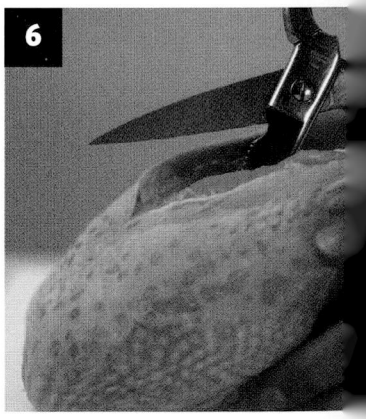

Slicing breast fillets

1 Cut or pull out the long strip of flesh lying on the inside of the breast. Slice it across the grain to the thickness required for your recipe. (Raw chicken should not be cut less than about 3mm/⅛in thick.)

2 Starting at the small tip of the breast, cut slices of the required thickness. Alternatively, cut into chunks or dice.

Perfect slicing

To make slicing easier, put breast fillets in the freezer for 30 minutes or so before slicing. The flesh will be much firmer and it will therefore be easier to slice it thinly.

Cutting escalopes

Escalopes are good for quick frying.

1 Cut or pull out the long strip of flesh lying on the inside of the breast fillet. (It can be used for stir-fries, stuffings, etc.)

2 Pressing the breast firmly on to the chopping board with the flat of one hand, carve a thin slice from underneath the breast using a sharp knife. (The knife blade should be parallel with the chopping board.) Remove that slice, then repeat until the breast meat is too small to slice.

3 To make escalopes, put the slices of chicken between two sheets of clingfilm or greaseproof paper and pound them with a meat mallet until they are about 3mm (⅛in) thick.

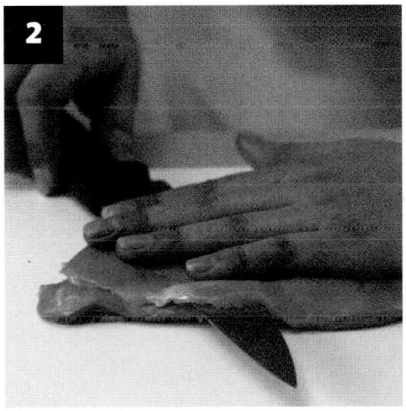

Skinning breast fillets

1 Firmly grab the flap of skin at the small end of the breast and pull towards the other end of the breast. Remove the skin and discard, then prepare or cook the fillet as required.

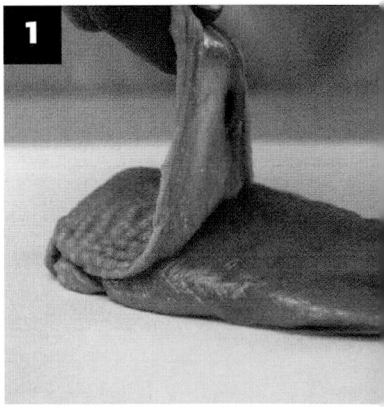

Cooking poultry

From the simplest, healthiest stir-frying, steaming and poaching to the most indulgent and luxurious deep-frying and roasting, there are numerous ways to make the most of the delicate taste of poultry.

Simple roast chicken

To serve four to six, you will need 1.4–1.6kg (3–3½lb) chicken, 5 garlic cloves, 4 lemon slices, juice of 2 lemons (squeezed halves put to one side), 2 tsp Dijon mustard, 4 sprigs each fresh rosemary and thyme, 1 sliced onion, 300ml (½ pint) chicken stock, 300ml (½ pint) dry white wine.

1 Make incisions all over the chicken except the breast. Loosen the breast skin. Crush 3 garlic cloves and slip under the skin with lemon slices, mustard and herbs.

2 Put the lemon halves in the cavity. Put the chicken in a roasting tin. Spoon 2 tbsp lemon juice into the cavity and pour the remaining juice over. Chill for a few hours. Take out of the refrigerator 30 minutes before cooking.

3 Preheat the oven to 200°C (180°C fan oven) mark 6. Put the chicken, breast down, on a rack in the tin. Add the onion, remaining garlic and 4 tbsp each stock and wine.

4 Roast for 20 minutes, turn and roast for 35 minutes or until juices run clear when the leg is pierced. Baste now and then, adding wine if needed.

5 Put the chicken on a platter and cover loosely with foil. Spoon off as much fat as possible, leaving behind the juices in the tin. Put the tin over a medium-high heat, add remaining stock and wine, and scrape up the sediment from the tin. Simmer for 5 minutes to make gravy. Strain.

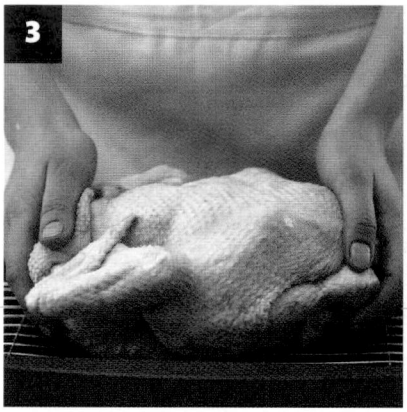

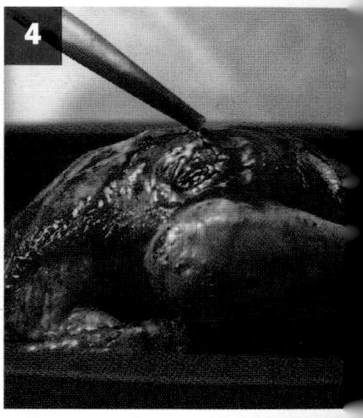

Roasting times

To calculate the roasting time for the chicken, weigh the bird and work it out at 20 minutes per 450g (1lb) plus 20 minutes, in an oven preheated to 180°C (160°C fan oven) mark 4. Test if it is cooked by piercing the thickest part of the leg with a skewer: the juices should run clear.

Carving

1 Hold the back of a carving fork against one side of the breast. Starting at the neck end, cut slices about 5mm (¼in) thick. Use the knife and fork to lift them on to a warmed serving plate.

2 To cut off the legs, cut the skin between the thigh and breast.

3 Pull the leg down to expose the joint between the thigh bone and ribcage, and cut through that joint. For small birds, cut through the joint between the thigh and drumstick.

4 To carve meat from the leg (for turkeys and very large chickens), remove it from the carcass as in step 2. Joint the two parts of the leg. Holding the drumstick by the thin end, stand it up on the carving board and carve slices roughly parallel with the bone. The thigh can be carved either flat on the board or upright.

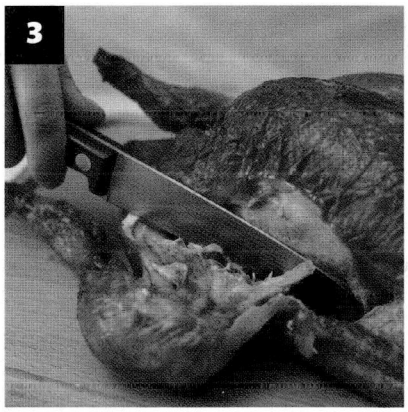

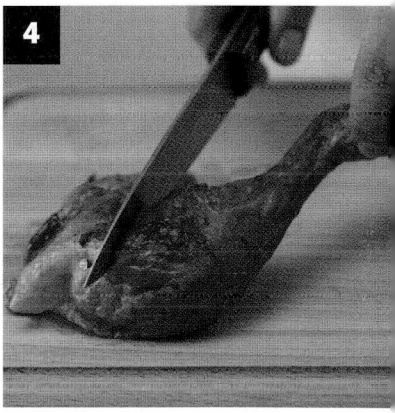

Cranberry and lemon stuffing

If you would like to cook the stuffing separately, try this recipe. You will need 25g (1oz) butter, 1 large onion, finely chopped, 1 garlic clove, crushed, 450g (1lb) best-quality sausages, 4 tbsp chopped parsley, 2 tbsp chopped sage, the zest of 2 lemons, 1 tbsp brandy or Calvados (optional), 75g (3oz) dried cranberries, salt and ground black pepper.

1 Melt the butter in a frying pan and sauté the onion for about 10 minutes or until softened but not coloured. Add the garlic and cook for 1 minute more, then transfer to a bowl and leave to cool.

2 Squeeze the sausage meat out of the skins into the bowl with the onions and garlic. Add all the remaining ingredients and season, then mix well, using your hands. Shape into 18 balls and place in muffin tins or pack into an oiled baking dish. Preheat the oven to 190°C (170°C fan oven) mark 5 and bake for 30 minutes or until cooked through and golden on top.

Pan-frying

This is a quick method for cooking chicken pieces and you can make a sauce with the pan juices at the end if you like.

1 Put in enough oil (or a mixture of oil and clarified butter) to fill the pan to a depth of about 5mm (¼in) and put the pan over a medium heat.

2 Season the chicken with salt and ground black pepper, then carefully add to the pan, flesh side down, and fry for 10–15 minutes until it's nicely browned. (Don't put too many pieces of chicken in the pan at once or the chicken will cook partly in its own steam.)

3 Turn the pieces over and cook on the skin side for another 10–15 minutes until the skin is brown and the flesh is cooked but still juicy all the way through.

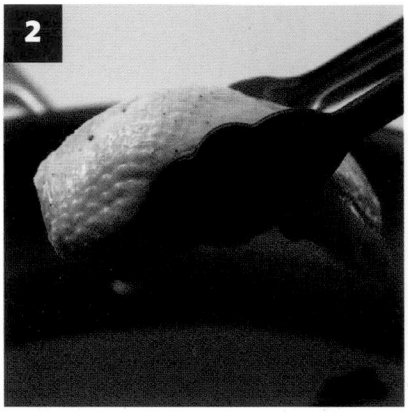

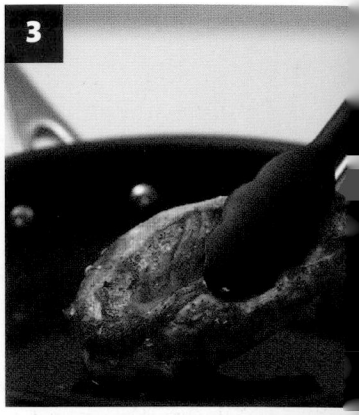

4 Remove the chicken from the pan using a pair of tongs and keep warm. Pour off the excess oil and deglaze the pan.

5 Make a simple gravy using wine, stock, herbs and some chopped garlic or onion (see page 18).

Cook's tips

- Don't rush the cooking by using a very high heat. If you need to speed things up, cover the pan during the first half of cooking.
- Don't let the poultry cook for too long, as it can quickly dry out and toughen over high heat.

Stir-frying

1 Cut the poultry into small, even-sized strips or dice no more than 5mm (¼in) thick. Heat a wok or large pan until very hot and add oil to coat the inside.

2 Add the chicken and cook, stirring constantly, until just done. Remove to a bowl. Cook the other ingredients you are using for the stir-fry, then return the poultry to the pan and cook for 1–2 minutes to heat through.

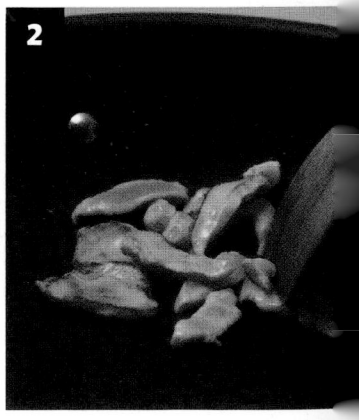

Deep-frying

1 Prepare the poultry for frying and chill. Prepare the seasoned flour, batter or coating (see page 80). Heat vegetable oil in a deep-fryer to 180°C (test by frying a small cube of bread; it should brown in 40 seconds). Start battering or coating each piece of poultry.

2 Using tongs, carefully lower the poultry into the oil. Don't add more than three or four pieces at a time (otherwise the temperature will drop and the poultry will take longer to cook and become greasy). Cook small chunks or strips for about 10 minutes, jointed pieces for about 15 minutes.

3 As the pieces become golden and crisp, remove them with a slotted spoon and drain on kitchen paper. Sprinkle with a little salt and serve immediately, or keep warm in the oven until everything is cooked.

Perfect frying

- Coat each piece of food well and make sure that they are completely covered in the coating.
- To speed up the cooking time, cut the chicken into strips or chunks.

Grilling

This method is perfect for cooking pieces of poultry such as breast fillets or for poultry strips or chunks threaded on to skewers.

1 Marinate (see page 117) the poultry pieces for 30 minutes, drain and pat dry. Alternatively, brush the poultry with a flavoured oil. Put the pieces on a wire rack over a grill pan or roasting tin, and set the pan under a preheated grill so that it is about 8cm (3¼in) from the heat source.

2 Every few minutes brush a little of the marinade or a teaspoon of oil over the poultry.

3 When cooked on one side, turn with tongs and cook the other side until cooked through. Avoid piercing the flesh when turning. Allow 12–20 minutes for a breast fillet or joint and 20–30 minutes for a spatchcocked bird. (There should be no pink juices when the flesh is pierced with a sharp knife.)

Casseroling

To serve four to six, you will need a jointed chicken, 3 tbsp oil, 1 onion, chopped, 2 garlic cloves, crushed, 2 celery sticks, chopped, 2 carrots, chopped, 1 tbsp plain flour, 2 tbsp chopped tarragon or thyme, chicken stock and/or wine, salt and pepper.

1 Preheat the oven to 180°C (160°C fan oven) mark 4. Cut the chicken legs and breasts in half.

2 Heat the oil in a flameproof casserole and brown the chicken all over. Remove and pour off the excess oil. Add the onion and garlic and brown for a few minutes. Add the vegetables, then stir in the flour and cook for 1 minute. Add the herbs and season. Add the chicken and pour in stock and/or wine to come three-quarters of the way up the poultry. Cook for 1–1½ hours.

Pot-roasting

To serve four to six, you will need 2 tbsp vegetable oil, 1 onion, cut into wedges, 2 rashers rindless streaky bacon, chopped, 1.4–1.6kg (3–3½lb) chicken, 2 small turnips, cut into wedges, 6 carrots, halved, 1 garlic clove, crushed, bouquet garni, 600ml (1 pint) chicken stock, 100ml (3½fl oz) dry white wine, small handful parsley, chopped, salt and pepper.

1 Preheat the oven to 200°C (180°C fan oven) mark 6. Heat the oil in a casserole dish. Fry the onion and bacon for 5 minutes. Set aside. Add the chicken, brown all over for 10 minutes, and set aside. Fry turnips, carrots and garlic for 2 minutes, then add the bacon, onion and chicken.

2 Add the bouquet garni, stock, wine and season. Bring to the boil and transfer to oven. Cook, basting now and then, for 1 hour 20 minutes or until juices run clear. Lift out the chicken, stir in parsley and carve.

Perfect pot-roasts

- Pot-roasting is the perfect way to cook almost any poultry or game bird apart from duck or goose, which are too fatty and do not give good results, and turkey, which are too large to fit in the average casserole dish.
- Make sure that you use a large enough casserole and that the bird doesn't fit too closely to the sides of the dish.
- Watch out for overcooking – the closed pot cooks birds almost as fast as an ordinary roast chicken in the oven would cook.
- Check the liquid level in the casserole from time to time. If it's too dry, add a little more. Water is fine, stock or wine is even better.
- Timings for pot-roasted poultry: about 45 minutes (for small birds such as poussin) or 1–1½ hours (for chicken or guinea fowl).

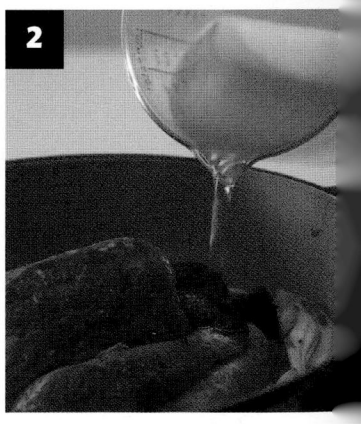

Steaming

1 Cut the poultry into thick shreds or chunks, or use thighs, drumsticks or halved breasts. Marinate (see below), if you like, for at least 1 hour.

2 Arrange the poultry in a single layer on a heatproof dish that is small enough to fit inside the steamer. Place in the steamer, cover and steam for 20–40 minutes until just cooked through.

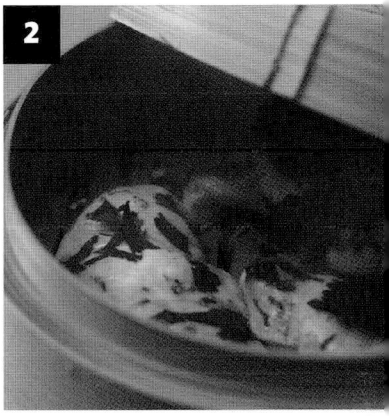

Poaching

The quick and gentle method of poaching will produce a light broth.

1 Brown the bird in oil if you wish (this is not necessary but will give a deeper flavour), then transfer to a pan that will hold it easily: a large frying pan or sauté pan is good for pieces, a large pan or casserole for a whole bird.

2 Add 1 roughly chopped onion, 2 crushed garlic cloves, 2 chopped carrots, 2 chopped celery sticks, 6 whole black peppercorns and 1 tsp dried mixed herbs, scattering them about the whole bird or between the pieces. Pour in just enough stock to cover, and simmer, uncovered, for about 1 hour (for a whole bird) or 30–40 minutes (for pieces).

3 Gently lift the bird out of the liquid. If you are planning to use the liquid as the basis for a sauce, reduce it by at least half.

Marinades

- Used to flavour the flesh, marinades will not penetrate poultry skin so remove the skin or cut slashes in it.
- Use just enough marinade to coat the poultry generously – drowning it is wasteful, as it runs off and most will be left in the bottom of the container.
- To make a simple marinade, combine olive oil, lemon juice and chopped garlic, pour over chicken and marinate in the refrigerator for at least 1 hour.
- To make a spicy marinade, combine 1 crushed garlic clove, 2 tbsp ground coriander, 2 tbsp ground cumin, 1 tbsp paprika, 1 deseeded and chopped hot red chilli, the juice of ½ lemon, 2 tbsp soy sauce and 8 thyme sprigs. Pour over 2kg (4½lb) chicken pieces, mix well and marinate in the refrigerator overnight.

Orange and Chicken Salad

SERVES 4
50g (2oz) cashew nuts
zest and juice of 2 oranges
2 tbsp marmalade
1 tbsp honey
1 tbsp oyster sauce
400g (14oz) roast chicken, shredded
a handful of chopped raw vegetables, such as cucumber, carrot, red and yellow pepper and Chinese leaves

PREPARATION TIME 15 minutes
COOKING TIME 10 minutes

PER SERVING
237 calories
8g fat (of which 2g saturates)
18g carbohydrate
0.5g salt

TECHNIQUES
see also zesting citrus fruits (page 207), making marmalade (page 407), roasting chicken (page 112), preparing vegetables (pages 170–182)

1 Put the cashew nuts in a frying pan and cook for 2–3 minutes until golden. Tip into a large serving bowl.

2 To make the dressing, put the orange zest and juice into the frying pan with the marmalade, honey and oyster sauce. Bring to the boil, stirring, then simmer for 2–3 minutes until slightly thickened.

3 Add the roast chicken to the serving bowl with the chopped raw vegetables. Pour the dressing over the salad, toss everything together and serve immediately.

Cook's tip

Toasting the cashew nuts in a dry frying pan before adding them to the salad brings out their flavour, giving them an intense, nutty taste and a wonderful golden colour.

Moroccan Spiced Chicken Kebabs

SERVES 4

2 tbsp olive oil
15g (½oz) flat-leafed parsley
1 garlic clove
½ tsp paprika
1 tsp ground cumin
zest and juice of 1 lemon
4 skinless chicken breasts, cut into bite-sized chunks

PREPARATION TIME 10 minutes, plus minimum 20 minutes marinating
COOKING TIME 10–12 minutes

PER SERVING

189 calories
7g fat (of which 1g saturates)
1g carbohydrate
0.2g salt

TECHNIQUES

see also preparing herbs (page 428), grilling poultry (page 115)

1 If using wooden skewers soak four in water for 30 minutes. Put the oil in a blender and add the parsley, garlic, paprika, cumin, lemon zest and juice. Whiz to make a paste.

2 Put the chicken in a medium-sized shallow dish and add the spice paste, then rub in and leave to marinate for at least 20 minutes. Preheat the grill to high.

3 Thread the marinated chicken on to skewers and grill for 10–12 minutes, turning every now and then, until the meat is cooked through.

Quick Chicken Stir-fry

SERVES 4

1 tsp groundnut oil
300g (11oz) chicken breast, sliced
4 spring onions, chopped
200g (7oz) medium rice noodles
100g (3½oz) mangetouts
200g (7oz) purple sprouting broccoli, chopped
2–3 tbsp sweet chilli sauce
freshly chopped coriander and lime wedges (optional) to garnish

PREPARATION TIME 10 minutes
COOKING TIME 15 minutes

PER SERVING

316 calories
3g fat (of which 1g saturates)
46g carbohydrate
0.5g salt

TECHNIQUES

see also preparing vegetables (pages 170–182), preparing rice noodles (page 263), stir-frying vegetables (page 185)

1 Heat the oil in a wok and add the chicken and spring onions. Stir-fry over a high heat for 5–6 minutes until the chicken is golden.

2 Meanwhile, cook the rice noodles in a large pan of boiling water according to the pack instructions. Add the mangetouts, broccoli and chilli sauce to the wok. Continue to stir-fry for 4 minutes.

3 Drain the noodles and add to the wok, then toss everything together. Scatter the chopped coriander over the top and serve with lime wedges, if you like, to squeeze over.

Sticky Chicken Thighs

SERVES 4

1 garlic clove, crushed
1 tbsp honey
1 tbsp Thai sweet chilli sauce
4 chicken thighs

PREPARATION TIME 5 minutes
COOKING TIME 20 minutes

PER SERVING

125calories
3g fat (of which 1g saturates)
4g carbohydrate
0.4g salt

TECHNIQUES

see also preparing garlic (page 171)

1 Preheat the oven to 200°C (180°C fan oven) mark 6. Put the garlic into a bowl with the honey and chilli sauce, and mix together. Add the chicken thighs and toss to coat.

2 Put into a roasting tin and roast for 15–20 minutes until the chicken is golden and cooked through.

Grilled Chicken with Mango Salsa

SERVES 4
4 skinless chicken breasts
juice of ½ lime
oil-water spray
salt and ground black pepper
rocket leaves to serve

For the salsa
1 mango, diced
1 small head of fennel, trimmed and diced
1 fresh chilli, deseeded and finely diced
1 tbsp balsamic vinegar
juice of ½ lime
2 tbsp freshly chopped flat-leafed parsley
2 tbsp freshly chopped mint

PREPARATION TIME 12 minutes
COOKING TIME 20 minutes

PER SERVING
165 calories
2g fat (of which trace saturates)
6g carbohydrate
0.2g salt

TECHNIQUES
see also preparing mangoes (page 210), preparing fennel (page 173), preparing chillies (page 177)

1 Put the chicken on a grill pan and season generously with salt and pepper. Pour over the lime juice and spray with the oil-water. Grill for 8–10 minutes on each side until cooked through and the juices run clear when pierced with a skewer. Set aside.

2 Combine all the salsa ingredients in a bowl and season generously with salt and pepper. Spoon alongside the chicken and serve with rocket leaves.

Stuffed Chicken Breasts

SERVES 4
oil to grease
150g (5oz) ball mozzarella
4 chicken breasts, about 150g (5oz) each
4 sage leaves
8 slices Parma ham
new potatoes and steamed spinach to serve

PREPARATION TIME 5 minutes
COOKING TIME 20 minutes

PER SERVING
270 calories
10g fat (of which 6g saturates)
trace carbohydrate
1g salt

TECHNIQUES
see also steaming vegetables (page 183)

1 Preheat the oven to 200°C (180°C fan oven) mark 6. Lightly grease a baking sheet. Slice the mozzarella into eight, then put two slices on each chicken piece. Top each with a sage leaf.

2 Wrap each piece of chicken in two slices of Parma ham, covering the mozzarella.

3 Put on to the prepared baking sheet and cook in the oven for 20 minutes. Serve with the potatoes and spinach.

Cook's tip

Sage has a naturally strong, pungent taste so you only need a little to flavour the chicken. Don't be tempted to add more than just one leaf to each one as too much will overpower the finished dish.

Chicken with Wine and Capers

SERVES 4
1 tbsp olive oil
15g (½oz) butter
4 small skinless chicken breasts
125ml (4fl oz) white wine
3 tbsp capers
juice of 1 lemon
15g (½oz) butter
1 tbsp freshly chopped parsley
lemon wedges to garnish
boiled rice to serve

PREPARATION TIME 5 minutes
COOKING TIME 25 minutes

PER SERVING
234 calories
10g fat (of which 5g saturates)
trace carbohydrate
0.3g salt

TECHNIQUES
see also chopping herbs (page 428), cooking rice (page 236)

1 Heat the oil and butter in a frying pan. Add the chicken breasts and fry over a medium heat for 10–12 minutes on each side until cooked right through. Transfer to a warm plate, cover and keep warm.

2 Add the wine and capers to the frying pan. Bring to the boil, then simmer for 2–3 minutes until the wine is reduced by half. Add the lemon juice and butter and stir in the parsley. Pour the sauce over the chicken, garnish with a lemon wedge and serve with boiled rice.

Mediterranean Chicken

SERVES 4

1 red pepper, deseeded and chopped
2 tbsp capers
2 tbsp freshly chopped rosemary
2 tbsp olive oil
4 skinless chicken breasts
salt and ground black pepper
rice or new potatoes to serve

PREPARATION TIME 5 minutes
COOKING TIME 20 minutes

PER SERVING
227 calories
8g fat (of which 1g saturates)
3g carbohydrate
0.2g salt

TECHNIQUES
see also seeding and chargrilling peppers (page 177)

1 Preheat the oven to 200°C (180°C fan oven) mark 6. Put the red pepper in a bowl with the capers, rosemary and oil. Season with salt and pepper and mix well.

2 Put the chicken breasts into an ovenproof dish and spoon the pepper mixture over the top. Roast for 15–20 minutes until the chicken is cooked through and the topping is hot. Serve with rice or new potatoes.

Cook's tip

Peppers are in season and at their sweetest and best in the summer and early autumn, so make this dish at that time of year to enjoy it at its very best.

Tarragon Chicken with Fennel

SERVES 4
1 tbsp olive oil
4 chicken thighs
1 onion, finely chopped
1 fennel bulb, finely chopped
juice of ½ lemon
200ml (7fl oz) hot chicken stock
200g carton crème fraîche
a small bunch tarragon, roughly chopped
salt and ground black pepper

PREPARATION TIME 10 minutes
COOKING TIME 45–55 minutes

PER SERVING
333 calories
26g fat (of which 15g saturates)
3g carbohydrate
0.5g salt

TECHNIQUES
see also preparing vegetables (pages 170–182), making chicken stock (page 34), chopping herbs (page 428), casseroling poultry (page 116)

1 Preheat the oven to 200°C (180°C fan oven) mark 6. Heat the oil in a large flameproof casserole. Add the chicken thighs and fry for 5 minutes or until brown, then remove and set them aside to keep warm.

2 Add the onion to the pan and fry for 5 minutes, then add the fennel and cook for 5–10 minutes until softened.

3 Add the lemon juice to the pan, followed by the stock. Bring to a simmer and cook until the sauce is reduced by half.

4 Stir in the crème fraîche and return the chicken to the pan. Stir once to mix, then cover and cook in the oven for 25–30 minutes. Stir the tarragon into the sauce, season to taste and serve.

Barbecued Marinated Poussins

SERVES 8
150ml (¼ pint) bourbon
15g (½oz) soft brown sugar
50ml (2fl oz) clear honey
50ml (2fl oz) tomato ketchup
2 tbsp grainy mustard
1 tbsp white wine vinegar
3 garlic cloves, crushed
1 tsp each salt and ground black pepper
4 poussins
chargrilled peppers, tomatoes and onions garnished with flat-leafed parsley to serve

PREPARATION TIME 30 minutes, plus overnight marinating
COOKING TIME 30 minutes

PER SERVING
246 calories
15g fat (of which 4g saturates)
4g carbohydrate
0.3g salt

TECHNIQUES
see also preparing poultry (page 108), making tomato ketchup (page 415), preparing garlic (page 171)

1 Mix the bourbon, sugar, honey, tomato ketchup and mustard together. Stir in the vinegar, garlic, salt and pepper.

2 Put the poussins, backbone uppermost, on a chopping board, then cut either side of the backbone with a pair of strong sharp scissors. Open out the poussins, cover them with clingfilm and flatten them slightly by tapping them with the base of a heavy pan. Put the poussins in a shallow non-metallic dish and pour the bourbon marinade over the top, then cover and chill overnight.

3 Thread the marinated poussins on to large skewers, keeping the remaining marinade to one side. Cook the poussins on the barbecue for 30 minutes or until cooked through, basting from time to time with leftover marinade. Reshape the poussins, if you like. Serve with the peppers, tomatoes and onions.

Guineafowl with Prunes

SERVES 6

225g (8oz) onion, roughly chopped
125g (4oz) carrot, roughly chopped
125g (4oz) celery, roughly chopped
6–8 guineafowl joints or cornfed chicken joints, 2kg (4½lb) total weight
750ml (1¼ pints) red wine
1 tsp black peppercorns, crushed
1 tbsp freshly chopped thyme
2 bay leaves
175g (6oz) ready-to-eat dried prunes
3 tbsp vegetable oil
3 garlic cloves, crushed
1 tsp harissa paste
1 tbsp tomato purée
2 tbsp plain flour
300ml (½ pint) chicken stock
225g (8oz) streaky bacon, cut in strips
2 apples, cored and sliced
salt and ground black pepper
mashed potato to serve

PREPARATION TIME 40 minutes, plus 4 hours marinating
COOKING TIME 1½ hours

PER SERVING
811 calories
49g fat (of which 14g saturates)
24g carbohydrate
1.7g salt

Get ahead

Cook up to the end of step 3, then cool and chill.
To use Bring to the boil and reheat in the oven at 180°C (160°C fan oven) mark 4 for 30–40 minutes.

1 Put the onion, carrot, celery, guineafowl or chicken, 600ml (1 pint) wine, peppercorns, thyme and bay leaves in a large bowl. Cover and marinate for at least 3–4 hours. Put the remaining wine in another bowl with the prunes. Cover and soak for 3–4 hours.

2 Preheat the oven to 170°C (150°C fan oven) mark 3. Drain and dry the joints (put the vegetables and wine to one side). Heat 2 tbsp oil in a large flameproof casserole. Cook the joints in batches, skin side down, over a medium heat until brown, then turn and brown the underside. Remove from pan and put to one side. Add the marinated vegetables (keep the marinade to one side) and stir-fry for 5 minutes. Add the garlic, harissa and tomato purée, and cook for 1 minute. Mix in the flour and cook for 1 minute. Pour in the reserved marinade and stock. Bring to the boil, stirring. Return the joints to the casserole, with the legs at the bottom. Bring to the boil, season well, cover and cook in the oven for 40 minutes.

3 Heat the remaining oil in a pan. Cook the bacon, stirring, for 5 minutes or until golden brown. Remove from pan and set aside. Cook the apple for 2–3 minutes on each side until golden. Put to one side. Remove the joints from the casserole. Strain the sauce and return to the pan with the joints. Add the prunes and any juices, the bacon and apple. Heat through in the oven for 10 minutes. Serve with mashed potato.

Turkey and Broccoli Stir-fry

SERVES 4

2 tbsp vegetable or sunflower oil
500g (1lb 2oz) turkey fillet, cut in strips
2 garlic cloves, crushed
2.5cm (1in) piece fresh root ginger, peeled and grated
1 broccoli head, chopped into florets
8 spring onions, finely chopped
140g (4½oz) button mushrooms, halved
100g (3½oz) beansprouts
3 tbsp oyster sauce
1 tbsp light soy sauce
125ml (4fl oz) hot chicken stock
juice of ½ lemon

PREPARATION TIME 15 minutes
COOKING TIME 7–11 minutes

PER SERVING
254 calories
8g fat (of which 1g saturates)
8g carbohydrate
1.3g salt

TECHNIQUES
see also preparing fresh spices (page 429), preparing vegetables (pages 170–182), making chicken stock (page 34)

1 Heat 1 tbsp oil in a large non-stick frying pan or wok and stir-fry the turkey strips for 4–5 minutes until golden and cooked through. Remove from the pan and set aside.

2 Heat the remaining oil in the same pan over a medium heat, then cook the garlic and ginger for 30 seconds, stirring all the time so that they don't burn. Add the broccoli, onions and mushrooms, increase the heat and cook for 2–3 minutes until the vegetables start to brown but are still crisp.

3 Return the turkey to the pan and add the beansprouts, oyster and soy sauces, stock and lemon juice. Cook for 1–2 minutes, tossing well to heat everything through.

Cook's tip

Grow your own beansprouts for this recipe following the technique on page 243.

Orange and Bay Turkey Crown

SERVES 8

2 onions, sliced
2 bay leaves, plus extra to garnish
2.7kg (6lb) oven-ready turkey crown
40g (1½oz) butter, softened
1 lemon, halved
2 tbsp all-purpose chicken seasoning
2 oranges, halved
150ml (¼ pint) dry white wine or chicken stock

PREPARATION TIME 20 minutes, plus 15 minutes resting
COOKING TIME 2½ hours

PER SERVING
181 calories
6g fat (of which 3g saturates)
3g carbohydrate
0.2g salt

TECHNIQUES
see also making gravy (page 18)

1 Preheat the oven to 190°C (170°C fan oven) mark 5. Arrange the onions in a large flameproof roasting tin, add the bay leaves and sit the turkey on top. Spread the butter over the turkey breast, then squeeze over the lemon. Throw the halves into the tin. Sprinkle over the seasoning then put the orange halves in the tin around the turkey.

2 Pour the wine or stock into the roasting tin, followed by 250ml (9fl oz) hot water. Cover the turkey loosely with a large sheet of foil. Make sure it's completely covered, but with enough space between the foil and the turkey for air to circulate.

3 Roast the turkey for 2 hours or until juices run clear when the meat is pierced with a skewer (see Cook's tip). Remove the foil and put the turkey back in the oven for 30 minutes or until golden.

4 Lift the turkey on to a warmed carving dish, cover loosely with foil to keep warm and leave it to rest for 15 minutes before carving. Keep the orange and lemon halves to garnish. Don't wash up the tin – you'll need it for making the gravy.

Cook's tip

To check that the turkey is cooked, pierce the thickest part of the crown with a skewer. Press the skin to release the juices – they should run clear and golden with no traces of pink. If there are any pink juices, put the turkey back in the oven for another 10–15 minutes until cooked.

Crispy Duck Salad

SERVES 8

6 duck legs, about 200g (7oz) each
2 fresh thyme sprigs
1 tsp peppercorns
2 bay leaves
2 tsp salt
125g (4oz) kumquats
125g (4oz) pecan nuts
finely grated zest and juice of 2 oranges
225g (8oz) cranberries
125g (4oz) caster sugar
4 tbsp white wine vinegar
9 tbsp sunflower oil
3 tbsp walnut oil
salt and ground black pepper
frisée leaves to serve

PREPARATION TIME 30 minutes, plus cooling and overnight chilling
COOKING TIME 1 hour 25 minutes

PER SERVING
614calories
54g fat (of which 10g saturates)
24g carbohydrate
0.1g salt

TECHNIQUES
see also zesting citrus fruits (page 207), making salad dressings (page 25)

1 Preheat the oven to 180°C (160°C fan oven) mark 4. Put the duck legs into a large flameproof casserole, cover with cold water and bring to the boil. Simmer for 10 minutes, skim the surface and add the thyme, peppercorns, bay leaves and salt. Cook in the oven for 45 minutes–1 hour until tender. Cool quickly in the liquor and chill overnight.

2 Quarter the kumquats. Put the nuts on a baking sheet and toast lightly under a grill. Put the orange zest in a frying pan with 200ml (7fl oz) orange juice, the cranberries and sugar. Bring to the boil and simmer for 5 minutes or until the cranberries are tender. Drain the juice into a pan, reserving the berries. Bring the juice to the boil and bubble until syrupy, then return the cranberries to the pan.

3 In a small bowl, whisk the vinegar and oils and season with salt and pepper. Add the kumquats to the cranberry mixture with the oil and vinegar dressing and the pecan nuts. Set aside. Skim the fat from the jellied duck liquor and set aside. Cut the duck into thick shreds, leaving the skin on. Just before serving, heat 1 tbsp reserved duck fat in a large non-stick frying pan and fry half the duck for 5 minutes or until crisp and brown. Keep warm and repeat with the remaining duck. To serve, toss the duck with the cranberry mixture and serve with salad leaves.

Marinated Duck with Prunes

SERVES 4
4 duck breasts
8 fat garlic cloves, unpeeled
8 ready-to-eat prunes
25g (1oz) butter
1 tsp plain flour
mashed potato to serve

For the marinade
1 carrot, finely chopped
2 shallots, finely chopped
1 fresh parsley sprig
1 fresh thyme sprig, plus extra to garnish
1 bay leaf
1 tsp black peppercorns
250ml (9fl oz) prune juice
125ml (4fl oz) red wine
4 tbsp brandy
4 tbsp olive oil
½ tsp salt

For the red cabbage
1 tbsp olive oil
1 red onion, halved and sliced
2 garlic cloves, crushed
1 large red cabbage, about 1kg (2¼lb), shredded
2 tbsp light muscovado sugar
2 tbsp red wine vinegar
8 juniper berries
¼ tsp allspice
300ml (½ pint) vegetable stock
2 pears, cored and sliced
salt and ground black pepper

PREPARATION TIME 30 minutes, plus overnight marinating and resting
COOKING TIME 1¼ hours

PER SERVING
654 calories
51g fat (of which 14g saturates)
38g carbohydrate
0.6g salt

1 Combine the marinade ingredients (setting aside half the prune juice) in a dish large enough to hold the duck breasts in a single layer, then add the duck. Cover and chill overnight, turning occasionally.

2 Soak four small wooden skewers in water. To make the red cabbage, heat the oil in a large pan, add the onion and fry for 5 minutes. Add the remaining ingredients except the pears. Season, bring to the boil, then cover and simmer for 30 minutes. Add the pears and cook for 15 minutes or until nearly all the liquid has evaporated and the cabbage is tender.

3 Boil the garlic for 10 minutes. Drain, peel and set aside. Remove the duck from the marinade and dry on kitchen paper. In a pan, bring the marinade to the boil, then reduce by half. Strain and keep warm. Push the prunes and garlic on to the skewers. Melt the butter in a large frying pan. Fry the duck, skin side down, for 8 minutes or until golden. Turn and cook for 3–4 minutes. Remove from pan and leave to rest for 10 minutes. Cook the skewers in the pan, turning, until the garlic colours. Remove and set aside. Add the flour to the pan and cook, stirring, for 2–3 seconds. Add the marinade and remaining prune juice and simmer, stirring, until it thickens and becomes glossy. Serve the duck and skewers with red cabbage and mashed potato. Garnish with thyme.

Goose with Roasted Apples

SERVES 8

6 small red onions
7 small red eating apples
5kg (11lb) oven-ready goose, washed, dried and seasoned inside and out
1 small bunch sage
1 small bunch rosemary
1 bay leaf
sea salt and ground black pepper

For the stock

giblets removed from the goose
1 carrot, chopped
1 celery stick, chopped
1 onion, quartered
1 bouquet garni
6 black peppercorns

For the gravy

30g pack Madeira Wine Gravy Mix
300ml (½ pint) red wine
200ml (7fl oz) giblet stock

PREPARATION TIME 30 minutes
COOKING TIME 4¼ hours

PER SERVING

646 calories
41g fat (of which 12g saturates)
11g carbohydrate
1g salt

1 For the stock, put the giblets in a pan, add the remaining ingredients and pour over 1.1 litres (2 pints) cold water. Cover and bring slowly to the boil, then simmer for 1 hour. Strain and keep the liquid to one side.

2 Preheat the oven to 230°C (210°C fan oven) mark 8. Quarter one of the onions and two of the apples and put inside the goose with half the sage and rosemary and the bay leaf. Tie the legs together and push a long skewer through the wings to tuck them in. Put the goose, breast side up, on a rack in a large roasting tin. Prick the breast all over and season. Put the remaining onions around the goose. Cover with foil. Cook for 15 minutes per 450g (1lb) plus 15 minutes (3 hours for a 5kg/11lb goose). Roast for 30 minutes. Lower the heat to 190°C (170°C fan oven) mark 5. Remove the fat from the tin, drizzle some over the goose, then chill the remainder in a jar (reserve for roasting potatoes). Roast the goose for 1 hour, remove fat again and chill. Cook the bird for 30 minutes, then remove the foil. Remove and chill fat again. Add the remaining apples. Sprinkle the goose with the remaining herbs and roast for 1 hour. Put on to a warm serving plate, cover with foil and leave to rest for 30 minutes. Remove the apples and onions and keep warm.

3 Make the gravy (see Finishing touches). Cut the remaining apples and onions into wedges and serve with the goose and gravy.

Finishing touches

To make the gravy, pour out all but 1 tbsp of the fat from the tin, then sprinkle in the gravy mix and whisk in the wine. Cook for 2 minutes, stirring, then whisk in the stock. Bring to the boil and pour in roasted apple juice, onion and juices from the tin. Simmer for 10 minutes until reduced to a clear sauce.

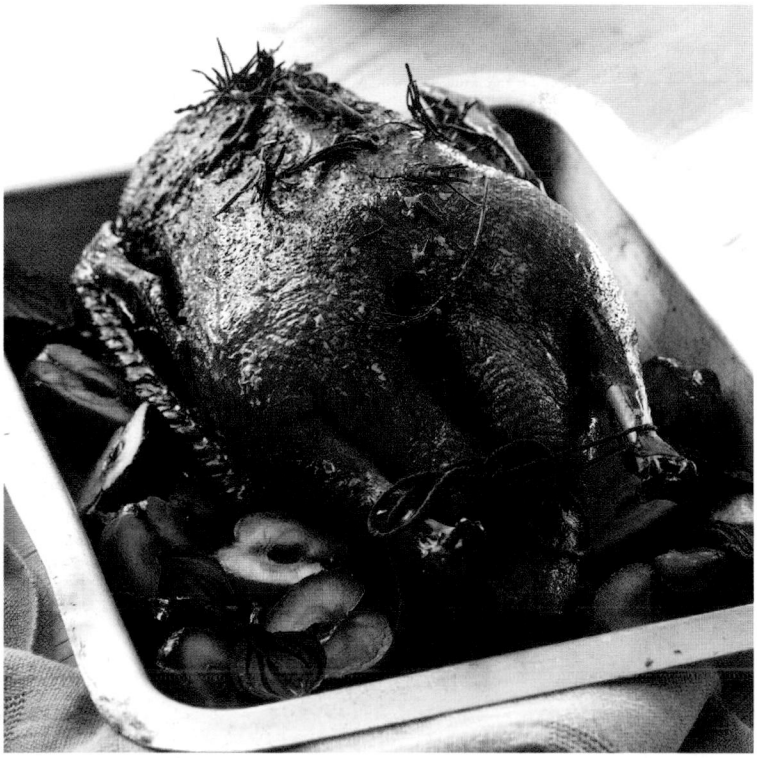

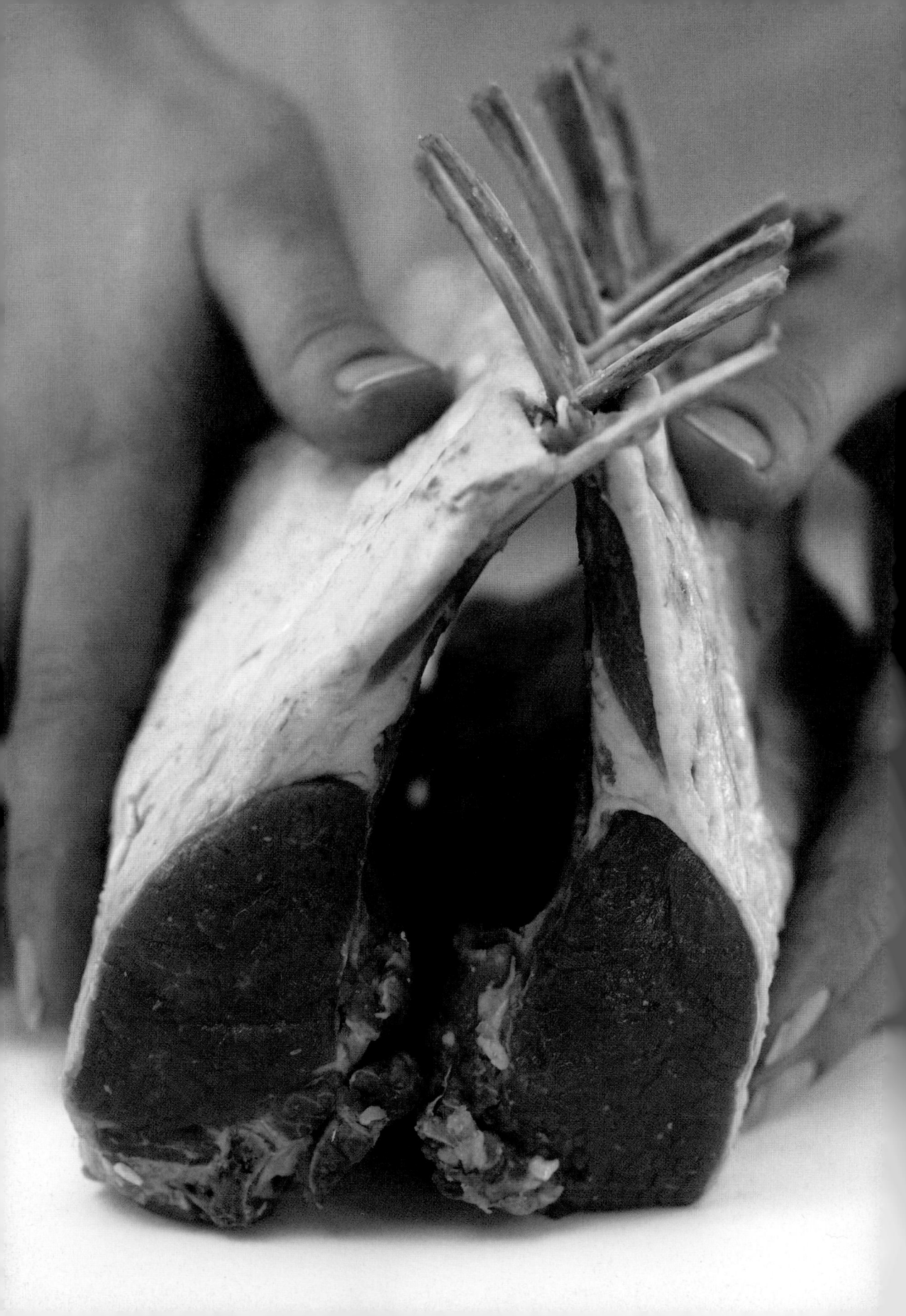

MEAT AND GAME

Beef, lamb, pork, ham and game such as rabbit and venison make wonderfully hearty, delicious meals and are easy to prepare and cook when you know how. The detailed step-by-step techniques guide you through all the basic preparation and cooking techniques with easy-to-follow photographs for perfect results every time. Packed with tips, hints and advice, ideas for stuffings and marinades, and handy tables of cooking times – this chapter provides everything you need to know about preparing and cooking meat. The recipe collection is packed with fabulous ideas too, including chunky Italian meatballs, Ginger and honey-glazed ham, Greek lamb and feta layer, Braised lamb shanks, Sweet chilli beef stir-fry, One-pot spicy beef and Roasted venison sausages.

Preparing beef

From trimming to tying joints to tenderising steaks and barding and larding to ensure the moistest, tenderest results, there are lots of simple techniques to make sure you make the most of your beef.

Boning

The joints you are mostly likely to want to bone are rib and sirloin so that they are easier to slice when cooked; they can also be rolled. The principle for preparing both joints is the same.

1 Put the joint on your chopping board with the bone facing down and the shorter vertebral bones facing upwards.

2 Use a long knife to make a thin cut all the way along the length of the spine. Cut towards the bone, working the knife between bone and meat until you reach the ribs.

3 Lift the meat in one hand and cut between the ribs and meat, cutting towards the bone, to remove the meat in a single piece. Trim off cartilage and fat.

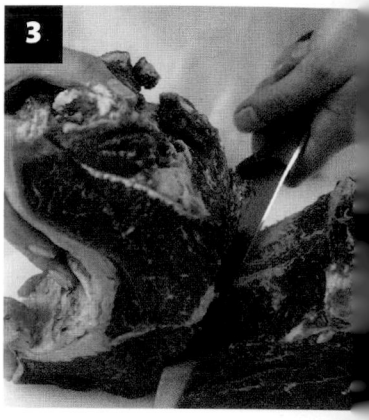

Barding

Lean joints of meat can be barded –wrapped in a thin layer of fat to moisten the meat during cooking. If the butcher hasn't done this for you, it's easy to do at home.

You will need string and 3–4 sheets of pork fat, preferably back fat, large enough to cover the whole joint, dried herbs, ground black pepper.

1 Season the meat with freshly ground black pepper and dried herbs if you like. Wrap the sheets of fat around the joint so that both the sides and ends are covered.

2 Tie a piece of string around the length of the joint. Turn it 90 degrees and tie another piece in the same way, so that the fat is held in place.

3 Starting at one end, loop string around the meat, tie it securely and cut off. Make another loop about 5cm (2in) from the first. Continue along the length of the joint.

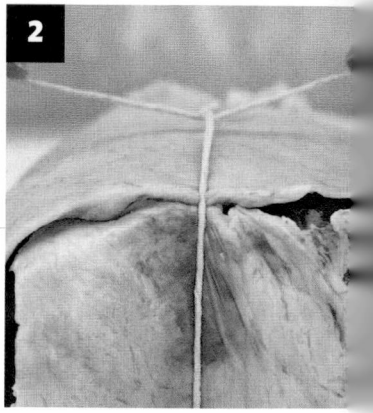

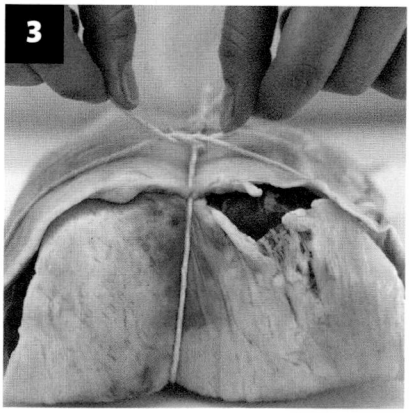

Larding

Threading narrow strips of fat through beef fillet is another way of guaranteeing juiciness. The fat is threaded through the joint using a larding needle.

1 Cut long strips of pork fat, preferably back fat, which will fit easily into the larding needle. Chill well or freeze.

2 Push the needle right through the joint, so that the tip sticks out at least 5cm (2in) through the other side.

3 Take a strip of fat, place it in the hollow of the larding needle, and feed it into the tip. When the fat can't go in any further, press down on the joint and pull the needle out. The fat should stay inside.

4 Repeat at 2.5cm (1in) intervals on all sides of the joint.

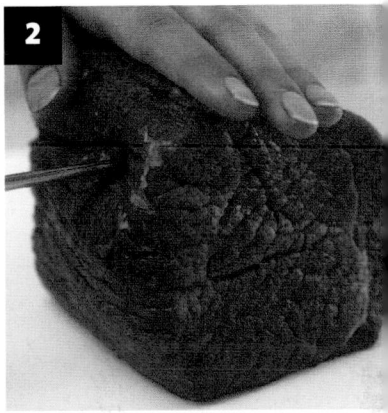

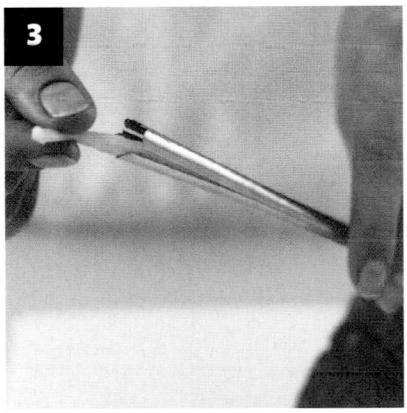

Cook's tips

- Larding is much easier if the strips of fat are very cold or even frozen.
- The strips of fat don't need to be as long as the joint; you can put several pieces of fat in a single larding channel.
- Use one strip per 2.5cm (1in), measuring the longer side of the joint.

Trimming tips

There are certain rules that apply to trimming most cuts of meat.

1 Trim away excess fat, leaving no more than 5mm (¼in) on steaks, chops and roasting cuts – a little fat will contribute juiciness and flavour. When preparing meat for cutting into chunks, try to separate the individual muscles, which can be identified by the sinews running between each muscle.

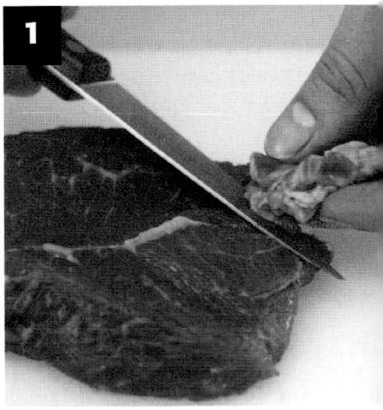

Trimming a joint

1 Cut off the excess fat to leave a thickness of about 5mm (¼in). This isn't necessary for very lean cuts.

2 Trim away any stray pieces of meat or sinew left by the butcher.

3 If the joint has a covering of fat, you can lightly score it – taking care not to cut into the meat – to help the fat drain away during cooking.

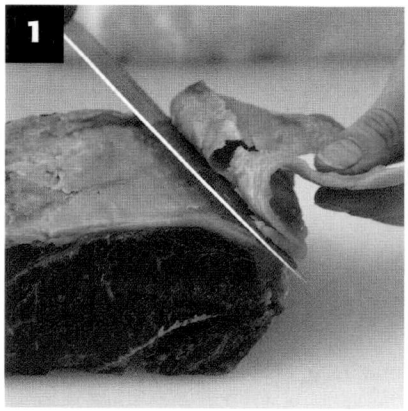

Tying

Tie the joint if you are using a boned and rolled joint, or if you have boned the joint but want to roast it using the bones as a 'roasting rack'.

1 Tie a piece of string around the length of the joint, securing it to the bones if you are using them. If you are cooking a boned and rolled joint, turn it 90 degrees then tie another piece in the same way.

2 Starting at one end of the joint, loop string around the meat and tie it securely and firmly. Cut it off and make another loop about 5cm (2in) from the first.

3 Continue tying the joint in this way along the whole length of the joint until neatly and firmly secured.

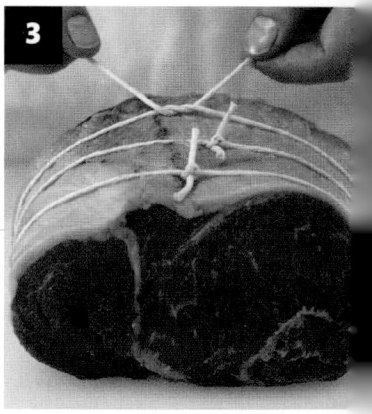

Seasoning

All joints can be seasoned for extra flavour. For pork, the meat should be seasoned and the rind rubbed with salt. Use a dry marinade (see page 147) or salt and black pepper.

1 Rub the joint with vegetable oil to help the seasonings stick.

2 Press on the seasonings in a thin, uniform layer.

Tenderising steak

Some cuts of steak benefit from tenderising. There are two ways to do it: by pounding or scoring.

1 To pound, lay the steaks in a single layer on a large piece of clingfilm or waxed paper. Lay another sheet on top of the slices and pound gently with a rolling pin, small frying pan or the flat side of a meat mallet.

2 Scoring is especially useful for cuts that have long, tough fibres, such as flank. It allows a marinade to penetrate more deeply into the meat. Lay the steak on the chopping board and, using a long, very sharp knife, make shallow cuts in one direction along the whole surface.

3 Make another set of cuts at a 45 degree angle to the first. Now turn the meat over and repeat on the other side.

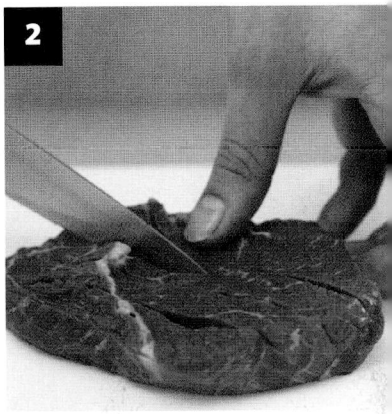

Using a mallet

You can tenderise very tough cuts of meat by beating them with the side of the meat mallet that has raised dimples on its surface. The dimples break down muscle fibre, effectively 'pre-chewing' it. Don't use clingfilm if you are tenderising with this method.

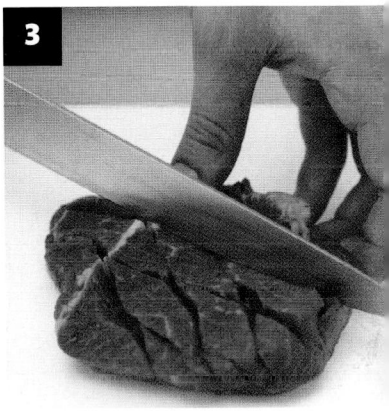

Mincing

If you don't have a mincer you can mince meat using a food processor or a knife.

1 Using a food processor Cut the meat into chunks about 2.5cm (1in) square. Put a handful of meat into the food processor and pulse for a few seconds at a time. Stop when the meat is just starting to form a ball on the sides of the bowl. Remove and set aside, and repeat with the remaining meat.

2 Using a knife This is an old-fashioned method but actually a really excellent one. Trim off all fat and sinews, and cut the meat into thin pieces. Chop with two large heavy knives or cleavers, using a decisive hammer action, until the meat resembles coarse mince.

Preparing lamb

From tender juicy noisettes of lamb for pan-frying to boned or butterflied leg of lamb for roasting, or rack of lamb tied in the French style or as an elegant guard or honour, lamb is wonderfully varied.

Butterflying a leg of lamb

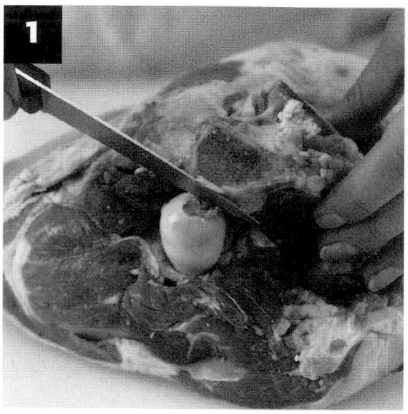

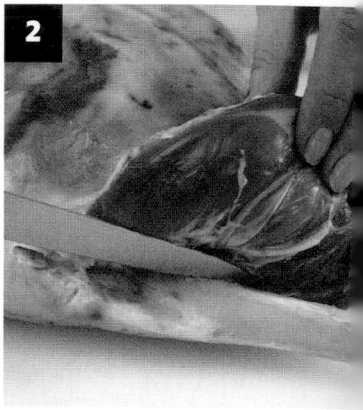

1 Place the leg of lamb on a chopping board with the meaty side facing down and the bone facing up. With the thick end facing towards you, see if the chunky end of the pelvic bone is in place. If it is, cut it out by working all around it with a boning or paring knife – always cutting towards the bone – then pull or twist it out.

2 Using a boning knife, cut a long slit right down to the bone, starting from the thin end, until you reach the joint. Then scrape and cut the meat from the bone, pulling it back with your fingers, until the bone is fully exposed.

3 Work the knife carefully around the bone, cutting away from the meat, to loosen it. Twist out the bone, then follow the same procedure with the other bone.

4 Flatten the meat with your hands. Holding one hand flat on the top of the thickest part, make a cut parallel with the chopping board about midway through. Cut to within 2.5cm (1in) of the edge, then fold it out as if opening a book.

5 Repeat with the other thick part of the leg and fold out. If you like, secure the flaps of meat with skewers to make cooking easier.

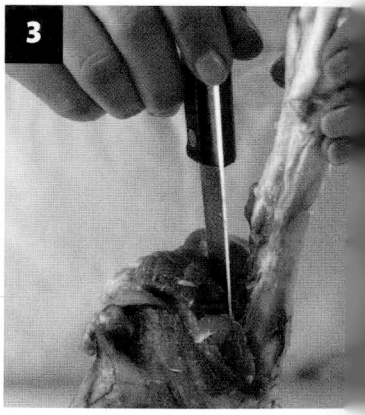

Tunnel-boning leg of lamb

Here, the leg is boned but left whole so the cavity can be stuffed. If necessary, cut out the pelvic bone as described above.

1 Starting from the thin end of the leg, insert a boning knife between the meat and bone, and run it around the bone to cut through the connective tissue and free the bone from the surrounding meat.

2 When you reach the joint, twist the bone and pull it out.

3 Turn the leg around and use the same technique to cut out the thick bone. When you reach the end of the bone, it should pull out easily.

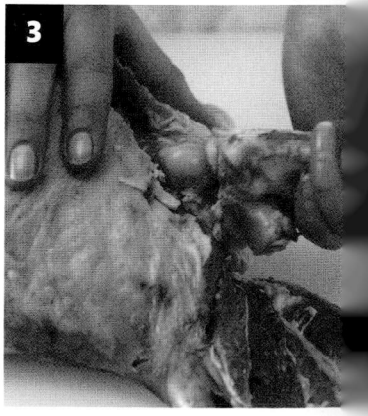

Preparing a rack of lamb

A rack of lamb comprises the seven or eight cutlets, chops from the neck end, served as a joint. It is one of the tastiest and most impressive lamb joints, and easy to prepare. You can cook it just as it comes from the butcher, or as a French-style rack.

1 If necessary, pull off the papery outer membrane from the fat side of the rack. Trim away the excess fat. Look for a long strip of cartilage on one end of the rack and cut it out if it is there. Do the same with a long strip of sinew running the length of the rack under the ribs.

2 Make a cut right down to the bone across the fat side of the rack about 2.5–5cm (1–2in) from the tips of the bones. Place the knife in that cut and, holding the knife almost parallel to the ribs, slice off the meat as a single piece to expose the ends of the bones.

3 Insert the knife between one pair of bared ribs at the point of the initial cut. Push through it to cut the meat between the ribs. Continue in the same way with the other ribs.

4 Slice down on both sides of each rib to remove the strips of meat. When you've finished, turn the rack bone side up and scrape off the papery membranes from the backs of the ribs. This will leave the top parts of the bones clean.

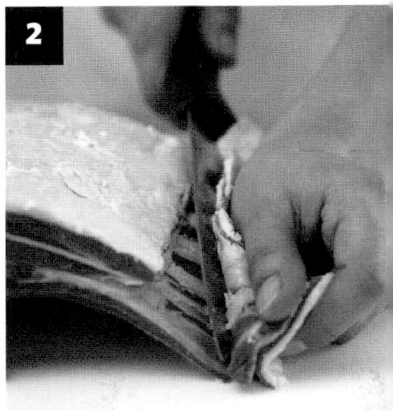

Roasting times

A rack of lamb should always be cooked at a fairly high temperature so that it browns well without overcooking the thin 'eye' meat. Preheat the oven to 220°C (200°C fan oven) mark 7 and cook for 25–30 minutes. If you are cooking a single rack, an alternative is to brown the fat side first; this means that you can cook it at a lower temperature, 180°C (160°C fan oven) mark 4.

Guard of honour

1 Prepare the racks as described for rack of lamb (see page 141) Place with the bases pressed together and the exposed end-bones interlocking.

2 Tie the joint using a piece of string vertically between every two ribs. Roast as it is, or stuff the space between the two racks and cook at 220°C (200°C fan oven) mark 7 for 30–35 minutes.

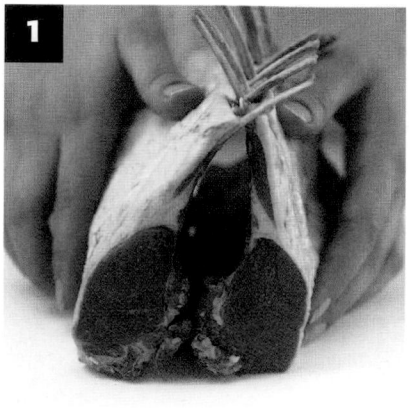

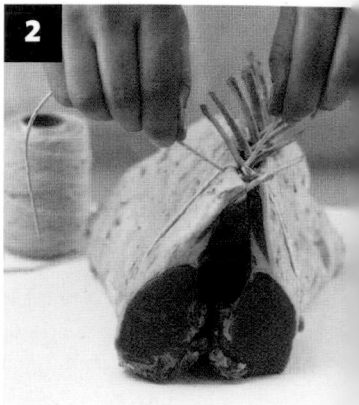

Noisettes of lamb

Loin of lamb can be boned, rolled and sliced to make noisettes (usually with a layer of fat on the meat), both delicious and elegant. Buy them ready prepared or ask the butcher to do it – or try this simple version.

1 Use a thin-bladed knife to scrape and cut along the backbone until the tenderloin falls away. Remove and save for a stir-fry.

2 Turn the loin around and cut between the backbone and eye meat, always cutting towards the bone. Remove the meat in a single piece and trim the excess fat.

3 Roll the flat apron of fat around the eye and tie it securely with string at 2.5cm (1in) intervals.

4 Slice the loin about 2.5cm (1in) thick. Grill (for 8–12 minutes) or pan-fry (for 6–10 minutes).

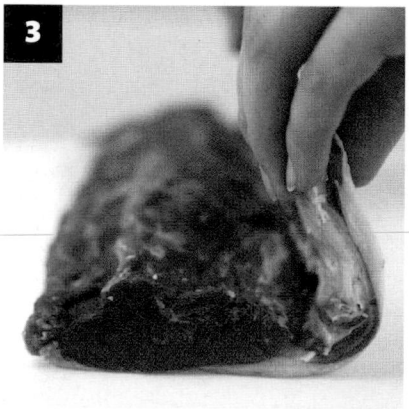

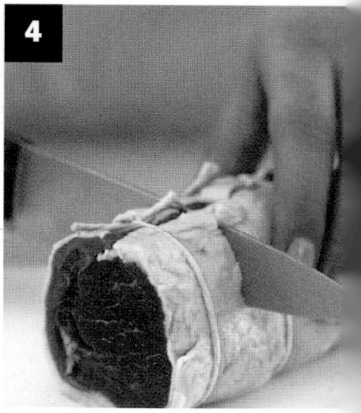

Cook's tips

- The small fillet on the underside of the loin is usually rolled up with the loin to make true noisettes. Otherwise, you can cut it off as a strip and use it (thinly sliced) in a stir-fry, while making this simplified version of noisettes of lamb, which will still be a delicious cut.
- Roast the boned loin as a whole piece rather than cutting it into individual noisettes.
- For a simpler version of medallions requiring no string, you can follow steps 1 and 2, then cut off all the fat and slice the meat. This may look a lot less elegant but is actually a much leaner cut and is therefore probably all the more desirable.

Preparing pork

From simple chops for stuffing to glorious tenderloin and crispy roast pork, the choice of techniques you can use with pork is endlessly varied and the results always delicious.

Removing the tenderloin

Like beef and lamb, pork has a piece of flesh running along the backbone on the other side of the ribs from the loin called the tenderloin. It is the most tender cut of all.

1 Place the loin skin side down on your chopping board and locate the long rounded strip of tenderloin meat. You can get your butcher to remove this for you, but it is also easy to do yourself.

2 Make a cut along the edge of the tenderloin closest to the backbone, taking care not to cut into the meat, then work the knife between meat and bone until you can pull away the tenderloin.

3 Cut off the thin strip of meat connected to the main section and save it for stock, if you like.

4 Using a sharp small knife, make a cut at the thick end of the tenderloin just underneath the thick, silvery membrane covering it on one side.

5 Taking care not to cut the meat, cut and pull off the membrane in long strips. Make sure every bit of membrane comes away. Trim away any loose scraps of meat, and tidy the ends if they look at all ragged.

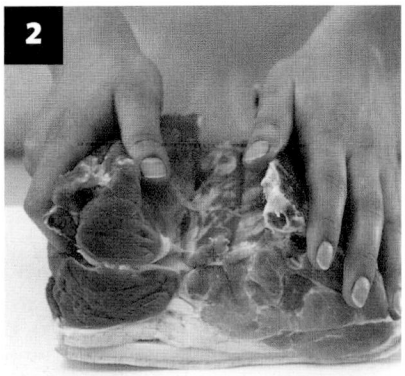

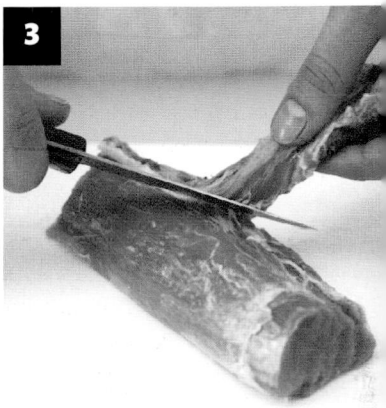

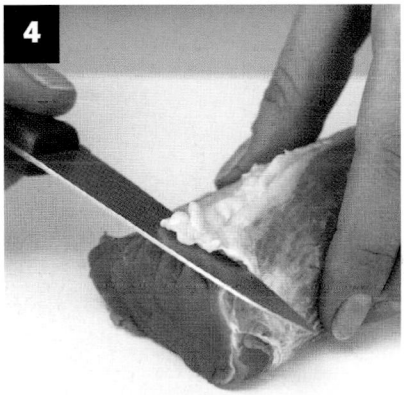

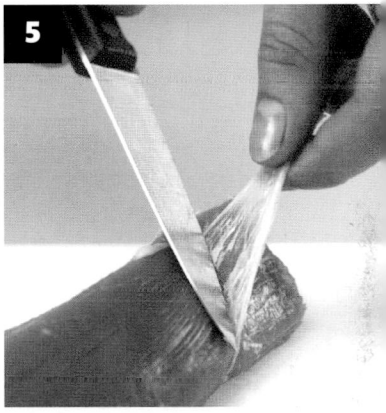

Cooking tenderloin

The tenderloin is most often cut into medallions (see page 144), but it can also be cooked in a single piece with or without stuffing. To cook it unstuffed, brown it well on all sides and then finish cooking in an oven preheated to 200°C (190°C fan oven) mark 6 for about 10 minutes. To stuff it, make a deep cut through the centre of the tenderloin, open it like a book, then pound it gently with a small frying pan or meat mallet to flatten it out. Put the stuffing in the centre of the meat, then roll it up and tie with string. (A quick stuffing can be made with chopped onion cooked gently in oil until soft with a little freshly chopped sage or rosemary.) Cook the stuffed tenderloin as you would unstuffed, but for a little longer.

Cutting medallions

1 Cut pork fillet into pieces about 1–2.5cm (½–1in) thick and lay them in a single layer on clingfilm or waxed paper.

2 Lay another sheet of clingfilm or waxed paper on top of the slices and pound gently with a rolling pin, small frying pan or the flat side of a meat mallet until they are about half their original thickness.

Stuffing chops

Chops at least 2.5cm (1in) thick can be stuffed for extra flavour. Loin chops are best for this; chump chops are also good.

1 Remove the rind (skin) and trim off all but about 5mm (¼in) of fat.

2 Press down with the flat of your hand and, using a small sharp knife, cut into the eye of the meat in the middle of the fat side of the chop.

3 Keep working the knife in until you reach the bone.

4 Cut through all of the eye meat to make a deep pocket. You can enlarge the pocket by cutting through some of the tail of the chop, but don't cut all the way through.

5 Shape the stuffing into thin flat patties if necessary. Open the pocket of the chop and slide the stuffing in, then secure with cocktail sticks.

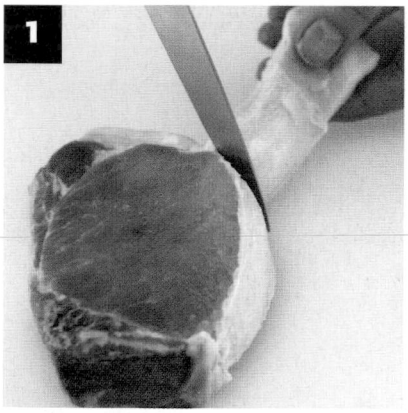

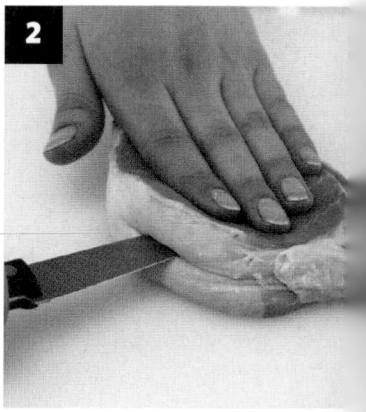

Easy stuffings

Don't overfill the chops or the stuffing will spill out. Try some of the following ideas:

- Slivered garlic cooked in butter
- Sage leaves
- Soft goat's cheese mashed with chopped herbs
- Apple sauce
- Slices of peeled lemon or orange

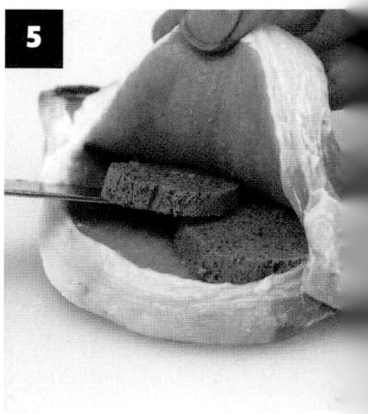

Pork loin

1 Using a long thin-bladed knife, cut a long slit into fat from rib end just below the rind (skin), taking off as little fat as you can. Work knife into fat to remove rind in single sheet. Trim off all but 5mm (¼in) of fat.

2 Using a long thin-bladed knife, cut into the meat as far as you can go.

3 Turn the loin around and place the knife flat on the ribs. Following the line of the ribs, and always cutting towards the bone, cut through the meat until you reach the vertebrae.

4 Use a small sharp knife to scrape the pieces of meat connecting the loin to the underlying bones, and remove the meat. Trim off any ragged scraps.

5 If you want a fully trimmed loin that doesn't need rolling, cut off the flap meat from the eye. Trim away any visible fat and sinews.

6 The loin may be rolled with or without stuffing. To stuff, shape the stuffing into a thin sheet or cylinder. Lay the loin with the fat side down on the chopping board, and put the stuffing on the line where the eye meets the flap meat.

7 Fold the flap of meat over the eye of loin and secure with skewers.

8 Tie the loin with string every 5cm (2in) and remove the skewers.

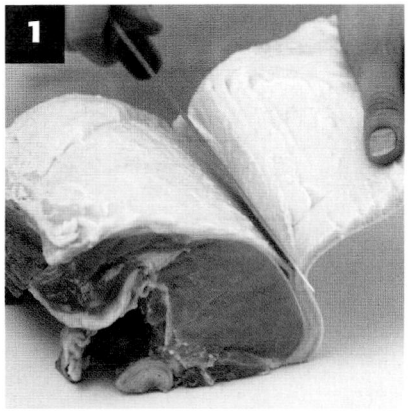

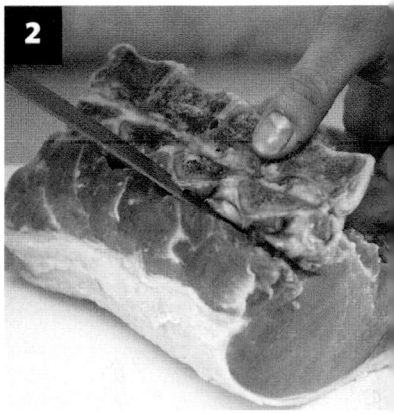

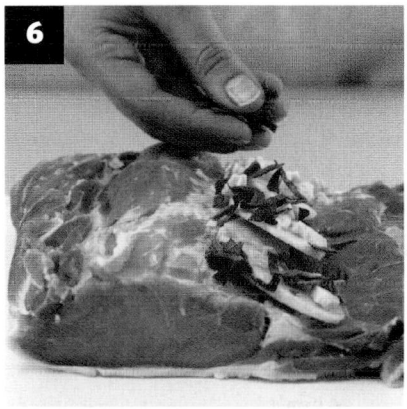

Cook's tips

- Roast a boned loin with the bones as a roasting rack – they add flavour to gravy.
- Save the rind to make pork scratchings. Roast at 200°C (180°C fan oven) mark 6 for 15–25 minutes.
- Butchers use a Stanley knife – available from DIY stores – to score pork rind, because it is so sharp.

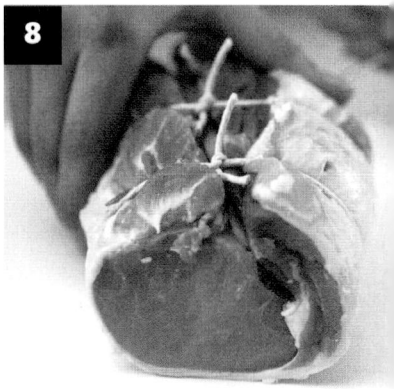

Preparing and cooking ham

Hams come in different sizes and cures. Some are sold cooked, while others are uncooked and some need to be soaked, so buy your ham from a butcher and ask his advice on preparation and cooking.

Baking

1 If the ham needs to be soaked, place it in a large container that will hold it comfortably with plenty of space for water. Pour over cold water to cover and weigh down the ham if necessary. Leave to soak overnight, then drain well.

2 Put the ham in a large flameproof casserole or stockpot, cover with cold water and bring to the boil. Skim off any surface scum. Simmer gently for 25 minutes per 450g (1lb), checking occasionally to make sure it is completely covered with water.

3 Leave to cool in the water. Transfer the ham to a roasting tin. (Reserve the stock for soup.)

4 Preheat the oven to 200°C (180°C fan oven) mark 6. Using a thin-bladed knife, remove the rind and neatly trim the fat so that there is a 5mm–1cm (¼–½in) layer of fat left on the meat.

5 Score the fat with parallel lines about 5cm (2in) apart, then score on the diagonal to make diamond shapes. Press a clove into the centre of each diamond.

6 Spread prepared English mustard as thinly and evenly as possible over the top of the ham. Sprinkle with soft brown sugar to make a light but even coating.

7 Bake the ham for about 30 minutes, until golden-brown.

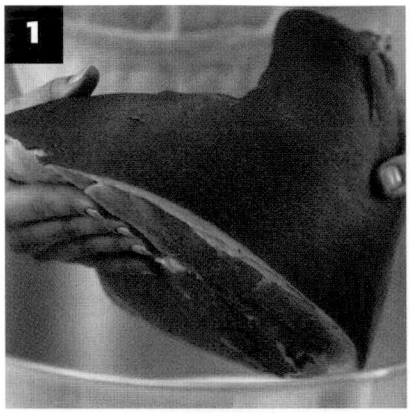

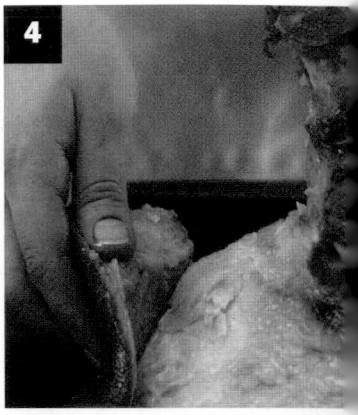

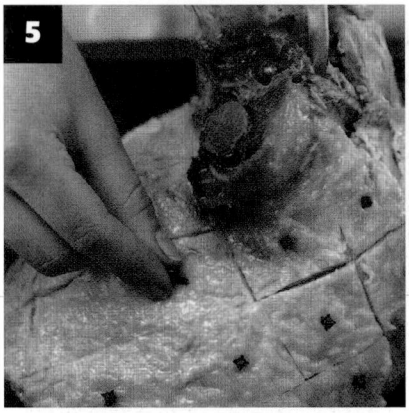

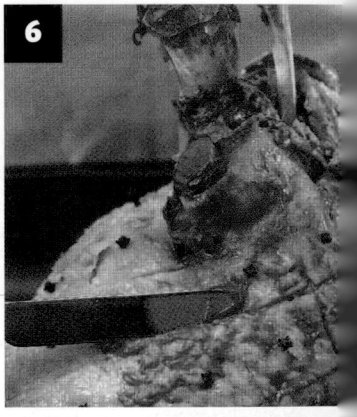

Cook's tips

- Do not let the water continue to boil or the meat will be tough.
- Add a few sprigs of parsley, a few peppercorns, a bay leaf and a chopped onion to the liquid.
- Or, braise in a covered casserole or bake in a tent of aluminium foil, if the ham is not too salty – 170°C (fan oven 150°C) mark 3.

Preparing hare and rabbit

Hare and rabbit are long thin animals with three sections of meat that need different types of cooking. This is reflected in the way that they are cut up for cooking.

Jointing

1 Chop off any pieces of bare bone from the legs, and trim away the thin pieces of flesh from the ribcage.

2 Using a large heavy knife, cut off the hind legs, then cut into two. Cut through the joint to separate the thigh from the ankle, and do the same with the forelegs.

3 If you are not cooking the saddle in a single piece, chop into three pieces of roughly equal size. For smaller pieces, cut each piece in half.

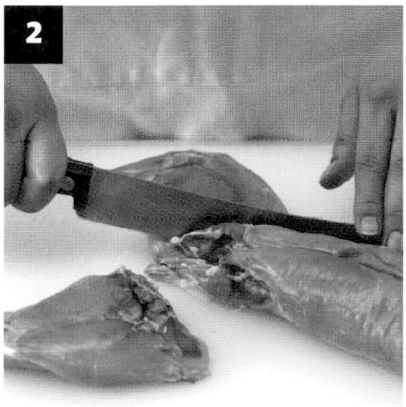

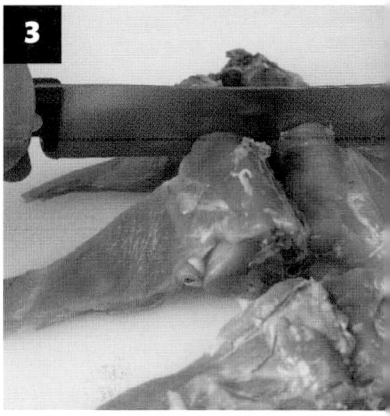

Marinades for meat

Meat is good for marinating, either wet or dry, because its large surface area allows maximum exposure to the marinade. Begin marinating at least 8 hours in advance for small pieces of meat and 24 hours for thick joints.

Wet marinades
Almost always contain some form of acid, which has a modest tenderising effect (especially in thin cuts such as steak). Dry marinated meat thoroughly to remove liquid from the surface, and cook the marinade (skimming off the oil if necessary) as a sauce or deglazing liquid. The following recipe is simple and quick to make:

Herb and garlic marinade This will marinate about 450g (1lb) meat. Use white wine for pork and rabbit, red for all other meats. You will need 2-3 garlic cloves, crushed, 1 celery stick, thinly sliced, 150ml (¼pint) red or white wine, 50ml (2fl oz) extra-virgin olive oil, 50ml (2fl oz) red or white wine vinegar, ¼ tsp dried herbs, 1 bay leaf.

1. Whisk all the ingredients together. Pour over the meat, coating it thoroughly, and chill for at least 8 hours. Turn the meat regularly to ensure it marinates evenly.
2. Before cooking, drain the meat and dry on kitchen paper.

Good additions to wet marinades:
Onions and shallots, chopped or sliced
Asian spices, such as Chinese five spice and star anise
Chilli
Sherry or sherry vinegar
Brandy

Dry marinades
These are useful for roasts and pot roasts. They don't penetrate far into the meat, but give an excellent flavour on and just under the crust. Make them with crushed garlic, dried herbs or spices, and plenty of freshly ground black pepper. Rub into the meat and marinate for at least 30 minutes or up to 8 hours.

Cooking meat and game

For perfectly cooked meat choose the appropriate method for the cut. Tender cuts need quick cooking, such as grilling, whereas tougher cuts benefit from slower cooking, such as pot-roasting.

Grilling

1 Preheat the grill to high while you dry the meat (if marinated) and put it on a wire rack in the grill pan. If it has not been marinated, salt lightly.

2 Put the grill pan under the heat. Thin cuts should be about 2.5cm (1 in) from the heat source, thicker cuts about 7.5cm (3in). Cook according to the table.

Grilling times

Note Cooking times are approximate, for a piece of meat 2.5cm (1in) thick.

Cut	Rare	Medium	Well done
Beef fillet	3–5 minutes	6–7 minutes	8–10 minutes
Other beefsteaks	5–6 minutes	8–12 minutes	15–18 minutes
Pork chops/steaks	8–10 minutes	10–14 minutes	
Lamb chops/steaks	8–10 minutes	10–14 minutes	
Lamb cutlets	6–10 minutes	8–12 minutes	

Griddling

1 Preheat the griddle for 3 minutes. Lightly brush the meat with vegetable oil on one side, then place on the griddle, oiled side down.

2 Cook for a few minutes. Lift the meat to see if it has formed blackened lines, then turn at a 45 degree angle to create a crisscross pattern. Repeat on the second side.

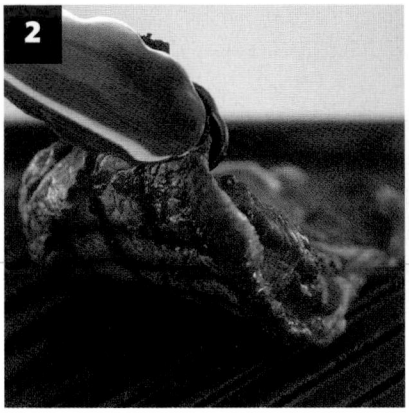

Perfect grills

- Get the griddle smoking hot before putting on the meat.
- You may find that you can cook without oil as long as you let the meat sear thoroughly before turning.

Stir-frying

1 Perfect for tender cuts. Trim the fat, then cut the meat into strips or dice no thicker than 5mm (¼in).

2 Heat a wok or large pan until hot and add oil to coat the inside. Add the meat and cook, stirring. Set aside. Cook the other ingredients you are using (such as vegetables and flavourings). Return the meat to the wok for 1–2 minutes, to heat through.

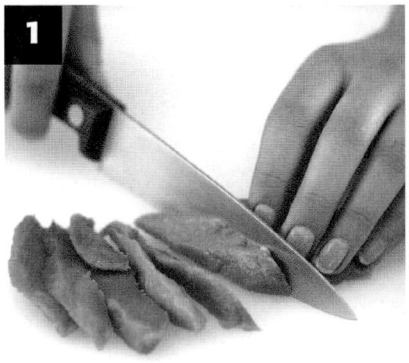

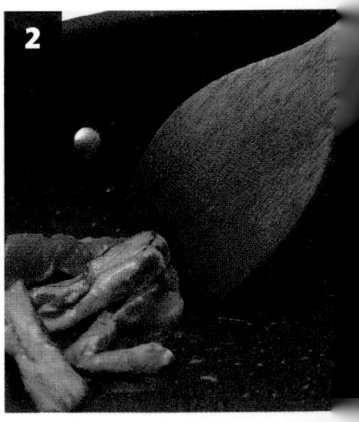

Pan-frying

1 Ideal for steaks or chops. Preheat a frying pan and season meat with salt.

2 Pour in enough vegetable oil to coat the base of the pan. Put in the meat without crowding. Do not move it for at least the first minute of cooking – it may stick.

3 When the meat is well browned, turn and cook on the other side.

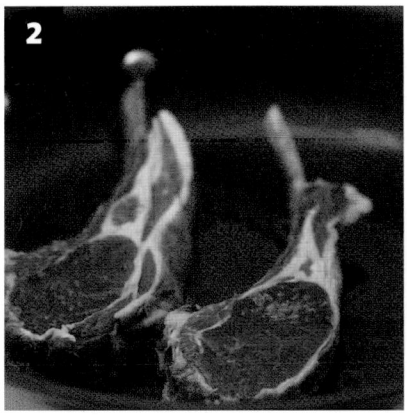

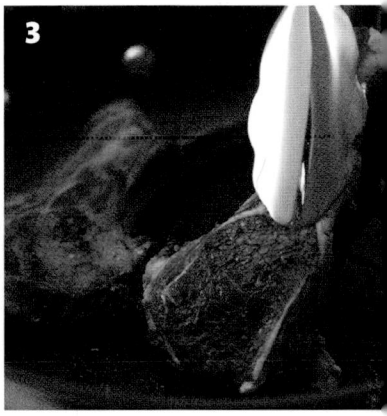

Braising and pot-roasting

Tougher cuts require slow cooking. Braises and pot roasts are similar but braises need more liquid.

To serve six, you will need 3 tbsp olive oil, 6 lamb shanks, 1 large onion, 3 carrots, 3 celery sticks, all thickly sliced, 2 garlic cloves, crushed, 2 × 400g cans chopped tomatoes, 150ml (5fl oz) white wine, salt and ground black pepper, 2 bay leaves.

1 Preheat the oven to 170°C (150°C fan oven) mark 3. Heat the oil in a large flameproof casserole and lightly brown the lamb shanks all over, two or three at a time. Remove from the pan and set aside. Add the onion, carrots, celery and garlic and cook until beginning to colour, then add the lamb, tomatoes and wine.

2 Stir well, season and add the bay leaves. Bring to the boil, cover, and transfer to the oven for 2 hours or until tender. Skim off fat if necessary.

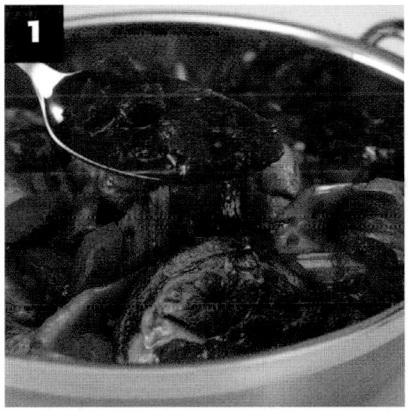

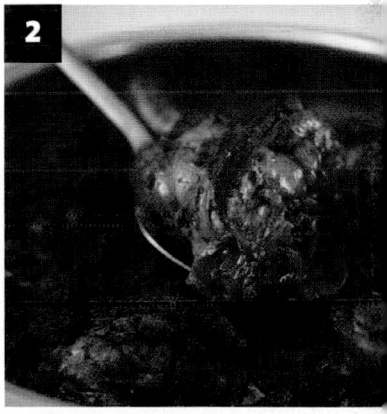

Perfect braising and pot-roasting

- Good cuts of beef include shin, chuck, blade, brisket and flank; good cuts of lamb include leg, shoulder, neck, breast and shank; good cuts of pork include shoulder, hand, spring, belly and loin.
- Casserole cooking can also be used with cuts you would normally roast. These simply need less time in the oven.
- Always use a low heat, and check regularly to make sure that there is enough liquid to keep the meat from catching on the casserole.
- Braises often improve by being cooked in advance and then gently reheated before serving. If you've braised a whole piece of meat, you can slice it before reheating.

Roasting and carving

Ensure the joint is cooked correctly and has time to rest before carving to allow the juices to redistribute and give moist, tender results. When carving joints, slice evenly through the meat.

There are two ways to carve leg of lamb. The first gives slices with a section of the browned crust; the second starts with slices that are well done and gets progressively rarer. Remove all string before carving.

Leg of lamb: method 1

1 Hold the shank and cut from that end, holding the knife flat on the bone, a couple of inches into the meat. Cut down on to the bone to remove that chunk and slice thinly.

2 Start cutting thin slices from the meat on the bone, starting at the cut left by the chunk you removed. Hold the knife at right angles to the bone, then cut at a slight angle as you reach the thicker sections of meat.

3 When you have taken off all the meat you can on that side, turn the leg and continue slicing at an angle until all the meat is removed.

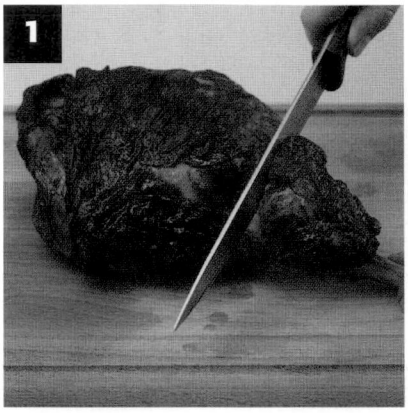

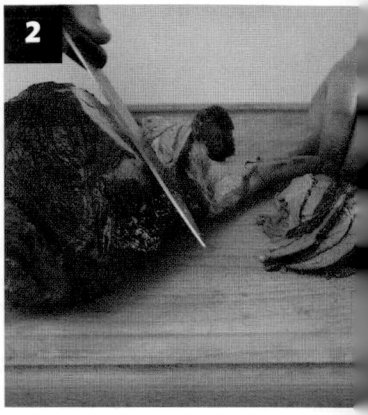

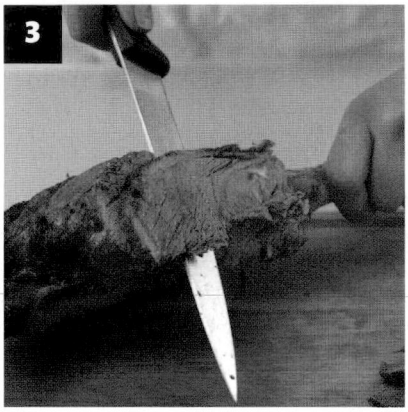

Leg of lamb: method 2

1 Hold the shank with the meatiest part of the leg facing up. Slice with the knife blade parallel to the bone. When you reach the bone, turn the leg over and continue slicing (knife blade parallel to the bone) until you reach the bone.

2 Remove the remainder of the meat from both sides in single pieces, and slice thinly.

Pork with crackling

1 It is much easier to slice pork if you first remove the crackling. Remove the strings and position the carving knife just under the skin on the topmost side of the joint. Work the knife under the skin, taking care not to cut into the meat, until you can pull it off with your fingers.

2 Slice the meat, then break the crackling into servings.

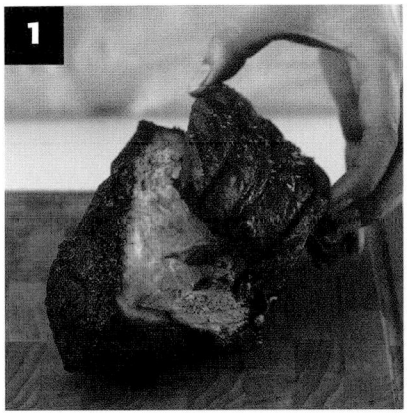

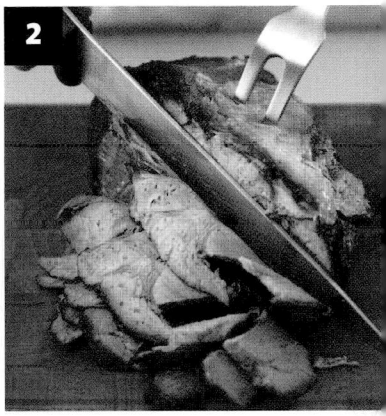

Perfect roasting

- Bring the meat to room temperature before cooking – remove from refrigerator 2–3 hours ahead.
- Cook on a wire rack, or on a bed of sliced vegetables, so that the fat drops away.
- Roast fat side up.
- Check pan juices to make sure they don't dry up and scorch – this will ruin the gravy. Pour water into the roasting tin and reduce extra liquid later.
- When cooked, loosely cover the meat with foil and leave to rest for 20 minutes before carving. This makes the meat juicier and easier to carve.

Roasting times

All these timings are designed as a rough guide. They are based on a large joint, such as rib of beef, leg of pork or leg of lamb, brought to room temperature before cooking. Smaller joints may take between 3 and 5 minutes more per 450g (1lb). Check the meat as it nears the end of its cooking time, and don't be surprised if it needs a few minutes more or less. Allow the meat to rest for at least 15 minutes before carving. A large joint can rest for 45 minutes without getting cold.

Beef	**Oven temperature**	**Timing per 450g (1lb)**
Rare	170°C (150°C fan oven) mark 3	12–15 minutes
Medium-rare	170°C (150°C fan oven) mark 3	15–18 minutes
Well done	170°C (150°C fan oven) mark 3	20–25 minutes
Lamb		
Medium-rare	180°C (160°C fan) mark 4	15–20 minutes
Well done	180°C (160°C fan) mark 4	20–25 minutes
Pork		
Note Many cooks give pork an initial blast of heat – 220°C (fan oven 200°C) mark 7 – for 15–20 minutes. If you do this, watch it carefully near the end of its cooking time.		
Medium-rare	190°C (170°C fan oven) mark 5	20–25 minutes
Well done	190°C (170°C fan oven) mark 5	25–30 minutes

Pork in Red Wine Sauce

SERVES 3–4

350g (12oz) pork fillet or tenderloin, well trimmed and cut diagonally into 1cm (½in) slices
1 tbsp freshly ground mixed peppercorns
oil-water spray
2 garlic cloves, crushed
1 red onion, chopped
200ml (7fl oz) red wine
300ml (½ pint) chicken stock
1 tsp redcurrant jelly
2 tsp Dijon mustard
salt and ground black pepper

For the herb couscous

175g (6oz) couscous
300ml (½ pint) vegetable stock
3–4 tbsp freshly chopped flat-leafed parsley
3–4 tbsp freshly chopped mint
2 tomatoes, deseeded and chopped

PREPARATION TIME 15 minutes
COOKING TIME 25 minutes

PER SERVING

351 calories for 3
6g fat (of which 2g saturates)
35g carbohydrate
0.8g salt
264 calories for 4
5g fat (of which 1g saturates)
27g carbohydrate
0.6g salt

TECHNIQUES

see also preparing pork tenderloin (page 143), preparing vegetables (pages 170–182), making stock (page 34), preparing couscous (page 241), chopping herbs (page 428)

1 To make the herb couscous, put the couscous into a large bowl. Bring the stock to the boil and add to the bowl. Season with salt and pepper and mix through with a fork. Cover with clingfilm and leave in a warm place for 10 minutes. Uncover, add the herbs and tomatoes, and check the seasoning.

2 Meanwhile, flatten the pork slightly with a rolling pin and sprinkle the ground mixed peppercorns on both sides.

3 Spray a heavy non-stick frying pan with the oil-water spray and heat until starting to smoke. Brown the pork medallions for 1–2 minutes on each side, then remove from the pan.

4 Lower the heat and add the garlic and onion to the pan. Cover and cook for 5 minutes or until soft. Add the wine, reduce by half, then pour in the stock and bubble for 7–10 minutes until the sauce has reduced by half.

5 Stir in the redcurrant jelly and mustard, and whisk until combined. Return the pork to the pan, bring the sauce to the boil and simmer for 2–3 minutes until the pork is cooked and the sauce is syrupy. Season and serve with the herb couscous.

Italian Meatballs

SERVES 4
50g (2oz) ready-made breadcrumbs
450g (1lb) minced lean pork
1 tsp fennel seeds, crushed
¼ tsp chilli flakes, or to taste
3 garlic cloves, crushed
4 tbsp chopped flat-leafed parsley
3 tbsp red wine
oil-water spray
salt and ground black pepper
oregano leaves to garnish
noodles to serve

For the tomato sauce
oil-water spray
2 large shallots, finely chopped
3 pitted black olives, shredded
2 crushed garlic cloves
2 pinches of chilli flakes
250ml (9fl oz) stock
500g carton passata
2 tbsp each freshly chopped flat-leafed parsley, basil and oregano

PREPARATION TIME 15 minutes
COOKING TIME 50 minutes

PER SERVING
248 calories
6g fat (of which 2g saturates)
20g carbohydrate
1.6g salt

TECHNIQUES
see also making breadcrumbs (page 308), mincing meat (page 139), chopping herbs (page 428), cooking noodles (page 263)

1 To make the tomato sauce, spray a pan with the oil-water spray and add the shallots. Cook gently for 5 minutes. Add the olives, garlic, chilli flakes and stock. Bring to the boil, cover and simmer for 3–4 minutes.

2 Uncover and simmer for 10 minutes or until the shallots and garlic are soft and the liquid syrupy. Stir in the passata and seasoning. Bring to the boil and simmer for 10–15 minutes, then stir in the herbs.

3 Meanwhile, put the breadcrumbs and remaining ingredients into a large bowl, season and mix together, using your hands, until thoroughly combined. (If you wish to check the seasoning, fry a little mixture, taste and adjust if necessary.)

4 With wet hands, roll the mixture into balls. Line a grill pan with foil, shiny side up, and spray with the oil-water spray. Cook the meatballs under a preheated grill for 3–4 minutes on each side. Serve with the tomato sauce and noodles, garnished with oregano.

Pork with Artichokes and Beans

SERVES 4

2 tbsp vegetable oil
2 pork fillets, about 275g (10oz) each, cut into 1cm (½in) slices
2 tbsp freshly chopped thyme
8 tbsp olive oil
400g can artichoke hearts, drained, rinsed and quartered
400g can flageolet beans, drained and rinsed
185g jar pitted green olives, drained and rinsed
juice of 1 lemon
salt and ground black pepper

PREPARATION TIME 10 minutes
COOKING TIME 8 minutes

PER SERVING
473 calories
36g fat (of which 6g saturates)
17g carbohydrate
3.7g salt

1 Heat the vegetable oil in a frying pan and fry the pork for 2 minutes on each side. Add the thyme and seasoning.

2 Meanwhile, heat the olive oil in a pan, add the artichokes and beans and cook for 3–4 minutes. Add the olives and lemon juice, and season with pepper.

3 Put the pork on top of the artichokes, beans and olives and serve.

Cumin-spiced Gammon

SERVES 4

large pinch each of ground cumin and paprika
2 tbsp olive oil
2 tsp light muscovado sugar
8 thin smoked gammon steaks, about 125g (4oz) each
2 large ripe papayas
zest and juice of 2 limes
½ red chilli, deseeded and finely chopped
20g (¾oz) fresh mint, finely chopped
steamed green beans to serve

PREPARATION TIME 5 minutes
COOKING TIME about 10 minutes

PER SERVING
566 calories
31g fat (of which 9g saturates)
4g carbohydrate
12.1g salt

TECHNIQUES
see also preparing papaya (page 211), zesting citrus fruits (page 207), preparing chillies (page 177), chopping herbs (page 428), preparing green beans (page 174)

1 Preheat the grill. In a small bowl, mix together the cumin, paprika, oil and half the sugar. Put the gammon on to a non-stick baking sheet, then brush the spiced oil over each side.

2 Grill the gammon for about 5 minutes on each side, basting once or twice with the juices.

3 Meanwhile, cut each papaya in half, then deseed and peel. Roughly chop half the flesh and put into a bowl. Purée the remaining fruit with the lime juice. Add to the bowl with the lime zest, chilli, mint and remaining sugar. Spoon the mixture on top of the gammon and serve with green beans.

Variations

- Use mango instead of the papaya. Make sure it's ripe before you buy it – give it a gentle squeeze to check.
- Try the spice rub and fruity relish with pork chops, or with meaty fish such as swordfish.

Ginger and Honey-glazed Ham

SERVES 8–10

4.5–6.8kg (10–15lb) unsmoked gammon on the bone
2 shallots, peeled and halved
6 cloves
3 bay leaves
2 celery sticks, cut into 5cm (2in) pieces
2 tbsp English mustard
5cm (2in) piece fresh root ginger, peeled and thinly sliced

For the glaze

225g (8oz) dark brown sugar
2 tbsp clear honey
8 tbsp brandy or Madeira

For the chutney

4 mangoes, peeled, sliced and chopped into 5cm (2in) chunks
1 tsp mixed spice
4 cardamom pods, seeds removed and crushed
½ tsp ground cinnamon
4 tbsp raisins

PREPARATION TIME 1 hour
COOKING TIME 5¾ hours

PER SERVING

550 calories for 8
19g fat (of which 6g saturates)
48g carbohydrate
5.5g salt
440 calories for 10
15g fat (of which 5g saturates)
38g carbohydrate
4.4g salt

TECHNIQUES

see also preparing ham (page 146), preparing vegetables (pages 170–182), preparing fresh spices (page 429), preparing mangoes (page 210)

1 Put the gammon in a large pan. Add the shallots, cloves, bay leaves, celery and cold water to cover. Bring to the boil, cover and simmer gently for about 5 hours. Remove any scum with a slotted spoon. Lift the ham out of the pan, discard the vegetables and herbs, and cool.

2 Preheat the oven to 200°C (180°C fan oven) mark 6. Using a sharp knife, carefully cut away the ham's thick skin to leave an even layer of fat. Score a diamond pattern in the fat and put the ham into a roasting tin. Smother evenly with the mustard and tuck the ginger into the scored fat.

3 To make the glaze, put the sugar, honey and brandy or Madeira into a pan and heat until the sugar has dissolved. Brush over the ham.

4 In a bowl, mix together the chutney ingredients, add any remaining glaze, then spoon around the ham.

5 Cook the ham for 30–40 minutes, basting every 10 minutes. Remove the ham from the roasting tin and put to one side. Stir the chutney and put it under the grill for 5 minutes to allow the mango to caramelise. Transfer the chutney to a side dish for serving.

Lamb with Orange and Mint

SERVES 4
4 tbsp olive oil
4 lamb steaks, about 700g (1lb 9oz) total weight
185g jar chargrilled sweet red peppers, drained and roughly chopped
50g (2oz) black olives
1 orange
juice of 1 lemon
1 small bunch mint, roughly chopped
salt and ground black pepper

PREPARATION TIME 10 minutes
COOKING TIME 20 minutes

PER SERVING
411 calories
28g fat (of which 10g saturates)
6g carbohydrate
1.1g salt

TECHNIQUES
see also chopping herbs (page 428)

1 Heat 2 tbsp oil in a large non-stick frying pan. Brown the lamb in the hot oil, turning occasionally until the meat has formed a deep golden-brown crust all over.

2 Lower the heat and add the peppers and olives to the pan. Chop up the orange, squeeze the juice directly into the pan and add the orange pieces for extra flavour. Add the lemon juice and the remaining oil.

3 Simmer for 5 minutes, stirring to break down the peppers a little. Stir the mint into the pan. Season to taste with salt and pepper and serve.

Greek Lamb and Feta Layer

SERVES 8 (MAKES 2 MEALS FOR 4)

5 tbsp olive oil
1 large onion, finely chopped
900g (2lb) lamb mince
2 garlic cloves, crushed
2 tbsp tomato purée
2 × 400g cans plum tomatoes in tomato juice
3 tbsp Worcestershire sauce
2 tbsp freshly chopped oregano
3 large potatoes, about 1kg (2¼lb) total weight
2 large aubergines, trimmed and cut into 5mm (¼in) slices
1kg (2¼lb) Greek yogurt
4 large eggs
50g (2oz) freshly grated Parmesan
pinch of freshly grated nutmeg
200g (7oz) feta cheese, crumbled
salt and ground black pepper

PREPARATION TIME 20 minutes
COOKING TIME 1 hour 50 minutes

PER SERVING
686 calories
45g fat (of which 20g saturates)
32g carbohydrate
1.8g salt

1 Heat 2 tbsp oil in a large pan, add the onion and cook over a low heat for 10 minutes or until soft. Put the mince in a large non-stick frying pan and cook over a high heat, breaking it up with a spoon, until no liquid remains and the lamb is brown, 10–15 minutes. Add the garlic and tomato purée, and cook for 2 minutes. Add the lamb to the onion with the tomatoes, Worcestershire sauce and oregano. Bring to the boil and season with salt and pepper. Simmer for 30–40 minutes until the lamb is tender.

2 Meanwhile, cook the potatoes in boiling salted water for 20–30 minutes until tender, then drain and cool. Peel and slice thickly. Preheat the oven to 180°C (160°C fan oven) mark 4. Brush the aubergine slices with the remaining oil. Preheat two non-stick frying pans and cook the aubergine slices for 2–3 minutes on each side until soft. Mix together the yogurt, eggs and half the Parmesan, season the sauce to taste with salt and pepper, then add the nutmeg.

3 Divide the lamb between two 1.4 litre (2½ pint) ovenproof dishes or eight individual dishes. Layer the potato, feta and aubergine on top. Pour the yogurt sauce over and sprinkle with the remaining Parmesan. Cook for 35–40 minutes until the top has browned and it's piping hot in the centre.

Freezing tip

When you have layered the lamb, vegetables, feta, yogurt sauce and Parmesan in the dishes at step 3, cool, wrap and freeze for up to three months.

Thaw overnight at cool room temperature. Cook at 190°C (170°C fan oven) mark 5 for 45–50 minutes until hot to the centre.

Lamb, Prune and Almond Tagine

SERVES 6

2 tsp each coriander and cumin seeds
2 tsp chilli powder
1 tbsp paprika
1 tbsp ground turmeric
5 garlic cloves, chopped
6 tbsp olive oil
1.4kg (3lb) lamb leg steaks
75g (3oz) ghee or clarified butter
2 large onions, finely chopped
1 carrot, roughly chopped
900ml (1½ pints) lamb stock
300g (11oz) ready-to-eat prunes
4 cinnamon sticks
4 bay leaves
50g (2oz) ground almonds
12 shallots
1 tbsp honey
salt and ground black pepper
toasted almonds and chopped flat-leafed parsley to garnish

PREPARATION TIME 20 minutes, plus minimum 5 hours marinating
COOKING TIME 2½ hours

PER SERVING
652 calories
44g fat (of which 16g saturates)
31g carbohydrate
0.6g salt

Cook's tip

To make clarified butter, heat butter in a small pan without colouring. Skim off the foam; the solids will sink. Pour the clear butter into a bowl through a lined sieve. Leave for 10 minutes. Pour into a bowl, leaving any sediment behind. Cool, then store in a jar in the refrigerator for up to six months.

1 Blend together the coriander, cumin, chilli powder, paprika, turmeric, garlic and 4 tbsp oil in a pestle and mortar or a blender. Coat the steaks with the paste and cover and chill for at least 5 hours.

2 Preheat the oven to 170°C (150°C fan oven) mark 3. Melt 25g (1oz) ghee or clarified butter in a large flameproof casserole, add the onions and carrot, and cook until soft. Remove and put to one side. Fry the lamb on each side in the rest of the ghee or butter. Add a little of the stock to the casserole and bring to the boil, scraping up the sediment from the bottom. Return the onion and carrot to the casserole and add 100g (3½oz) prunes. Add the remaining stock to the pan with the cinnamon sticks, bay leaves and ground almonds. Season, cover and cook in the oven for 2 hours or until the meat is really tender.

3 Meanwhile, fry the shallots in the remaining oil and the honey until they turn a deep golden brown. Add to the casserole 30–40 minutes before the end of the cooking time.

4 Take the lamb out of the sauce and put to one side. Bring the sauce to the boil, bubble and reduce to a thick consistency. Return the lamb to the casserole, add the remaining prunes, then bubble for 3–4 minutes. Garnish with almonds and parsley.

Braised Lamb Shanks

SERVES 6

6 small lamb shanks
450g (1lb) shallots
2 medium aubergines, cut into small dice
2 tbsp olive oil
3 tbsp harissa
pared zest of 1 orange and juice of 3 large oranges
200ml (7fl oz) medium sherry
700g jar passata
300ml (½ pint) hot vegetable or lamb stock
75g (3oz) ready-to-eat dried apricots
75g (3oz) cherries
large pinch of saffron
couscous and French beans (optional) to serve

PREPARATION TIME 20–25 minutes
COOKING TIME 2¾ hours

PER SERVING

355 calories
16g fat (of which 6g saturates)
23g carbohydrate
1.2g salt

TECHNIQUES

see also preparing vegetables (pages 170–182), zesting citrus fruits (page 207), making stock (page 34), preparing couscous (page 241)

Cook's tip

Cooking lamb shanks in a rich, fruity vegetable sauce at a low heat in the oven makes the meat deliciously tender.

1 Preheat the oven to 170°C (150°C fan oven) mark 3. Heat a large flameproof casserole and brown the lamb shanks all over. Allow 10–12 minutes to do this, as the better the colour now the better the flavour of the finished dish.

2 Remove the lamb and set aside. Add the shallots, aubergines and oil to the casserole. Return the casserole to the hob and cook everything together over a high heat, stirring from time to time, until the shallots and aubergines are golden and beginning to soften.

3 Lower the heat and add the lamb and all the other ingredients. The liquid should come halfway up the shanks. Bring to the boil, then cover tightly and put in the oven for 2½ hours. Test the lamb with a fork – it should be so tender it almost falls off the bone.

4 If the cooking liquid looks too thin, remove the lamb to a heated serving plate, then bubble the sauce on the hob until reduced and thickened. Return the lamb to the casserole. Serve with couscous and French beans, if you like.

Roast Lamb with Orange

SERVES 4

zest and juice of 1 orange, plus extra wedges to garnish
2 garlic cloves, sliced
3 large fresh rosemary sprigs
1 tbsp olive oil
1.25kg (2lb 12oz) leg of lamb
3 tbsp marmalade
1 tbsp plain flour
150ml (¼ pint) water
salt and ground black pepper
1 bunch watercress to garnish
roast vegetables to serve

PREPARATION TIME 20 minutes
COOKING TIME 1 hour 25 minutes

PER SERVING
581 calories
38g fat (of which 12g saturates)
14g carbohydrate
0.4g salt

TECHNIQUES
see also zesting citrus fruit (page 207), preparing garlic (page 171), roasting vegetables (page 189)

1 Preheat the oven to 180°C (160°C fan oven) mark 4. In a bowl, mix together the orange zest, garlic, the leaves from two rosemary sprigs and the oil. Season with salt and pepper. Put the lamb joint on a chopping board and make several slits all over it. Stuff the mixture into the slits. Put the lamb on a metal rack in a roasting tin and roast for 1¼ hours. Baste the joint with the lamb juices from the tin from time to time.

2 About 10–15 minutes before the end of the cooking time, brush the top of the joint with the marmalade. Insert a few rosemary leaves into each slit in the meat.

3 Remove the joint from the oven, wrap loosely in foil and allow to rest for 10–15 minutes.

4 Put the roasting tin on the hob, skim off any surface fat and discard, leaving the lamb juices. Increase the heat and stir in the flour. Add the water and the orange juice and bring to the boil, then lower the heat and simmer, stirring occasionally, for about 8 minutes or until thick. Season to taste.

5 Serve the lamb joint with the gravy and roast vegetables, garnished with orange wedges and watercress.

Sweet Chilli Beef Stir-fry

SERVES 4

1 tsp chilli oil
1 tbsp soy sauce
1 tbsp clear honey
1 garlic clove, crushed
1 large red chilli, halved, deseeded and chopped
400g (14oz) lean beef, cut into strips
1 tsp sunflower oil
1 broccoli head, shredded
200g (7oz) mangetouts, halved
1 red pepper, halved, deseeded and cut into strips
soba noodles or rice to serve

PREPARATION TIME 10 minutes
COOKING TIME 10–11 minutes

PER SERVING

271 calories
12g fat (of which 4g saturates)
10g carbohydrate
0.9g salt

TECHNIQUES

see also preparing vegetables (pages 170–182), cooking noodles (page 263), cooking rice (page 236), stir-frying meat (page 148)

1 Put the chilli oil in a medium-sized shallow bowl. Add the soy sauce, honey, garlic and chilli, and stir well. Add the strips of beef and toss in the marinade.

2 Heat the sunflower oil in a wok over a high heat until it is very hot. Cook the strips of beef in two batches, then remove them from the pan and set to one side. Wipe the pan with kitchen paper to remove any residue.

3 Add the broccoli, mangetouts, red pepper and 2 tbsp water. Stir-fry for 5–6 minutes until starting to soften. Return the beef to the pan to heat through. Serve with noodles or rice.

Cook's tip

Allow 50g (2oz) uncooked noodles or rice per person.

One-pot Spicy Beef

SERVES 4

2 tsp sunflower oil
1 large onion, roughly chopped
1 garlic clove, finely chopped
1 small red chilli, finely chopped
2 red peppers, roughly chopped
2 celery sticks, diced
400g (14oz) lean beef mince
400g can chopped tomatoes
2 × 400g cans mixed beans, drained
1–2 tsp Tabasco sauce
2–3 tbsp roughly chopped coriander to garnish (optional)

To serve

salsa (see Cook's tip)
soft flour tortilla or basmati rice – 50g (2oz) per person

PREPARATION TIME 15 minutes
COOKING TIME about 40 minutes

PER SERVING

412 calories
13g fat (of which 5g saturates)
42g carbohydrate
1.7g salt

TECHNIQUES

see also preparing vegetables (pages 170–182), mincing meat (page 139), chopping herbs (page 428)

Cook's tip

To make a quick salsa, peel and roughly chop ½ ripe avocado. Put in a bowl with 4 roughly chopped tomatoes, 1 tsp olive oil and the juice of ½ lime. Mix well.

1 Heat the oil in a large frying pan. Add the onion to the pan with 2 tbsp water. Cook for 10 minutes or until softened. Add the garlic and chilli, and cook for a further 1–2 minutes until golden. Add the red peppers and celery and cook for 5 minutes.

2 Add the beef to the pan and brown all over. Add the tomatoes, beans and Tabasco sauce, then simmer for 20 minutes. Garnish with coriander, if you like, and serve with salsa accompanied by a tortilla or rice.

Braised Beef

SERVES 4

175g (6oz) smoked pancetta or smoked streaky bacon, cubed
2 medium leeks, thickly sliced
1 tbsp olive oil
450g (1lb) braising steak, cut into 5cm (2in) pieces
1 large onion, finely chopped
2 carrots and 2 parsnips, thickly sliced
1 tbsp plain flour
300ml (½ pint) red wine
1–2 tbsp redcurrant jelly
125g (4oz) chestnut mushrooms, halved
ground black pepper
freshly chopped flat-leafed parsley to garnish

PREPARATION TIME 20 minutes
COOKING TIME about 3½ hours

PER SERVING
524 calories
25g fat (of which 9g saturates)
27g carbohydrate
1.6g salt

TECHNIQUES
see also preparing vegetables (pages 170–182)

Freezing tip

Complete to the end of step 4, without the garnish. Put in a freezerproof container, cool and freeze for up to three months.

Thaw overnight at cool room temperature. Preheat the oven to 180°C (160°C fan oven) mark 4. Bring to the boil on the hob, cover tightly and reheat in the oven for about 30 minutes or until piping hot.

1 Preheat the oven to 170°C (150°C fan oven) mark 3. Fry the pancetta or bacon in a shallow flameproof casserole for 2–3 minutes until golden. Add the leeks and cook for a further 2 minutes or until the leeks are just beginning to colour. Remove with a slotted spoon and set aside.

2 Heat the oil in the casserole. Fry the beef in batches for 2–3 minutes until a rich golden colour on all sides. Remove from the casserole and set aside. Add the onion and fry over a gentle heat for 5 minutes or until golden. Stir in the carrots and parsnips and fry for 1–2 minutes.

3 Return the beef to the casserole and stir in the flour to soak up the juices. Gradually add the wine and 300ml (½ pint) water, then stir in the redcurrant jelly. Season with pepper and bring to the boil. Cover with a tight-fitting lid and cook in the oven for 2 hours.

4 Stir in the fried leeks, pancetta and mushrooms, re-cover and cook for a further 1 hour or until everything is tender. Serve scattered with chopped parsley.

Fillet of Beef with Roquefort Sauce

SERVES 6

125g (4oz) Roquefort cheese, crumbled
125g (4oz) unsalted butter, softened
900g (2lb) fillet beef
7 tbsp vegetable oil
2 garlic cloves, crushed
2 large aubergines, 400g (14oz) each, cut lengthways into 1cm (½in) slices
150g (5oz) onion, finely chopped
150ml (¼ pint) medium-dry sherry
750ml (1¼ pints) meat stock
lemon juice to taste
salt and ground black pepper
fresh rosemary sprigs, baby spinach and beetroot shavings to garnish

For the polenta

900ml (1½ pints) milk
pinch of salt
140g (4½oz) polenta
4 tbsp olive oil
75g (3oz) finely grated Parmesan

PREPARATION TIME 30 minutes
COOKING TIME about 1 hour 10 minutes

PER SERVING

610 calories
46g fat (of which 2g saturates)
7g carbohydrate
1.1g salt

Cook's tip

Cook a whole fillet of beef for 30 minutes for rare, 35 minutes for medium-rare and 40 minutes for well done.

1 Preheat the oven to 220°C (200°C fan oven) mark 7. Gently stir the cheese into the butter. Cover and chill. Season the beef. Heat 1 tbsp oil in a frying pan for 1–2 minutes. Brown the beef for 1–2 minutes on each side. Leave to cool. Rub the beef with garlic. Brush each side of the aubergines with oil and fry in a non-stick frying pan for 4–5 minutes on each side until golden, then cool. Wrap the aubergine around the beef and tie at intervals with string. Season and set aside. Heat 2 tbsp oil in the pan and cook the onion for 10 minutes or until golden. Add the sherry, bring to the boil and bubble to reduce by half. Add the stock, bring to the boil again and bubble for 10–15 minutes until reduced by half. Set aside. Roast the beef for 30–40 minutes (see Cook's tip). Cover and set aside in a warm place for 10 minutes.

2 For the polenta, pour the milk into a large pan, add salt and bring to the boil. Remove from the heat and add the polenta in a slow stream, stirring constantly. Simmer, stirring, for 5 minutes. Remove from the heat and stir in the olive oil and Parmesan. Season and set aside.

3 To finish, reheat the sherry stock mixture, whisking in the reserved Roquefort butter a little at a time. Add the lemon juice. Remove the string from the beef and thickly slice. Stir any pan juices into the sauce. Garnish and serve with the polenta and Roquefort sauce.

Roasted Venison Sausages

SERVES 6

12 venison sausages
2 tbsp redcurrant jelly
1 tsp lemon juice
400g (14oz) red onions, chopped
2 tbsp olive oil
4 tbsp red wine vinegar
2 tbsp demerara sugar
1 tsp juniper berries, crushed
mashed potatoes to serve

PREPARATION TIME 10 minutes
COOKING TIME 35 minutes

PER SERVING

538 calories
40g fat (of which 16g saturates)
32g carbohydrate
3g salt

TECHNIQUES

see also preparing onions (page 170), mashing potatoes (page 184)

1 Preheat the oven to 220°C (200°C fan oven) mark 7. Put the sausages into a small roasting tin. Mix together the redcurrant jelly and lemon juice and spoon over the sausages. Roast for 35 minutes, turning once.

2 Gently fry the onions in the oil for 15–20 minutes. Add the vinegar, sugar and juniper berries, and continue cooking for 5 minutes or until the onions are really tender.

3 Serve the sausages with the red onion marmalade.

Rabbit Casserole with Prunes

SERVES 6

175g (6oz) ready-to-eat pitted prunes
300ml (½ pint) red wine
3–4 tbsp olive oil
about 2.3kg (5lb) rabbit joints
1 large onion, chopped
2 large garlic cloves, crushed
5 tbsp Armagnac
450ml (¾ pint) light stock
few sprigs fresh thyme or 1 tsp dried thyme
2 bay leaves
140ml (4½fl oz) double cream
125g (4oz) brown-cap mushrooms, sliced
salt and ground black pepper
fresh thyme sprigs to garnish

PREPARATION TIME 20 minutes, plus 4 hours soaking
COOKING TIME 1¼ hours

PER SERVING

538 calories
26g fat (of which 13g saturates)
5g carbohydrate
0.3g salt

TECHNIQUES

see also jointing rabbit (page 147), preparing vegetables (pages 170–182), making stock (page 34)

1 Put the prunes and wine into a bowl. Cover and leave for about 4 hours, then strain, keeping the wine and prunes to one side.

2 Preheat the oven to 170°C (150°C fan oven) mark 3. Heat 3 tbsp oil in a flameproof casserole. Brown the rabbit joints a few at a time, then remove from the casserole. Add the onion and garlic with a little more oil, if necessary, and lightly brown. Return the rabbit to the casserole, add the Armagnac and warm through. Carefully light the Armagnac with a taper or long match, then shake the pan gently until the flames subside.

3 Pour in the stock and the wine from the prunes, and bring to the boil. Add the sprigs of thyme (tied together), or the dried thyme, to the casserole with the bay leaves and plenty of seasoning. Cover the casserole tightly. Bake for about 1 hour or until tender.

4 Lift the rabbit out of the juices and keep warm. Boil the cooking juices until reduced by about a half. Add the cream and mushrooms and continue boiling for 2–3 minutes. Stir in the prunes and warm through. Adjust the seasoning and spoon the sauce over the rabbit to serve. Garnish with sprigs of fresh thyme.

7 VEGETABLES

Nutritious, mouthwatering and essential to a healthy diet – vegetables are a must in every kitchen. From basic peeling, slicing, shredding, chopping and dicing to podding, coring, seeding and stuffing, the easy-to-follow techniques section explains every type of preparation for the various families of vegetables. The cooking section guides you through the essentials, including boiling, steaming, sautéing, stir-frying, deep-frying, braising, stewing, griddling, roasting and mashing, with essential tips and useful tables of cooking times. The recipes offer a choice of dishes for every occasion – from salads such as Winter coleslaw and Mixed leaf salad to Mediterranean kebabs, Sprouts and pancetta, Mixed vegetable tempura, Thai vegetable curry, Chilli onions with goat's cheese and Roasted stuffed peppers.

Preparing onions and shallots

Similar in shape, aroma and flavour, onions and shallots are prepared in very similar ways. Their pungent taste makes them excellent flavouring ingredients.

Onions

1 Cut off the tip and base of the onion. Peel away all the layers of papery skin and any discoloured layers underneath.

2 Put the onion cut side down on the chopping board, then, using a sharp knife, cut the onion in half from tip to base.

3 **Slicing** Put one half on the board with the cut surface facing down and slice across the onion.

4 **Chopping** Slice the halved onions from the root end to the top at regular intervals. Next, make 2–3 horizontal slices through the onion, then slice vertically across the width.

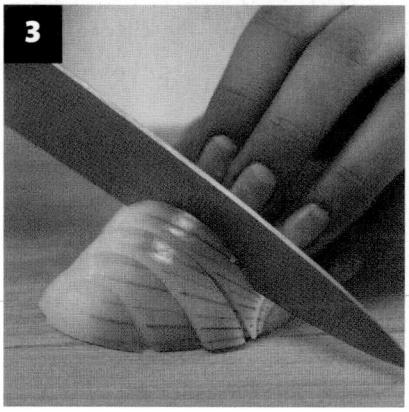

Shallots

As shallots are much smaller than onions, they are easier to slice and dice in the following way.

1 Cut off the tip and trim off the ends of the root. Peel off the skin and any discoloured layers beneath.

2 Holding the shallot with the root end down, use a small, sharp knife to make deep parallel slices almost down to the base while keeping the slices attached to it.

3 **Slicing** Turn the shallot on its side and cut off slices from the base.

4 **Dicing** Make deep parallel slices at right angles to the first slices. Turn it on its side and cut off the slices from the base. You should now have fine dice, but chop any larger pieces individually.

Cook's tips

- When buying onions, press the neck end with a fingertip. If it is not rock-hard, the onion may be soft in the centre and therefore not at its best.
- To keep your hands from getting an onion smell, use your fingertips to hold the onion and touch the cut surfaces as little as possible.

Preparing garlic and leeks

Although garlic and leeks are also members of the onion family and share the same familiar pungent flavour and aroma, they are prepared in quite different ways to onions and shallots.

Garlic

1 Put the clove on the chopping board and put the flat side of a large knife on top of it. Press down firmly on the flat of the blade to crush the clove and break the papery skin.

2 Cut off the base of the clove and slip the garlic out of its skin. It should come away easily.

3 Slicing Using a rocking motion with the knife tip on the board, slice the garlic as thinly as you need.

4 Shredding and chopping Holding the slices together, shred them across the slices. Chop the shreds if you need chopped garlic.

5 Crushing After step 2, the whole clove can be put into a garlic press. To crush with a knife, roughly chop the peeled cloves and put them on the board with a pinch of salt.

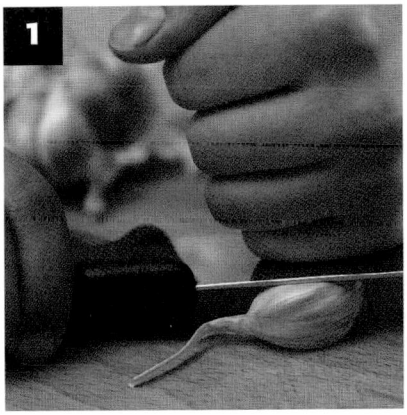

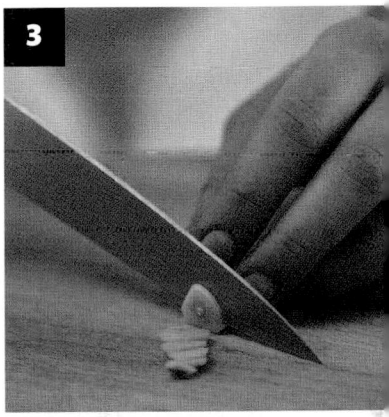

6 Press down hard with the edge of a large knife tip (with the blade facing away from you), then drag the blade along the garlic while still pressing hard. Continue to do this, dragging the knife tip over the garlic to make a purée.

Leeks

As some leeks harbour a lot of grit and earth between their leaves, they need careful cleaning.

1 Cut off the root and any tough parts of the leek. Make a cut into the leaf end of the leek, about 7.5cm (3in) deep.

2 Hold under the cold tap while separating the cut halves to expose any grit. Wash well, then shake dry. Use the green tops for stock.

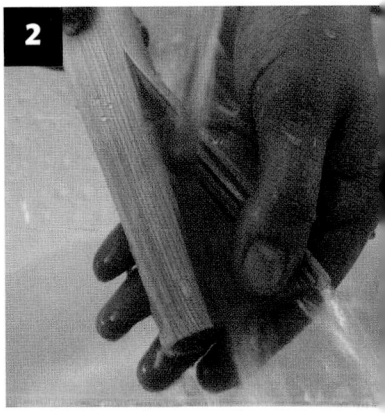

Preparing shoots, stems and corn

The delicate flavours of artichokes, asparagus and fennel are excellent in salads, main dishes or first courses. Celery is a useful vegetable for flavouring stocks and soups too.

Whole artichokes

1 Snap off the stalk so that it's level with the base of the leaves. Tear off any dry or discoloured leaves, and rinse in cold water.

2 Put the artichokes in a pan of salted water with 1 tsp lemon juice and weigh them down with a bowl so that they are completely covered. Boil for 40–45 minutes until an outer leaf pulls off easily.

Artichoke hearts

1 Heat a pan of salted water with 1 tbsp lemon juice per 1 litre (1¾ pints) of water.

2 Remove the stalk and outer leaves, then cut off the remaining leaves and trim away the green parts from the base. Rub with lemon juice and cook for 15–20 minutes until tender.

3 Drain, then scoop out the choke.

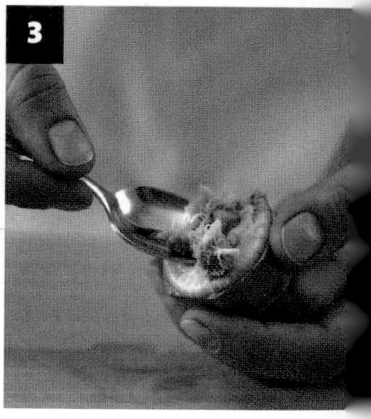

Asparagus

1 Cut the asparagus spears about 5cm (2in) from the stalk end, or where the white and green sections meet. Or cut off the stalk end and peel with a vegetable peeler or small sharp knife.

2 Heat a large pan of salted water that will hold the asparagus in a single layer. Put in the spears and cook for 5–10 minutes until tender.

Cook's tips

- To prepare, snap off the woody tip of the stem; it will snap in just where the stem becomes tender.
- To roast, drizzle with olive oil, a few spoonfuls water and a little salt and roast for 12 minutes at 200°C (180°C fan oven) mark 6.

Celery

1 To remove the strings in the outer green stalks, trim the ends and cut through the base to separate the stalks. Set aside the inner ones.

2 Cut into the base of the green outer stalks with a small knife and catch strings between the blade and your thumb. Pull up towards the top of the stalk to remove the string. Continue along the outside of stalk.

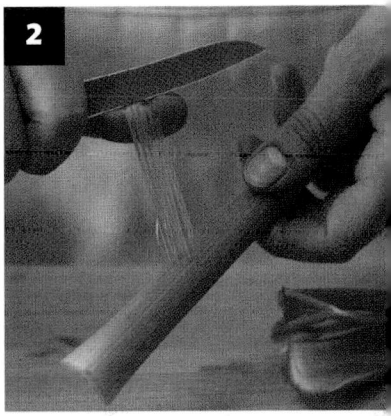

Fennel

1 Trim off the top stems and the base of the bulbs. Remove the core with a small, sharp knife if necessary.

2 The outer leaves may be discoloured and can be scrubbed gently in cold water, or you can peel away the discoloured parts with a knife or a vegetable peeler. Slice the fennel or cut it into quarters, according to your recipe.

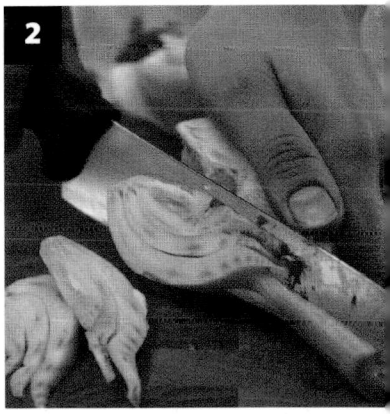

Corn on the cob

Like peas, the sugar in corn starts to turn to starch soon after picking so it is best eaten as soon as possible after picking or buying. To bake, microwave or barbecue corn, leave it in its husk. To boil, you will need to remove it from its husk.

1 To husk, pull away the green papery husks from the ear, a few at a time, until the whole ear is exposed.

2 Grasp the stalk and snap it off, taking all the husks with it. Rub the cob firmly with your hand to remove all the silky threads.

3 Removing the kernels Hold the ear upright in a large bowl, with the stalk sitting on the base of the bowl. Using a thin-bladed knife, cut off the kernels from top to bottom, turning the cob until they are all removed.

Preparing peas, beans and pods

Quick and simple preparation means that you can enjoy summertime favourites, such as sweet young peas, mangetouts, beans and okra at their best.

Peas

1 Hold the pea pod in one hand with the stem pointing towards you. Press the curved 'seam' at the top of the pod to pop it open, and insert the tip of a thumbnail between the two halves to open up the pod.

2 Using your thumb, gently push the peas into a bowl. Rinse the peas in cold water before using.

Cook's tips

- Cook peas as soon as possible after shelling.
- Allow 1kg (2¼lb) unshelled peas or broad beans for four servings.
- Mangetouts and sugarsnaps can be eaten whole. Top and tail; older specimens may benefit from stringing.

Broad beans

1 Hold the pod in one hand with the stem pointing towards you. Insert the tip of a thumbnail between the two halves and open up the pod. Using your thumb, gently push the beans into a bowl.

2 For older beans, it is best to remove the skin. Make a shallow nick in the skin of each bean, then pull off the skin and discard.

Runner beans

1 Small tender runner beans can be topped and tailed. Larger ones need to be stringed. Cut through the stem end so you can catch string between knife blade and finger.

2 Pull off the string and discard. Cut on the diagonal into 5cm (2in) pieces or into fine strips lengthways using a bean slicer or a sharp knife.

Other beans

- Fine (French) beans simply need to be topped and tailed: snip off both ends to remove the stem and tail.
- Bobby beans – a thicker form of bean – can be topped and tailed if tender. Larger ones may need to be stringed.

Okra

1 For cooking okra whole Wash and remove any wispy black 'hair' on the pods. Trim the end of the caps, taking care not to pierce the pods.

2 For cooking okra split If you want the gelatinous texture inside the pod for thickening a stew, okra should be split. Wash well and remove any wispy black 'hair'. Trim the end of the caps and cut in half lengthways, from tip to cap.

Mushrooms

There are many different types of these edible fungi. The most common are cultivated white mushrooms, but there are also numerous wild varieties.

Cultivated mushrooms

Button, white, chestnut and flat mushrooms are all prepared in a similar way.

1 Wipe with a damp cloth or pastry brush to remove any dirt.

2 With button mushrooms, cut off the stalk flush with the base of the cap. For other mushrooms, cut a thin disc off the end of the stalk and discard. Chop or slice mushrooms.

3 If stuffing the mushrooms, snap off the stalk instead, then chop finely and use in the stuffing.

Wild and shitake

Wild mushrooms are typically dirtier than cultivated mushrooms and need careful cleaning and trimming. Fill a bowl with cold water. Immerse the mushroom and shake vigorously to loosen dirt. Dry the mushroom carefully on kitchen paper and check for any remaining specks of dirt. Shiitake have a hard stalk that needs to be removed. Cut this from the softened mushroom, using a sharp knife.

Dried

Soaking in hot water softens the mushrooms to make them usable. Put the mushrooms in a bowl and cover with hot but not boiling water. Leave to soak for 15–40 minutes (or according to the instructions on the pack) until the mushroom caps are soft and flexible. Rinse under cold water, checking for any dirt that might be trapped.

Preparing vegetable fruits

Tomatoes and full-flavoured Mediterranean vegetable fruits such as aubergines and peppers add a rich flavour to many dishes. Each have their individual preparation techniques.

Peeling tomatoes

1 Fill a bowl or pan with boiling water. Using a slotted spoon, add the tomato for 15–30 seconds, then remove to a chopping board.

2 Use a small sharp knife to cut out the core in a single cone-shaped piece. Discard the core.

3 Peel off the skin; it should come away easily depending on ripeness.

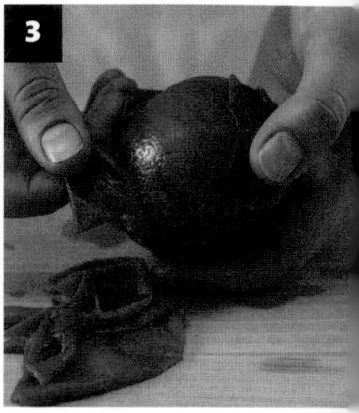

Cutting tomatoes

1 Use a small sharp knife to cut the core out in a single cone-shaped piece. Discard the core.

2 **Wedges** Halve the tomato and then cut into quarters or into three.

3 **Slices** Hold the tomato with the cored side on the chopping board for greater stability and use a serrated knife to cut into slices.

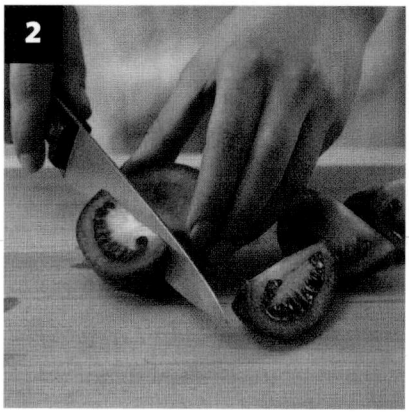

Seeding tomatoes

1 Halve the tomato through the core. Use a small, sharp knife or a spoon to remove the seeds and juice. Shake off the excess water.

2 Chop the tomato as required for your recipe and place in a colander for a minute or two, to drain off any excess liquid.

Cook's tip

If you are using tomatoes in a sauce that will be cooked for a long time, you can just roughly chop them without peeling and then, if you prefer it smooth, sieve the sauce after cooking.

Seeding peppers

The seeds and white pith of peppers taste bitter so should be removed.

1 Cut the pepper in half vertically and snap out the white pithy core and seeds. Trim away the rest of the white membrane with a knife.

2 Alternatively, cut off the top of the pepper, then cut away and discard the seeds and white pith.

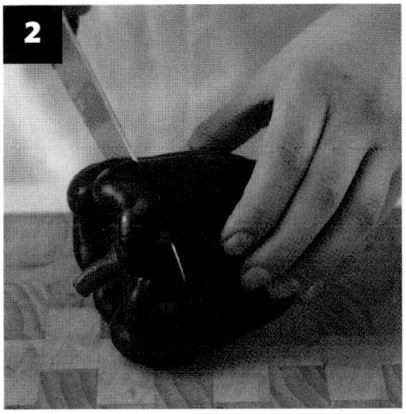

Skinning

Some people find pepper skins hard to digest. To peel raw peppers, use a swivel-handled peeler to cut off strips down the length of the pepper. Use a small knife to cut out any parts of skin that the peeler could not reach.

Chargrilling peppers

Charring imparts a smoky flavour and makes peppers easier to peel.

1 Hold the pepper, using tongs, over the gas flame on your hob (or under a preheated grill) until the skin blackens, turning until black all over.

2 Put in a bowl, cover and leave to cool (the steam will help to loosen the skin). Peel.

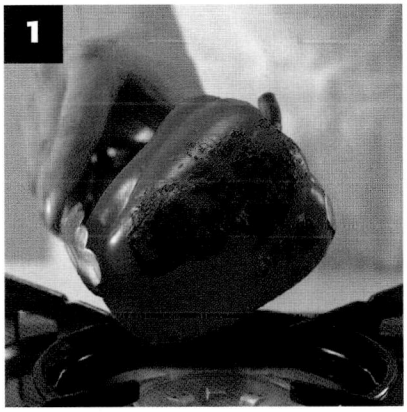

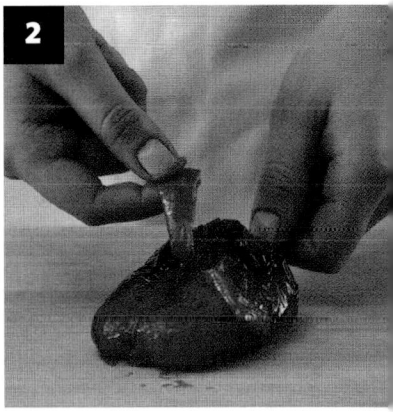

Chillies

Always wash your hands thoroughly with soap and water immediately after handling chillies.

1 Cut off the cap and slit open lengthways. Using a spoon, scrape out the seeds and the pith. (These are the hottest parts of the chilli.)

2 For diced chilli, cut into thin shreds lengthways, then cut crossways.

Avocados

Prepare avocados just before serving because their flesh discolours quickly once exposed to air.

1 Halve the avocado lengthways and twist the two halves apart. Tap the stone with a sharp knife, then twist to remove the stone.

2 Run a knife between the flesh and skin and pull away. Slice the flesh.

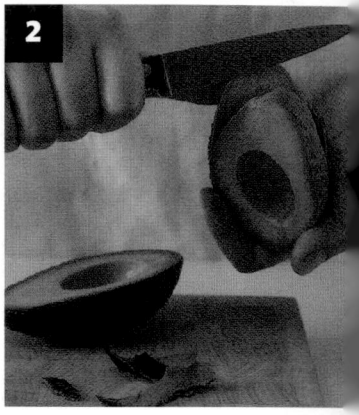

Cutting aubergines

1 Trim the aubergine to remove the stalk and end.

2 **Slicing** Cut the aubergine into slices as thick as the pieces you will need for your recipe.

3 **Cutting and dicing** Stack the slices and cut across them to the appropriate size for fingers. Cut in the opposite direction for dice.

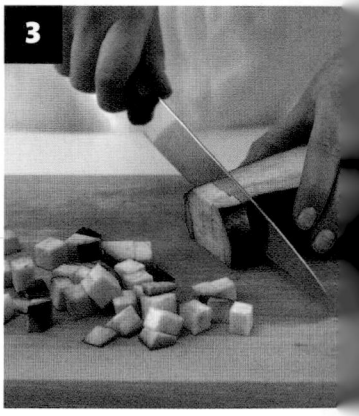

Stuffing aubergines

1 To hollow out an aubergine for stuffing, cut off the stem and halve the aubergine lengthways.

2 Make deep incisions in the flesh, using a crisscross pattern, being careful not to pierce the skin.

3 Using a spoon, scoop out the flesh, leaving the skin intact, and use according to your recipe.

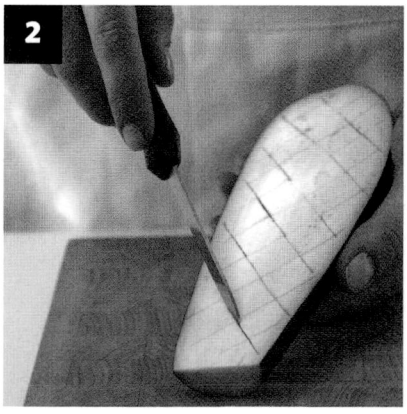

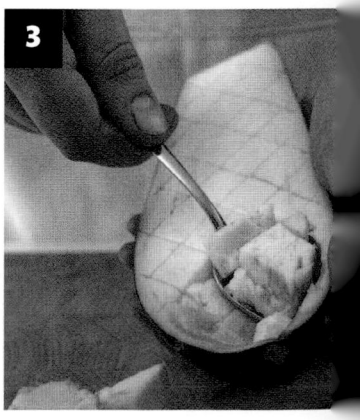

Courgettes

Cutting diagonally is an ideal, all-purpose shape if using courgettes in a stir-fry.

1 After washing under the cold tap, dry the courgette well and trim the base and the stem.

2 Trim off a piece at the base at a 45 degree angle, then repeat with the remaining courgette.

Stuffing

- To stuff courgettes whole, trim the base, then halve lengthways.
- To stuff courgettes in sections, trim the base and stem, then cut into 7.5cm (3in) sections. Stand on one end and use a melon baller to scoop out the flesh.

Peeling and cutting squash

1 For steaming, baking or roasting, keep the chunks fairly large – at least 2.5cm (1in) thick. Peel with a swivel-handled peeler or a chef's knife.

2 Halve the squash, then use a knife to cut through some of the fibrous mass connecting the seeds with the wall of the central cavity. Scoop out the seeds and fibres with a spoon, then cut the flesh into pieces.

Cooking squash in the skin

1 Wash the squash, then cut in half or quarters.

2 Use a knife to cut through some of the fibrous mass connecting the seeds with the wall of the central cavity, then use a spoon to scoop out the seeds and fibres.

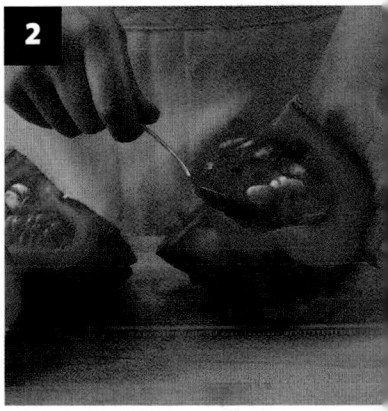

Preparing cabbage and broccoli

Cauliflower, cabbage and broccoli – the cruciferous vegetables – make crisp, healthy and tasty accompaniments to main courses as well as working well in stir-fries and other vegetable dishes.

Cabbage

The crinkly leaved Savoy cabbage may need more washing than other varieties, because its open leaves catch dirt more easily than the tightly packed white and red cabbage. The following method is suitable for all cabbages.

1 Pick off any of the outer leaves that are dry, tough or discoloured. Cut off the base and, using a small sharp knife, cut out as much as possible of the tough inner core in a single cone-shaped piece.

2 If you need whole cabbage leaves, peel them off one by one. As you work your way down, you will need to cut out more of the core.

3 If you are cooking the cabbage in wedges, cut it in half lengthways then cut the pieces into wedges of the required size.

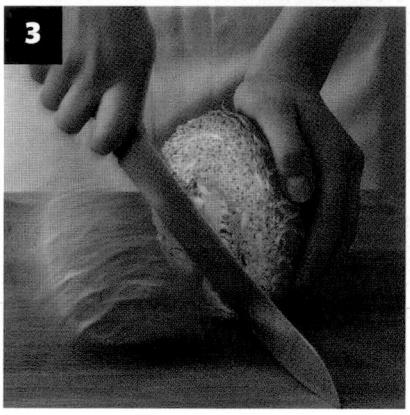

Shredding

If you want fine shreds, you can make them easily on the shredding disc of a food processor. To do it by hand, cut the cabbage into quarters before slicing with a large cook's knife.

Broccoli

1 Slice off the end of the stalk and cut 1cm (½in) below the florets.

2 Peel the thick, woody skin from the stalks and slice in half or quarters lengthways. Cut off equal-sized florets with a small knife. If the florets are very large, or if you want them for a stir-fry, you can halve them by cutting lengthways through the stalk and pulling the two halves apart.

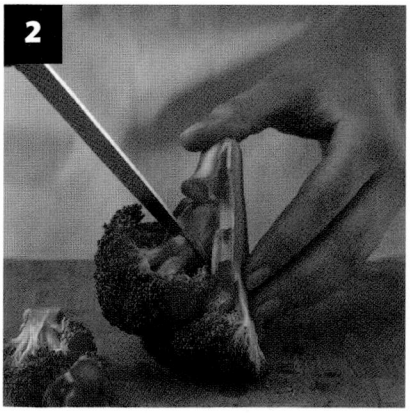

Cauliflower

First cut off the base and remove the outer leaves, then cut out the tough inner core in a cone-shaped piece. Cut off the florets in the same way as for broccoli. Don't cut away too much of the stalk or the florets will fall apart.

Preparing roots and tubers

All roots and tubers are prepared in roughly the same way. Some should always be peeled, whereas for others peeling is optional – it will depend mostly on how you plan to cook them.

Peeling roots and tubers

1 Using a swivel-headed peeler is the best method to peel most roots and tubers. However, celeriac has thick, irregular skin and is easier to peel using a knife.

2 Using a sharp knife, trim the ends off the vegetable.

3 Peel off the skin in long strips using a vegetable peeler.

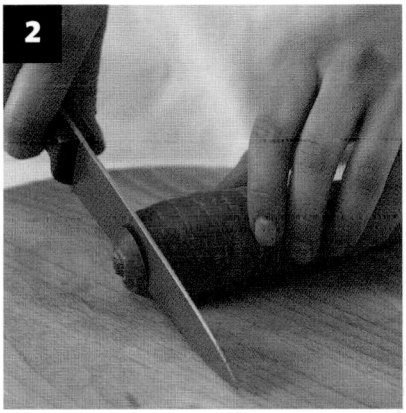

What to peel

Not all vegetables need to be peeled. Some vegetables become discoloured after peeling, and need to be placed in acidulated water (water and lemon juice) to slow the discolouration down.

- Beetroot are unpeeled when left whole, but peeled if sliced or shredded. They can be scrubbed if organic, otherwise peel.
- Celeriac needs to be peeled and then put into acidulated water.
- Potatoes can be peeled or scrubbed. If peeled, put them immediately into cold water.
- Salsify needs to be peeled and then put into acidulated water.
- Sweet potatoes can be peeled or scrubbed. If peeled, put them immediately into cold water.
- Turnips need to be peeled and then put into acidulated water.

Coring parsnips

Large parsnips have a tough woody core that takes longer to cook so it can be removed.

1 Trim both ends and use a sharp knife to halve the parsnip lengthways.

2 Run the knife along both sides of the core. Cut into the thick end of the parsnip, between core and walls, and gently work it up the core.

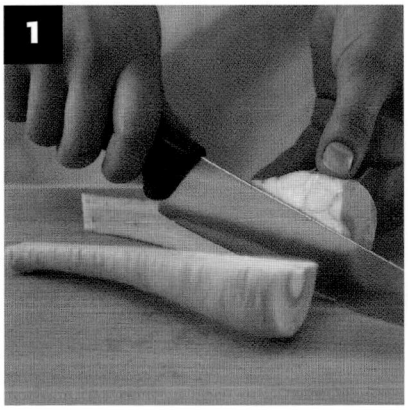

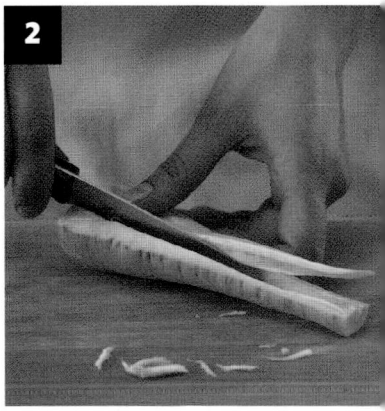

Slicing and dicing

Root vegetables often need to be cut into small pieces and a slice-and-stack approach works well.

1 First, peel and cut off the ends.

2 Cut slices off each of the rounded sides to make four flat surfaces that are stable on the chopping board.

3 Hold steady with one hand and cut lengthways into even slices so they are lying in a flat stack.

4 To dice the shreds, turn the stack at right angles and cut through in the opposite direction.

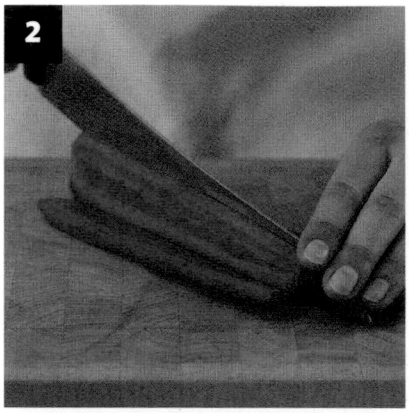

Preparing beetroot

When you are peeling or preparing raw beetroot, wear rubber gloves and work over a plate rather than a chopping board, as the beetroot colour will stain your hands and the board. Be careful of your clothing, too, as the juice can stain.

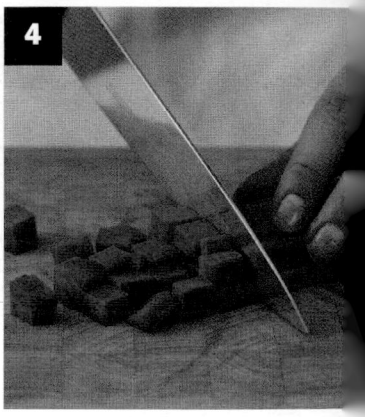

Slicing with a mandolin

1 Put the mandolin on a chopping board and set the blade to the required thickness. Push the pieces of vegetable across the blade with a swift, decisive motion, taking care to protect your fingers.

2 To make julienne (matchsticks), use either the fine or coarse julienne blade and swiftly push the pieces of vegetable across the blade.

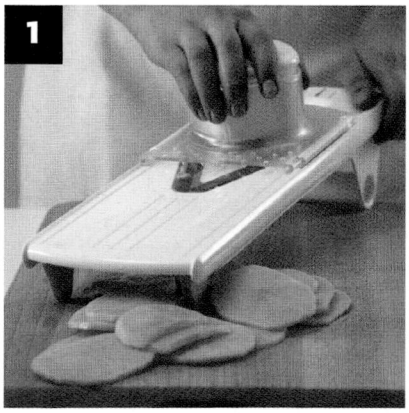

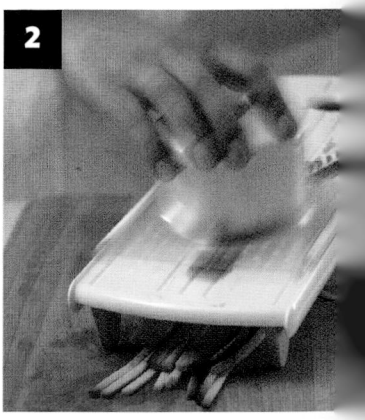

Cooking vegetables

Vegetables can be boiled, fried, sautéed, roasted, braised, stir-fried or steamed, providing endless variety. Some methods are more suited to certain vegetables than others, as explained below.

Boiling

This technique is suitable for most vegetables, but time them carefully as they can disintegrate or turn mushy if overcooked.

1 Prepare the vegetables and put them in plenty of salted cold water.

2 Cover, bring to boil, then reduce the heat and simmer until cooked. Drain in a colander.

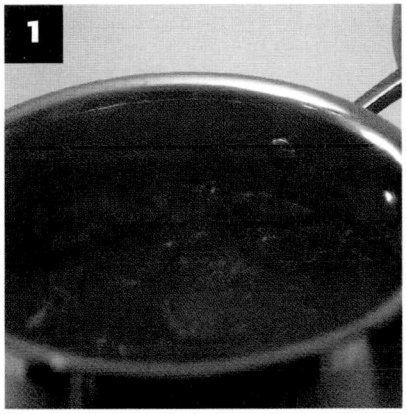

Boiling times

Note All timings are for peeled vegetables sliced about 2.5cm (1in) thick, except where noted.

Vegetable	Timing	Vegetable	Timing
Beetroot (whole)	1–2 hours	Potatoes	15–20 minutes
Carrots	10–20 minutes	Potatoes, new	10 minutes
Celeriac	20–25 minutes	Salsify	10–20 minutes
Corn on the cob	10–15 minutes	Sweet potatoes	10–15 minutes
Green beans	4–8 minutes	Turnips	15–20 minutes

Cook's tip

- Don't boil very thin pieces of root vegetable – they are more likely to absorb a lot of water and disintegrate.
- Small new potatoes are the only type that takes well to boiling whole. Larger ones can start to disintegrate before they are fully cooked.

Steaming

This is a healthy cooking method, cooking the vegetables until just tender while retaining their nutrients.

1 Put the vegetables in a steamer basket set over a pan of simmering water, being careful that the water does not touch the basket.

2 Cover and cook until the vegetables are just tender.

Steaming times

Note For soft results, add 2–3 minutes.

Vegetable	Timing
Leaf spinach	1–2 minutes
Peas, beans, carrots, cabbage, cauliflower and broccoli florets,	about 5 minutes
Root vegetables	5–10 minutes

Steaming tips

- Use an uncrowded steamer so that air can circulate.
- Cut root vegetables into chunks or dice.
- Toss the vegetables now and then during steaming.
- If steaming frozen vegetables, move them around occasionally.

Mashing potatoes

To serve four, you will need 900g (2lb) floury potatoes such as Maris Piper, 125ml (4fl oz) full-fat milk, 25g (1oz) butter.

1 Peel the potatoes and cut into even-sized chunks. Put in a pan of cold salted water to cover, then bring to the boil and simmer for 15–20 minutes until just tender. Test with a skewer or small knife. Drain well.

2 Return the potatoes to the pan and cover with a clean teatowel for 5 minutes. Alternatively, warm the potatoes over a very low heat until all the moisture has evaporated.

3 Pour the milk into a small pan and bring to the boil. Pour on to the potatoes with the butter and season.

4 Mash the potatoes until smooth, light and fluffy.

Crushing potatoes

To serve six, you will need 18 new potatoes, halved, 3 large garlic cloves, chopped, 225ml (8fl oz) olive oil, 8 tbsp chopped flat-leafed parsley, salt and black pepper.

1 Boil the potatoes until just soft. Drain. Heat the garlic in the oil until it starts to sizzle. Roughly mash the potatoes with a fork. Spoon over the oil. Season and add the herbs.

Perfect mash

- To mash vegetables you can use a mouli-légumes, a potato masher, or a ricer. The mouli and ricer give the smoothest results.
- Mashing and crushing are also suitable for parsnips, sweet potatoes and celeriac.

Sautéing

Sautéing browns vegetables lightly.

1 Cut into uniform pieces. Coat the base of a heavy-based pan with oil until medium-hot. Add the vegetables, toss quickly to coat with oil. Season.

2 Cover the pan and cook for 2–3 minutes until they start to soften. Remove the lid and stir every minute or so while the vegetables cook.

Sautéing times

Cooking times vary according to type of vegetable and thickness. Add 2–3 minutes more for softer results.

Vegetable	Timing
Carrots	5–8 minutes
Celery	4–5 minutes
Mushrooms	3–5 minutes
Onions	6–8 minutes
Spinach	2–4 minutes

Stir-frying

Stir-frying is perfect with non-starchy vegetables, as the quick cooking preserves their colour, freshness and texture. You will need 450g (1lb) vegetables, 1–2 tbsp vegetable oil, 2 garlic cloves, crushed, 2 tbsp soy sauce, 2 tsp sesame oil.

1 Cut the vegetables into even-sized pieces. Heat the oil in a large wok or frying pan until smoking-hot. Add the garlic and cook for a few seconds, then remove and set aside.

2 Add the vegetables to the wok, and toss and stir them. Keep them moving constantly as they cook, which will take 4–5 minutes.

3 When the vegetables are just tender, but still with a slight bite, turn off the heat. Put the garlic back into the wok and stir well. Add the soy sauce and sesame oil, toss and serve.

Perfect stir-frying

- Cut everything into small pieces of uniform size so that they cook quickly and evenly.
- If you're cooking onions or garlic with the vegetables, don't keep them in the high heat for too long or they will burn.
- Add liquids towards the end of cooking so they don't evaporate.

Deep-frying

Carrots, broccoli, onions, courgettes, aubergines, mushrooms and cauliflower are all good deep-fried.

1 Prepare the vegetables and cut into small pieces (no more than 2cm (¾in) thick). If washed, dry well.

2 Heat vegetable oil in a deep-fryer to 190°C (a small cube of bread should brown in 20 seconds).

3 Coat the vegetables with flour, then dip into batter (page 80).

4 Fry in batches, a few pieces at a time, until the batter is crisp and golden brown. Don't put too many vegetables in the pan at once (if you do, the temperature drops and the vegetables take longer to cook and become greasy). Drain on kitchen paper before serving.

Making potato chips

1 Heat vegetable oil in a deep-fryer to 160°C (a cube of bread should brown in 60 seconds). Cut potatoes into chips and dry on kitchen paper. Fry in batches for 6–7 minutes until soft. Drain on kitchen paper.

2 Turn up heat to 190°C (bread will brown in 20 seconds). Fry till golden brown. Drain well, sprinkle with salt and serve immediately.

Making vegetable crisps

1 Using a mandolin, slice the potatoes or root vegetables very thinly. Heat vegetable oil in a deep-fryer to 190°C (a small cube of bread should brown in 20 seconds).

2 Gently lower the sliced vegetables into the oil and stir or shake the frying basket to separate them. Fry until golden, then lift out and drain on kitchen paper.

Frying potatoes

- Potatoes never need to be coated in batter.
- Use floury potatoes – Maris Piper is the best variety.
- Dry the sliced potatoes thoroughly before frying. Water on the surface can cause the fat to splatter.

Braising

1 Prepare the vegetables (see box right). Pack tightly in an ovenproof dish. Preheat the oven to 180°C (160°C fan oven) mark 4. Dot generously with butter and season with salt.

2 Pour in stock to come halfway up the vegetables. Cover and bake for 30–40 minutes until the vegetables are soft. Baste them with the buttery stock a few times during cooking.

Perfect braises

- Carrots, fennel, leeks, celeriac, celery and cabbage are good braised.
- Leave vegetables whole or cut into chunks. Shred cabbage, then lightly fry before braising.
- Cook the vegetables in a single layer.

Stewing

1 Cut the vegetables into large bite-sized pieces, no more than about 5cm (2in) square. Put them into a heatproof casserole (for oven cooking) or a heavy-based pan (for hob cooking). Add salt and pepper and flavourings if you like (see box below), and mix well.

2 Preheat the oven to 180°C (160°C fan oven) mark 4 if you are cooking in the oven.

3 Pour in stock to come about three-quarters of the way up the vegetables. Cover the dish with a lid or foil and cook for 30–40 minutes until the vegetables are tender but not disintegrating.

4 Turn the vegetables once during cooking, and baste with the juices a few times.

Perfect stews

- Any vegetable can be stewed; be careful not to overcook it.
- Ideal flavourings for stewed vegetables include garlic, shallots, curry powder (or Indian spices), and chilli sauce or chopped chilli.
- Potatoes will thicken the dish a little as they release some of their starch.

Griddling and grilling

A few vegetables are perfect for cooking on a griddle or under the grill. Those that work well in both methods are courgettes and aubergines. Peppers (whole or halved) can be grilled and so can fennel, onions and sweet potatoes with careful slicing. Brush all vegetables with oil and use a medium-high heat.

To serve four, you will need 450g (1lb) courgettes, cut lengthways into 5mm (¼in) slices, or quartered if small, about 6 tbsp extra-virgin olive oil, ½ lemon, a small handful of fresh dill, finely chopped.

1 Preheat the griddle over a medium to high heat. Brush the courgettes with oil.

2 Cook the courgettes without disturbing them until they have deep brown seared lines underneath, about 2–3 minutes.

3 Turn them and griddle until seared underneath and tender, but still with a hint of bite.

4 Remove to a serving plate and squeeze over lemon juice to taste. Scatter with dill, and serve.

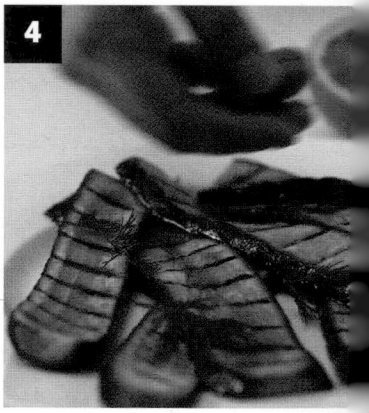

Perfect griddling

- Vegetables have a lovely flavour when cooked on the griddle as well as attractive browned lines if you use a ridged griddle.
- The choice of vegetable is crucial in griddling: you have to use something that has a fairly even surface so that it will lie flat on the griddle and won't break up when it's turned. Top choices include sliced courgettes, aubergines, fennel and onion, whole small onions, large field mushrooms and asparagus.
- Don't slice the vegetables too thickly or they will burn before they get fully cooked – 1cm (½in) should be the maximum thickness.
- Lay the vegetables on a work board and brush them with oil so that it coats them thoroughly.Turn once when they have browned underneath

Roasting potatoes

To serve eight to ten, you will need 1.8kg (4lb) potatoes, peeled and cut into large chunks, 3 tbsp vegetable oil, 75g (3oz) unsalted butter, 6 rosemary sprigs, 6 garlic cloves, salt and ground black pepper.

1 Preheat the oven to 200°C (180°C fan oven) mark 6. Put the potatoes in a pan of salted water, cover, bring to the boil, and simmer for 5–6 minutes until they start to soften. Drain and return to the pan over a low heat. Shake until the potatoes are dry and a little fluffy.

2 Heat the oil and butter in a roasting tin. Put the potatoes in the tin with the rosemary and garlic. Toss to cover evenly in oil and butter, and season. Cook for 1 hour, turning from time to time until the potatoes are brown and crisp. Adjust the seasoning and serve.

Roasting other vegetables

Many vegetables are excellent when roasted, as long as they contain enough starch to brown well. Brush them with extra-virgin olive oil and season. Timings are for a 200°C (180°C fan oven) mark 6 oven.

Aubergines (halved)	30–40 minutes
Beef tomatoes (halved)	10–20 minutes
Courgettes (halved)	20–30 minutes
Green or yellow peppers (halved)	30–40 minutes
Mushrooms (large)	20–30 minutes
Onions (quartered, halved or small)	20 minutes

Roasting butternut squash

To serve four, you will need 2 squash, quartered and seeded, 2 tbsp olive oil, 2 tbsp thyme, 1 red chilli, seeded and chopped, 25g (1oz) butter.

1 Preheat the oven to 220°C (200°C fan oven) mark 7. Drizzle the squash with oil. Roast for 40 minutes.

2 Combine the thyme, chilli and butter and dot over the squash.

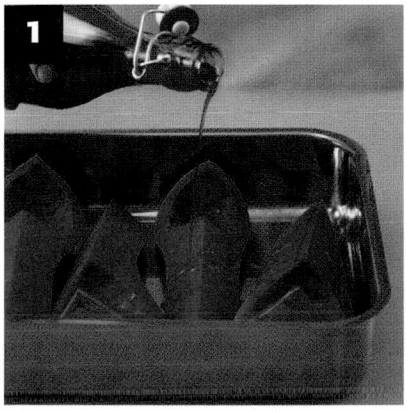

Winter Coleslaw

SERVES 6

4 oranges
400g can chickpeas, drained and rinsed
450g (1lb) carrots, coarsely grated
½ red cabbage, about 550g (1¼lb), finely shredded
75g (3oz) sultanas
6 tbsp freshly chopped coriander
4 tbsp extra-virgin olive oil
3 tbsp red wine vinegar
salt and ground black pepper

PREPARATION TIME 15 minutes

PER SERVING

265 calories
10g fat (of which 1g saturates)
38g carbohydrate
0.4g salt

TECHNIQUES

see also preparing vegetables (pages 170–182), chopping herbs (page 428), making salad dressings (page 25)

1 Using a sharp knife, cut a thin slice of peel and pith from each end of the oranges. Place, cut side down, on a plate and cut off the peel and pith in strips. Remove any remaining pith. Cut out each segment leaving the membrane behind. Squeeze the remaining juice from the membrane into a bowl.

2 Put the orange segments and juice in a serving bowl with the chickpeas, carrots, cabbage, sultanas and coriander.

3 Add the oil and vinegar, and season well with salt and pepper. Toss everything together to coat thoroughly. Store the coleslaw in a sealable container in the refrigerator for up to two days.

Mixed Leaf Salad

SERVES 8

3 round lettuce hearts, roughly shredded
100g (3½oz) watercress
2 ripe avocados, roughly chopped
1 box salad cress, chopped
100g (3½oz) sugarsnap peas, roughly sliced
4 tbsp vinaigrette dressing

PREPARATION TIME 15 minutes

PER SERVING

144 calories
12g fat (of which 2g saturates)
4g carbohydrate
0.2g salt

TECHNIQUES

see also preparing vegetables (pages 170–189)

1 Put the lettuce hearts into a bowl and add the watercress, avocados, salad cress and sugarsnap peas.

2 Toss in the vinaigrette dressing and serve immediately.

Variations

Try any of the dressings on page 25 instead of a simple vinaigrette. Balsamic dressing, herb dressing, garlic dressing and blue cheese dressing would all make good alternatives.

Summer Vegetable Salad

SERVES 10

900g (2lb) mixed green vegetables, such as French beans, peas, sugarsnap peas, asparagus and broccoli
¼ cucumber, halved, deseeded and sliced
1 tbsp freshly chopped flat-leafed parsley
salt

For the dressing

1 tbsp white wine or sherry vinegar
1 tsp English mustard powder
3 tbsp extra-virgin olive oil

PREPARATION TIME 10 minutes
COOKING TIME about 10 minutes

PER SERVING

54 calories
4g fat (of which 1g saturates)
3g carbohydrate
0g salt

TECHNIQUES

see also preparing vegetables (pages 170–182), chopping herbs (page 428), making salad dressings (page 25)

1 Cook the beans in a large pan of boiling salted water for 5 minutes, then add all the other vegetables. Bring the water back to the boil and cook for a further 3–4 minutes. Drain well and put immediately into a bowl of ice-cold water.

2 Whisk the dressing ingredients together.

3 To serve, drain the vegetables, then toss in the dressing with the cucumber and parsley.

Get ahead

Make the recipe to the end of step 2 up to one day ahead. Chill the dressing and keep the cooked vegetables, covered in cold water, until needed.
To use Complete the recipe.

Roasted Root Vegetable Salad

SERVES 4

1 butternut squash, halved, deseeded and cubed
1½ large carrots, cut into chunks
3 fresh thyme sprigs
1½ tbsp olive oil
2 red onions, cut into wedges
1 tbsp balsamic vinegar
410g can chickpeas, drained and rinsed
25g (1oz) pinenuts, toasted
100g (3½oz) wild rocket
salt and ground black pepper

PREPARATION TIME 20 minutes
COOKING TIME 40 minutes

PER SERVING
290 calories
14g fat (of which 2g saturates)
33g carbohydrate
0.7g salt

TECHNIQUES
see also preparing vegetables (pages 170–182), toasting nuts (page 218)

1 Preheat the oven to 190°C (170°C fan oven) mark 5. Put the squash and carrots into a large deep roasting tin. Scatter over the thyme and drizzle with 1 tbsp oil. Season with salt and pepper and roast for 20 minutes.

2 Take the tin out of the oven, give it a good shake to make sure the vegetables aren't sticking, then add the onions. Drizzle the remaining oil over and toss to coat. Continue to roast for 20 minutes or until all the vegetables are tender.

3 Remove the roasted veg from the oven and discard any twiggy bits of thyme. Drizzle the vinegar over, stir in and set aside to cool.

4 To serve, put the chickpeas into a large serving bowl. Add the cooled vegetables, the pinenuts and rocket (putting some to one side for a garnish). Toss everything together and garnish with a little rocket.

Get ahead

Make to the end of step 3 up to two days ahead. Put in a container. Cool, cover and chill.
To use Complete the recipe.

Asparagus with Lemon Dressing

SERVES 5
finely grated zest of ½ lemon
2 tbsp lemon juice
3 tbsp extra-virgin olive oil
pinch of golden caster sugar
250g (9oz) fine-stemmed asparagus, ends trimmed
salt and ground black pepper

PREPARATION TIME 15 minutes
COOKING TIME 5 minutes

PER SERVING
73 calories
7g fat (of which 1g saturates)
1g carbohydrate
0g salt

TECHNIQUES
see also zesting citrus fruits (page 207), making salad dressings (page 25), preparing asparagus (page 172)

1 Put the lemon zest into a screwtopped jar, add the lemon juice, oil and sugar, then shake to mix.

2 Half-fill a frying pan with boiling salted water. Add the asparagus, then cover and simmer for 5 minutes or until just tender.

3 Remove the asparagus with a large draining spoon. If serving the asparagus cold, plunge it into a large bowl of iced water (this will help to keep its bright green colour), then drain.

4 To serve, arrange the asparagus in a concentric pattern in a large shallow bowl, with tips outwards and ends overlapping in the centre. Season with salt and pepper and drizzle with the dressing.

Mediterranean Kebabs

SERVES 4

1 large courgette, cut into chunks
1 red pepper, deseeded and cut into chunks
12 cherry tomatoes
125g (4oz) halloumi cheese, cubed
100g (3½oz) natural yogurt
1 tsp ground cumin
2 tbsp olive oil
squeeze of lemon
1 lemon, cut into eight wedges
couscous tossed with freshly chopped flat-leafed parsley to serve

PREPARATION TIME 15 minutes
COOKING TIME 10 minutes

PER SERVING

177 calories
13g fat (of which 5g saturates)
8g carbohydrate
1.2g salt

TECHNIQUES

see also preparing courgettes (page 179), preparing peppers (page 177), preparing couscous (page 241) chopping herbs (page 428)

1 Preheat the grill. Put the courgette into a large bowl with the red pepper, cherry tomatoes and halloumi cheese. Add the yogurt, cumin, oil and a squeeze of lemon. Mix together.

2 Take eight skewers and push a lemon wedge on to each one, then divide the vegetables and cheese among the skewers. Grill the kebabs, turning regularly, for 8–10 minutes until the vegetables are tender and the halloumi is nicely charred. Serve with couscous.

Cook's tip

If using wooden skewers, soak them in water for at least 30 minutes before using to prevent them burning during grilling.

Lemon and Orange Carrots

SERVES 8
900g (2lb) carrots, cut into long batons
150ml (¼ pint) orange juice
juice of 2 lemons
150ml (¼ pint) dry white wine
50g (2oz) butter
3 tbsp light muscovado sugar
4 tbsp freshly chopped coriander to garnish

PREPARATION TIME 5 minutes
COOKING TIME 10–15 minutes

PER SERVING
127 calories
6g fat (of which 3g saturates)
17g carbohydrate
0.2g salt

TECHNIQUES
see also preparing root vegetables (page 181), chopping herbs (page 428)

1 Put the carrots, orange and lemon juices, wine, butter and sugar in a pan. Cover and bring to the boil.

2 Remove the lid and cook until almost all the liquid has evaporated – this should take about 10 minutes. Serve sprinkled with the coriander.

Freezing tip

Cook the carrots for only 5 minutes and cool. Freeze with the remaining liquid.
To use Thaw for 5 hours and reheat in a pan for 5–6 minutes or microwave on High 900W for 7–8 minutes.

Sprouts and Pancetta

SERVES 8

900g (2lb) Brussels sprouts, halved, with bases trimmed
1 tbsp olive oil
130g pack cubetti di pancetta
2 shallots, chopped
250g (9oz) chestnuts
15g (½oz) butter
pinch of freshly grated nutmeg
salt

PREPARATION TIME 15 minutes
COOKING TIME 15 minutes

PER SERVING
174 calories
9g fat (of which 3g saturates)
17g carbohydrate
0.6g salt

TECHNIQUES
see also preparing shallots (page 170), preparing chestnuts (page 220)

1 Bring a pan of salted water to the boil and blanch the Brussels sprouts for 2 minutes. Drain and refresh with a little cold water.

2 Heat the oil in a wok and fry the pancetta until golden. Add the shallots and stir-fry for about 5 minutes. Return the Brussels sprouts to the pan with the chestnuts and stir-fry for another 5 minutes to heat through.

3 Add the butter and nutmeg, and toss well. Serve immediately.

Freezing tip

Fry the pancetta and shallots and leave to cool, then add the chestnuts and freeze.
To use Thaw for 1 hour. Blanch the sprouts as in the recipe, then cool in iced water. Stir-fry the chestnut mixture for 1 minute and follow the recipe.

Spinach with Tomatoes

SERVES 6
2 garlic cloves, crushed
25g (1oz) butter
450g (1lb) baby plum tomatoes, halved
250g (9oz) baby spinach leaves
25g (1oz) butter
a large pinch of freshly grated nutmeg
salt and ground black pepper

PREPARATION TIME 10 minutes
COOKING TIME 15 minutes

PER SERVING
85 calories
7g fat (of which 5g saturates)
3g carbohydrate
0.3g salt

TECHNIQUES
see also preparing vegetables (pages 170–182)

1 Cook the garlic in the butter until just soft, then add the tomatoes and cook for 4–5 minutes.

2 Put the spinach and a little water into a clean pan, cover and cook for 2–3 minutes. Drain well, chop roughly and stir into the tomatoes.

3 Add the butter and gently heat through. Season well with salt and pepper, stir in the nutmeg and serve.

Mixed Vegetable Tempura

SERVES 6

1.8 litres (3¼ pints) vegetable oil
150g pack Tempura Mix
330ml bottle of Japanese lager (or a substitute lager)
40g (1½oz) sesame seeds
1 tsp salt
150g (5oz) sweet potato, cut into fine matchsticks
1 onion, cut into wedges
150g (5oz) baby leeks, washed and cut into 5cm (2in) pieces
1 red pepper, deseeded and cut into 12 wedges
200g (7oz) fine green beans, trimmed
Thai sweet chilli dipping sauce

PREPARATION TIME 20 minutes
COOKING TIME 20 minutes

PER SERVING

282 calories
16g fat (of which 2g saturates)
27g carbohydrate
0.9g salt

TECHNIQUES

see also making tempura batter (page 80), preparing vegetables (pages 170–182), deep-frying vegetables (page 186)

1 Heat the oil in a deep-fat fryer on the chip setting, or until 190°C. Preheat the oven to 110°C (90°C fan oven) mark ¼. Put the pack of tempura mix into a bowl and gradually whisk in the lager to make a smooth batter. Add the sesame seeds and salt.

2 Drop six pieces of vegetable into the tempura batter to coat, then, using a draining spoon, put into the hot oil. Cook for 3 minutes or until golden and puffy. Drain on kitchen paper, then keep warm in the oven. Repeat with the remaining vegetables. Serve with a bowl of chilli dipping sauce.

Variations

Other good vegetables for using for tempura include broccoli and cauliflower florets, yellow peppers, cut into wedges, and carrots and butternut squash, cut into fine matchsticks.

Thai Vegetable Curry

SERVES 4

2–3 tbsp Thai red curry paste
2.5cm (1in) piece fresh root ginger, peeled and finely chopped
50g (2oz) cashew nuts
400ml can coconut milk
3 carrots, cut into thin batons
1 broccoli head, cut into florets
20g (¾oz) fresh coriander, roughly chopped
zest and juice of 1 lime
2 large handfuls of washed spinach leaves
basmati rice to serve

PREPARATION TIME 15 minutes
COOKING TIME 15 minutes

PER SERVING

203 calories
12g fat (of which 2g saturates)
16g carbohydrate
0.6g salt

TECHNIQUES

see also preparing fresh spices (page 429), making coconut milk (page 221), preparing vegetables (pages 170–182), chopping herbs (page 428), cooking rice (page 236)

1 Put the curry paste into a large pan. Add the ginger to the pan with the cashew nuts. Stir over a medium heat for 2–3 minutes.

2 Add the coconut milk, cover and bring to the boil. Stir the carrots into the pan and simmer for 5 minutes, then add the broccoli florets and simmer for a further 5 minutes or until the vegetables are tender.

3 Stir the coriander and lime zest into the pan with the spinach. Squeeze the lime juice over and serve with basmati rice.

Chilli Onions with Goat's Cheese

SERVES 6

75g (3oz) unsalted butter, softened
2 medium red chillies, deseeded and finely diced
1 tsp crushed chillies
6 small red onions, peeled
3 × 100g goat's cheese logs, with rind
salt and ground black pepper
balsamic vinegar to serve

PREPARATION TIME 15 minutes
COOKING TIME 45 minutes

PER SERVING
276 calories
23g fat (of which 16g saturates)
5g carbohydrate
0.9g salt

TECHNIQUES
see also preparing chillies (page 177)

1 Preheat the oven to 200°C (180°C fan oven) mark 6. Put the butter into a small bowl. Beat in the diced and crushed chillies, and season well with salt and pepper. Cut off the root of one of the onions, sit it on its base, then make several deep cuts in the top to create a star shape, slicing about two-thirds of the way down the onion. Do the same with the other five onions, then divide the chilli butter equally among them, pushing it down into the cuts.

2 Put the onions into a small roasting tin, cover with foil and bake for 40–45 minutes until soft. About 5 minutes before they are ready, slice each goat's cheese into two, leaving the rind intact, then put on a baking sheet and bake for 2–3 minutes. Put the onion on top of the goat's cheese and serve drizzled with balsamic vinegar.

Mushroom and Aubergine Tian

SERVES 2

100g (3½oz) butter
1 bunch spring onions, sliced
450g (1lb) fennel, roughly chopped
4 tbsp freshly chopped tarragon
50g (2oz) pinenuts, toasted
150g (5oz) goat's cheese
200g (7oz) fresh breadcrumbs
zest of 1 lemon, juice of 1½ lemons
2 medium eggs, beaten
25g (1oz) dark muscovado sugar
2 onions, finely chopped
3 tbsp balsamic vinegar
1 celery stick, chopped
4 tbsp freshly chopped oregano
75g pack dried cranberries
125g (4oz) vacuum-packed chestnuts, chopped
350g (12oz) small chestnut mushrooms
1 small aubergine, about 250g (9oz), thinly sliced
1 courgette, about 140g (4½oz), thinly sliced
½ red onion, cut into thin wedges, root intact
3 tbsp olive oil
2 portabella or large flat mushrooms
100ml (3½fl oz) port
150ml (¼ pint) vegetable stock
4 tbsp redcurrant jelly
2 strips orange peel, finely sliced
salt and ground black pepper
fresh oregano sprigs to garnish

PREPARATION TIME 30 minutes
COOKING TIME 50 minutes

PER SERVING
898 calories
43g fat (of which 16g saturates)
102g carbohydrate
1g salt

TECHNIQUES
see also toasting nuts (page 218), making breadcrumbs (page 308)

1 Heat 75g (3oz) butter in a pan. Cook the spring onions for 3 minutes. Add the fennel, cook for 5 minutes and cool. Add the tarragon, pinenuts, cheese, 140g (4½oz) breadcrumbs, zest and juice of 1 lemon and the eggs. Season with salt and pepper and mix well. Reserve 8 tbsp, then freeze the rest. Melt the remaining butter and the sugar in a pan. Cook the onions until soft. Add the vinegar and celery, bring to the boil and cook for 1 minute. Cool. Add the oregano, cranberries, remaining breadcrumbs, chestnuts and chestnut mushrooms. Season and mix well. Reserve 8 tbsp, then freeze the rest. Brush the aubergine, courgette and red onion with 2 tbsp oil. Heat a non-stick frying pan and fry them in batches.

2 Preheat the oven to 200°C (180°C fan oven) mark 6. Lay half the aubergine slices overlapping on top of each mushroom. Divide the fennel stuffing between the mushrooms and season. Top with mushroom and chestnut stuffing, and season. Arrange courgette slices over the stuffing, overlapping them, then top with onion wedges. Wrap a thick foil band around each mushroom to keep the stuffing in place. Put in an ovenproof dish, drizzle the remaining oil over and bake for 40 minutes.

3 Put the port, stock, redcurrant jelly, peel and remaining lemon juice in a pan. Bring to the boil. Simmer until syrupy. Remove the foil from the mushrooms, garnish with oregano and drizzle with the sauce.

Roasted Stuffed Peppers

SERVES 4

4 Romano peppers
40g (1½oz) butter
350g (12oz) chestnut mushrooms, roughly chopped
3 tbsp olive oil
4 tbsp finely chopped chives
100g (3½oz) feta cheese
50g (2oz) fresh white breadcrumbs
25g (1oz) freshly grated Parmesan
salt and ground black pepper

PREPARATION TIME 20 minutes
COOKING TIME 50 minutes

PER SERVING
375 calories
25g fat (of which 11g saturates)
27g carbohydrate
1.5g salt

TECHNIQUES
see also preparing vegetables (pages 170–182), chopping herbs (page 428), making breadcrumbs (page 308)

1 Preheat the oven to 180°C (160°C fan oven) mark 4. Halve the peppers, keeping the stalks on, and carefully cut out the seeds. Use a little of the butter to grease a shallow ovenproof dish and put in the peppers side by side, ready to be filled.

2 Fry the mushrooms in the remaining butter and 1 tbsp oil until they are golden and there's no excess liquid left in the pan. Stir in the chives, then spoon the mixture into the pepper halves.

3 Crumble the feta cheese over the mushrooms. Mix the breadcrumbs and Parmesan in a bowl, then sprinkle over the top.

4 Season with salt and pepper and drizzle with the remaining oil, then roast for 45 minutes or until golden and tender. Serve warm.

Freezing tip

Prepare up to the end of step 3 and freeze in a freezerproof container for up to one week.

Thaw the peppers overnight in the refrigerator and complete the recipe.

FRUIT AND NUTS

Fresh, sweet, juicy fruit can be prepared and cooked in many different ways. The step-by-step techniques guide opens by showing you how to peel, core, slice, pit, seed and hull all the different fruits and then demonstrates the basic cooking techniques from poaching, stewing and pan-frying to deep-frying, baking and grilling – along with essential advice on making smoothies and purées. This is followed by an essential guide to preparing nuts, including special advice on preparing chestnuts and coconut. The recipe section puts these techniques to work in dishes such as Fruit kebabs with spiced pear dip, Strawberry compote, Barbecued figs with Marsala and American-style plum cobbler.

Preparing orchard fruits

When they are used for cooking, all these fruits are usually peeled and cored. Quince is very hard and is always cooked, never eaten raw – unlike its relatives, the apple and pear.

Apples and quinces

1 To core an apple, push an apple corer straight through the apple from the stem to base. Remove the core and use a small sharp knife to pick out any stray seeds or seed casings. To core a quince, halve the quince and then cut out the core.

2 To peel, hold the fruit in one hand and run a swivel peeler under the skin, starting from the stem end and moving around the fruit, taking off the skin until you reach the base. (Quinces for making jelly do not need to be peeled.)

3 To slice, halve the cored apple. For flat slices, hold the apple cut side down and slice with the knife blade at right angles to the hollow left by the core. For crescent-shaped slices, stand the fruit on its end and cut slices into the hollow as if you were slicing a pie.

Preserving colour

Apples and quinces are easy to work with because they are very firm-fleshed, but their flesh starts to discolour quickly and turn brown when exposed to air. Toss with lemon juice if you are not going to use the prepared fruit immediately.

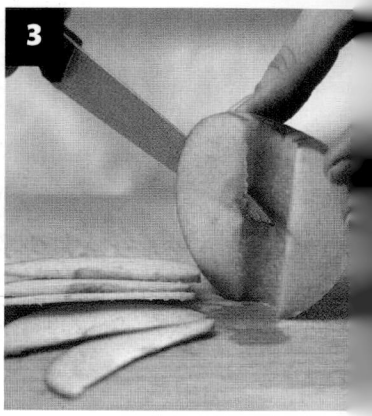

Pears

1 To core, use a teaspoon to scoop out the seeds and core through the base of the pear. Trim away any remaining fragments with a small knife. If you halve or quarter the pear, remove any remaining seeds.

2 To peel, cut off the stem. Peel off the skin in even strips from tip to base. If not using immediately, toss the pears in lemon juice.

3 To slice, halve the cored, peeled pear lengthways. Check for any remaining fragments of core, then slice with the pear halves lying cut side down on the board.

4 To make pear fans, slice at closely spaced intervals from the base to about 2.5cm (1in) from the tip, making sure you don't cut all the way through.

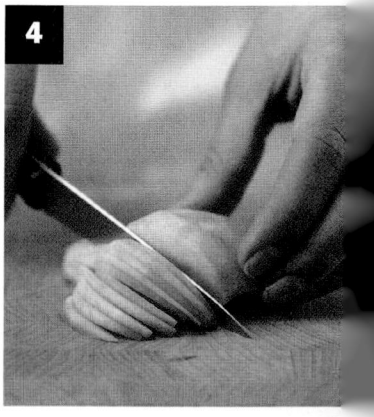

Preparing citrus fruits

Citrus zest is an important flavouring and is simple to prepare. The segments or slices of citrus are also used in recipes and need to be prepared so that no skin, pith or membrane remains.

Zesting

1 Wash and thoroughly dry the fruit. Using a vegetable peeler, cut away the zest (the coloured outer layer of skin) taking care to leave behind the bitter white pith. Continue until you have removed as much as you need.

2 Stack the slices of zest on a board and shred or dice as required using a sharp knife.

Easy zesting

- To use a zester, press the blade into the citrus skin and run it along the surface to take off long shreds.
- To use a grater, rub the fruit over the grater, using a medium pressure to remove the zest without removing the white pith.

Segmenting

1 Cut off a slice at both ends of the fruit, then cut off the peel, just inside the white pith.

2 Hold fruit over a bowl to catch the juice and cut between the segments just inside the membrane to release the flesh. Continue until all the segments are removed. Squeeze the juice from the membrane into the bowl and use as required.

Slicing

1 Cut off a slice at both ends of the fruit, then cut off the peel, just inside the white pith as described above.

2 Gently hold the fruit on its side on the chopping board and use a serrated knife to cut slices no less than 5mm (¼in) thick.

Sprayed fruit

Most citrus fruit is sprayed with wax and fungicides or pesticides. When using the zest, wash the lemon with a tiny drop of washing-up liquid and warm water, then rinse with clean water.

Preparing stone fruits

The most difficult aspect of dealing with stone fruits is that really ripe fruits can be very soft. Handle them with care whenever you are lucky enough to find fully ripe fruits.

Pitting cherries

1 To eat raw, cherries need only to be stemmed and washed. If your recipe requires you to remove the stones, a cherry stoner will do this neatly, but it is important to take care to position the fruit correctly on the cherry stoner.

2 First, remove the stems from the cherries, and then wash the fruits and pat dry on kitchen paper.

3 Put each cherry on the stoner with the stem end facing up. Close the stoner and gently press the handles together so that the metal rod pushes through the fruit, pressing out the stone.

4 Alternatively, if you do not have a cherry stoner, cut the cherries in half and remove the stones with the tip of a small, pointed knife.

Stoning larger fruits

Peaches, nectarines, plums, greengages and apricots can all be handled in the same way.

1 Following the cleft along one side of the fruit, cut through to the stone all around the fruit.

2 Twist gently to separate the halves. Ease out the stone with a small knife. Rub the flesh with lemon juice.

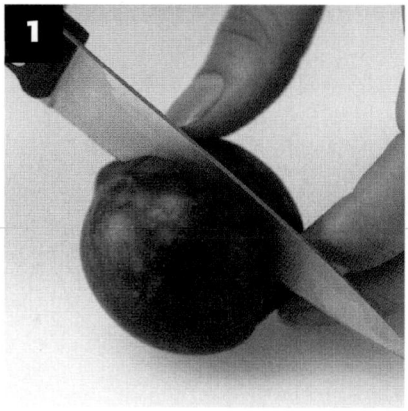

Peeling peaches

1 Peaches may be peeled for use in desserts. Put in a bowl of boiling water for 15 seconds–1 minute (depending on ripeness). Don't leave in the water for too long, as heat will soften the flesh. Put in cold water.

2 Work a knife between the skin and flesh to loosen the skin, then gently pull to remove. Rub the flesh with lemon juice.

Preparing berries and currants

Soft fruits – strawberries, blackberries, raspberries and currants – are generally quick to prepare. Always handle ripe fruits gently as they can be delicate.

Washing berries

Most soft fruits can be washed very gently in cold water. Shop-bought blackberries will usually have the hull removed. If you have picked blackberries yourself the hulls and stalks may still be attached, so pick over the berries carefully and remove any that remain. Raspberries are very delicate so handle very carefully; remove any stalks and hulls. Leave strawberries whole.

1 Place the berries in a bowl of cold water and allow any small pieces of grit, dust or insects to float out.

2 Transfer the fruit to a colander and rinse gently under fresh running water. Drain well, then leave to drain on kitchen paper.

Hulling strawberries

1 Wash the strawberries gently and dry on kitchen paper. Remove the hull (the centre part that was attached to the plant) from the strawberry using a strawberry huller or a small sharp knife.

2 Put the knife into the small, hard area beneath the green stalk and gently rotate to remove a small, cone-shaped piece.

Stripping currants

Blackcurrants, redcurrants and whitecurrants can all be stripped quickly and simply from the stem in the same way.

1 Using a fork, strip all the currants off the stalks by running the fork down the length of the stalk.

2 Put the currants into a colander and wash them gently.

Preparing exotic fruits

Sweet, fragrant exotic fruits are wonderful eaten raw but are also delicious in numerous desserts. Each fruit is unique and requires its own individual preparation technique.

Pineapples

1 Cut off the base and crown of the pineapple, and stand the fruit on a chopping board.

2 Using a medium-sized knife, peel away a section of skin going just deep enough to remove all or most of the hard, inedible 'eyes' on the skin. Repeat all the way around.

3 Use a small knife to cut out any remaining traces of the eyes.

4 You can buy special tools for coring pineapples but a 7.5cm (3in) biscuit cutter or an apple corer works just as well. Cut the peeled pineapple into slices.

5 Place the biscuit cutter directly over the core and press down firmly to remove the core. If using an apple corer, cut out in pieces, as it will be too wide to remove in one piece.

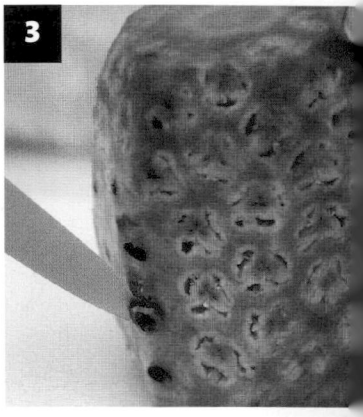

Mangoes

1 Cut a slice to one side of the stone in centre. Repeat on the other side.

2 Cut parallel lines into the flesh of one slice, almost to the skin. Cut another set of lines to cut the flesh into squares.

3 Press on the skin side to turn the fruit inside out, so that the flesh is thrust outwards. Cut off the chunks as close as possible to the skin. Repeat with the other half.

Papaya

1 Using a sharp knife, halve the fruit lengthways and use a teaspoon to scoop out the shiny black seeds and fibres inside the cavity.

2 If using in a salad, peel the fruit using a swivel-headed vegetable peeler, then gently cut in half using a sharp knife. Remove the seeds using a teaspoon and slice the flesh, or cut into cubes.

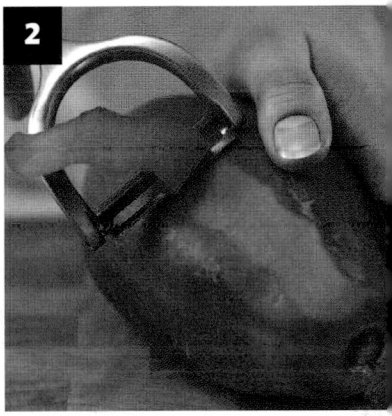

Passion fruit

1 The seeds are edible but if you want the fruit for a purée, you will need to sieve them. Halve the passion fruit and scoop the seeds and pulp into a food processor or blender. Process for 30 seconds, until the mixture looks soupy.

2 Pour into a sieve over a bowl, and press down hard on pulp with the back of a spoon to release the juice.

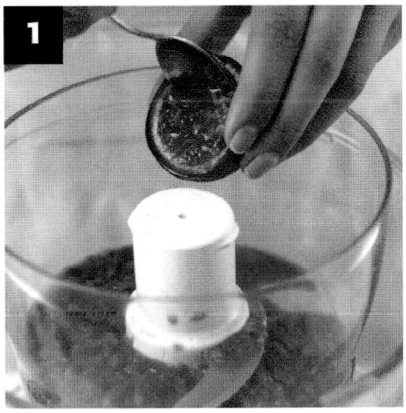

Pomegranate

1 Cut off base of fruit, trying not to cut into cells containing seeds, and make four shallow cuts into the skin with a small sharp knife. Break the pomegranate in half, then quarters.

2 Bend the skin of each quarter backwards to push the seeds out into a bowl. Remove any left behind with a teaspoon. Remove any of the bitter pith that remains on the seeds.

Cook's tip

To extract the juice, roll the pomegranate on a board, then halve over a bowl and let the juice drip out. Put the pulp in a sieve and press the seeds lightly to extract the juice. Do not press hard or the juice will have a bitter taste.

Take care: the juice stains.

Preparing other fruits

There are several other fruits, including melons, gooseberries, grapes and figs, that do not fit into any particular category or family of fruit. They are simple to prepare and delicious to eat.

Melons

1 Halve the melon by cutting horizontally through the middle.

2 Use a spoon to scoop out the seeds and fibres, and pull or cut out any that remain.

3 **Balling** Cut into the flesh close to the hollow left by the seeds with a melon baller to scoop out a ball. Continue along the perimeter of the hollow until you have come full circle. Keep scooping until you have scooped out all of the soft flesh. (Avoid the harder flesh just under the skin.)

4 **Slicing** Cut each seeded half into slices of the required thickness. Trim off the skin in a single piece, taking care to remove the harder flesh just inside it (the knife will meet more resistance here than when it meets the softer flesh).

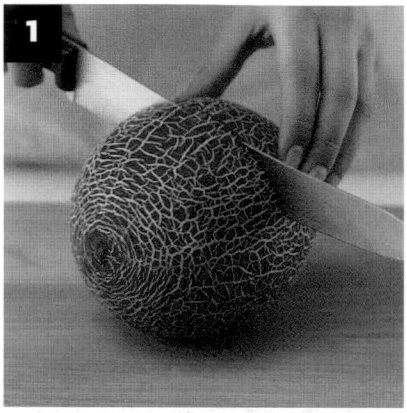

Gooseberries

Gooseberries should always be cooked and sweetened.

1 Remove the stems and flower ends, and put in a pan. Add sugar to taste – about 50g (2oz) per 125g (4oz) fruit for a dessert, 25g (1oz) per 125g (4oz) for a sauce. Pour in water to a quarter the depth of the fruit.

2 Cook over a medium heat, stirring occasionally, until about half the berries have collapsed.

Grapes

1 Seeding grapes Cut grapes in half from stalk-end to base. Remove seeds.

2 Peeling grapes Keep grapes in bunches and dip into boiling water for 10 seconds, then iced water for another 10 seconds.

3 Remove from the stalk and catch a piece of skin between your thumb and the knife and pull to remove.

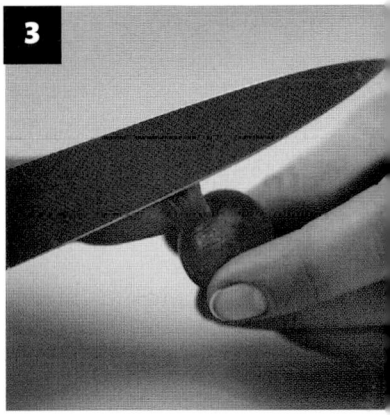

Figs

1 Washing One of the most fragile of fruits, figs call for very careful handling. To wash, put the fig in a bowl of cold water and, holding it loosely, shake briefly underwater. Gently rub the skin to remove any traces of grit then dry gently but thoroughly with kitchen paper.

2 Peeling Cut off the stem end, taking care not to cut into any of the flesh. Starting from the stalk end, catch a piece of skin between your thumb and the blade of a small sharp knife. Pull down to remove a strip of skin, then catch another piece of skin and remove it. Continue until peeled.

3 Halving and quartering Figs can be cooked under the grill or in a tart. Either way, it is best to leave the skin on but to cut the figs into pieces. Trim off the stem, then halve the fig lengthways. For quarters, cut both halves lengthways again.

4 Removing the pulp If you are making a sauce, purée or coulis, you need to remove the pulp from the fig. Halve the fruit lengthways. Starting from the base, use a teaspoon to dig into the flesh just underneath the skin. Follow the contours of the skin to scoop out the flesh in a single piece, taking care not to mash the pulp or cut the skin.

Cook's tip

Figs have a very soft, edible skin which helps keep the fruit together if you are cooking it. If you are in doubt about whether figs should be peeled, cut off a small section of skin and eat it. If it's chewy and leathery, peel it. If it is soft and tender, it doesn't need to be peeled.

Cooking fruit

Most fruits taste marvellous raw, although a few always need to be cooked. Nearly all fruits make superb desserts when they are baked, poached, stewed, deep-fried or pan-fried.

Poaching

To serve four, you will need 300g (11oz) sugar, 4 ripe pears, 1 lemon, halved.

1 Put the sugar in a large measuring jug and fill with cold water to make 1 litre (1½ pints). Transfer to a pan and heat gently, stirring now and then, until the sugar has dissolved.

2 Peel and halve the pears, and gently toss with lemon juice.

3 Pour the sugar syrup in a wide-based pan and bring up to a simmer. Put in the pears, cut sides down. They should be completely covered with syrup; add a little more syrup if necessary.

4 Simmer the fruit very gently for 30–40 minutes until the pears are soft when pierced with a knife. Serve hot, warm or cold.

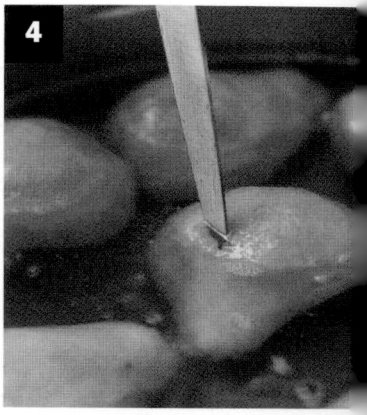

Oven poaching

- You can poach fruit in the oven as well. Put the pears in a shallow ovenproof dish and add the syrup as described. Cook at 150°C (130°C fan oven) mark 2 for 30–40 minutes.
- Under-ripe fruit takes much longer to cook than ripe fruit. Test for doneness regularly, especially in the final stages of cooking.

Cook's tips

Pears, apples and stone fruits are all well suited to gentle poaching in a sugar syrup. The secrets to successful poaching are to:

- never let the liquid boil rapidly
- never overcook the fruit.

Stewing

To serve four, you will need 450g (1lb) prepared fruit (chunks of apples and rhubarb, whole gooseberries, halved plums), 1 tbsp lemon juice, sugar (see box on Sweetening, right).

1 Put the fruit in a non-stick stainless steel pan with the sugar. Add flavourings and 2 tbsp water. Bring to the boil over a medium heat, then turn down the heat and simmer gently, partly covered, until the fruit is soft, stirring often.

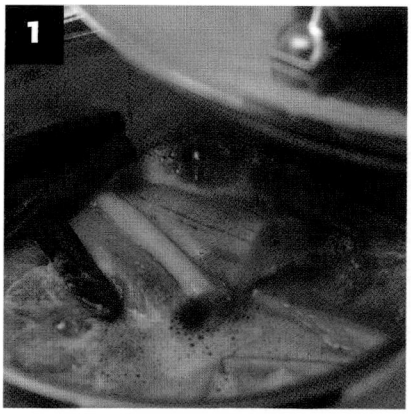

Sweetening

The type of fruit, its ripeness and personal taste will dictate how much sugar is required. However, as a general rule:

- Fruit that you can eat raw will need less sugar.
- Fruits that you wouldn't eat raw such as rhubarb will need more sugar.

Pan-frying

Suitable for apples, pineapple, bananas and stone fruits, this can make a quick dessert or a tasty side dish for pork and game.

To serve four, you will need 450g (1lb) fruit, 25g (1oz) unsalted butter, 4 tbsp golden caster sugar, 1 tbsp lemon juice.

1 Prepare fruit and cut into pieces no more than 2cm (¾in) thick.

2 Melt the butter in a heavy frying pan and add the fruit. Stir to coat with butter, then cover and cook just long enough to heat through.

3 Uncover the pan and sprinkle on the sugar. Stir to coat well, and continue cooking, stirring regularly, until the fruit is soft but not mushy. Sprinkle with the lemon juice and toss just before serving.

Deep-frying

Bananas and apples are best-known for deep-frying, but other fruits are equally good if coated in batter, too. Other good choices for cooking this way include pears, pineapple and skinned peaches or nectarines.

1 Heat vegetable oil in a deep-fryer to 190°C (test by frying a small cube of bread; it should brown in about 20 seconds).

2 Cut the fruit into small pieces, about 1cm (½in) thick. Dry them completely on kitchen paper if they have been washed.

3 Coat the fruit with icing sugar, then dip into the batter (page 80).

4 Fry, a few pieces at a time, until the batter is crisp and golden brown.

5 Lift out the fruit using a slotted spoon and drain well on kitchen paper before serving.

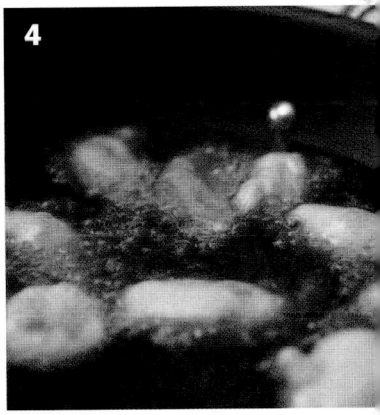

Perfect frying

- Make sure the oil is at the correct temperature.
- Don't crowd the pieces in the pan (if you do, the temperature drops and the fruit takes longer to cook and becomes greasy).
- If you have washed the fruit, dry it thoroughly before coating.
- Don't coat the fruit with batter more than a couple of minutes before cooking.

Baking

The key to success to baking fruit is in keeping the cooking time short, so that the delicate flesh of the fruit doesn't break down completely. Preheat the oven to 200°C (180°C fan oven) mark 6.

1 Prepare the fruit and put in a single layer in a buttered baking dish or individual dishes. Put a splash of water in the bottom of the dish(es). (For extra flavour, you can use fruit juice or wine instead of water, if you prefer.) Sprinkle the tops with sugar (and other flavourings such as spices, citrus zest or vanilla, if you like). Dot with butter.

2 Bake the fruit until just tender when pierced with a knife or skewer, this should take 15–25 minutes depending on the fruit and the size of the pieces. Leave to rest for a few minutes before serving.

Good fruits for baking

Fruit	Preparation
Apples (dessert or cooking)	cored and halved or quartered
Apricots	whole or halved and stoned
Bananas	peeled and halved, or in their skins
Berries	whole
Nectarines and peaches	halved and stoned
Pears	cored and halved or quartered
Pineapple	cored and cut into large chunks
Plums	whole or halved and stoned

Grilling

Cooking fruit under the grill is a quick and delicious method.

1 Preheat the grill to high. Prepare the fruit and put in the grill pan (or a roasting tin) in a single layer. Sprinkle generously with sugar.

2 Set the grill pan under the grill about 10cm (4in) from the heat. Grill until the top is lightly caramelised and the fruit has softened, 5–8 minutes. Serve hot or warm.

Making smoothies and purées

Fruit, whether cooked or raw, can be transformed into a smooth sauce by puréeing. It also makes a healthy breakfast or snack that is bursting with flavour when used in a smoothie.

Making smoothies

To serve four, you will need 4 passion fruit, 150ml (¼ pint) low-fat yogurt, 4 bananas, 225g (8oz) grapes.

1 Halve the passion fruit and scoop the pulp into a blender. Add the remaining ingredients. Crush 8 ice cubes and add to the blender.

2 Process until smooth and pour into glasses. Serve immediately.

Puréeing in a blender

Some fruit can be puréed raw, while others are better cooked. Wait until cooked fruit cools.

1 Put a large spoonful of fruit in the jug and blend until smooth, then add another spoonful and blend again. Add rest of fruit in batches.

2 For a very smooth purée, pass the fruit through a fine sieve.

Puréeing using a mouli

The fine plate of a mouli-légumes does a good job of puréeing, although it is slightly more laborious than a blender.

1 Set the mouli over a bowl and, working in batches, ladle in the fruit.

2 Turn the handle until the fruit has gone through, then repeat until all the fruit has been puréed.

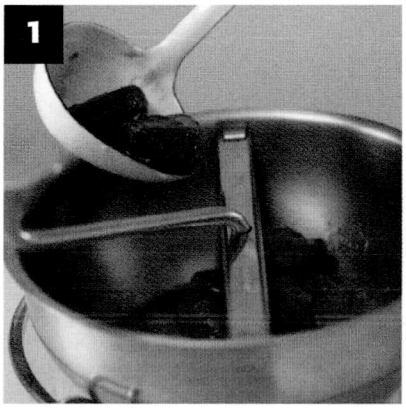

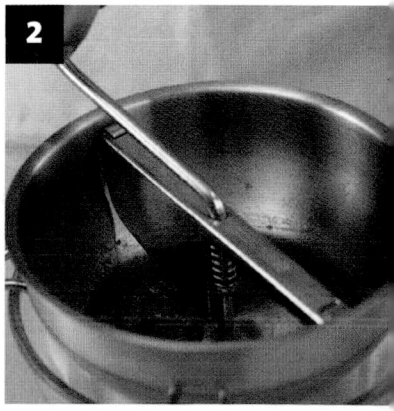

Preparing nuts

Most nuts are sold ready-prepared, but if you plan to store them for any length of time, choose nuts in their shells, which keep for longer.

Blanching and skinning

After nuts have been shelled, they are still coated with a skin, which, although edible, tastes bitter. This is easier to remove if the nuts are blanched or toasted.

1 Blanching Put the shelled nuts in a bowl and cover with boiling water. Leave for 2 minutes.

2 Drain and remove the skins either by rubbing between your hands in a teatowel or squeezing between your thumb and index finger.

3 Toasting This also improves the flavour. Preheat the oven to 200°C (180°C fan oven) mark 6. Put the shelled nuts on a baking sheet in a single layer, and bake for 8–15 minutes until the skins are lightly coloured. Remove skins by rubbing in a teatowel or squeezing between thumb and index finger.

Storing nuts

Because of their high fat content, nuts do not keep particularly well and turn rancid if kept for too long.

- Always buy nuts from a store with a high turnover of stock so you know they're likely to be fresh.
- Store in an airtight container in a cool, dark place, or in the refrigerator, and use quickly.

Chopping

Unless you want very large pieces, the easiest way to chop nuts is in the food processor. Only chop about 75g (3oz) of nuts at a time.

1 Put the nuts in a food processor and pulse at 10-second intervals.

2 Chop to the size of coarse breadcrumbs. Store in an airtight container for up to two weeks.

Slicing and slivering

Although you can buy sliced and slivered nuts, it's easy enough to make your own.

1 Put the nuts on a board. Using a chef's knife, carefully slice the nuts as thinly as required.

2 To make slivers, carefully cut the slices in the same way to make narrow matchsticks.

Making spiced nuts

These simply toasted nuts with a spicy, oily coating are great served with drinks.

To make a 500ml jar, you will need 4 tbsp vegetable oil, 2 tsp caster sugar, 2 tsp English mustard powder, 2 tsp garam masala, ½ tsp hot chilli powder, 350g (12oz) mixed nuts (almonds, pecan nuts, cashew nuts, hazelnuts, Brazil nuts), 50g (2oz) pumpkin seeds, 50g (2oz) sunflower seeds, 1 tsp sea salt.

1 Preheat the oven to 200°C (180°C fan oven) mark 6. Pour the vegetable oil into a roasting tin and heat for 3 minutes.

2 Meanwhile, mix together the sugar, mustard, garam masala and chilli powder, then add to the oil in the tin and roast for 1 minute.

3 Add the nuts and seeds to the tin, and stir to coat thoroughly in the spices, then roast for 10–15 minutes until golden.

4 Transfer the nuts to a bowl lined with kitchen paper, sprinkle with salt, and leave to cool. Serve immediately, or store in an airtight container for up to two weeks.

Preparing chestnuts

A richly flavoured nut, the chestnut is used for stuffings and other sweet and savoury dishes. Chestnuts need to be cooked and peeled before eating or using as an ingredient.

Slitting the shells

Whatever you are planning to do with chestnuts, they need to be cut open first.

1 Using a very sharp small knife, make a slit in the flat side of the nut, through the skin but not too deeply into the flesh.

2 Make a second cut across the first to make a cross-shaped cut.

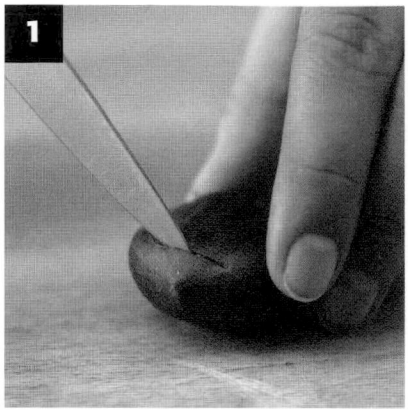

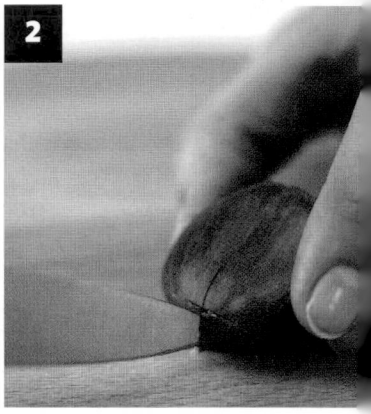

Boiling

This is the simplest way to prepare chestnuts for stuffings or for cooking.

1 Put scored chestnuts in a pan and cover with water. Bring to the boil, then simmer for 15–20 minutes until half-cooked. (They will feel soft but with some resistance at the centre.)

2 Drain. When cool enough to handle, skin using a small knife.

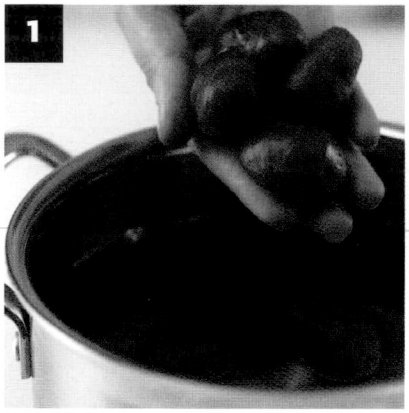

Roasting

These are best eaten immediately but can also be used for stuffings.

1 Preheat the oven to 200°C (180°C fan oven) mark 6. Slit the shells.

2 Put the nuts in a roasting pan in a single layer and bake for 20–25 minutes until the flesh is cooked and the edges of the cuts are slightly blackened. Cool a little, then peel.

Cook's tips

After skinning boiled chestnuts, you can cook them further:

- Fry gently in butter in a covered pan.
- Simmer in salted water or stock until just tender.
- For stuffings, chop using a knife or food processor.

Preparing coconut

The moist flesh of fresh coconut can be eaten as it is or grated to use in recipes. Check the coconut for freshness when you buy it by shaking it to make sure it has liquid inside.

Cracking

1 Find the three 'eyes' on one end and make holes with a skewer or screwdriver. Drain the juice into a bowl or jug.

2 Crack the shell by hitting between the eyes with a hammer or cleaver, then tap around the circumference. Break open, then split into smaller pieces. Using a small sharp knife, dig out flesh by cutting just under shell.

Grating

In countries where fresh coconut is extensively used, cooks use a special grater that produces perfectly fluffy shreds. You can grate coconut by hand or in the food processor.

1 By hand A rotary grater is easier to use than a flat grater because of the tough fibres of the coconut. Cut the coconut into pieces and feed through the grater.

2 Using a food processor Cut the coconut into fairly small pieces and process no more than a handful at a time. Pulse the processor until the coconut forms dry, fluffy shreds.

Making coconut milk

1 Weigh the grated coconut flesh and put it into a bowl. Pour over 100ml (3½fl oz) boiling water for each 100g (3½oz) coconut. Leave to stand for 30 minutes.

2 Line a large sieve with a double layer of muslin and pour the liquid through it. Gather up the four corners of the muslin and twist hard to squeeze out every bit of juice.

Exotic Fruit Salad

SERVES 6

1 pineapple, about 900g (2lb), peeled, cored and cut into chunks
2 papaya, deseeded, peeled and sliced
1 Galia melon, deseeded, and flesh cut into chunks
mint and lemongrass stalks (optional) to decorate

For the syrup

125g (4oz) caster sugar
6 fresh mint sprigs
¼ tsp ground Chinese five-spice powder
2 small fresh bay leaves
4 lemongrass stalks, split in half and bruised
½ tsp grated fresh root ginger

PREPARATION TIME 30 minutes, plus minimum 1 hour infusion and 2 hours chilling
COOKING TIME 7 minutes

PER SERVING

187 calories
1g fat (of which 0g saturates)
47g carbohydrate
0.1g salt

TECHNIQUES

see also preparing pineapples (page 210), preparing papaya (page 211), preparing melons (page 212)

1 To make the syrup, put the sugar in a pan with 600ml (1 pint) water and the remaining syrup ingredients. Heat gently until the sugar has dissolved. Bring to the boil and simmer for 5 minutes. Remove from the heat and set aside to infuse for at least 1 hour.

2 Put all the fruit in a bowl, strain the cooled syrup over the top, then cover and chill for at least 2 hours. Decorate with mint, and lemongrass stalks, if you want, to serve.

Spiced Nectarines

SERVES 4
4 tbsp clear honey
2 star anise
1 tbsp freshly squeezed lemon juice
4 ripe nectarines, halved and stoned
good-quality vanilla ice cream to serve

PREPARATION TIME 5 minutes, plus cooling

PER SERVING
105 calories
0g fat (of which 0g saturates)
25g carbohydrate
0g salt

TECHNIQUES
see also stoning fruits (page 208)

1 Put the honey, star anise and lemon juice in a heatproof bowl. Stir in 150ml (¼ pint) boiling water and leave until just warm.

2 Add the nectarines or peaches to the bowl of warm honey syrup and leave to cool. Transfer to a glass serving dish. Serve with a scoop of vanilla ice cream.

Variation

If you don't have any nectarines, use ripe peaches instead. It's best to remove the peaches' tougher skin first, so peel them following the technique on page 208, then complete the recipe as above.

Fruit Kebabs with Spiced Pear Dip

MAKES 6

3 large fresh figs, each cut into quarters
1 large ripe mango, skin and stone removed, flesh cut into cubes
1 baby pineapple or 2 thick slices, skin removed and flesh cut into cubes
1 tbsp dark clear honey

For the spiced pear dip

150g (5oz) ready-to-eat dried pears, soaked in hot water for about 30 minutes
juice of 1 orange
1 tsp finely chopped fresh root ginger
½ tsp vanilla extract
50ml (2fl oz) very low-fat plain yogurt
½ tsp ground cinnamon, plus extra to dust
1 tsp dark clear honey
25g (1oz) hazelnuts, toasted and roughly chopped

PREPARATION TIME 20 minutes, plus 30 minutes soaking
COOKING TIME 8 minutes

PER SERVING
129 calories
3g fat (of which trace saturates)
25g carbohydrate
0g salt

Get ahead

Complete step 1 to end of line 4. Cover and chill for up to two days. Make kebabs as in step 2. Cover and chill for up to one day.
To use Drizzle the dip with honey, sprinkle with toasted nuts and dust with cinnamon. Allow the chilled kebabs to come to room temperature. Finally, complete step 2.

1 Soak six 20.5cm (8in) wooden skewers in water for 30 minutes. To make the dip, drain the pears and put in a food processor or blender with the orange juice, ginger, vanilla extract, yogurt, cinnamon and 50ml (2fl oz) water, and whiz until smooth. Spoon the dip into a bowl. Drizzle with the honey, sprinkle with the toasted hazelnuts and dust with a little ground cinnamon. Cover and set aside in a cool place until ready to serve.

2 Preheat the grill to its highest setting. To make the kebabs, thread alternate pieces of fruit on to the skewers, using at least two pieces of each type of fruit per skewer. Put the skewers on a foil-covered tray. Drizzle with honey and grill for about 4 minutes on each side, close to the heat, until lightly charred. Serve warm or at room temperature with the spiced pear dip.

Elderflower and Fruit Jelly

SERVES 6
2–3 tbsp elderflower cordial
200g (7oz) caster sugar
4 gelatine leaves
150g (5oz) raspberries
150g (5oz) halved seedless grapes

PREPARATION TIME 15 minutes, plus minimum 4 hours chilling
COOKING TIME 10 minutes

PER SERVING
184 calories
0g fat (of which 0g saturates)
42g carbohydrate
0g salt

TECHNIQUES
see also preparing berries (page 209), seeding grapes (page 213)

1 Put the elderflower cordial into a large pan and add 750ml (1¼ pints) water and the sugar. Heat gently, stirring to dissolve the sugar.

2 Soak the gelatine leaves in cold water for 5 minutes. Lift out the gelatine, squeeze out the excess water, then add the liquid to the pan. Stir to dissolve, then strain into a jug.

3 Divide the raspberries and grapes among six 200ml (7fl oz) glass dishes. Pour the liquid over the fruit, then cool and chill for at least 4 hours or overnight.

Cook's tips

- Gelatine is available in leaf and powdered forms. Both must be soaked in liquid to soften before being dissolved in a warm liquid. Always add dissolved gelatine to a mixture that is warm or at room temperature – if added to a cold liquid, it will set in fine threads and spoil the final texture of the dish.
- Gelatine is derived from meat bones, but there are also several vegetarian alternatives such as agar agar and gelazone.

Lemon and Passion Fruit Fool

SERVES 6
6 tbsp good-quality lemon curd
4 ripe passion fruits
140ml (4½fl oz) double cream
1 tbsp icing sugar
200g (7oz) Greek yogurt
toasted flaked almonds to decorate

PREPARATION TIME 20 minutes

PER SERVING
244 calories
18g fat (of which 10g saturates)
21g carbohydrate
0.1g salt

TECHNIQUES
see also preparing passion fruit (page 211), slivering nuts (page 219)

1 Put the lemon curd into a small bowl. Halve the passion fruit and spoon the pulp into a sieve resting over a bowl. Stir to separate the seeds from the juice. Add 1 tbsp of the passion fruit juice to the lemon curd and mix well.

2 In a large bowl, whip the cream with the icing sugar until soft peaks form. Stir in the yogurt.

3 Put a dollop of yogurt cream into each of four small glasses. Layer with a spoonful of lemon curd mixture and 1 tsp passion fruit juice. Repeat to use up all the ingredients. Scatter over some toasted flaked almonds and serve immediately.

Cook's tip

Using a good-quality lemon curd will make all the difference to the final flavour of this fool. Making your own is easy, follow the technique on page 409.

Strawberry Compote

SERVES 10
340g jar raspberry conserve
juice of 2 large oranges
juice of 2 lemons
1 tbsp rosewater
700g (1lb 9oz) strawberries, hulled and thickly sliced
250g (9oz) blueberries

PREPARATION TIME 15 minutes, plus overnight chilling
COOKING TIME 10 minutes

PER SERVING
126 calories
0g fat (of which 0g saturates)
32g carbohydrate
0g salt

TECHNIQUES
see also hulling strawberries (page 209)

1 Put the contents of the jar of raspberry conserve into a pan with the orange and lemon juices. Add 150ml (¼ pint) boiling water. Stir over a low heat to melt the conserve, then leave to cool.

2 Stir in the rosewater and taste – you may want to add a squeeze more lemon juice if it's too sweet. Put the strawberries and blueberries into a large serving bowl. Strain over the raspberry conserve mixture. Cover and chill overnight. Remove the bowl from the refrigerator about 30 minutes before serving.

Summer Gratin

SERVES 4

3 ripe peaches, halved, stoned and sliced
225g (8oz) wild strawberries or raspberries
3 tbsp Kirsch or Eau de Vie de Mirabelle
4 large egg yolks
50g (2oz) sugar

PREPARATION TIME 15 minutes
COOKING TIME 15 minutes

PER SERVING
168 calories
4g fat (of which 1g saturates)
27g carbohydrate
0g salt

TECHNIQUES
see also stoning fruit (page 208), preparing berries (page 209), separating eggs (page 52)

1 Put the peach slices in a bowl with the strawberries or raspberries and 2 tbsp Kirsch or Eau de Vie.

2 Put the egg yolks, sugar, remaining Kirsch and 2 tbsp water in a heatproof bowl set over a pan of barely simmering water. Whisk for 5–10 minutes or until the mixture leaves a trail and is warm in the centre. Remove from the heat. Preheat the grill.

3 Arrange the fruit in four shallow heatproof dishes and spoon the sauce over. Cook under the grill for 1–2 minutes or until light golden. Serve immediately.

Rustic Blackberry and Apple Pie

SERVES 6

200g (7oz) plain flour, plus extra to dust
125g (4oz) chilled unsalted butter, diced
1 medium egg, beaten
75g (3oz) golden caster sugar, plus 3 tbsp
pinch of salt
500g (1lb 2oz) eating apples, quartered, cored and cut into chunky wedges
300g (11oz) blackberries
¼ tsp ground cinnamon
juice of 1 small lemon

PREPARATION TIME 25 minutes, plus minimum 15 minutes chilling
COOKING TIME 40 minutes

PER SERVING
372 calories
19g fat (of which 11g saturates)
49g carbohydrate
0.4g salt

TECHNIQUES
see also making pastry (pages 278–279), preparing apples (page 206), preparing berries (page 209)

1 Pulse the flour and butter in a food processor until it resembles coarse crumbs. (Alternatively, rub the fat into the flour by hand or using a pastry cutter.) Add the egg, 2 tbsp sugar and the salt, and pulse again to combine, or stir in. Wrap in clingfilm and chill for at least 15 minutes. Meanwhile, preheat the oven to 200°C (180°C fan oven) mark 6.

2 Put the apples, blackberries, 75g (3oz) sugar, the cinnamon and lemon juice in a bowl and toss together, making sure the sugar dissolves in the juice.

3 Grease a 25.5cm (10in) enamel or metal pie dish. Using a lightly floured rolling pin, roll out the pastry on a large sheet of baking parchment to a 30.5cm (12in) circle. Lift up the paper, upturn the pastry on to the pie dish and peel away the paper.

4 Put the prepared fruit in the centre of the pie dish and fold the pastry edges up and over the fruit. Sprinkle with the remaining sugar and bake in the oven for 40 minutes or until the fruit is tender and the pastry golden.

Variation

To save time, use 450g (1lb) ready-made chilled or thawed frozen shortcrust pastry.

Drunken Pears

SERVES 4
4 Williams or Comice pears
140g (4½oz) granulated sugar
300ml (½ pint) dry red wine
150ml (¼ pint) sloe gin
1 cinnamon stick
zest of 1 orange
6 star anise
Greek yogurt or whipped cream to serve (optional)

PREPARATION TIME 20 minutes
COOKING TIME 50 minutes

PER SERVING
305 calories
trace fat (of which 0g saturates)
52g carbohydrate
0g salt

TECHNIQUES
see also preparing pears (page 206), zesting citrus fruit (page 207)

1 Peel the pears, cut out the calyx at the base of each and leave the stalks intact. Put the sugar, wine, sloe gin and 300ml (½ pint) water into a small pan and heat gently until the sugar dissolves.

2 Bring to the boil and add the cinnamon stick, orange zest and star anise. Add the pears, then cover and poach over a low heat for 30 minutes or until tender.

3 Lift the pears into a bowl and reduce the liquid to about 200ml (7fl oz) or until syrupy. Pour over the pears and serve warm or chilled with Greek yogurt or whipped cream, if you like.

Barbecued Figs with Marsala

SERVES 6
12 large ripe figs
melted butter, to brush
1 cinnamon stick, roughly broken
6 tbsp clear Greek honey
6 tbsp Marsala
crème fraîche to serve

PREPARATION TIME 10 minutes
COOKING TIME 20 minutes

PER SERVING
151 calories
1g fat (of which 0g saturates)
34g carbohydrate
0.1g salt

TECHNIQUES
see also preparing figs (page 213)

1 Make a small slit in each fig, three-quarters of the way through. Take two sheets of foil large enough to hold the figs in one layer. With the shiny side uppermost, lay one piece on top of the other and brush the top piece all over with the melted butter.

2 Stand the figs in the middle of the foil and scatter over the broken cinnamon stick. Bring the sides of the foil together loosely, leaving a gap at the top, and pour in the honey and Marsala. Finally, scrunch the edges of the foil together so that the figs are loosely enclosed.

3 Put the foil parcel on the barbecue and cook over medium hot coals for about 10–15 minutes, depending on how ripe the figs are, until very tender.

4 Just before serving, open up the foil slightly at the top and barbecue for a further 2–3 minutes to allow the juices to reduce and become syrupy.

5 Serve the figs immediately with a large dollop of crème fraîche and the syrupy juices spooned over.

Get ahead

Although they are best served immediately, the figs can also be cooked in advance, then popped on the barbecue to warm through just before eating.

Rhubarb and Pear Crumble

SERVES 8

450g (1lb) rhubarb, cut into 2.5cm (1in) pieces
2 ripe pears, peeled, cored and roughly chopped
75g (3oz) Demerara sugar
1 tsp ground cinnamon
50g (2oz) chilled butter
75g (3oz) self-raising flour
2 shortbread fingers
50g (2oz) whole hazelnuts
500g (1lb 2oz) Greek yogurt to serve

PREPARATION TIME 25 minutes
COOKING TIME 40–45 minutes

PER SERVING

262 calories
17g fat (of which 7g saturates)
25g carbohydrate
0.3g salt

TECHNIQUES

see also preparing pears (page 206)

1 Preheat the oven to 180°C (160°C fan oven) mark 4. Put the fruit into a small shallow baking dish and sprinkle over 25g (1oz) sugar and the cinnamon. Mix together well.

2 Next, make the crumble mixture. Put the butter in a food processor, add the flour and remaining sugar and whiz until it looks like rough breadcrumbs. (Alternatively, rub the fat into the flour by hand or using a pastry cutter, then stir in the sugar.)

3 Break the shortbread fingers into pieces and add to the processor with the hazelnuts (or crush the shortbread with a rolling pin and chop the hazelnuts). Whiz again for 4–5 seconds until the crumble is blended but still looks rough. Sprinkle the crumble over the fruit, spreading it up to the edges and pressing down with the back of a wooden spoon.

4 Bake in the oven for 40–45 minutes until the topping is golden brown and crisp. Serve with yogurt.

Variation

Creamy vanilla custard is another traditional accompaniment to fruit crumbles. Make your own using the recipe and technique on page 26.

American-style Plum Cobbler

SERVES 6

900g (2lb) plums, halved and stones removed
150g (5oz), golden caster sugar, plus 3 tbsp
1 tbsp cornflour
250g (9oz) self-raising flour
100g (3½oz) chilled unsalted butter, diced
175ml (6fl oz) buttermilk or whole natural yogurt

PREPARATION TIME 25 minutes
COOKING TIME 40 minutes

PER SERVING
451 calories
15g fat (of which 9g saturates)
76g carbohydrate
0.3g salt

TECHNIQUES
see also stoning fruit (page 208)

1 Preheat the oven to 200°C (180°C fan oven) mark 6. Cut the plums into chunky wedges. Tip into an ovenproof dish measuring 25.5 × 18 × 7.5cm (10 × 7 × 3in) and toss together with 3 tbsp sugar and the cornflour.

2 Whiz the flour, butter and 100g (3½oz) sugar in a food processor until the mixture forms fine crumbs. (Alternatively, rub the fat into the flour by hand or using a pastry cutter, then stir in the sugar.) Add the buttermilk or yogurt and blend for a few seconds until just combined.

3 Scatter clumps of the squidgy dough over the plums, leaving some of the fruit exposed. Sprinkle the cobbler with the remaining sugar and bake in the oven for 40 minutes or until the fruit is tender and the topping is pale golden.

Finishing touches

A scoop of vanilla ice cream makes an indulgent addition to a bowl of plum cobbler. Try making your own homemade ice cream using the recipe and technique on page 388.

RICE, GRAINS AND PULSES

Wholesome and healthy, grains, beans, lentils and pulses can be a nutritious staple in your everyday diet. So easy to prepare, the step-by-step technique section explains how to prepare and cook perfect rice every time, including making risotto, paella and sushi, and cooking other grains such as couscous, bulgur wheat, barley, quinoa, wheat grain and polenta. It also shows you how easy it is to soak, cook and sprout your own beans. The recipes put these basic skills to good use in wonderful dishes such as Salmon and coriander kedgeree, Spiced chicken pilau, Prawn and lemon risotto, Cheesey polenta with tomato sauce, Summer couscous, Spicy pork and bean stew, and Chicken with chorizo and beans.

Cooking rice

There are two main types of rice: long-grain and short-grain. Short-grain rice is used for dishes such as risotto, sushi and paella. Long-grain rice is used as an accompaniment.

Preparing long-grain rice

Long-grain rice needs no special preparation, though basmati should be washed to remove excess starch.

1 Put in a bowl and cover with cold water. Stir until this becomes cloudy, then drain and repeat the washing process until the water is clear.

2 Soak the rice for 30 minutes, then drain before cooking.

Cooking long-grain rice

1 Measure the rice by volume and put it in a pan with a pinch of salt with twice the volume of boiling water (or boiling stock).

2 Bring to the boil. Turn the heat down to low, and set the timer for the time stated on the pack. It needs to cook al dente: tender but with a hint of bite at the centre.

3 When the rice is cooked, fluff up the grains by gently tossing with a fork; this keeps the grains from sticking together. The rice can be left, covered, for a few minutes.

Perfect rice

- Use 50–75g (2–3oz) raw rice per person – or measure by volume 50–75ml (2–2½fl oz).
- If you cook a lot of rice, you may want to invest in a special rice steamer. They are available in Asian supermarkets and some kitchen shops and give good, consistent results.

Variation

Cooking the rice in stock, with additional aromatics such as herbs, garlic or spices, will add flavour.

Making risotto

Italian risotto is made with medium-grain arborio, vialone nano or carnaroli rice, which release starch to give a rich, creamy texture. It is traditionally cooked on the hob, but can also be cooked in the oven.

Basic risotto

To serve four, you will need 1 onion, chopped, 50g (2oz) butter, 900ml (1½ pints) hot chicken stock, 225g (8oz) risotto rice, 50g (2oz) freshly grated Parmesan, plus extra to serve.

1 Gently fry the onion in the butter for 10–15 minutes until it is very lightly coloured. Heat the stock in a pan and keep at a simmer. Add the rice to the butter and stir for 1–2 minutes until well coated.

2 Add a ladleful of stock and stir constantly until absorbed. Add the remaining stock a ladleful at a time, stirring, until the rice is al dente (tender but still with bite in the centre), about 20–30 minutes. Note: you may not need all the stock.

3 Stir in the grated Parmesan and serve immediately, with extra cheese passed separately.

Perfect risotto

- Use home-made stock, preferably with minimal salt – the stock cooks away, so the salt will be concentrated in the finished dish.
- Make sure the stock is hot while you are ladling it into the rice.

Easy oven risotto

This method has the advantage over classic risotto because it requires no attention or stirring during cooking.

To serve four, you will need 40g (1½oz) unsalted butter, 1 garlic clove, finely chopped, 1 onion, finely chopped, 1 rosemary sprig, leaves finely chopped, 225g (8oz) risotto rice, 900ml (1½ pints) hot chicken stock, 50g (2oz) freshly grated Parmesan.

1 Preheat the oven to 150°C (130°C fan) mark 2. Melt half the butter in a flameproof casserole and fry the garlic, onion and rosemary for 8 minutes until soft and golden.

2 Add the rice and stir for 2 minutes. Pour over the stock, bring to the boil, cover and bake for 20 minutes. To serve, stir in the remaining butter and the cheese.

Making paella

No two Spanish cooks make this classic dish in exactly the same way and the choice and quantities of ingredients vary from home to home. It is usually made in a large flat pan with a dimpled bottom.

Simple paella

Traditionally, paella is made using a medium-grain rice but this version uses long-grain rice.

To serve six, you will need about 1 litre (1¾ pints) chicken stock, ½ tsp saffron, 6 boneless skinless chicken thighs, 5 tbsp extra-virgin olive oil, 1 large onion, chopped, 4 large garlic cloves, crushed, 1 tsp paprika, 2 red peppers, sliced, 400g can chopped tomatoes, 350g (12oz) long-grain rice, 200ml (7fl oz) dry sherry, 500g (1lb 2oz) cooked mussels, 200g (7oz) cooked tiger prawns, the juice of ½ lemon, salt and ground black pepper, lemon wedges and parsley sprigs to serve.

1 Heat the stock, then add the saffron and leave to infuse for 30 minutes. Meanwhile, cut the chicken thighs into three pieces.

2 Heat half the oil in a large frying pan and, working in batches, fry the chicken for 3–5 minutes until pale golden brown. Set the chicken aside.

3 Lower the heat slightly and add the remaining oil. Fry the onion for 5 minutes until soft. Add the garlic and paprika and stir for 1 minute. Add chicken, peppers and tomatoes.

4 Stir in the rice, then add one-third of the stock and bring to the boil. Season with salt and pepper.

5 Reduce heat to a simmer. Cook, uncovered, stirring continuously, until most of the liquid is absorbed.

6 Add the remaining stock a little at a time, letting it become absorbed into the rice before adding more. (This should take about 25 minutes.) Add the sherry and continue cooking for another 2 minutes – the rice should be quite wet, as it will continue to absorb liquid.

7 Add the mussels and prawns to the pan, including all their juices, with the lemon juice. Stir them in and cook for 5 minutes to heat through. Adjust the seasoning and garnish with lemon wedges and sprigs of fresh parsley.

Making sushi

Japanese sushi is made with special short- or medium-grain rice, which has a higher moisture content and stickier consistency, making it perfect for rolling up inside seaweed to make elegant sushi rolls.

Classic sushi rolls

To make four rolls (24 pieces), you will need 150g (5oz) Japanese sushi rice, 2 tbsp rice vinegar, 4 tbsp mirin (rice wine), 1 tbsp caster sugar, 4 sheets nori (seaweed), 1 tbsp wasabi paste, soy sauce, wasabi and pickled ginger to serve.

For the filling you will need 150g (5oz) smoked salmon, ½ cucumber, 2 large spring onions.

1 Put the rice in a pan with 350ml (12fl oz) cold water. Bring to the boil, cover, and simmer for 10 minutes or until the water has evaporated. Remove from the heat and stir in the vinegar, mirin and sugar. Leave to cool, then fluff up with chopsticks.

2 Cut the salmon into long thin strips. Peel and seed the cucumber and cut into strips. Thinly shred the spring onions.

3 Lay a sheet of nori, shiny side down, in the centre of a sushi mat. Spread a quarter of the rice across two-thirds of the nori.

4 Make an indentation along the top of the rice and spread with a little wasabi paste, then lay a quarter of the salmon, cucumber and spring onion across the width.

5 Using your thumbs to pick up the mat, roll it away from you, pressing gently but firmly on the filling as you roll to make a neat cylinder. Unroll the mat and repeat with the remaining nori and fillings.

6 Wet the blade of a very sharp knife. Trim the ends of each roll, cut each one into three equal-sized pieces, then cut each third in half at an angle. Serve with soy sauce, wasabi and pickled ginger.

Cooking other grains

With any grain, the cooking time depends heavily on how the grain has been processed. Both wheat and barley come in several forms, so you need to check which type you have bought.

Couscous

Often mistaken for a grain, couscous is actually a type of pasta that originated in North Africa. It is perfect for serving with stews and casseroles, or making into salads. The tiny pellets do not require cooking and can simply be soaked.

1 Measure the couscous in a jug and add 1½ times the volume of hot water or stock.

2 Cover the bowl and leave to soak for 5 minutes. Fluff up with a fork before serving.

3 If using for a salad, leave the couscous to cool completely before adding the other salad ingredients.

Bulgur wheat

A form of cracked wheat, bulgur has had some or all of the bran removed. It is pre-boiled during manufacturing and may be boiled, steamed or soaked. It is good served as a grain or used in salads.

1 Simmering bulgur Cover in water by about 2.5cm (1in). Bring to the boil, then simmer for 10–15 minutes until just tender. Drain well.

2 Steaming bulgur Place the bulgur in a steamer lined with a clean teatowel and steam over boiling water for 20 minutes or until the grains are soft.

3 Soaking bulgur Put the bulgur in a deep bowl. Cover with hot water and mix with a fork. Leave to steep for 20 minutes, checking to make sure there is enough water. Drain and fluff up with a fork.

Barley

There are three types of barley, all of which may be cooked on their own, or in a soup or stew.

1 Whole barley Soak the barley overnight in twice the volume of water, then drain well. Put the barley in a heavy-based pan, pour over boiling water and simmer for about 1½ hours or until tender. Check the liquid, adding more if necessary.

2 Scotch (pot) barley Rinse well, then simmer gently in boiling water for 45–50 minutes until tender.

3 Pearl barley This barley has had all of its outer husk removed, and needs no soaking. Rinse the barley and put it into a pan with twice the volume of water. Bring to the boil. Turn down the heat and simmer until tender, 25–30 minutes.

Quinoa

This nutritious South American grain makes a great alternative to rice.

1 Put the quinoa in a bowl of cold water. Mix well, soak for 2 minutes and drain. Put in a pan with twice its volume of water. Bring to the boil.

2 Simmer for 20 minutes. Remove from heat, cover and leave to stand for 10 minutes.

Wheat grain

Also known as whole wheat and wheat berries, wheat grain needs to be soaked overnight and long, slow simmering. You can sometimes find pre-cooked varieties that will cut down on soaking and cooking time.

1 Soak the wheat grain overnight in twice the volume of water, then drain well.

2 Measure the grain in a measuring cup, then put in a heavy-based pan with twice the volume of water (or use unsalted stock instead of water to add flavour to the grain).

3 Bring to the boil and simmer until tender, about 45 minutes. Check the liquid regularly to make sure it is not boiling away, and add more if necessary. Drain well.

Quantities

Allow 50–75g (2–3oz) raw grain per person. Or, if measuring by volume, allow 50–75ml (2–2½fl oz).

Cooking polenta

This classic Italian staple made of coarse ground cornmeal may be cooked to make a grainy purée to be served immediately, or cooled and then fried or grilled. Here are some quick ways to cook it.

Traditional polenta

1 Fill a pan with 1.1 litres (2 pints) water and add ¼ tsp salt. Pour in 225g (8oz) polenta and set it over the heat.

2 As the water starts to heat up, stir the polenta. Bring to the boil, reduce the heat to a simmer and continue cooking, stirring every few minutes, for 15–20 minutes until it comes away from the sides of the pan.

Grilling polenta

1 Make traditional polenta (see above), then pour into an oiled baking dish. Smooth the surface with a spatula and leave to cool.

2 Cut polenta into squares and brush the pieces with olive oil.

3 Preheat the grill or frying pan and cook for 5–10 minutes until hot and browned on both sides.

Baking polenta

1 Preheat the oven to 200°C (180°C fan oven) mark 6. Fill a pan with 1.1 litres (2 pints) water and add ¼ tsp salt. Pour in 225g (8oz) polenta and set it over the heat. Bring to the boil, stirring, then simmer for 5 minutes.

2 Pour the polenta into an oiled baking dish, cover with foil and bake for 45–50 minutes. Brown under grill.

Perfect polenta

- Use coarse cornmeal if you want a slightly gritty texture, or fine cornmeal for a smooth texture.
- If you are serving the traditional polenta straight from the pan, have all the other dishes ready – the polenta needs to be eaten straightaway otherwise it becomes thick and difficult to serve.

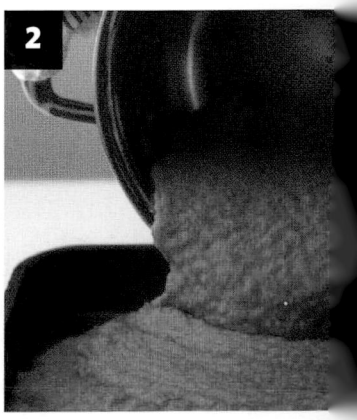

Using beans and lentils

Many dried beans and peas need to be soaked overnight before cooking, and doing so will shorten their cooking time. However, quicker-cooking lentils do not need soaking.

Cooking beans

1 Pick through the beans to remove any grit or small stones.

2 Put the beans in a bowl or pan and pour over cold water to cover generously. Leave to soak for at least 8 hours, then drain. (If you are in a hurry, pour over boiling water and leave the beans to cool in the water for 1–2 hours.)

3 Put the soaked beans in a large pan and add water to cover by at least 5cm (2in). Bring to the boil and boil rapidly for 10 minutes.

4 Skim off the scum that rises to the top, and leave to simmer until the beans are soft inside. They should be tender but not falling apart. Check the water periodically to make sure there's enough to keep the beans well covered. Drain well. If using in a salad, allow to cool completely.

Cooking times

These vary for dried beans. Older beans will take longer to cook, so use them within their best-before date.

Chickpeas	1–2 hours
Red kidney, cannellini, borlotti, butter, flageolet beans	1–3 hours
Red lentils	20 minutes
Lentils, green	30–40 minutes

Sprouting beans

Mung beans, green or Puy lentils and afalfa are all popular for home sprouting and are good in salads and stir-fries. You will only need about 3 tbsp beans to sprout at one time.

1 Pick through the beans to remove any grit or stones, then soak in cold water for at least 8 hours. Drain and place in a clean (preferably sterilised) jar. Cover the top with a dampened piece of cloth, secure and leave in a warm, dark place.

2 Rinse the sprouting beans twice a day. The sprouts can be eaten when there is about 1cm (½in) of growth, or they can be left to grow for a day or two longer. When they are sprouted, leave the jar on a sunny windowsill for about 3 hours – this will improve both their flavour and their nutrients. Then rinse and dry them well. They can be kept for about three days in the refrigerator. Always rinse the beans well before using them.

Salmon and Coriander Kedgeree

SERVES 4

1 tbsp olive oil
4 shallots, chopped
225g (8oz) basmati rice
450ml (¾ pint) hot fish stock
100g (3½oz) frozen peas
300g (11oz) hot-smoked salmon flakes
a handful of freshly chopped coriander
salt and ground black pepper
lime wedges to serve

PREPARATION TIME 15 minutes
COOKING TIME 20–25 minutes

PER SERVING

392 calories
12g fat (of which 2g saturates)
49g carbohydrate
0.3g salt

TECHNIQUES

see also preparing shallots (page 170), chopping herbs (page 428)

1 Heat the oil in a large pan over a low heat and fry the shallots for 5 minutes or until soft. Add the rice and stir to mix everything together. Pour in the stock. Cover and cook for 10 minutes over a low heat until the rice is almost cooked and most of the liquid has been absorbed.

2 Add the peas and salmon and cook, uncovered, for 2–3 minutes until the peas are tender. Season with salt and pepper, scatter over the chopped coriander and serve with lime wedges to squeeze over.

Cook's tip

Basmati rice is prized for its delicate fragrant flavour. Its long grains are firm and separate when cooked, not sticky, making it perfect for this tasty kedgeree.

Spiced Egg Pilau

SERVES 4
200g (7oz) basmati or wild rice
150g (5oz) frozen peas
4 medium eggs
200ml (7fl oz) coconut cream
1 tsp mild curry paste
1 tbsp sweet chilli sauce
1 tbsp smooth peanut butter
1 large bunch coriander, roughly chopped
mini poppadums and mango chutney to serve

PREPARATION TIME 2 minutes
COOKING TIME 15 minutes

PER SERVING
483 calories
26g fat (of which 17g saturates)
48g carbohydrate
0.4g salt

TECHNIQUES
see also chopping herbs (page 428)

1 Put the rice into a pan with 450ml (¾ pint) boiling water over a low heat and cook for 15 minutes or until just tender. Add the frozen peas for the last 5 minutes of cooking time.

2 Meanwhile, put the eggs into a large pan of boiling water and simmer for 6 minutes, then drain and shell.

3 Put the coconut cream, curry paste, chilli sauce and peanut butter into a small pan and whisk together. Heat the sauce gently, stirring, without allowing it to boil.

4 Drain the rice and stir in the chopped coriander and 2 tbsp of the sauce.

5 Divide the rice among four bowls. Cut the eggs into halves and serve on the rice, spooning the remaining coconut sauce over the top. Serve with the poppadums and chutney.

Spiced Chicken Pilau

SERVES 4

2 tbsp olive oil
2 garlic cloves, crushed
2 onions, sliced
2 tbsp medium curry powder
6 skinless boneless raw chicken thighs, or 450g (1lb) skinless cooked chicken, cut into strips
350g (12oz) – or a measuring jug filled to 450ml (¾ pint) – American easy-cook rice
2 tsp salt
pinch of saffron
50g (2oz) sultanas
225g (8oz) ripe tomatoes, roughly chopped
50g (2oz) pinenuts, toasted

PREPARATION TIME 15 minutes
COOKING TIME 35–40 minutes

PER SERVING

649 calories
18g fat (of which 2g saturates)
87g carbohydrate
2.8g salt

TECHNIQUES

see also preparing vegetables (pages 170–182), preparing poultry (page 108–111), toasting nuts (page 218)

Cook's tip

The word pilau comes from the Persian *pilaw*. The dish originated in the east and consists of rice flavoured with spices and cooked in stock, to which vegetables, poultry and fish have been added.

1 Heat the oil in a large heavy-based pan (a paella pan is ideal). Add the garlic and onions, then cook for 5 minutes to soften. Remove half the onions and set aside.

2 Add the curry powder and cook for 1 minute, then add the chicken and stir. Cook for 10 minutes if the meat is raw, or for 4 minutes if you're using cooked chicken, stirring from time to time until browned.

3 Add the rice to the pan, stir to coat in the oil, then add 900ml (1½ pints) boiling water, the salt and saffron. Cover and bring to the boil, then turn the heat down low and cook for 20 minutes or until the rice is tender and most of the liquid is absorbed.

4 Stir in the reserved onions and the sultanas, tomatoes and pinenuts. Cook for a further 5 minutes to warm through, then serve.

Prawn and Lemon Risotto

SERVES 4

225g (8oz) sugarsnap peas, sliced diagonally
175g (6oz) baby courgettes, sliced diagonally
2 tbsp olive oil
1 onion, finely chopped
¼ tsp saffron (optional)
225g (8oz) arborio (risotto) rice
1 garlic clove, crushed
225g (8oz) brown-cap mushrooms, quartered
zest and juice of 1 lemon
750ml (1¼ pints) hot fish, chicken or vegetable stock
300g (11oz) cooked peeled prawns
3 tbsp finely chopped chives
salt and ground black pepper
spring onion curls (see Cook's tips) and grated lemon zest to garnish

PREPARATION TIME 15 minutes
COOKING TIME 40 minutes

PER SERVING
396 calories
8g fat (of which 1g saturates)
57g carbohydrate
0.6g salt

TECHNIQUES
see also preparing vegetables (pages 170–182), making stock (page 34)

Cook's tips

- Adding the stock gradually gives the risotto its deliciously creamy texture.
- To make spring onion curls, thinly slice the onions lengthways, soak in ice-cold water for 30 minutes, then drain well.

1 Put the sugarsnap peas and courgettes in a large pan of boiling salted water, then bring to the boil. Cook for 1–2 minutes, then drain and plunge into ice-cold water.

2 Heat the oil in a medium non-stick pan, then add the onion and saffron, if using. Cook over a medium heat for 10 minutes or until soft. Add the rice, garlic and mushrooms, and cook, stirring, for 1–2 minutes. Season with salt and pepper.

3 Add the grated lemon zest and about one-third of the stock (see Cook's tips). Simmer gently, stirring frequently, until most of the liquid has been absorbed. Add another one-third of the stock, then repeat the process.

4 Add the remaining stock. Cook, stirring, for 10 minutes or until the rice is tender and most of the stock has been absorbed. Add the prawns, drained vegetables, 1–2 tbsp lemon juice and the chives, then heat for 3–4 minutes. Garnish with spring onion curls and grated lemon zest.

Fruity Rice Pudding

SERVES 6

125g (4oz) pudding rice
1.1 litres (2 pints) full-fat milk
1 tsp vanilla extract
3–4 tbsp caster sugar
200ml (7fl oz) whipping cream
12 tbsp wild lingonberry sauce

PREPARATION TIME 10 minutes, plus 30 minutes cooling and minimum 1 hour chilling
COOKING TIME 1 hour

PER SERVING
352 calories
21g fat (of which 13g saturates)
34g carbohydrate
0.2g salt

1 Put the rice in a pan with 600ml (1 pint) cold water, bring to the boil and simmer until the liquid has evaporated. Add the milk, bring to the boil and simmer for 45 minutes or until the rice is very soft and creamy. Leave to cool.

2 Add the vanilla extract and sugar to the rice. Lightly whip the cream and fold through the pudding. Chill for 1 hour.

3 Divide a third of the rice mixture among six glass tumblers, top with a spoonful of lingonberry sauce and repeat the process, finishing with a spoonful of lingonberry sauce. Chill until ready to serve.

Variation

Although wild lingonberry sauce is recommended here, a spoonful of any fruit sauce or compote such as strawberry or blueberry will taste delicious.

Cheesy Polenta with Tomato Sauce

SERVES 6
oil to grease
225g (8oz) polenta
4 tbsp freshly chopped herbs, such as oregano, chives and flat-leafed parsley
100g (3½oz) freshly grated Parmesan
salt and ground black pepper
fresh Parmesan shavings to serve

For the tomato and basil sauce
1 tbsp vegetable oil
3 garlic cloves, crushed
500g carton creamed tomatoes or passata
1 bay leaf
sprig of fresh thyme
caster sugar
3 tbsp freshly chopped basil, plus extra to garnish

PREPARATION TIME 15 minutes, plus cooling
COOKING TIME 45 minutes

PER SERVING
246 calories
9g fat (of which 4g saturates)
30g carbohydrate
0.5g salt

TECHNIQUES
see also making polenta (page 242), chopping fresh herbs (page 428)

Get ahead

Complete to the end of step 3. Cover and chill separately for up to two days.
To use Complete the recipe.

1 Lightly oil a 25.5 × 17cm (10 × 6½in) dish. In a large pan, bring 1.1 litres (2 pints) water and ¼ tsp salt to the boil. Sprinkle in the polenta, whisking constantly. Reduce the heat and simmer, stirring frequently, for 10–15 minutes until the mixture leaves the sides of the pan.

2 Stir in the herbs and Parmesan, and season to taste with salt and pepper. Turn into the prepared dish and leave to cool.

3 Next, make the tomato and basil sauce. Heat the oil in a pan and fry the garlic for 30 seconds (do not brown). Add the creamed tomatoes or passata, the bay leaf, thyme and a large pinch of sugar. Season with salt and pepper, bring to the boil and simmer, uncovered, for 5–10 minutes. Remove the bay leaf and thyme sprig, and add the chopped basil.

4 To serve, cut the polenta into pieces and lightly brush with oil. Preheat a griddle and fry for 3–4 minutes on each side, or grill under a preheated grill for 7–8 minutes on each side. Serve with the tomato and basil sauce, fresh Parmesan shavings and chopped basil.

Summer Couscous

SERVES 4

175g (6oz) baby plum tomatoes, halved
2 small aubergines, thickly sliced
2 large yellow peppers, deseeded and roughly chopped
2 red onions, cut into thin wedges
2 fat garlic cloves, crushed
5 tbsp olive oil
250g (9oz) couscous
400g can chopped tomatoes
2 tbsp harissa paste
25g (1oz) toasted pumpkin seeds (optional)
1 large bunch coriander, roughly chopped
salt and ground black pepper
warm flatbreads and Greek yogurt to serve

PREPARATION TIME 10 minutes
COOKING TIME about 20 minutes

PER SERVING
405 calories
21g fat (of which 3g saturates)
49g carbohydrate
0g salt

TECHNIQUES
see also preparing vegetables (pages 170–182), toasting nuts (page 218), chopping herbs (page 428)

1 Preheat the oven to 230°C (210°C fan oven) mark 8. Put the vegetables and garlic into a large roasting tin, drizzle over 3 tbsp oil and season with salt and pepper. Toss to coat. Roast for 20 minutes or until tender.

2 Meanwhile, put the couscous into a separate roasting tin and add 300ml (½ pint) cold water. Leave to soak for 5 minutes. Stir in the tomatoes and harissa, and drizzle with the remaining oil. Pop in the oven next to the vegetables for 4–5 minutes to warm through.

3 Stir the pumpkins seeds, if you like, and the coriander into the couscous and season. Add the vegetables, stir through and serve with warm flatbreads and a dollop of Greek yogurt.

Roasted Tomato Bulgur Salad

SERVES 6
175g (6oz) bulgur wheat
700g (1lb 9oz) cherry tomatoes or baby plum tomatoes
8 tbsp extra-virgin olive oil
a handful each of mint and basil, roughly chopped, plus fresh basil sprigs to garnish
3–4 tbsp balsamic vinegar
1 bunch spring onions, sliced
salt and ground black pepper

PREPARATION TIME 15 minutes, plus 30 minutes soaking
COOKING TIME 15 minutes

PER SERVING
265 calories
16g fat (of which 2g saturates)
29g carbohydrate
0g salt

TECHNIQUES
see also chopping herbs (page 428)

1 Put the bulgur wheat in a bowl and add boiling water to cover by 1cm (½in). Leave to soak for 30 minutes.

2 Preheat the oven to 220°C (200°C fan oven) mark 7. Put the tomatoes in a small roasting tin, drizzle with half the oil and add half the mint. Season with salt and pepper, and roast for 10–15 minutes until beginning to soften.

3 Put the remaining oil and the vinegar into a large bowl. Add the warm pan juices from the roasted tomatoes and the soaked bulgur wheat.

4 Stir in the remaining chopped herbs and the spring onions, and check the seasoning. (You may need a little more vinegar depending on the sweetness of the tomatoes.)

5 Carefully toss in the tomatoes and serve garnished with basil sprigs.

Cook's tip

Bulgur wheat is widely used in Middle Eastern cooking and has a light, nutty flavour and texture. It is available in several different sizes – from coarse to fine.

Simple Bean Salad

SERVES 6

2 tbsp olive oil
2 garlic cloves, sliced
2 × 400g cans flageolet beans, drained and rinsed
extra-virgin olive oil to drizzle
2 tbsp fresh pesto sauce
lemon juice to taste
a small handful of basil leaves, bruised
salt and ground black pepper

PREPARATION TIME 5 minutes, plus 10–15 minutes marinating
COOKING TIME 5 minutes

PER SERVING
208 calories
10g fat (of which 2g saturates)
21g carbohydrate
1.2g salt

TECHNIQUES
see also slicing garlic (page 171), making pesto (page 21)

1 Put the olive oil into a small pan and fry the garlic until golden. Stir in the flageolet beans, then leave to marinate in the oil for 10–15 minutes.

2 When ready to serve, drizzle a little extra-virgin olive oil over the beans until generously coated. Add the pesto sauce and lemon juice to taste and season with salt and pepper, then stir in the basil leaves.

Variations

This uses flageolet beans, but cannelini, haricot or borlotti beans would all work well.

Mushroom and Bean Hotpot

SERVES 6

3 tbsp olive oil
700g (1lb 9oz) chestnut mushrooms, roughly chopped
1 large onion, finely chopped
2 tbsp plain flour
2 tbsp mild curry paste
150ml (¼ pint) dry white wine
400g can chopped tomatoes
2 tbsp sun-dried tomato paste
2 × 400g cans mixed beans, drained and rinsed
3 tbsp mango chutney
3 tbsp roughly chopped fresh coriander and mint

PREPARATION TIME 15 minutes
COOKING TIME 30 minutes

PER SERVING
280 calories
10g fat (of which 1g saturates)
34g carbohydrate
1.3g salt

TECHNIQUES
see also preparing vegetables (pages 170–182), chopping herbs (page 428)

1 Heat the oil in a large pan and fry the mushrooms and onion until the onion is soft and dark golden. Stir in the flour and curry paste, then cook for 1–2 minutes before adding the wine, tomatoes, sun-dried tomato paste and beans.

2 Bring to the boil, then simmer gently for 30 minutes or until most of the liquid has reduced. Stir in the chutney and herbs before serving.

Spicy Pork and Bean Stew

SERVES 4

3 tbsp olive oil
400g (14oz) pork escalopes, cubed
1 red onion, sliced
2 leeks, cut into chunks
2 celery sticks, cut into chunks
1 tbsp harissa paste
1 tbsp tomato purée
400g can cherry tomatoes
300ml (½ pint) hot vegetable or chicken stock
400g can cannellini beans, drained and rinsed
1 marinated red pepper, sliced
salt and ground black pepper
chopped flat-leafed parsley to garnish
Greek yogurt and lemon wedges to serve

PREPARATION TIME 15 minutes
COOKING TIME 50–55 minutes

PER SERVING

373 calories
14g fat (of which 3g saturates)
32g carbohydrate
1.2g salt

TECHNIQUES

see also preparing vegetables (pages 170–182), making stock (page 34)

1 Preheat the oven to 180°C (160°C fan oven) mark 4. Heat 2 tbsp oil in a flameproof casserole and fry the pork in batches until golden. Remove from the pan and set aside.

2 Heat the remaining oil in the pan and fry the onion for 5–10 minutes until softened. Add the leeks and celery, and cook for about 5 minutes. Return the pork to the pan, and add the harissa and tomato purée. Cook for 1–2 minutes, stirring all the time. Add the tomatoes and stock. Season well with salt and pepper. Bring to the boil, then transfer to the oven. Cook for 25 minutes.

3 Add the drained beans and red pepper to the mixture and put back in the oven for 5 minutes to warm through. Garnish with parsley and serve with a dollop of Greek yogurt and lemon wedges for squeezing over.

Cook's tip

For a simple accompaniment, serve with chunks of crusty baguette or wholegrain bread.

Chicken with Chorizo and Beans

SERVES 6

1 tbsp olive oil
12 chicken pieces (6 drumsticks and 6 thighs)
175g (6oz) Spanish chorizo sausage, cubed
1 onion, finely chopped
2 large garlic cloves, crushed
1 tsp mild chilli powder
3 red Romano peppers, cut in half, deseeded and very roughly chopped
400g (14oz) passata
2 tbsp tomato purée
300ml (½ pint) chicken stock
2 × 410g cans butter beans, drained and rinsed
200g (7oz) baby new potatoes, halved
1 small bunch thyme
1 bay leaf
200g (7oz) baby-leaf spinach

PREPARATION TIME 10 minutes
COOKING TIME about 1 hour 10 minutes

PER SERVING
626 calories
22g fat (of which 7g saturates)
42g carbohydrate
3.5g salt

TECHNIQUES
see also jointing chicken (page 110), preparing vegetables (page 170)

1 Preheat the oven to 190°C (170°C fan oven) mark 5. Heat the oil in a large flameproof casserole and brown the chicken all over. Remove from the pan and set aside. Add the chorizo to the casserole and fry for 2–3 minutes until its oil starts to run.

2 Add the onion, garlic and chilli powder, and fry over a low heat for 5 minutes or until soft.

3 Add the peppers and cook for 2–3 minutes until soft. Stir in the passata, tomato purée, stock, beans, potatoes, thyme sprigs and bay leaf. Cover and simmer for 10 minutes.

4 Return the chicken and any juices to the casserole pan. Bring to a simmer, then cover and cook in the oven for 30–35 minutes. If the sauce looks thin, return the casserole to the hob over a medium heat and simmer to reduce until nicely thick.

5 Remove the thyme and bay leaf, and stir in the spinach until it wilts. Serve the casserole immediately.

Aubergine and Lentil Curry

SERVES 4

3 tbsp olive oil
2 aubergines, cut into 2.5cm (1in) chunks
1 onion, chopped
2 tbsp mild curry paste
3 × 400g cans chopped tomatoes
200ml (7fl oz) hot vegetable stock
150g (5oz) red lentils
100g (3½oz) spinach leaves
25g (1oz) fresh coriander, roughly chopped
2 tbsp Greek 0 per cent fat yogurt

PREPARATION TIME 10 minutes
COOKING TIME 40–45 minutes

PER SERVING

335 calories
15g fat (of which 3g saturates)
39g carbohydrate
0.2g salt

TECHNIQUES

see also preparing vegetables (pages 170–182), making stock (page 34), chopping herbs (page 428)

1 Heat 2 tbsp oil in a large pan and fry the aubergine chunks until golden. Remove from the pan and set aside.

2 Heat the remaining oil and fry the onion for 8–10 minutes until soft. Add the curry paste and stir-fry for a further 2 minutes.

3 Add the tomatoes, stock, lentils and aubergine to the pan. Bring to the boil, then reduce the heat to a low simmer, half-cover with a lid and simmer for 25 minutes or according to the lentil pack instructions.

4 At the end of cooking, stir through the spinach, coriander and yogurt. Serve.

Cook's tip

When buying aubergines, choose those that are firm, shiny and blemish-free, with a bright green stem.

Chickpea Curry

SERVES 6

2 tbsp vegetable oil
2 onions, finely sliced
2 garlic cloves, crushed
1 tbsp ground coriander
1 tsp mild chilli powder
1 tbsp black mustard seeds
2 tbsp tamarind paste
2 tbsp sun-dried tomato paste
750g (1lb 10oz) new potatoes, quartered
400g can chopped tomatoes
1 litre (1¾ pints) hot vegetable stock
250g (9oz) green beans, trimmed
2 × 400g cans chickpeas, drained and rinsed
2 tsp garam masala
salt and ground black pepper

PREPARATION TIME 20 minutes
COOKING TIME 40–45 minutes

PER SERVING
251 calories
9g fat (of which 1g saturates)
32g carbohydrate
1.5g salt

TECHNIQUES
see also preparing vegetables (pages 170–182), making vegetable stock (page 34)

1 Heat the oil in a pan and fry the onions for 10–15 minutes until golden – when they have a good colour they will add depth of flavour. Add the garlic, coriander, chilli, mustard seeds, tamarind paste and sun-dried tomato paste. Cook for 1–2 minutes until the aroma from the spices is released.

2 Add the potatoes and toss in the spices for 1–2 minutes. Add the tomatoes and stock, and season with salt and pepper. Cover and bring to the boil. Simmer, half covered, for 20 minutes or until the potatoes are just cooked.

3 Add the beans and chickpeas, and continue to cook for 5 minutes or until the beans are tender and the chickpeas are warmed through. Stir in the garam masala and serve.

Cook's tip

Tamarind paste has a very sharp, sour flavour and is widely used in Asian and South-east Asian cooking. It is available in jars from large supermarkets and Asian stores.

10 PASTA AND NOODLES

Providing plenty of energy and low in fat, Italian pasta and Asian noodles are easy to cook and a real stand-by in most people's kitchens. The easy-to-follow techniques show you how to make your own fresh pasta – rolling, cutting, stuffing and shaping it – as well as simply cooking dried pasta and noodles. The recipe section is packed with delicious ideas from the simplest Fusilli with chilli and tomatoes, Pasta with pesto and beans and Quick and easy carbonara to more complex dishes such as Mixed mushroom cannelloni, Spinach and cheese lasagne, Chilli beef noodle salad and Salmon laksa curry.

Making fresh pasta

Although you can buy very good-quality fresh pasta, it's easy and fun to make at home. And although a pasta machine will make quick work of rolling and cutting, you can do it all by hand.

Making pasta by hand

To make pasta for 3–4 servings, you will need 300–400g (11–14oz) flour (see Cook's tip), 4 medium eggs, beaten, 1 tbsp extra-virgin olive oil.

1 Sieve 300g (11oz) of the flour on to a clean worksurface. Make a well in the centre, then add the eggs and oil. Draw in the flour until the mixture resembles breadcrumbs.

2 When the flour and eggs are combined, knead the dough for 5–10 minutes until dry, smooth and elastic. Wrap in clingfilm and leave to rest for 1 hour.

3 Dust the dough and worksurface with flour and roll out until you can see the worksurface through it.

4 Hang the pasta over a rolling pin and leave to dry until it no longer feels damp, then cut (see opposite).

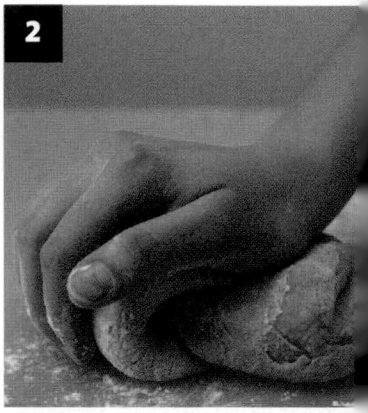

Cook's tips

- For the best results, use Italian '00' strong flour.
- When you're rolling out the pasta, have something ready to hang it on – a clothes drier or a rolling pin is perfect for this.

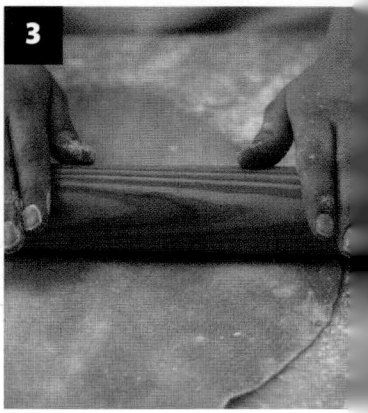

Using a pasta machine

1 Make the pasta dough as above and leave to rest for 1 hour. Cut the dough into small pieces that will fit through the machine's rollers. Dust with flour. Set the rollers as wide apart as they will go, then feed the dough through. Repeat two or three times, folding the dough into three after each roll.

2 Narrow the rollers and repeat. Continue until the pasta is of the right thickness, then cut as required.

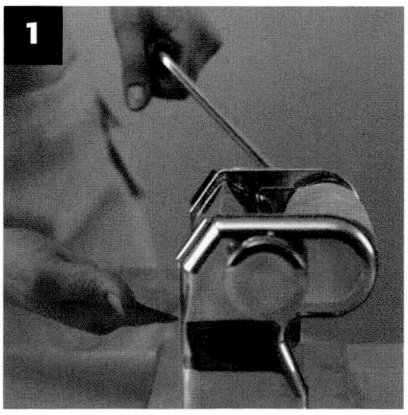

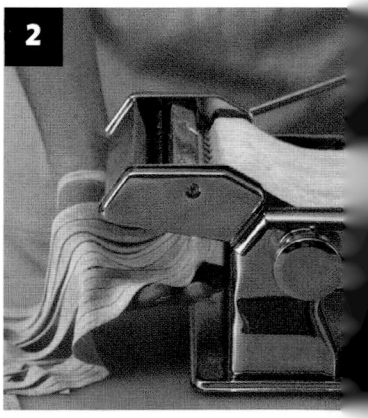

Cutting pasta with a knife

1 Lay the sheet of dough on a floured worksurface and dust lightly with flour. Lift one edge and fold it over, then keep folding to make a long, flat cigar-shape.

2 Cut the dough into strips of the required width. Unfold and leave them to dry on a clean teatowel for a few minutes before cooking.

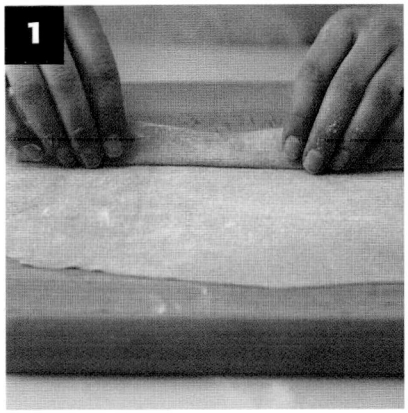

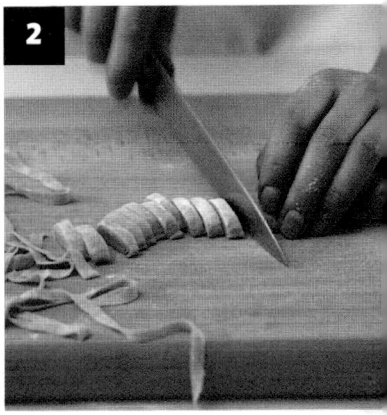

Filling ravioli

1 Lay a sheet of dough over a ravioli tray and gently press into the indentations. Place teaspoonfuls of filling into the hollows. Be particularly careful not to overfill the ravioli as the filling may leak out during cooking.

2 Lay a second sheet of pasta on top of the first.

3 Using a circular cutter, cut a row between the lumps of filling in one direction, then cut in the other direction to make squares. Press the edges to seal the dough.

4 Separate the ravioli, dust very lightly with flour, and cover with a clean teatowel until needed. This will help prevent the ravioli drying out while you are preparing more of them.

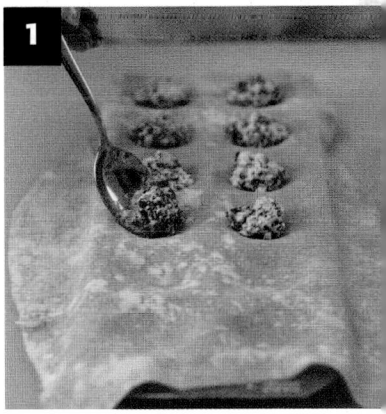

Making shaped pasta

1 Roll out just one sheet of dough at a time. If you roll out more than one sheet at a time, the others might start drying out while you are cutting and filling the first.

2 Trim one edge to make a straight line, then cut a strip from the straight edge to the width of the pasta you want to make. Cut into pieces no bigger than 5cm (2in) square.

3 Place a teaspoonful of filling at the centre of one square, then fold over to make a triangle. Do not overfill.

4 Fold the topmost corner of the triangle down, then fold the other two edges over to leave a hollow space in the middle of the pasta. Press the two folded corners together firmly. Repeat with the remaining pasta and filling.

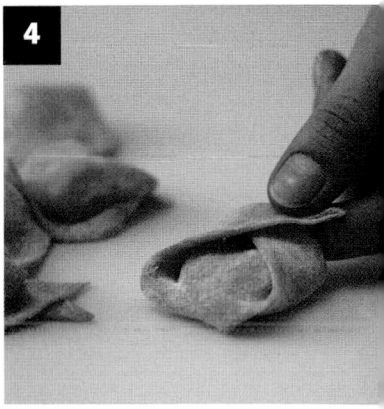

Cooking pasta

This simple task has attracted a number of mistaken ideas, such as adding oil to the water, rinsing the pasta after cooking and adding salt only at a certain point. The basics couldn't be simpler.

Cooking dried pasta

1 Heat the water with about 1 tsp salt per 100g (3½oz) of pasta. Cover the pan to speed up boiling.

2 When the water has reached a rolling boil, put in all the pasta.

3 Stir well for 30 seconds, to keep the pasta from sticking either to itself or the pan. Once boiling, set the timer for 2 minutes less than the recommended cooking time on the pack and cook uncovered.

4 Check the pasta when the timer goes off, then every 60 seconds until it is cooked al dente: tender with a little bite at the centre. Scoop out a cup of cooking water (it may be useful for loosening up a thick sauce).

5 Drain the pasta well in a colander. Transfer to a serving bowl, and toss immediately with your chosen sauce.

Perfect pasta

- Use about 1 litre (1¾ pints) of water per 100g (3½oz) of pasta.
- Rinse the pasta *only* if you are going to cool it for serving as salad, then dry well and toss with oil.
- If a recipe calls for cooking the pasta with the sauce after it has boiled, undercook the pasta slightly when boiling it.

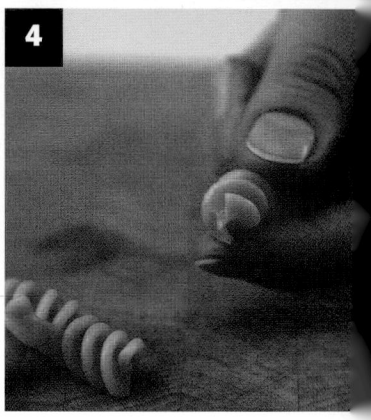

Cooking fresh pasta

Fresh pasta is cooked in the same way as dried, but for a shorter time.

1 Bring the water to the boil.

2 Add the pasta to the boiling water all at once and stir well. Set the timer for 2 minutes and keep testing every 30 seconds until the pasta is cooked al dente: tender but with a little bite in the centre.

Filled pasta

This is the only type of pasta that needs oil in the cooking water – the oil reduces friction, which could tear the wrappers and allow the filling to come out. Use 1 tbsp for a large pan of water.

Cooking Asian-style noodles

Asian wheat or egg noodles are similar to pasta in both what they are made of and how they are cooked, while rice and cellophane noodles require different preparation.

Wheat noodles

These are the sturdiest and most versatile of Asian noodles and are particularly good for stir-fries.

1 Bring a pan of water to the boil and put the noodles in.

2 Agitate the noodles using chopsticks or a fork to separate them (this is especially important if they're dried noodles in a block). This can take a minute or even more.

3 Continue boiling until the noodles are cooked al dente: tender but with a little bite in the centre.

4 Drain well and then rinse in cold water and toss with a little oil if you are not using them immediately.

Perfect noodles

- If you plan to re-cook the noodles after the initial boiling or soaking – for example, in a stir-fry – it's best to undercook them slightly.
- When cooking noodles sold as a block or nest, use a pair of forks or chopsticks to untangle the strands from the moment they go into the water.

Rice noodles

There are different ways of preparing these no-cook noodles, some calling for warm-water soaking and others for hot-water soaking. In both cases, the procedure is the same.

1 Cover the noodles with water and soak until they are al dente: tender but with a little bite in the centre. Drain well and toss with a little oil if you are not using them immediately.

Fusilli with Chilli and Tomatoes

SERVES 4

350g (12oz) fusilli or other short pasta
4 tbsp olive oil
1 large red chilli, deseeded and finely chopped
1 garlic clove, crushed
500g (1lb 2oz) cherry tomatoes
2 tbsp freshly chopped basil
50g (2oz) Parmesan shavings
salt and ground black pepper

PREPARATION TIME 10 minutes
COOKING TIME 15 minutes

PER SERVING

479 calories
17g fat (of which 4g saturates)
69g carbohydrate
0.4g salt

TECHNIQUES

see also cooking pasta (page 262), preparing chillies (page 177), preparing garlic (page 171), chopping herbs (page 428)

1 Cook the pasta in a large pan of boiling salted water according to the pack instructions. Drain.

2 Meanwhile, heat the oil in a large frying pan, add the chilli and garlic, and cook for 30 seconds. Add the tomatoes, season and cook over a high heat for 3 minutes or until the skins begin to split.

3 Add the chopped basil and drained pasta, and toss together. Sprinkle the Parmesan shavings over and serve.

Cook's tip

The easiest way to make Parmesan shavings is by using a vegetable peeler. Hold the piece of cheese in one hand and pare off wafer thin strips of cheese using the peeler.

Pasta with Pesto and Beans

SERVES 4

350g (12oz) trofie or other dried pasta shapes
175g (6oz) fine green beans, roughly chopped
175g (6oz) small salad potatoes, such as Anya, thickly sliced
2 × 125g cartons fresh pesto sauce
freshly grated Parmesan to serve

PREPARATION TIME 5 minutes
COOKING TIME 15 minutes

PER SERVING
688 calories
35g fat (of which 8g saturates)
74g carbohydrate
0.7g salt

TECHNIQUES
see also cooking pasta (page 262), preparing green beans (page 174), making pesto (page 21)

1 Bring a large pan of water to the boil. Add the pasta, bring back to the boil and cook for 5 minutes.

2 Add the beans and potatoes to the pan and continue to boil for a further 7–8 minutes until the potatoes are just tender.

3 Drain the pasta, beans and potatoes in a colander, then tip everything back into the pan and stir in the pesto sauce. Serve scattered with freshly grated Parmesan.

Cook's tip

This combination of pasta, potatoes, green beans and pesto is a speciality of Liguria on the East coast of Italy. Traditionally, it is made with the twisted pasta shape known as trofie.

Penne with Smoked Salmon

SERVES 4
350g (12oz) penne
200ml carton half-fat crème fraîche
140g pack smoked salmon, roughly chopped
20g pack dill, finely chopped
salt and ground black pepper
lemon wedges to serve (optional)

PREPARATION TIME 5 minutes
COOKING TIME 12–15 minutes

PER SERVING
432calories
11g fat (of which 6g saturates)
67g carbohydrate
1.7g salt

TECHNIQUES
see also cooking pasta (page 262), chopping herbs (page 428)

1 Bring a large pan of water to the boil. Add the pasta, bring back to the boil and cook for 12 minutes or according to the instructions on the pack.

2 Meanwhile, put the crème fraîche into a large bowl. Add the smoked salmon and dill. Season well and mix together. Gently stir through the drained penne and serve immediately with lemon wedges, if you like, to squeeze over.

Quick and Easy Carbonara

SERVES 4
350g (12oz) tagliatelle
150g (5oz) smoked bacon, chopped
1 tbsp olive oil
2 large egg yolks
140ml (4½fl oz) double cream
50g (2oz) freshly grated Parmesan
2 tbsp chopped parsley

PREPARATION TIME 5 minutes
COOKING TIME 10 minutes

PER SERVING
671calories
37g fat (of which 18g saturates)
66g carbohydrate
1.8g salt

TECHNIQUES
see also cooking pasta (page 262), separating eggs (page 52), chopping herbs (page 428)

1 Bring a large pan of water to the boil. Add the pasta, bring back to the boil and cook for 4 minutes or according to the instructions on the pack.

2 Meanwhile, fry the bacon in the oil for 4–5 minutes. Add to the drained pasta and keep hot.

3 Put the egg yolks in a bowl, and add the cream. Whisk together. Add to the pasta with the Parmesan and parsley. Toss well.

Chilli Bolognese

SERVES 4

1 tbsp olive oil
1 large onion, finely chopped
½ large red chilli, deseeded and thinly sliced
450g (1lb) minced beef or lamb
125g (4oz) smoked bacon lardons
3 roasted red peppers, drained and finely chopped
400g can chopped tomatoes
125ml (4fl oz) red wine
300g (11oz) spaghetti
25g (1oz) freshly grated Cheddar or Gruyère cheese
2 tbsp freshly chopped flat-leafed parsley (optional)
salt and ground black pepper

PREPARATION TIME 15 minutes
COOKING TIME 26–38 minutes

PER SERVING

761 calories
33g fat (of which 13g saturates)
74g carbohydrate
1.4g salt

TECHNIQUES

see also preparing vegetables (pages 170–182), mincing meat (page 139), cooking pasta (page 262), chopping herbs (page 428)

1 Heat the oil in a large pan over a medium heat. Add the onion and chilli, and fry for 5–10 minutes until soft and golden. Add the beef or lamb and lardons, and stir over the heat for 5–7 minutes until well browned.

2 Stir in the red pepper, tomatoes and wine. Season, bring to the boil, then simmer over a low heat for 15–20 minutes.

3 Meanwhile, cook the spaghetti according to the pack instructions, then drain.

4 Just before serving, stir the grated cheese, parsley, if using, and the sauce into the spaghetti.

Stuffed Pasta Shells

SERVES 6

2 tbsp olive oil
1 large onion, finely chopped
a few sprigs of fresh rosemary or oregano, chopped, plus extra to garnish (optional)
125g (4oz) small flat mushrooms, sliced, or 1 small aubergine, diced
6 plump coarse sausages, skinned
175ml (6fl oz) red wine
300ml (½ pint) passata
4 tbsp sun-dried tomato paste
sugar to taste, if necessary
250g (9oz) large dried pasta shells, such as conchiglioni rigati
140ml (4½fl oz) half-fat single cream (optional)
salad to serve

PREPARATION TIME 15 minutes
COOKING TIME about 1 hour

PER SERVING
358 calories
17g fat (of which 6g saturates)
43g carbohydrate
1.4g salt

TECHNIQUES
see also preparing vegetables (pages 170–182), cooking pasta (page 262)

1 Preheat the oven to 180°C (160°C fan oven) mark 4. Heat the oil in a deep frying pan. Stir in the onion and rosemary or oregano and cook over a gentle heat for 10 minutes or until the onion is soft and golden. Add the mushrooms or aubergine and cook over a medium heat until the vegetables are soft and beginning to brown at the edges. Tip the onion mixture into a bowl.

2 Crumble the sausagemeat into the hot pan and stir over a high heat with a wooden spoon, breaking the meat up as you do so, until browned all over. Reduce the heat slightly and pour in the wine. Leave to bubble and reduce by about half. Return the onion mixture to the pan and add the passata and sun-dried tomato paste. Bubble gently for another 10 minutes. Add a pinch of sugar if the sauce tastes a little sharp.

3 While the sauce is simmering, cook the pasta shells in plenty of boiling water for 10 minutes or until just tender. Drain well and run under the cold tap to cool.

4 Fill the shells with the sauce and put in a shallow ovenproof dish. Drizzle over any extra sauce and the cream, if using, and bake for 30 minutes or until piping hot. Sprinkle with extra herbs if you want to and serve with a big bowl of salad.

Mixed Mushroom Cannelloni

SERVES 4

6 sheets fresh lasagne
3 tbsp olive oil
1 small onion, finely sliced
3 garlic cloves, sliced
20g pack fresh thyme, finely chopped
225g (8oz) chestnut or brown-cap mushrooms, roughly chopped
125g (4oz) flat-cap mushrooms, roughly chopped
2 × 125g goat's cheese logs, with rind
350g carton cheese sauce
salt and ground black pepper

PREPARATION TIME 15 minutes
COOKING TIME 46–55 minutes

PER SERVING

623 calories
37g fat (of which 18g saturates)
47g carbohydrate
1.9g salt

TECHNIQUES

see also preparing vegetables (pages 170–182)

1 Preheat the oven to 180°C (160°C fan oven) mark 4. Cook the lasagne in boiling water until just tender. Drain well and run under cold water to cool. Keep covered with cold water until ready to use.

2 Heat the oil in a large pan and add the onion. Cook over a medium heat for 7–10 minutes until the onion is soft. Add the garlic and fry for 1–2 minutes. Keep a few slices of garlic to one side. Keep a little thyme for sprinkling over later, then add the rest to the pan with the mushrooms. Cook for a further 5 minutes or until the mushrooms are golden brown and there is no excess liquid in the pan. Season, remove from the heat and set aside.

3 Crumble one of the goat's cheese logs into the cooled mushroom mixture and stir together. Drain the lasagne sheets and pat dry with kitchen paper. Spoon 2–3 tbsp of the mushroom mixture along the long edge of each lasagne sheet leaving a 1cm (½in) border. Roll up the pasta sheets and cut each roll in half. Put the pasta in a shallow ovenproof dish and spoon over the cheese sauce. Slice the remaining goat's cheese into thick rounds and arrange across the middle of the pasta rolls. Sprinkle the reserved garlic and thyme on top. Cook in the oven for 30–35 minutes until golden and bubbling.

Cook's tip

Lasagne sheets wrapped around a filling are used here to make cannelloni, but you can also buy dried cannelloni tubes, which can easily be filled using a teaspoon.

Spinach and Cheese Lasagne

SERVES 6

125g (4oz) fresh or frozen leaf spinach, thawed
40g (1½oz) fresh basil, roughly chopped
250g (9oz) ricotta cheese
5 pieces marinated artichokes, drained and chopped
350g carton cheese sauce
175g (6oz) Dolcelatte cheese, roughly diced
9 sheets fresh egg lasagne
25g (1oz) pinenuts, toasted

PREPARATION TIME 30 minutes
COOKING TIME 50–55 minutes

PER SERVING

422 calories
21g fat (of which 10g saturates)
43g carbohydrate
1.6g salt

TECHNIQUES

see also chopping herbs (page 428), toasting nuts (page 218)

1 Preheat the oven to 180°C (160°C fan oven) mark 4. Chop the spinach finely (if it was frozen, squeeze out the excess liquid first). Put in a bowl with the basil, ricotta cheese, artichokes and 6 tbsp cheese sauce. Mix well.

2 Beat the Dolcelatte into the remaining cheese sauce. Layer the ricotta mixture, lasagne, then cheese sauce into a 23 × 23cm (9 × 9in) ovenproof dish. Repeat to use up the remainder.

3 Cook the lasagne for 40 minutes. Sprinkle over the pinenuts and put back in the oven for a further 10–15 minutes until golden.

Cook's tip

Dolcelatte is an Italian cheese and has a much milder flavour than other blue cheeses such as Stilton and Roquefort. It also has a deliciously rich, creamy texture.

Chilli Beef Noodle Salad

SERVES 4

150g (5oz) dried rice noodles
juice of 1 lime
1 lemongrass stalk, outside leaves discarded, finely chopped
1 red chilli, deseeded and chopped
2 tsp finely chopped fresh root ginger
2 tsp caster sugar
2 garlic cloves, crushed
1 tbsp Thai fish sauce
3 tbsp extra-virgin olive oil
50g (2oz) rocket (wild if possible)
125g (4oz) sliced cold roast beef
125g (4oz) sunblush tomatoes, chopped (these are partly dried and not as dehydrated as sun-dried)
salt and ground black pepper

PREPARATION TIME 15 minutes, plus 15 minutes soaking

PER SERVING

290 calories
12g fat (of which 2g saturates)
36g carbohydrate
0.8g salt

TECHNIQUES

see also preparing rice noodles (page 263), preparing chillies (page 177), preparing fresh spices (page 429)

1 Put the noodles in a large bowl and pour over boiling water to cover. Put to one side for 15 minutes.

2 Meanwhile, in a small bowl, whisk together the lime juice, lemongrass, chilli, ginger, sugar, garlic, fish sauce and oil. Season.

3 While they are still warm, drain the noodles well, put in a large bowl and toss with the dressing. Allow to cool.

4 Just before serving, toss the rocket leaves, sliced beef and chopped tomatoes through the noodles.

Salmon Laksa Curry

SERVES 4

1 tbsp olive oil
1 onion, finely sliced
3 tbsp laksa paste
200ml (7fl oz) coconut milk
900ml (1½ pints) hot vegetable stock
200g (7oz) baby corn, halved lengthways
600g (1lb 5oz) piece skinless salmon fillet, cut into 1cm (½in) slices
225g pack baby leaf spinach, washed
250g pack medium rice noodles
salt and ground black pepper

For the garnish

2 spring onions, sliced diagonally
2 tbsp freshly chopped coriander
2 limes, cut into halves

PREPARATION TIME 15 minutes
COOKING TIME 22 minutes

PER SERVING

607 calories
24g fat (of which 4g saturates)
59g carbohydrate
2.6g salt

TECHNIQUES

see also preparing onions (page 170), making coconut milk (page 221), making stock (page 34)

1 Heat the oil in a large pan, then add the onion and fry over a medium heat for 10 minutes, stirring, until golden. Add the laksa paste and cook for 2 minutes.

2 Add the coconut milk, stock and baby corn, and season. Bring to the boil, reduce the heat and simmer for 5 minutes.

3 Add the salmon slices and spinach, stirring to immerse them in the liquid. Cook for 4 minutes or until the fish is opaque to the centre.

4 Meanwhile, put the noodles in a large bowl, pour boiling water over and soak for 30 seconds. Drain, then stir into the curry. Pour into bowls and garnish with the onions, coriander and lime. Serve immediately.

Thai Noodles with Prawns

SERVES 4

4–6 tsp Thai red curry paste
175g (6oz) medium egg noodles (wholewheat if possible)
2 small red onions, chopped
1 lemongrass stalk, trimmed and sliced
1 Thai red chilli, deseeded and finely chopped
300ml sachet low-fat coconut milk
400g (14oz) raw tiger prawns, peeled
4 tbsp freshly chopped coriander
salt and ground black pepper
torn coriander to garnish

PREPARATION TIME 10 minutes
COOKING TIME 5 minutes

PER SERVING

343 calories
11g fat (of which 2g saturates)
40g carbohydrate
1g salt

TECHNIQUES

see also preparing onions (page 170), preparing chillies (page 177), making coconut milk (page 221), preparing prawns (page 83), chopping herbs (page 428)

1 Put 2 litres (3½ pints) boiling water into a large pan, add the curry paste, noodles, onions, lemongrass, chilli and coconut milk. Bring to the boil, and add the prawns and chopped coriander. Simmer for 2–3 minutes until the prawns turn pink. Season to taste.

2 Serve in large bowls sprinkled with the torn coriander.

Cook's tip

Don't overcook this dish, or the noodles will taste soggy and the prawns tough.

Pork and Noodle Stir-fry

SERVES 4

1 tbsp sesame oil
5cm (2in) piece fresh root ginger, peeled and grated
2 tbsp soy sauce
1 tbsp fish sauce
½ red chilli, finely chopped
450g (1lb) stir-fry pork strips
2 red peppers, halved, deseeded and roughly chopped
250g (9oz) baby corn, halved lengthways
200g (7oz) sugarsnap peas, halved
300g (11oz) beansprouts
250g pack rice noodles

PREPARATION TIME 10 minutes
COOKING TIME 7–8 minutes

PER SERVING

509 calories
9g fat (of which 2g saturates)
69g carbohydrate
3.4g salt

TECHNIQUES

see also preparing fresh spices (page 429), preparing vegetables (pages 170–182), sprouting beans (page 243), preparing rice noodles (page 263)

1 Put the oil into a large bowl. Add the ginger, soy sauce, fish sauce, chilli and pork strips. Mix well and leave to marinate for 10 minutes.

2 Heat a large wok until hot. Lift the pork out of the marinade with a slotted spoon and add to the pan. Stir-fry over a high heat for 5 minutes. Add the red peppers, corn, sugarsnap peas, beansprouts and remaining marinade, and stir-fry for a further 2–3 minutes until the pork is cooked.

3 Meanwhile, bring a large pan of water to the boil and cook the noodles according to the pack instructions.

4 Drain the noodles, tip into the wok and toss together, then serve immediately.

11 PASTRY

Crisp pastries, tempting pies and luscious tarts are one of the most enticing treats to come out of the home kitchen. The easy-to-follow techniques section provides an invaluable guide to making all the basic types of pastry, lining tart and pie tins, baking blind, and toping, sealing and finishing pies. There are also essential cook's tips, plus advice on making and using choux and filo pastries. The recipe section utilises these basic skills in a collection of fabulous sweet and savoury pies and tarts including Mushroom baskets, Salmon, dill and potato pastries, Leek and ham galette, Chicken and artichoke pie, Cinnamon custard tart, Pear and cranberry strudel, Berry millefeuilles and Easy pear and toffee tarte tatin.

Making pastry

Shortcrust, sweet pastry, puff and flaky pastry are the four most frequently used pastries and are delicious when home made. Shortcrust is the most simple and quick to prepare.

Shortcrust pastry

Used for tarts and pies.

To make 125g (4oz) pastry, you will need 125g (4oz) plain flour, pinch of salt, 50g (2oz) unsalted butter, cut into small pieces, 1 medium egg yolk.

1 Sift the flour and salt into a bowl and add the butter. Using the fingertips or a pastry cutter, rub or cut the butter into the flour until the mixture resembles fine breadcrumbs.

2 Using a fork, mix in the egg yolk and 1½ tsp water until the mixture holds together; add a little more water if necessary. Knead lightly to form a firm dough.

3 Gather the dough in your hands and lightly knead.

4 Form the pastry into a ball, wrap tightly in clingfilm and chill for at least 1 hour before using. (This allows the pastry to 'relax' and prevents shrinkage when it is baked.)

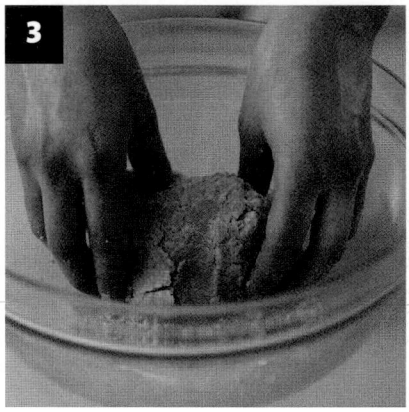

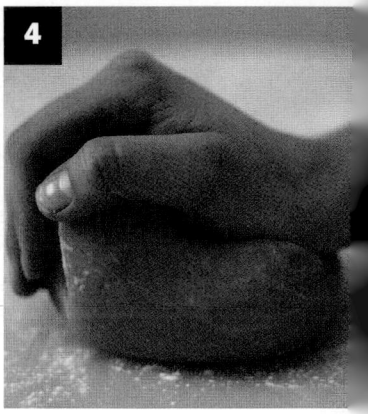

Sweet shortcrust pastry

Used for sweet tarts and pies.
To make 125g (4oz) pastry, you will need 125g (4oz) plain flour, pinch of salt, 50g (2oz) unsalted butter, cut into pieces, 2 medium egg yolks, 50g (2oz) caster sugar.

1 Make as for shortcrust pastry above, adding the sugar with the egg yolks at step 3.

Using a food processor

1 You can make shortcrust or sweet shortcrust using a food processor. Put the dry ingredients into the food processor and pulse quickly to mix. Cut the butter into small pieces and add. Process until the mixture resembles breadcrumbs – do not over-process.

2 Add the egg yolk(s) and a little water if necessary, and pulse until the mixture just comes together. Continue as step 4 for shortcrust.

Puff pastry

If you can, make this a day ahead.

To make 450g (1lb) pastry, you will need 450g (1lb) strong white bread flour, pinch of salt, 450g (1lb) butter, chilled, 1 tbsp lemon juice.

1 Sift the flour and salt into a bowl. Cut dice 50g (2oz) butter. Flatten the rest into a 2cm (¾in) thick slab. Rub the diced butter into the flour. Using a knife, stir in the lemon juice and about 300ml (½ pint) cold water to make a soft elastic dough. Knead on a lightly floured surface until smooth. Cut a cross through half the depth.

2 Open out the 'flaps'. Roll out the dough, keeping the centre four times as thick as the flaps.

3 Put the slab of butter in the centre and fold the flaps over it. Gently roll out to make a rectangle measuring 40.5 × 20.5cm (16 × 8in).

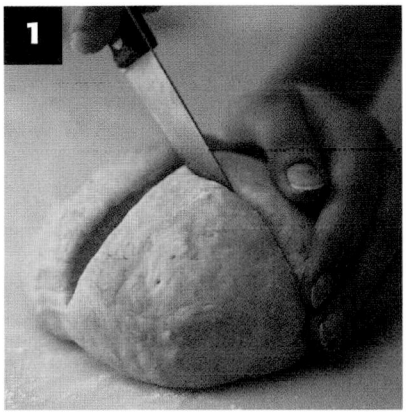

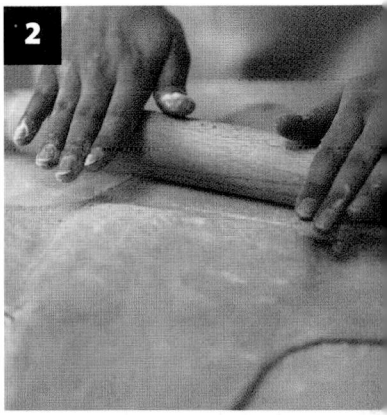

4 Mark off three equal sections from top to bottom. Fold the bottom third of the pastry up over the middle and the top third down. Wrap in clingfilm and chill for 30 minutes (or freeze 5–10 minutes).

5 Repeat the rolling, folding, resting and turning four more times, ensuring the folded edges are to the sides each time. Chill for at least 30 minutes before baking.

Rough puff pastry

Rough puff doesn't rise as much as puff pastry but is quicker to make. To make 225g (8oz), you will need 225g (8oz) plain flour, pinch of salt, 175g (6oz) butter, 1 tsp lemon juice.

1 Sift the flour and salt into a bowl. Cut the butter into 2cm (¾in) cubes and add to the flour. Mix lightly to coat the butter with flour. Using a knife, stir in the lemon juice and 100ml (3½fl oz) water to make a soft elastic dough.

2 Turn out the dough on to a lightly floured worksurface and knead until smooth. Roll out to a rectangle 30.5 × 10cm (12 × 4in). Mark off three equal sections from top to bottom. Fold the bottom third over the middle and the top third down. Press the edges with a rolling pin to seal. Wrap in clingfilm and chill for 30 minutes (or freeze for 5–10 minutes).

3 Repeat the rolling, folding, resting and turning five more times, ensuring the folded edges are to the sides. Chill for 30 minutes before baking.

Quantities

Tart tins vary in depth, which affects the quantity of pastry needed. The following quantities are approximate.

Tart tin size	Pastry
18cm (7in)	125g (4oz)
20cm (9in)	175g (6oz)
23cm (9in)	200g (7oz)
25cm (10in)	225g (8oz)

Using pastry

A light touch and a little care with rolling and lifting your prepared dough will ensure your pastry case or pie crust is crisp and perfect. It's worth taking your time for the best results.

Lining tart and pie tins

1 Working carefully, roll out chilled dough on a floured worksurface to make a sheet at least 5cm (2in) larger than the tart tin or pie dish. Roll the dough on to the rolling pin, then unroll it on to the tin, covering it completely with an even overhang all round. Don't stretch the dough.

2 Lift the hanging dough with one hand while you press it gently but firmly into the base and sides of the tin. Don't stretch the dough while you're pressing it down.

3 For a tart case, roll the rolling pin over the tin and remove the excess dough for later use. For a pie dish ensure the pastry covers the lip of the dish.

4 Push the dough into and up the sides of the tin or dish, so that the dough rises a little over the edge.

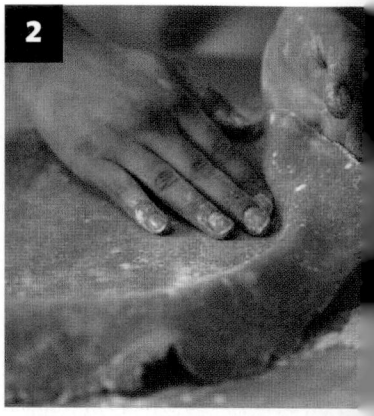

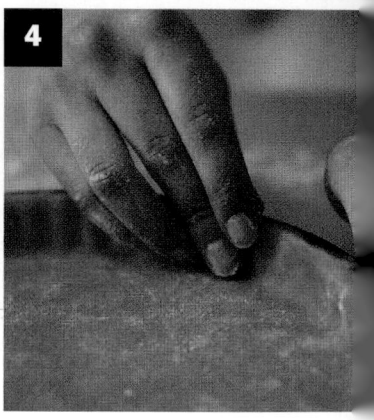

Baking blind

Cooking the pastry before filling gives a crisp result.

1 Preheat the oven according to the recipe. Prick the pastry base with a fork. Cover with foil or greaseproof paper 8cm (3¼in) larger than the tin.

2 Spread baking beans on top. Bake for 15 minutes. Remove the foil or paper and beans and bake for 5–10 minutes until light golden.

Topping

Covered pies need a lid of equal thickness to the base.

1 Roll out the pastry on a floured worksurface to about 2.5cm (1in) larger than the baking tin or dish. Roll on to the rolling pin, then unroll over the pie with an even overhang.

2 Using a small knife, cut off the overhang just outside the rim.

Sealing

1 Using your thumb and index finger, pinch the base and top of the pastry dough all the way round the rim. You don't need to squeeze hard, just firmly enough to stick them together. If the pie has no base, just press the top down on the rim of the tin or dish.

2 Use a fork to make decorative fluting marks on the rim.

Finishing

1 If you want to make decorations for the pie using leftover pastry, cut them out using pastry cutters and put them in place, using a little water to stick them to the pastry.

2 Brush the top of the pastry with beaten egg if you wish. Cut two slits in the top of the pie using a small, sharp knife to let the steam escape during baking.

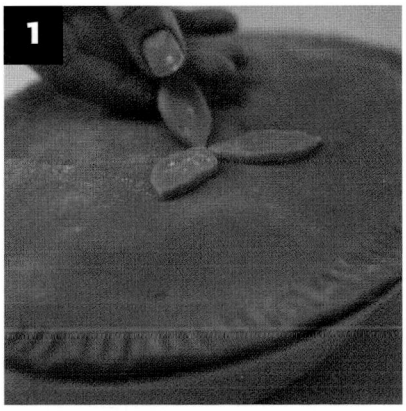

Using choux

This soft pastry is usually spooned or piped and is excellent for making cream-filled buns, profiteroles and savouries. It contains a lot of water so it puffs up beautifully and is wonderfully light and airy.

Choux buns

To make eight choux buns, you will need 65g (2½oz) plain flour, 50g (2oz) butter, cubed, 150ml (¼ pint) sparkling water, 1 tbsp golden caster sugar, 2 medium eggs, beaten.

1 Sift the flour on to a sheet of greaseproof paper. Melt the butter, water and sugar in a heavy-based pan, and bring to the boil. Turn off the heat and tip in the flour all at once.

2 Beat thoroughly with a wooden spoon until the mixture forms a smooth ball in the centre of the pan. Turn the ball out into a bowl and leave to cool for 15 minutes. Preheat the oven to 220°C (190°C fan oven) mark 7.

3 Gradually beat in the eggs, adding a little at a time, and whisk until the mixture is shiny.

4 Sprinkle water on to a non-stick baking sheet and put the mixture on it in eight large spoonfuls. Make sure they aren't too close together. Bake for 30 minutes until the buns are risen and golden-brown. Turn off the oven.

5 Pierce a small hole in each bun so that air can escape, then return the sheet to the oven for 15 minutes. Cool on a wire rack.

Perfect choux

- Before you start, have all the ingredients carefully measured and in place.
- Tip in all the flour at once, then leave the mixture to cool before beating in the eggs gradually.
- Use a dampened baking sheet (the steam will help the pastry to rise), and don't open the oven door for the first 20 minutes of baking, as the cold air will make the pastry sink.

Using filo

Making filo pastry is time-consuming, but ready-made filo is an excellent alternative. The delicate sheets of pastry are usually brushed with butter, then layered and filled to create crisp, golden treats.

Baklava

To serve six to eight, you will need 175g (6oz) shelled unsalted pistachio nuts, 125g (4oz) pinenuts, 1 tsp ground cinnamon, ½ tsp ground cloves, pinch of freshly grated nutmeg, 2 tbsp caster sugar, 225g (8oz) filo pastry, 75g (3oz) unsalted butter, melted. For the syrup: 2 cardamom pods, bruised, grated zest and juice of ½ lemon, 225g (8oz) clear honey, 2 tbsp rosewater (optional).

1 Whiz the nuts and spices in a food processor until coarsely ground. Add the sugar. Preheat oven to 170°C (150°C fan oven) mark 3.

2 Grease an 18 × 25.5cm (7 × 10in) baking tin. Brush a sheet of filo with butter and press it into the tin.

3 Repeat with half the filo sheets.

4 Scatter nut mixture on top of the pastry sheets, then top with more buttered filo until all used.

5 Cut the pastry in a diamond pattern, cutting down to the base of the tin. Drizzle over any remaining butter. Bake for 30 minutes. Increase the heat to 220°C (200°C fan oven) mark 7 and bake for 15 minutes until the top is crisp and golden.

6 Meanwhile, put the cardamom, lemon and honey in a pan and add 150ml (¼ pint) water. Bring to the boil, simmer for 5 minutes. Strain and stir in the rosewater, if using. Drizzle with half the syrup. Leave to cool, cut into diamonds and drizzle over the rest.

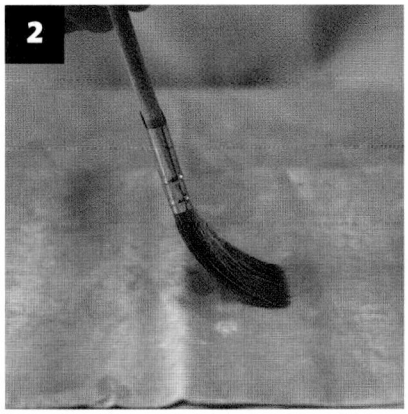

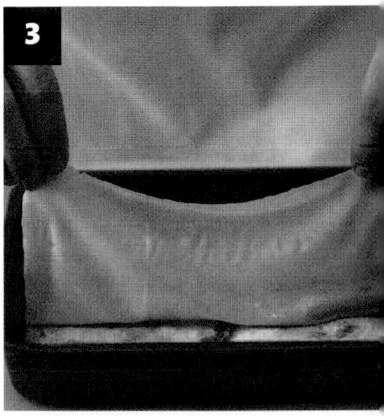

Cook's tips

- Filo pastry is often sold frozen: if you plan to put it into the freezer at home, get it home quickly so that it doesn't defrost.
- Defrost it completely before you start to work with it, otherwise it can crack or crumble. The best way to do this is to leave it to thaw overnight in the refrigerator.
- As you work, cover the unused sheets with a clean damp teatowel to prevent them from drying out.

Camembert and Tomato Tarts

SERVES 4
½ × 375g pack ready-rolled puff pastry
2 tbsp black olive tapenade
200g (7oz) cherry tomatoes, halved
75g (3oz) Camembert, sliced
crisp green salad to serve

PREPARATION TIME 10 minutes
COOKING TIME 15–20 minutes

PER SERVING
253 calories
17g fat (of which 4g saturates)
19g carbohydrate
1.1g salt

TECHNIQUES
see also making puff pastry (page 279)

1 Preheat the oven to 220°C (200°C fan oven) mark 7. Cut the puff pastry into four pieces. Put on to a baking sheet and cook for 8–10 minutes until risen. Press down the centres of the tarts slightly with the back of a fish slice, then spread with the tapenade.

2 Top with the tomatoes and sliced Camembert. Put back into the oven for a further 7–8 minutes. Serve with a crisp green salad.

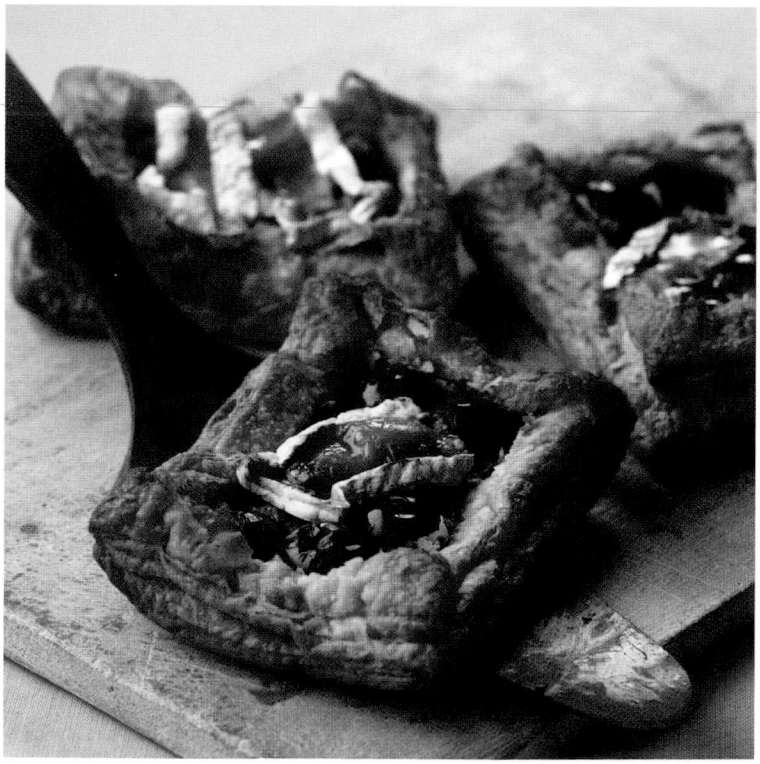

Cook's tip

Tapenade is a strongly flavoured paste made from puréed olives, capers, anchovies, garlic and olive oil and is a speciality of Provence in southern France.

Mushroom Baskets

SERVES 6
250g (9oz) plain flour, plus extra to dust
150g (5oz) chilled butter, cubed
1 large egg

For the filling
15g (½oz) dried mushrooms
50g (2oz) butter
225g (8oz) onion, finely chopped
450g (1lb) mixed mushrooms, sliced
1 garlic clove, crushed
300ml (½ pint) medium-dry sherry
285ml (9½fl oz) double cream
salt and ground black pepper
fresh thyme sprigs to garnish

PREPARATION TIME 40 minutes, plus 50 minutes chilling
COOKING TIME 50 minutes

PER SERVING
659calories
48g fat (of which 29g saturates)
37g carbohydrate
0.5g salt

TECHNIQUES
see also making pastry (pages 278–279), using dried mushrooms (page 175), preparing vegetables (pages 170–182)

Freezing tip

The baskets can be frozen at the end of step 1.
To use Thaw and then complete the recipe.

1 To make the pastry, whiz the flour and butter in a food processor until the mixture resembles fine breadcrumbs. Add the egg and pulse (or stir in) until the mixture comes together. Knead lightly on a floured surface and shape into six balls. Wrap and chill for 30 minutes. Roll out the pastry on a lightly floured worksurface and line six loose-based tart cases 8.5cm (3¼in) across the base and 3cm (1¼in) high. Prick the bases and chill for 20 minutes. Meanwhile, preheat the oven to 200°C (180°C fan oven) mark 6. Line the pastry bases with greaseproof paper and baking beans, and bake for 10 minutes. Remove the paper and beans and bake for 5 minutes or until cooked. Reduce the oven temperature to 180°C (160°C fan oven) mark 4.

2 To make the filling, soak the dried mushrooms in 300ml (½ pint) boiling water for 10 minutes. Heat the butter in a pan, add the onion and cook for 10 minutes. Add the fresh mushrooms and garlic, cook for 5 minutes, remove from the pan and set aside. Put the dried mushrooms and their liquid in the pan with the sherry. Bring to the boil, bubble for 10 minutes, add the cream and cook for 5 minutes or until syrupy. To serve, warm the pastry in the oven for 5 minutes. Add the reserved mushrooms to the sauce, season and heat through. Pour into the cases and garnish with thyme, then serve with salad.

Goat's Cheese Parcels

SERVES 6, MAKES 12

125g (4oz) fresh spinach leaves
2 tbsp sunflower oil
1 onion, finely chopped
1 large garlic clove, chopped
250g (9oz) soft goat's cheese
270g pack filo pastry, thawed if frozen
50g (2oz) butter, melted
sesame seeds to sprinkle
salt and ground black pepper
rocket to garnish

PREPARATION TIME 45 minutes, plus 10 minutes cooling and 20 minutes chilling
COOKING TIME 10 minutes

PER SERVING
345 calories
22g fat (of which 12g saturates)
26g carbohydrate
0.8g salt

TECHNIQUES
see also preparing vegetables (pages 170–182)

1 Plunge the spinach into a pan of boiling water, bring back to the boil, bubble for 1 minute then drain and run it under very cold water. Once cold, squeeze out all the excess liquid and chop finely. Put to one side.

2 Heat the oil in a pan, add the onion and garlic, and cook until translucent, then allow to cool. Combine the spinach, onion mixture and goat's cheese in a bowl, and season generously.

3 Cut the filo pastry into twenty-four 12.5cm (5in) squares. Brush one square with melted butter, cover with a second square and brush with more melted butter. Put to one side and cover with a damp teatowel to prevent drying out. Repeat with the remaining squares, to make 12 sets.

4 Put a dessertspoonful of the filling in the centre of each square and join up the corners to form a square parcel. Brush the pastry with a little more butter, sprinkle with sesame seeds and chill for 20 minutes. Meanwhile, preheat the oven to 220°C (200°C fan oven) mark 7.

5 Bake for about 5 minutes or until the pastry is crisp and brown at the edges. Arrange on serving plates and garnish with rocket.

Cook's tip

Be sure to keep the filo pastry covered with a damp cloth while making the pastries to prevent it drying out and cracking while you work.

Salmon, Dill and Potato Pastries

SERVES 6, MAKES 12

1 potato, about 125g (4oz), peeled and cut into 5mm (¼in) cubes
285ml (9½fl oz) single cream
2 tbsp freshly chopped dill
250g (9oz) skinned salmon fillet, cut into 5mm (¼in) cubes
plain flour to dust
680g pack puff pastry, thawed if frozen
1 medium egg, beaten
salt and ground black pepper

PREPARATION TIME 40 minutes, plus 20 minutes cooling and 10 minutes chilling
COOKING TIME 25 minutes

PER SERVING
616 calories
42g fat (of which 7g saturates)
47g carbohydrate
1g salt

TECHNIQUES
see also chopping herbs (page 428), skinning fish (page 77), making puff pastry (page 279)

1 Put the potato in a pan with the cream, bring to the boil and simmer gently for 5 minutes or until the potato is almost tender. Cool, then add the dill and salmon, and season well.

2 Roll out the pastry on a lightly floured surface to 3mm (⅛in) thick, then stamp out twelve rounds 7.5cm (3in) in diameter and twelve rounds 9.5cm (3¾in) in diameter.

3 Put the smaller rounds on a baking sheet, brush the edges with cold water and spoon about 2 tbsp of the salmon mixture into the centre. Top with the larger rounds, seal and crimp the edges, then cut a steam hole in the centre. Chill for 10 minutes.

4 Put a baking tray in the oven and preheat to 220°C (200°C fan oven) mark 7. Brush the pastries with the beaten egg and put on to the hot baking tray. Cook for 20 minutes or until crisp and brown. Serve warm.

Freezing tip

After baking, cool, pack and freeze.
To use Thaw at cool room temperature for 2–3 hours and warm at 200°C (180°C fan oven) mark 6 for 5 minutes.

Winter Roasted Vegetable Tart

SERVES 4

250g (9oz) ready-rolled shortcrust pastry, removed from refrigerator 5 minutes before using
1 small red onion, cut into six wedges
1 raw baby beetroot, peeled and thickly sliced
1 baby aubergine, quartered
1 small red apple, quartered, cored and cut into chunky slices
1 garlic clove, crushed
juice of ½ lemon
1 tsp freshly chopped thyme
1 tbsp olive oil
125g (4oz) cranberry and red onion marmalade (see below)
25g (1oz) chestnut mushrooms, halved
50g (2oz) chestnuts, cooked and peeled
1 tbsp redcurrant jelly, warmed
salt and ground black pepper

For the savoury marmalade

2 tbsp olive oil
500g (1lb 2oz) red onions, sliced
juice of 1 orange
1 tbsp pickling spice
150g (5oz) dark muscovado sugar
150ml (¼ pint) ruby port
450g (1lb) fresh cranberries

PREPARATION TIME for the marmalade, 10 minutes, plus chilling; for the tart, 20 minutes
COOKING TIME for the marmalade, 1 hour 5 minutes; for the tart, 1 hour

PER SERVING

553calories
27g fat (of which 7g saturates)
68g carbohydrate
0.8g salt

TECHNIQUES

see also preparing chestnuts (page 220), lining tart tins (page 280)

1 To make the marmalade, heat the oil in a pan and gently fry the onions for 5 minutes. Add the orange juice, spice, sugar and port, and simmer gently for 40 minutes. Add the cranberries and cook over a medium heat for 20 minutes. Cool and chill until required.

2 Preheat the oven to 200°C (180°C fan oven) mark 6. Place an 11.5 × 20.5cm (4½ × 8in) loose-based tart tin on a baking sheet. Line the tin with the pastry, prick the base, line with baking parchment and fill with baking beans. Bake for 15 minutes, remove the paper and beans and cook for 5 minutes until golden. Cool and remove from the tin.

3 For the filling, put the onion, beetroot, aubergine, apple and garlic into a roasting tin. Squeeze over the lemon juice, scatter over the thyme and drizzle with oil, then roast for 20 minutes. Put in a bowl, then cool.

4 Preheat the oven to 200°C (180°C fan oven) mark 6. Put the cooked pastry case on a baking sheet. Spoon the 125g (4oz) marmalade over the base. (Leftover marmalade can be stored in the refrigerator for up to two days.) Arrange the roasted vegetables and mushrooms on top of the tart. Chop the chestnuts and sprinkle them on top, then season. Brush warmed redcurrant jelly over the vegetables and cook for 20 minutes. Serve hot.

Leek and Ham Galette

SERVES 4

25g (1oz) butter, plus extra to grease
350g (12oz) medium leeks, trimmed and cut into 2cm (¾in) thick slices
25g (1oz) plain flour, plus extra to dust
50ml (2fl oz) milk
1 tbsp freshly chopped marjoram
50g (2oz) Beaufort or Gruyère cheese, cubed, plus 2 tbsp, grated
150g pack good-quality cooked sliced ham, thickly shredded
225g pack chilled puff pastry
½ medium egg, beaten with a pinch of salt
salt and ground black pepper

PREPARATION TIME 30 minutes, plus 20 minutes cooling
COOKING TIME 40 minutes

PER SERVING
395 calories
25g fat (of which 6g saturates)
29g carbohydrate
2g salt

Freezing tip

At step 3, line 8, cover in clingfilm and freeze on the baking tray. When firm, remove from the baking tray. Wrap in baking parchment, and then in clingfilm. **To use** Thaw for 3 hours at cool room temperature on baking parchment. Put a flat baking tray in the oven to preheat to 220°C (200°C fan oven) mark 7 and complete step 3 of the recipe. Put the galette on the hot tray (this will keep the pastry base crisp) and bake for 40 minutes.

1 Preheat the oven to 220°C (200°C fan oven) mark 7. Grease a baking sheet. Cook the leeks in boiling salted water for 2–3 minutes until just beginning to soften. Drain, keeping the cooking liquid to one side. Plunge the leeks into cold water, drain and dry well on kitchen paper.

2 Melt the butter in a pan, take off the heat and mix in the flour to form a smooth paste. Mix in 225ml (8fl oz) leek water and the milk, stirring until smooth. Bring to the boil, simmer for 1–2 minutes, cover and cool for 20 minutes or until cold. Add the marjoram, leeks, cubed cheese and ham, and season.

3 Roll out the pastry on a lightly floured surface to a 30.5 × 33cm (12 × 13in) rectangle. Cut into two rectangles, one 15 × 30.5cm (6 × 12in) and the other 18 × 30.5cm (7 × 12in). Put the smaller piece on to the baking sheet. Spoon on the ham mixture, leaving a 2cm (¾in) pastry border all the way around. Brush the border with beaten egg. Cover the filling with the larger pastry rectangle and press the edges together. Cut slashes in the top of the pastry to prevent the filling seeping out. Crimp the edges of the pastry to seal, then cover and freeze for 20 minutes or until firm. Remove from the freezer, brush again with the beaten egg, make a good-sized steam hole in the centre and sprinkle with the grated cheese. Bake for 20–30 minutes until brown and crisp.

Chicken and Artichoke Pie

SERVES 4

3 skinless chicken breasts, about 350g (12oz)
150ml (¼ pint) dry white wine
225g (8oz) reduced-fat soft cheese with garlic and herbs
400g can artichoke hearts in water
4 sheets filo pastry, about 40g (1½oz), thawed if frozen
olive oil
1 tsp sesame seeds
salt and ground black pepper
fresh thyme to garnish (optional)

PREPARATION TIME 20 minutes
COOKING TIME 45 minutes

PER SERVING

241calories
9g fat (of which 5g saturates)
7g carbohydrate
0.2g salt

TECHNIQUES

see also using filo pastry (page 283)

1 Preheat the oven to 200°C (180°C fan oven) mark 6. Put the chicken and wine in a pan and bring to the boil, then cover and simmer for 10 minutes. Set the chicken aside. Add the cheese to the wine and mix until smooth. Bring to the boil, then simmer until thickened.

2 Cut the chicken into bite-sized pieces. Drain and quarter the artichokes, and add to the sauce with the chicken. Season and mix well.

3 Put the mixture in a shallow ovenproof dish. Brush the pastry lightly with oil, scrunch slightly and put on top of the chicken. Sprinkle with sesame seeds.

4 Cook for 30–35 minutes until crisp. Serve garnished with thyme, if you like.

Variation

Replace the artichoke hearts with 225g (8oz) brown-cap mushrooms, cooked in a little water with seasoning and lemon juice.

Cinnamon Custard Tart

SERVES 8

250g (9oz) plain flour, plus extra to dust
100g (3½oz) butter
100g (3½oz) icing sugar
4 large eggs
450ml (¾ pint) milk
285ml (9½fl oz) double cream
1 vanilla pod, split
1 cinnamon stick, crumbled
275g (10oz) caster sugar
1 mango, 1 small pineapple, 2 clementines and 125g (4oz) kumquats to serve

PREPARATION TIME 50 minutes, plus 1 hour chilling and 20–30 minutes standing
COOKING TIME 1½ hours

PER SERVING
664 calories
34g fat (of which 20g saturates)
87g carbohydrate
0.4g salt

1 Pulse the flour, butter and icing sugar in a food processor until the mixture forms fine crumbs. (Alternatively, rub the fat into the flour by hand or using a pastry cutter, then stir in the icing sugar.) Beat one egg and add to the flour mixture with 1 tbsp water. Process (or stir) until the crumbs make a dough. Wrap in clingfilm and chill for 30 minutes. Use the pastry to line a 23cm (9in) loose-based tart tin. Prick the base and line with greaseproof paper and baking beans. Chill for 30 minutes. Preheat the oven to 200°C (180°C fan oven) mark 6. Put on a baking tray and bake for 15 minutes. Remove the paper and beans and cook for 10–15 minutes until the base is cooked. Lightly whisk the remaining eggs. Use 1 tbsp egg to brush over the pastry. Return to the oven for 2 minutes. Reduce the temperature to 150°C (130°C fan oven) mark 2.

2 Bring the milk, cream, vanilla and cinnamon slowly to the boil. Leave to infuse for 20 minutes. Mix the whisked eggs with 150g (5oz) caster sugar. Stir the milk into the egg mixture, strain into a jug and pour into the tart. Cook for 40–50 minutes until the filling has just set. Turn the oven off and leave the tart in the oven for 15 minutes. Remove and cool in the tin for 20–30 minutes. Transfer to a wire rack to cool.

3 Make the caramelised fruit (see Finishing touches). Cut the tart into portions and spoon the fruit over the top to serve.

Finishing touches

To decorate, cut the fruits into thick slices and arrange on two non-stick baking sheets. Put the remaining caster sugar in a small, heavy-based pan. Cook over a low heat until the sugar begins to dissolve, then turn up the heat and cook to a pale caramel. Cool a little and drizzle over the fruit. Allow to set. The caramel will stay brittle for 1–2 hours. Cut the tart into portions and spoon the fruit over the top just before serving.

Pear and Cranberry Strudel

SERVES 8

zest and juice of 1 lemon
25g (1oz) golden caster sugar
1 tbsp fresh white breadcrumbs
1 tsp ground cinnamon
125g (4oz) fresh cranberries
550g (1¼lb) Williams or Comice pears, cored and sliced
50g (2oz) Brazil nuts, chopped and toasted
7 sheets filo pastry, thawed if frozen
75g (3oz) butter, melted
icing sugar to dust
thick cream to serve

PREPARATION TIME 20 minutes
COOKING TIME 40–45 minutes

PER SERVING

190 calories
12g fat (of which 6g saturates)
19g carbohydrate
0.2g salt

TECHNIQUES

see also zesting citrus fruits (page 207), making breadcrumbs (page 308), preparing pears (page 206), preparing nuts (page 218)

1 Preheat the oven to 190°C (170°C fan oven) mark 5. Grease a large baking sheet. Mix the lemon zest with 1 tbsp caster sugar, the breadcrumbs and cinnamon, and put to one side. Put six cranberries to one side, then toss the rest with the pears, lemon juice and nuts. Mix in the breadcrumb mixture.

2 Lay a clean teatowel on a board and put three sheets of filo pastry on it, each overlapping the other by 12.5cm (5in) to make a rectangle measuring 56 × 48cm (22 × 19in). Brush with melted butter, then put three more sheets on top and brush again.

3 Spoon the pear mixture along the nearest, longest length and roll up. Trim the edges, then carefully lift on to the prepared baking sheet so that the seam is underneath. Brush the remaining sheet of filo pastry with butter, fold in half and cut out six holly leaves. Arrange three each together on the log and brush with melted butter. Sprinkle the strudel with the remaining caster sugar and bake for 40–45 minutes, covering with foil if the top browns too quickly.

4 Take out of the oven, arrange the reserved cranberries on the holly leaves and dust the strudel heavily with icing sugar. Serve at once with a dollop of thick cream.

Berry Millefeuilles

SERVES 8
550g (1¼lb) puff pastry
3 tbsp caster sugar
50g (2oz) hazelnuts, toasted and chopped
450g (1lb) strawberries, hulled
50g (2oz) icing sugar, sifted
1 tsp lemon juice

For the custard
1 vanilla pod, split
450ml (¾ pint) milk
4 large egg yolks
125g (4oz) caster sugar
50g (2oz) plain flour, sifted
225g (8oz) raspberries
1 tbsp lemon juice
285ml (9½fl oz) double cream
125g (4oz) icing sugar, sifted

PREPARATION TIME 40 minutes, plus 4 hours chilling and standing
COOKING TIME 40 minutes

PER SERVING
828 calories
57g fat (of which 23g saturates)
65g carbohydrate
1.4g salt

Get ahead

To make the custard, scrape the vanilla seeds into a pan. Add the pod and milk, bring to the boil, then set aside for 30 minutes. Whisk the yolks and 75g (3oz) sugar until pale. Mix in the flour. Strain in quarter of the milk, mix, then stir in the remainder. Return to the pan and bring to the boil over a gentle heat, stirring. Pour into a bowl, cover with clingfilm, cool and chill for 3–4 hours. Sprinkle the raspberries with the remaining sugar and lemon juice.

1 First make the custard (see Getting ahead).

2 Cut the pastry into three and roll each piece on a lightly floured surface into an 18 × 35.5cm (7 × 14in) rectangle. Put each rectangle on a baking sheet, prick and chill for 30 minutes. Preheat the oven to 220°C (200°C fan oven) mark 7. Bake for 10 minutes, then turn over and cook for another 3 minutes. Sprinkle each sheet with 1 tbsp sugar and one-third of the nuts. Return to the oven and cook for 8 minutes until the sugar melts. Cool slightly, then transfer to wire racks to cool.

3 Beat the custard until smooth; whip the cream until thick, then fold into the custard with the raspberries and juices. Cover and chill. Put the icing sugar in a small bowl, then stir in 2 tbsp water. Trim each pastry sheet to 15 × 30.5cm (6 × 12in), then drizzle with the icing. Leave for 15 minutes.

4 Meanwhile, blend the strawberries with the icing sugar and lemon juice, then sieve and chill. Spoon half the custard mixture over a sheet of pastry. Put another sheet on top and spoon over the remaining custard. Top with the final sheet and press down lightly. Leave for 30 minutes before slicing. Serve with the strawberry sauce.

Caramelised Orange Tart

SERVES 8
225g (8oz) plain flour, plus extra to dust
pinch of salt
125g (4oz) butter, diced
2 tbsp golden icing sugar
1 medium egg yolk, beaten

For the filling
juice of 1 lemon
juice of 1 orange
zest of 2 oranges
75g (3oz) butter
225g (8oz) golden granulated sugar
3 medium eggs, beaten
75g (3oz) ground almonds
2 tbsp orange liqueur
a few drops of orange food colouring (optional)

To decorate
100g (3½oz) golden caster sugar
pared zest of 1 orange, cut into slivers

PREPARATION TIME 15 minutes, plus 10 minutes chilling
COOKING TIME 45 minutes

PER SERVING
556 calories
29g fat (of which 14g saturates)
70g carbohydrate
0.5g salt

TECHNIQUES
see also separating eggs (page 52), zesting citrus fruits (page 207)

1 Pulse the flour, salt, butter and icing sugar in a food processor until the mixture forms fine crumbs. (Alternatively, rub the fat into the flour by hand or using a pastry cutter, then stir in the icing sugar.) Beat the egg yolk and 2 tbsp cold water and add to the flour mixture. Process (or stir) until the crumbs make a dough. Knead lightly, wrap and chill.

2 To make the filling, put the juices, orange zest, butter, sugar and eggs in a heavy-based pan and heat gently, stirring, until thickened. Stir in the almonds, liqueur and food colouring, if using. Set aside.

3 Preheat the oven to 200°C (180°C fan oven) mark 6. Roll out the dough on a floured surface and use to line a 23cm (9in) tin. Prick the base with a fork. Cover and chill for 10 minutes. Line the pastry case with greaseproof paper and fill with baking beans. Bake blind for 15 minutes; remove the paper and beans and bake for 5 minutes. Reduce the oven temperature to 180°C (160°C fan oven) mark 4. Pour the filling into the pastry case and bake for 20 minutes or until just firm. Cool.

4 To decorate, dissolve 50g (2oz) sugar in a pan with 300ml (½ pint) water. Add the orange zest. Simmer for 10–15 minutes until the liquid has reduced and the peel is tender. Drain. Sprinkle the rest of the sugar over the tart. Caramelise under the grill, cool, then spoon the peel around the edge.

Plum and Cardamom Pie

SERVES 6
plain flour to dust
250g (9oz) ready-rolled sweet shortcrust pastry
900g (2lb) mixed yellow and red plums, halved, stoned and quartered
2–3 green cardamom pods, split open, seeds removed and crushed or chopped
50–75g (2–3oz) caster sugar, plus extra to dust
beaten egg or milk for glazing
cream or vanilla ice cream to serve

PREPARATION TIME 15 minutes, plus 30 minutes cooling
COOKING TIME 30 minutes

PER SERVING
275 calories
12g fat (of which 4g saturates)
41g carbohydrate
0.4g salt

TECHNIQUES
see also making shortcrust pastry (page 278), stoning fruits (page 208), making vanilla ice cream (page 388)

1 Heat a flat baking sheet in the oven at 220°C (200°C fan oven) mark 7. On a lightly floured worksurface, roll the pastry a little thinner into a rough circle about 30.5cm (12in) diameter. Put it on a floured baking sheet, without a lip if possible.

2 Pile the fruit in the centre of the pastry and sprinkle with the cardamom seeds and sugar (if the plums are tart you'll need all of it, if ripe and sweet use a little less). Fold in the pastry edges and pleat together around the plums.

3 Brush the pastry with beaten egg or milk and sprinkle with sugar. Put on the preheated sheet and bake for 30 minutes until the pastry is golden brown and the plums just tender. The juices will begin to bubble a little from the pie as it cooks.

4 Leave the pie to cool for 10 minutes, then carefully loosen the pastry around the edges. Cool for another 20 minutes before transferring very carefully to a serving plate. Sprinkle the pie with a little extra sugar and serve warm with cream or vanilla ice cream.

Easy Pear and Toffee Tarte Tatin

SERVES 6
4 small rosy pears
8 tbsp dulce de leche toffee sauce
225g (8oz) sheet ready-rolled puff pastry
flour to dust
thick cream or vanilla ice cream to serve

PREPARATION TIME 15 minutes
COOKING TIME 25–30 minutes

PER SERVING
294 calories
12g fat (of which 2g saturates)
46g carbohydrate
0.5g salt

TECHNIQUES
see also making dulce de leche (page 373), making puff pastry (page 279), making vanilla ice cream (page 388)

1 Preheat the oven to 200°C (180°C fan oven) mark 6. Quarter the pears – no need to peel them – and cut out the cores. Put into a large non-stick frying pan and add the toffee sauce. Cook over a medium heat for 5 minutes or until the pears are well coated and the sauce has turned a slightly darker shade of golden brown.

2 Tip the pears and the sauce into a 20.5cm (8in) round non-stick sandwich or tart tin. Arrange the pears skin side down in a circle and leave to cool for 10 minutes.

3 Unroll the puff pastry, rolling it out wider on a floured surface, if necessary. Lay it over the pears and press down on to the edge of the tin. Trim off any excess pastry. Prick the pastry all over and bake the tart for 20–25 minutes until the pastry is well risen and golden.

4 Leave the tart to cool for 5 minutes. To turn out, hold a large serving plate or baking sheet over the tart, turn over and give a quick shake to loosen. Lift off the tin. Serve the tart immediately, cut into thick wedges, with cream or vanilla ice cream.

Baked Apple and Lemon Tartlets

SERVES 8

3 medium eggs
pinch of salt
300g (11oz) plain flour, plus extra to dust
75g (3oz) icing sugar
300g (11oz) butter
700g (1lb 9oz) Bramley or Granny Smith's apples, peeled, cored and thinly sliced
zest and juice of 2 lemons
225g (8oz) caster sugar
1 tsp arrowroot
caster sugar and cinnamon to dust
clotted cream to serve

PREPARATION TIME 40 minutes, plus 50 minutes chilling
COOKING TIME 45–50 minutes

PER SERVING
615 calories
34g fat (of which 20g saturates)
77g carbohydrate
0.6g salt

TECHNIQUES
see also making pastry (pages 278–279), preparing apples (page 206), zesting citrus fruits (page 207)

1 Beat one egg with a pinch of salt then set aside 1 tbsp. Whiz the flour, icing sugar and 175g (6oz) butter in a food processor until the mixture resembles fine crumbs. Add the remaining beaten egg with 3 tbsp water; pulse until the pastry comes together. Divide into eight balls and chill for 30 minutes. Roll out the pastry on a lightly floured worksurface and line eight 8cm (3¼in) base, 3cm (1¼in) deep, fluted, loose-based tartlet tins. Prick the bases and chill for 20 minutes. Meanwhile, preheat the oven to 200°C (180°C fan oven) mark 6. Line the tins with greaseproof paper and baking beans and cook for 15 minutes. Remove the weighted paper, brush the pastry with reserved beaten egg and cook for 2–3 minutes. Set aside. Reduce the oven temperature to 180°C (160°C fan oven) mark 4.

2 Toss the apples in 2 tbsp lemon juice. Fry in 25g (1oz) melted butter for 1–2 minutes. Spoon into the pastry cases. Soften the remaining butter. Process with the caster sugar (or use an electric hand mixer) for 3 minutes or until soft and pale. Add the lemon zest, arrowroot and remaining two eggs. Blend for 2 minutes. With the food processor or mixer running, add the remaining lemon juice. Blend for 1 minute. Pour over the apples. Dust with caster sugar and bake for 45–50 minutes until the pastry is golden and the apples start to caramelise. Serve warm or cold with clotted cream, dusted with cinnamon.

Freezing tip

Bake the tarts, then cool, wrap and freeze.
To use Put back in the tins, then thaw overnight at room temperature. Reheat at 200°C (180°C fan oven) mark 6 for 7–10 minutes.

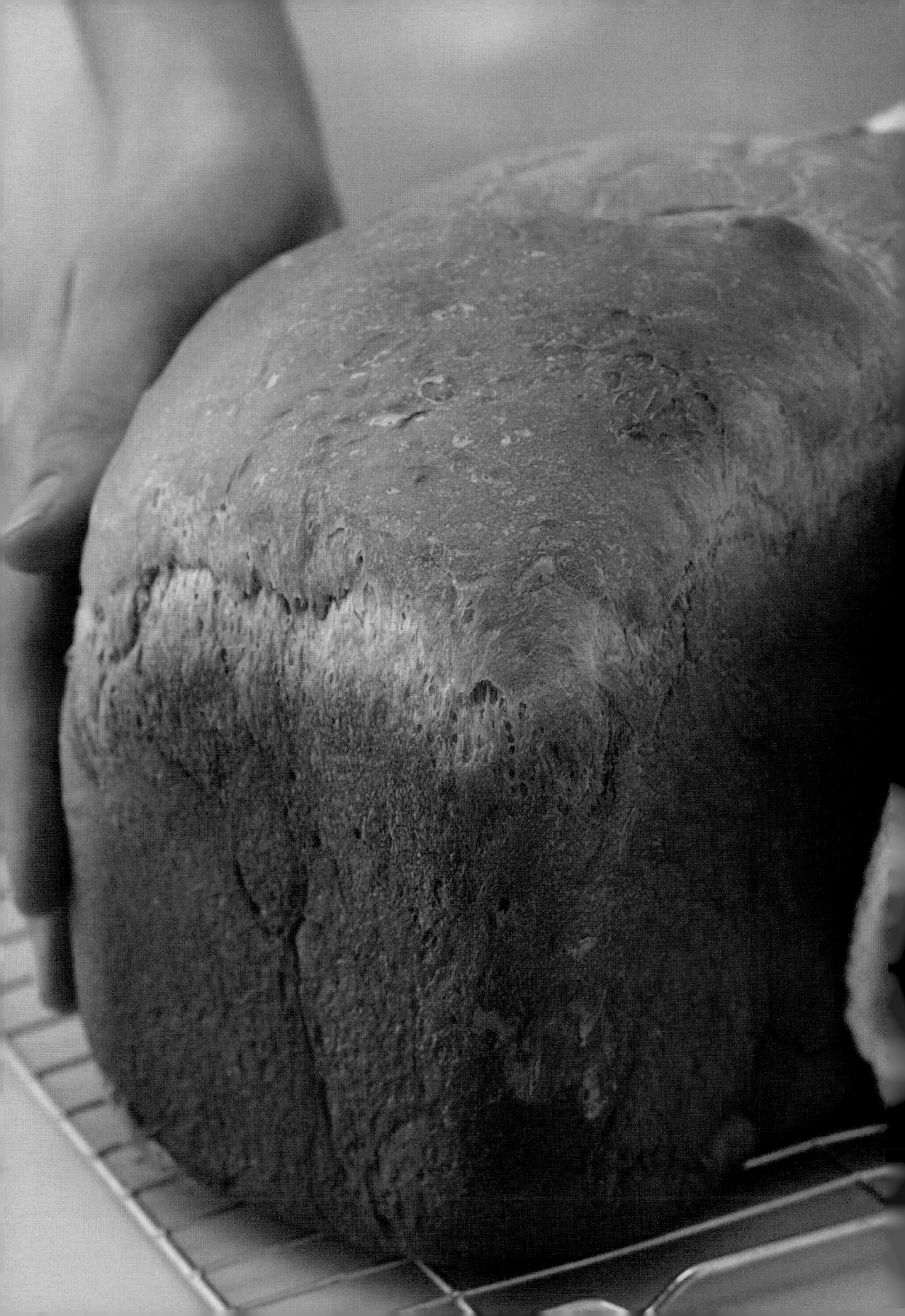

12 SWEET AND SAVOURY BREADS

Very little beats the smell of freshly baked bread. This chapter provides you with all the know-how you will ever need from how to make the simplest white and brown loaves to using a bread machine and making other classic loaves such as sourdough, soda bread and flatbread to topped breads such as pizza and focaccia. Packed with advice on basic bread-making ingredients including yeast, troubleshooting tips, and hints on achieving perfect results every time, there's even a section on using bread as an ingredient, including making breadcrumbs, bruschetta, wraps and sandwiches. The recipe section includes more complex loaves and bread recipes including Black olive bread, Walnut and garlic bread, Warm cornbread, Sweet mocha bread, Kugelhopf, Garlic Cheese Pizza and Panettone Pudding.

Bread basics

Baking bread is one of the greatest pleasures of the kitchen, and one of the simplest. Simple loaves provide the foundation for further experimentation, so they are the best place to start with bread-making.

White farmhouse loaf

You will need 700g (1lb 9oz) strong plain white flour, 1 tbsp salt, 1 tsp golden caster sugar, 1½ tsp fast-action (easy-blend) dried yeast, a little vegetable oil.

1 Sift the flour into a large bowl and stir in the salt, sugar and yeast. Make a well in the middle and stir in 450ml (¾ pint) warm water to make a soft sticky dough, adding a little extra water if necessary.

2 Knead thoroughly for 10 minutes until the dough is smooth and elastic, then shape into a ball and put into an oiled bowl.

3 Cover and leave to rise for 1–2 hours until doubled in size.

4 Knock back the dough for 2–3 minutes on a lightly floured surface, by pressing down with your knuckles to expel any air. Shape into a large oval loaf and transfer to a floured baking sheet. Cover loosely with lightly oiled clingfilm and leave to prove (rise) for a further 30 minutes.

5 Preheat the oven to 230°C (210°C fan) mark 8. Slash the top of the loaf with a very sharp knife, dust with flour and bake for 15 minutes.

6 Reduce the heat to 200°C (180°C fan) mark 6 and bake for a further 15–20 minutes until the bread is risen and sounds hollow when tapped underneath. Cool on a wire rack.

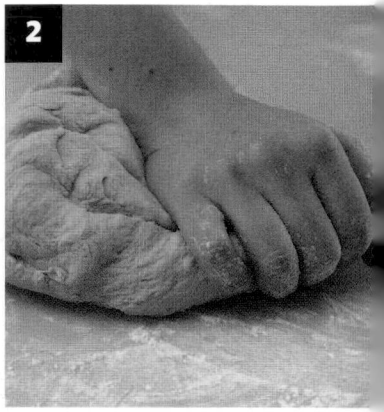

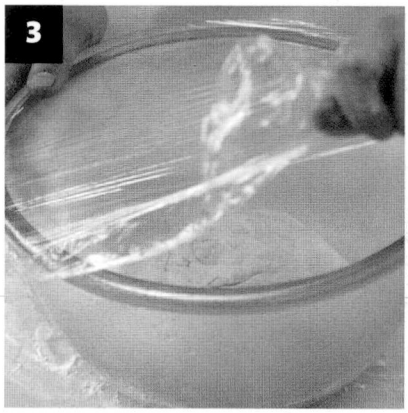

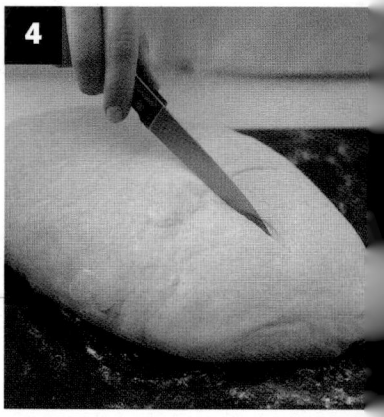

Making bread

Yeast Fresh yeast is activated when blended with warm liquid. Dried yeast needs sugar to activate it (no sugar is needed if using milk): blend the yeast with a little of the water plus sugar (or milk) and leave for 15 minutes to froth. Fast-action (easy-blend) dried yeast is sprinkled directly into the flour and the liquid added afterwards. As a rough guide, for 700g (1lb 9oz) flour use 15g (½oz) fresh yeast, 1 tbsp dried yeast or a 7g sachet (2 tsp) fast-action dried yeast.

Liquid This needs to be slightly warm to the fingertips. Milk gives bread a softer texture than water.

Flour Use strong white or wholemeal flour, or Granary flour.

Salt This controls fermentation, strengthens the gluten, which gives the bread its texture, and adds flavour.

Fats Some recipes use fat for flavour and to improve keeping quality.

Shaping loaves

The shape and size of bread can be varied almost endlessly after the first rise. After the second rising, the dough is ready to bake. Understanding the basics will ensure success.

Simple rolls

1 After knocking back, cut the dough into even pieces, each about 40g (1½oz). Roll each piece with the palm of hand on lightly floured work surface to make a ball.

2 Place on a greased baking sheet, seam side down, and press down slightly. Cover with clingfilm and leave to prove for 30 minutes before baking.

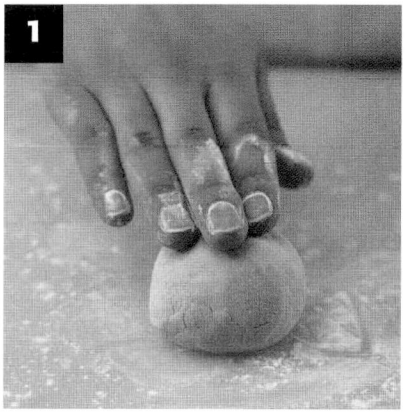

Long loaves

1 After knocking back, cut the dough into pieces, each weighing about 200g (7oz). Roll one piece until it is about 40.5cm (16in) long. Transfer to a baking sheet, seam side down. Repeat with remaining pieces.

2 Cover with oiled clingfilm and leave to prove (rise) for 30 minutes. Slash 3–4 times before baking.

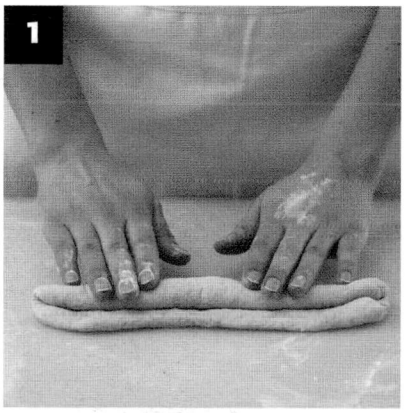

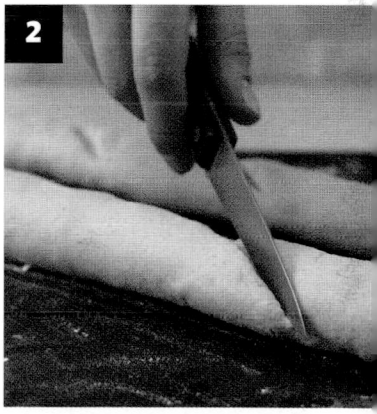

Perfect baking

- Make sure shaped dough has risen sufficiently – usually to double.
- Always oil or flour the loaf tin or baking sheet, to prevent sticking.
- Make sure the oven is at the correct temperature before baking.
- Bake on a preheated ceramic baking stone (from good kitchen shops) if possible, even if the bread is in a loaf tin. The heat of the stone will give the bread a crisp base.

Troubleshooting

The loaf hasn't risen enough:

- Not enough liquid was added.
- The yeast was not fresh.
- The dough was left to prove (rise) for too long causing it to collapse during baking.

The loaf is too dense in texture:

- The dough was not allowed to rise.
- Not enough or too little liquid.
- Dough not kneaded long enough.

Cooling

If baked bread is left for too long either in the loaf tin or on the baking sheet, steam will gather and, as a result, the underneath will start to become soggy. To prevent this, always remove the loaf immediately and put it on a wire rack. Then leave it to cool completely before slicing as you like.

Using a bread machine

Bread machines are now becoming extremely popular as a way for busy people to enjoy home-baked bread. As well as baking loaves, the machine can make doughs for all kinds of shaped breads.

Mixed grain loaf

You will need 1 tsp fast-action (easy-blend) dried yeast, 300g (11oz) strong white bread flour, 100g (3½oz) strong wholemeal bread flour, 50g (2oz) bulgur wheat, 25g (1oz) millet grain, 2 tbsp linseed, 2 tbsp porridge oats or wheat flakes, plus extra to sprinkle, 1½ tsp salt, 1 tbsp golden caster sugar, 25g (1oz) butter, 350ml (12fl oz) water.

1 Put the ingredients in the bread bucket following the guidelines in the manufacturer's manual. (Most machines specify adding the liquid(s) first followed by the dry ingredients and yeast.

2 Fit the bucket into the bread machine and set to the programme recommended in the manual for a large multigrain loaf with the crust of choice. Press start and leave the bread to mix and rise.

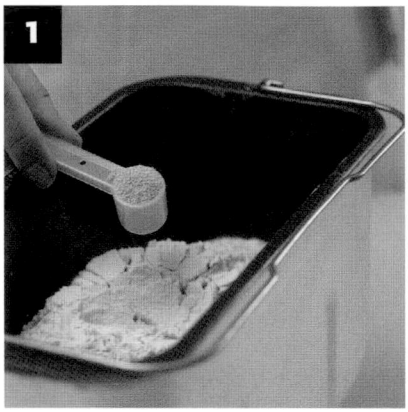

3 Before baking, brush top of risen bread dough with water and sprinkle with oats or wheat flakes.

4 After baking, remove the loaf from the bread machine as soon as it is cooked and place on a wire rack to cool.

Which machine?

Bread machines knead, prove and bake, but models vary. Most will bake different sizes of loaf as well as different breads, and some have a special 'beep' function to tell you when to add other ingredients during the dough cycle. Most machines allow you to select your preferred crust colour, and some have a timer so that you can set the machine to bake bread ready for a selected time, such as first thing in morning.

Perfect machine-baked bread

- Always follow the bread machine instructions carefully; it is essential that the ingredients go into the machine in the order stated, as the yeast must not come into contact with the liquid until the machine begins to mix.
- Measure out all the ingredients carefully, as exact quantities are essential for a perfect loaf.
- Avoid lifting the lid during the rising and baking cycles as this may cause the loaf to sink.
- The loaf is best removed from the machine as soon as it is baked, otherwise it will become soggy.
- Use recipes that have been designed for bread machine use only, as conventional bread recipes use different quantities of ingredients and are not converted easily.

Making classic breads

There are numerous classic breads – from a simple brown loaf made with wholemeal flour and distinctive-tasting sourdough to unleavened flatbreads and unyeasted soda breads and scones.

Brown loaf

You will need 300g (11oz) strong white bread flour, 200g (7oz) strong wholemeal flour, 15g (½oz) fresh yeast or 1 tsp dried yeast, 2 tsp salt.

1 Sift flours into a bowl and make a well in centre. Pour in 325ml (11fl oz) water. Sprinkle over the yeast and mix in a little of the flour to make a batter. Sprinkle salt over the dry flour, so that it doesn't come into contact with the yeast. Cover and leave for 20 minutes.

2 Mix to make soft dough and knead 10 minutes until smooth and elastic. Shape into a ball and place in a lightly oiled bowl. Cover and leave ¾–1½ hours until doubled in size.

3 Punch the dough to knock back on lightly floured surface by pressing with your knuckles to expel the air.

4 Knead for 2–3 minutes, then shape and put in a greased 900g (2lb) loaf tin or on a lightly floured baking sheet. Cover, and leave to rise for ¾–1½ hours until doubled.

5 Preheat the oven to 200°C (180°C fan oven) mark 6. Bake for 50 minutes–1 hour if using a loaf tin, or 45–50 minutes on baking sheet.

6 Tap the bottom of loaf: it should sound hollow. Cool on a wire rack.

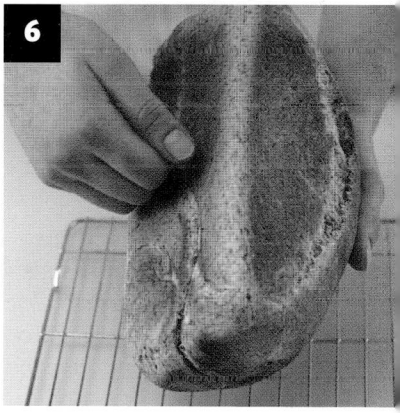

Sourdough

Old-fashioned sourdough has a close texture and a deliciously tangy flavour. You can adapt a basic bread recipe to make sourdough bread. Simply use 125ml (4fl oz) of the starter (see below) in place of each 15g (½oz) fresh yeast or 1 tsp dried yeast called for in a recipe.

1 For the starter, you will need 15g (½oz) fresh yeast or 1 tsp dried yeast, 450ml (¾ pint) water, about 225g (8oz) strong white bread flour.

2 Mix the ingredients to a thick, pourable batter. Then cover the bowl with a clean damp cloth and leave at room temperature for between three and five days. During this time, the starter will ferment and, as a result, it will take on the distinctive and sought-after sourdough flavour that characterises this bread, which is what it is all about.

Cook's tip

Sourdough starter keeps well but must be 'refreshed'. Keep the starter covered in the refrigerator and whisk in a handful of flour and a small cup of water every day – this provides fresh nutrients for the yeast and aids its leavening properties.

Soda bread

You will need 350g (12oz) plain wholemeal flour, 125g (4oz) coarse oatmeal, 2 tsp bicarbonate of soda, 1 tsp salt, 300ml (½ pint) buttermilk, 1 tsp clear honey, 2–3 tbsp milk, plus extra to brush.

1 Preheat the oven to 200°C (180°C fan oven) mark 6. Combine the dry ingredients in a bowl and make a well in the middle.

2 Gradually beat in the buttermilk, honey and just enough milk to form a soft dough. Knead for 5 minutes or until smooth.

3 Shape into a 20.5cm (8in) round and place on a lightly oiled baking sheet. Cut a cross on top. Brush with milk and bake for 30–35 minutes until slightly risen; it should sound hollow when tapped on its base.

Spicy griddled flatbread

You will need 300g (11oz) strong white bread flour, 175g (6oz) gram flour, 1 tsp salt, 2 tsp dried yeast, 2 tsp ground cumin, ½ tsp golden caster sugar.

1 Mix the flours together in a large bowl, then stir in the remaining ingredients. Make a well in the middle and gradually work in 250–300ml (9fl oz–½ pint) water to make a soft dough.

2 Knead the dough for about 10 minutes or until it becomes smooth and slightly elastic. Transfer to an oiled bowl, cover, and leave to rise for 1–1½ hours until doubled in size.

3 Punch the dough to knock it back and divide into 12 equal pieces. Roll out each piece to make a small oval, about 7.5 × 15cm (3 × 6in), and put on well-floured baking sheets.

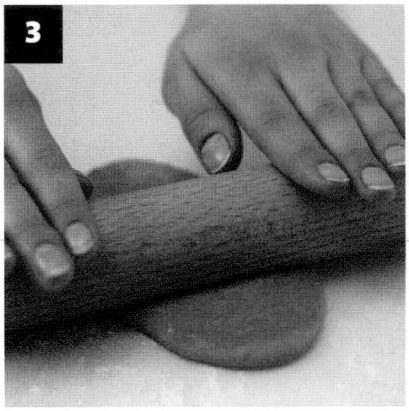

4 Spray the breads lightly with water, cover loosely, and leave to rise for another 15 minutes.

5 Preheat a lightly oiled flat griddle, or the grill, and cook the breads, a few at a time, until they're puffed up and golden (1–2 minutes). Turn and cook the underside for another 30–60 seconds. Cover and keep warm while you cook the remaining breads. Eat as soon as possible.

Cook's tips

- If grilling the breads, position the rack about 10cm (4in) from the heat so that they have room to puff up.
- If you need to speed things up, use a food processor for step 1.

Enriched breads

An enriched dough contains more fat, and often milk and sugar or honey. A typical recipe would have 50g (2oz) butter rubbed into every 225g (8oz) flour, plus 1 egg and 100ml (3½fl oz) milk.

1 Mix the ingredients in normal way.

2 Knead and shape, then bake and cool in the usual way.

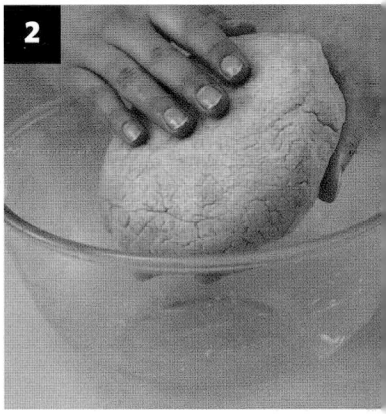

Scones

To make eight scones, you will need 225g (8oz) self-raising flour, pinch of salt, 75g (3oz) butter at room temperature, cut into small pieces, 40g (1½oz) golden caster sugar, 1 large egg, 4–10 tbsp buttermilk or soured milk (milk with lemon juice).

1 Preheat the oven to 220°C (200°C fan oven) mark 7. Sift the flour and salt into a bowl. Add the butter and rub it in until the mixture looks like breadcrumbs. Stir in the sugar.

2 Put the egg in a jug and beat in 2 tbsp of the buttermilk or soured milk. Make a well in centre of the flour mixture and pour in the egg mixture. Using a round-bladed knife, gradually stir in. Bring the dough together with your hands – it should be soft but not sticky; if too dry, add a drop more liquid. Shape the dough into a ball and pat into a round.

3 Flour worksurface and rolling pin, and roll out the dough to 2.5cm (1in) thick. Dip a 5cm (2in) cutter in flour, and cut out 8 rounds.

4 Arrange the scones on a floured baking sheet. Lightly brush with milk and dust with flour.

5 Bake at top of oven for 10–12 minutes until well risen and golden. Cool on wire rack for 5 minutes.

Making pizza and focaccia

Whereas pizza has a rich topping, focaccia's topping is much lighter. The dough takes only about 10 minutes to make and needs just one rise, so it can be ready to use within an hour.

Pizza

For one pizza, you will need 225g (8oz) strong white bread flour, 7g sachet fast-action (easy-blend) dried yeast, ½ tsp salt, 4 tbsp extra virgin olive oil, cornmeal or flour, to sprinkle.

1 Sift the flour into a large bowl, stir in the yeast and salt, and make a well in the centre. Pour 150ml (¼ pint) water into the well with 1 tbsp of the oil. Use your fingertips or a large spoon to stir together.

2 Turn on to a lightly floured surface and knead for 5 minutes or until the dough is smooth. It should be quite soft. Lightly oil the mixing bowl, put in the dough and turn it over to coat in the remaining oil. Cover with oiled clingfilm or a clean teatowel. Put in a warm, draught-free place to rise for 45 minutes or until doubled in size.

3 Preheat the oven to 240°C (220°C fan oven) mark 9. Quickly punch the dough to knock it back, then roll it out into a circle or rectangle about 1cm (½in) thick.

4 Sprinkle a baking sheet fairly generously with cornmeal or plain flour. Roll the dough over the rolling pin and lift it on to the baking sheet, then unroll and spread with sauce.

5 Add your choice of toppings (see right) and bake for 20–25 minutes until the rim is crusty and the topping is bubbling.

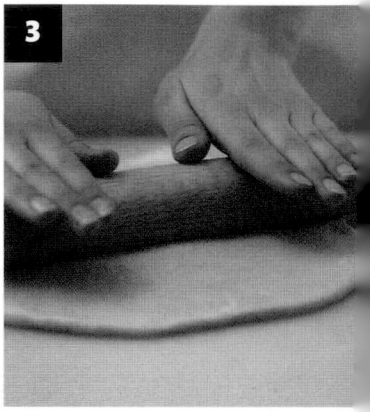

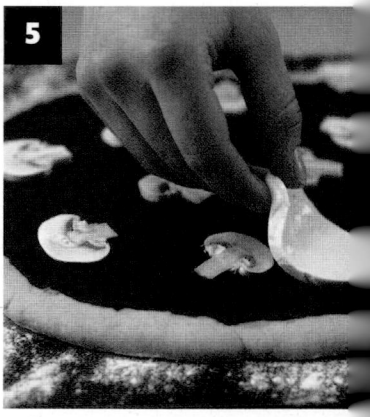

Perfect pizzas

- Pizza should not be a heavy dish so add toppings with a light hand.
- If you can't get good mozzarella, use another cheese instead – Taleggio, Fontina, or even just good Cheddar all work well.
- A ceramic baking stone (from good kitchen shops) is extremely useful for cooking pizza, to help cook the pizza evenly and give crunchiness to the base. (Put the stone into the oven before preheating.)

Toppings

Scatter one or two of the following on top of a basic cheese and tomato topping:

- Pancetta bits or slices of prosciu
- Rocket leaves
- Dried chilli flakes
- Capers
- Sliced sun-dried tomatoes
- Pepperoni slices
- Roasted peppers
- Artichoke hearts, drained and quartered
- Sliced mushrooms.

Focaccia

A very popular Italian bread, focaccia scores high as a tasty comfort food. It is made from pizza dough, pressed into a roughly rectangular shape, a little thicker than pizza, and then topped with salt, extra-virgin olive oil and your choice of herbs.

You will need 1 quantity of pizza dough, 2 tbsp extra virgin olive oil, a small handful of fresh herbs (basil, rosemary, flat-leafed parsley or thyme), roughly torn, 2 tsp coarse sea salt.

1 Roll the pizza dough into a rectangle about 2.5cm (1in) thick. Place it in a shallow baking tin or on a baking sheet, and leave to rise for 30 minutes.

2 Preheat the oven to 200°C (180°C fan oven) mark 6.

3 Dimple the surface of the bread by gently pressing a finger into the dough at regular intervals.

4 Drizzle the oil all over the top of the bread.

5 Scatter on your chosen herbs, then sprinkle with sea salt.

6 Bake for 30–35 minutes until the bread is well risen and golden brown in colour.

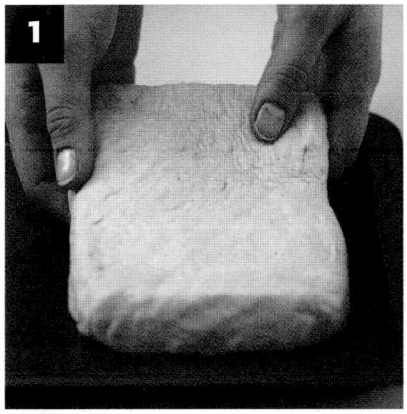

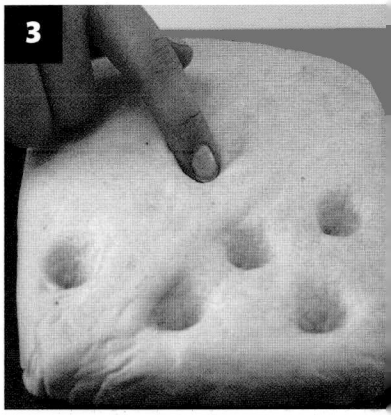

Seasonings

These should be scattered on with a light hand. Remember, they are a seasoning, not a main ingredient.

- Garlic, finely chopped
- Onions, thinly sliced
- Shallots, finely chopped
- Cracked black pepper
- Olives, roughly chopped
- Anchovies, finely chopped
- Dried herbs, such as oregano
- Sun-dried tomatoes, chopped
- Capers, finely chopped

Cooking with bread

Bread is delicious eaten on its own, but it's also invaluable as an ingredient – whether processed into breadcrumbs, toasted and turned into bruschetta, made into wraps or sandwiches, or used in salads.

Fresh breadcrumbs

Used for stuffings or as a topping, these are best made just before using.

1 Cut off the crusts and discard. Chop the bread roughly.

2 Working in batches, put handfuls of bread in a food processor or blender, and whiz until it becomes fine crumbs. Use as soon as possible or freeze for up to one month.

Dried crumbs

Used for coating fish, meat and poultry before frying, dried breadcrumbs can be made from stale bread or from slices of bread dried in the oven at 200°C (180°C fan oven) mark 6 for 5–10 minutes. Break into pieces, and whiz in the food processor.

Garlic bruschetta

To make six, you will need 3 garlic cloves, 6 thick slices bread, 5 tbsp virgin olive oil.

1 Heat a griddle until hot. Peel the garlic and bruise, then halve and rub on both sides of the bread.

2 Brush both sides of the bread with oil. Put on the griddle, press down and cook until golden brown.

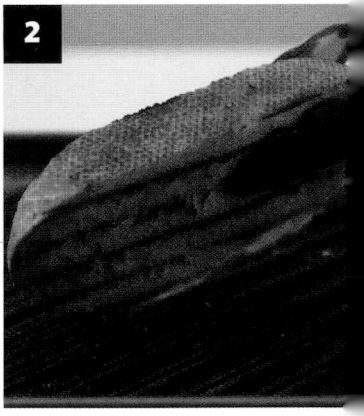

Simple chicken wrap

Wraps are best made with a finely chopped filling so that the wrapper can fold around it easily.

You will need 1 tsp salt, 1 tsp ground black pepper, 2 cooked chicken breasts, finely chopped, 1 carrot, grated, 1 avocado, chopped, a small handful of rocket leaves, the juice of ½ lemon, 3 tbsp mayonnaise, 4 soft tortillas.

1 Put the salt and pepper in a bowl, then add the chicken, carrot, avocado and rocket and mix well.

2 In a separate bowl, combine the lemon juice and mayonnaise, then spread it over the tortillas. Divide the chicken mixture evenly between them and roll up tightly. Serve whole, or cut in half.

Steak sandwich

For four sandwiches, you will need 2 sirloin steaks, 1 tbsp olive oil, 4 large mushrooms, sliced, 1 red onion, sliced, 1 tbsp Dijon mustard, 25g (1oz) butter, 2 ciabattas, halved and split, salt and ground black pepper.

1 Heat a frying pan. Rub the steaks with 1 tsp oil, and season. Cook for 2 minutes per side for rare, 3–4 minutes for medium.

2 Remove the steaks and leave to rest for 5 minutes. Lower the heat and heat remaining oil in the pan. Stir-fry the vegetables for 5 minutes or until tender. Add the mustard and butter and remove from the heat.

3 Thinly slice the steak and divide among the two ciabattas. Top with the vegetables and the top half of the bread and serve.

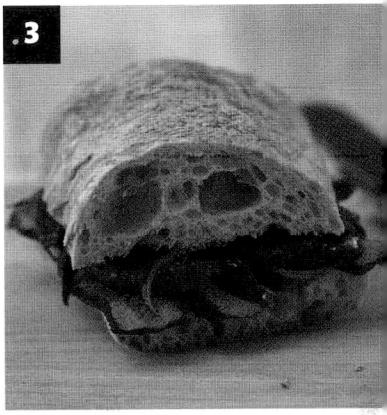

Tuscan bread salad

You will need 6–8 thick slices of country-style bread, about 250g (9oz) total weight, 3–4 large ripe tomatoes, 1 small or ½ large cucumber, 1 medium red onion, a small handful of fresh basil leaves, torn, home-made dressing made with 3 tbsp red wine vinegar and 6 tbsp extra virgin olive oil, salt and ground black pepper.

1 Cut or tear the bread into pieces and put into a large bowl. Slice the vegetables into pieces a little smaller than the bread, and add to the bowl with the basil.

2 Whisk the dressing, then pour about 7 tbsp of this over the salad.

3 Toss well, and leave to stand for 30 minutes–2 hours, depending on the freshness of the bread, tossing from time to time. Taste the salad, adjust seasoning and serve.

Perfect results

- This salad is best made in the summer, when tomatoes are ripe and juicy and have the best flavour.
- The bread can be either fresh or stale; if stale, soak with the other ingredients for at least 2 hours before making up the salad.

Salt and Pepper Rolls

MAKES 16

675g (1½lb) strong white bread flour, plus extra to dust
7g sachet fast-action dried yeast
1 tsp sea salt flakes, plus extra to sprinkle
1 tsp each red and green peppercorns
2 tbsp olive oil, plus extra to grease
1 medium egg, beaten, to glaze

PREPARATION TIME 40 minutes, plus 2 hours rising
COOKING TIME 30–35 minutes

PER ROLL
157 calories
2g fat (of which trace saturates)
33g carbohydrate
0.3g salt

TECHNIQUES
see also bread basics (page 300)

1 Sift the flour into a large warmed bowl. Stir in the yeast. Crush the salt and peppercorns in a pestle and mortar and stir into the flour. Make a well in the centre of the flour, then pour in the oil and enough water – about 500ml (almost 1 pint) – to make a soft dough. (Alternatively, if using an electric hand mixer, put the flour, yeast, salt, peppercorns, oil and water in the bowl and knead to a soft dough with a dough hook.)

2 Put the dough in an oiled bowl, cover with oiled clingfilm and leave in a warm place until doubled in size.

3 Knead the dough on a floured board for about 5 minutes. Again, put in an oiled bowl, cover with oiled clingfilm and leave in a warm place until doubled in size.

4 Punch the dough to knock back, then knead for 1 minute. Divide into 16 pieces and shape into rolls. Put on greased baking sheets, spaced well apart, cover with oiled clingfilm and leave for 30 minutes or until spongy. Preheat the oven to 220°C (200°C fan oven) mark 7.

5 Brush the rolls with egg, sprinkle with a little salt and bake for 30–35 minutes until golden.

Freezing tip

At step 5, bake for 25 minutes. Cool and freeze.
To use Warm in the oven at 200°C (180°C fan oven) mark 6 or thaw for 1 hour and warm at the same temperature for 4–5 minutes.

Black Olive Bread

MAKES 2 LOAVES

2 tsp traditional dried yeast
500g (1lb 2oz) strong white bread flour, plus extra to dust
2 tsp coarse salt, plus extra to sprinkle
6 tbsp extra-virgin olive oil, plus extra to grease
100g (3½oz) black olives, pitted and chopped

PREPARATION TIME 40 minutes, plus 2 hours rising
COOKING TIME 30–35 minutes

PER LOAF

601 calories
21g fat (of which 3g saturates)
16g carbohydrate
0.7g salt

TECHNIQUES

see also cooling and troubleshooting (page 301)

1 Put 150ml (¼ pint) hand-hot water into a jug, stir in the yeast and leave for 10 minutes or until foamy.

2 Put the flour into a bowl or in a food processor, then add the salt, yeast mix, 200ml (7fl oz) warm water and 2 tbsp oil to the bowl and use a dough hook to mix. Continue mixing for 2–3 minutes to make a soft smooth dough. Put the dough in a lightly oiled bowl; cover with oiled clingfilm and a teatowel. Leave in a warm place for 45 minutes or until doubled in size. Punch the dough to knock out the air, then knead on a lightly floured worksurface for 1 minute. Add the olives and knead until combined.

3 Divide in half, shape into rectangles and put into two greased tins, each around 15 × 25.5 × 4 cm (6 × 10 × 1½in). Cover with clingfilm and leave in a warm place for 1 hour or until the dough is puffy. Preheat the oven to 200°C (180°C fan oven) mark 6.

4 Press your finger into the dough 12 times, drizzle over 2 tbsp oil and sprinkle with salt. Bake for 30–35 minutes until golden. Drizzle with the remaining oil and cover with a cloth for a softer crust. Cut into slices and serve warm.

Freezing tip

Wrap and freeze after sprinkling with salt at step 4.
To use Bake the dough from frozen at 200°C (180°C fan oven) mark 6 for 35–40 minutes until cooked through.

Walnut and Garlic Bread

SERVES 8

oil to grease
500g (1lb 2oz) strong white bread flour with kibbled grains of rye and wheat, plus extra to dust
7g sachet fast-action dried yeast
2 tsp salt
2 tbsp malt extract
50g (2oz) butter, softened
3 garlic cloves, crushed
100g (3½oz) walnut pieces
1 tbsp milk

PREPARATION TIME 20 minutes, plus 45 minutes rising
COOKING TIME 1 hour 50 minutes

PER SERVING

359 calories
15g fat (of which 4g saturates)
52g carbohydrate
1.3g salt

TECHNIQUES

see also preparing garlic (page 171)

1 Lightly grease a 20.5cm (8in) springform tin. Put the flour, yeast and salt into the bowl of a freestanding mixer with a dough hook attachment. Add 300ml (½ pint) lukewarm water and 1 tbsp malt extract, then mix to a pliable dough. Increase the speed and machine-knead for 5 minutes.

2 Lightly dust a surface with flour, turn out the dough and roll into a rectangle measuring about 40.5 × 28cm (16 × 11in). Mix together the butter and garlic, and spread over the dough. Scatter the walnuts over and, starting at the long edge, roll up into a sausage. Cut into eight slices and put in the tin. Cover with lightly oiled clingfilm and leave to rise in a warm place for 45 minutes or until doubled in size. Preheat the oven to 220°C (200°C fan oven) mark 7 and put a baking sheet in to heat.

3 Remove the clingfilm, cover the bread with foil, and put on the hot baking sheet. Bake for 20 minutes. Reduce the oven temperature to 200°C (180°C fan oven) mark 6 and bake for 1 hour 10 minutes.

4 Mix the milk with the remaining malt extract and brush the glaze over the bread. Bake, uncovered, for 5 minutes or until golden brown. Leave in the tin to cool slightly, then remove and serve warm.

Freezing tip

At step 3 turn the oven down to 200°C (180°C fan oven) mark 6 and continue to bake for a further 40 minutes. Remove from the oven and cool in the tin. Freeze for up to one month.
To use from frozen, cover with foil, put on a hot baking sheet and bake at 220°C (200°C fan oven) mark 7, for 45 minutes. Continue with the recipe.

Warm Cornbread

SERVES 8
oil to grease
125g (4oz) plain flour
175g (6oz) polenta or cornmeal
1 tbsp baking powder
1 tbsp caster sugar
½ tsp salt
285ml (9½fl oz) buttermilk, or equal quantities of natural yogurt and milk, mixed together
2 medium eggs
4 tbsp extra-virgin olive oil

PREPARATION TIME 10 minutes
COOKING TIME 25–30 minutes, plus 5 minutes resting

PER SERVING
229 calories
8g fat (of which 1g saturates)
32g carbohydrate
1.3g salt

1 Preheat the oven to 200°C (180°C fan oven) mark 6. Generously grease a 20.5cm (8in) square shallow tin.

2 Put the flour into a large bowl, then add the polenta or cornmeal, baking powder, sugar and salt. Make a well in the centre and pour in the buttermilk or yogurt and milk mixture. Add the eggs and oil, then stir together until evenly mixed.

3 Pour into the tin, then bake for 25–30 minutes until firm to the touch. Double check by plunging a skewer into the centre; if it comes out clean, the cornbread is done.

4 Leave the cornbread to rest in the tin for 5 minutes, then turn out and cut into chunky triangles. Serve warm with butter.

Sweet Mocha Bread

MAKES 1 LOAF (10 SLICES)

425g (15oz) strong white bread flour, plus extra to dust
1 tsp salt
7g sachet fast-action dried yeast
150g (5oz) golden caster sugar
3 large eggs
150ml (¼ pint) double cream
50g (2oz) butter, melted
oil to grease
4 tbsp instant coffee granules
200g (7oz) good-quality plain chocolate, semi-sweet such as Bournville, chopped
50g (2oz) pecan nuts

PREPARATION TIME 25 minutes, plus 2 hours rising
COOKING TIME 45 minutes

PER SLICE

477 calories
24g fat (of which 12g saturates)
62g carbohydrate
0.6g salt

TECHNIQUES

see also bread basics (page 300), choosing chocolate (page 357), lining tins (page 322)

1 Sift the flour and salt into a bowl. Stir in the yeast and 75g (3oz) sugar. In a separate bowl, lightly beat the eggs, cream and butter. Make a well in the flour and pour in the egg mixture. Mix to a soft dough. Turn out on to a lightly floured worksurface and knead for 5–10 minutes until smooth and elastic. Transfer to an oiled bowl, cover with oiled clingfilm and leave in a warm place to rise until doubled in size. Meanwhile, put 50g (2oz) sugar in a small pan with 5 tbsp water and heat gently until the sugar dissolves. Stir in the coffee. Bring to the boil. Simmer for 1 minute. Cool.

2 Grease and line a 20.5cm (8in) springform tin. Turn the dough on to a lightly floured surface and divide into four. Roll one piece to a 25.5cm (10in) round. Press into the base of the tin so the edges come slightly up the sides. Scatter over 50g (2oz) chocolate. Spoon over one-third of the coffee syrup. Roll out another piece of dough. Lay it over the first, letting the excess dough come up the sides and pinching it into the first layer. Repeat, finishing with dough. Brush with water and scatter with the nuts.

3 Cover with lightly oiled clingfilm and leave to rise until the dough nearly reaches the top of the tin. Preheat the oven to 220°C (200°C fan oven) mark 7. Bake for 15 minutes, then reduce the oven temperature to 170°C (150°C fan oven) mark 3. Cover with foil and bake for 30 minutes. Remove from the oven and transfer to a wire rack.

Sweet Cherry Bread

SERVES 8

oil to grease
350g (12oz) strong white bread flour, plus extra to dust
½ tsp salt
2 tsp ground mixed spice
1 tbsp cinnamon
25g (1oz) caster sugar
25g (1oz) fresh yeast or 15g (½oz) fast-action dried yeast
75g (3oz) unsalted butter, diced
200ml (7fl oz) milk, warmed
125g (4½oz) white almond paste, roughly chopped
125g (4½oz) glacé cherries
3 tbsp honey, warmed
75g (3oz) icing sugar, sifted

PREPARATION TIME 40 minutes, plus 2½ hours rising
COOKING TIME 40 minutes

PER SERVING
310 calories
4g fat (of which trace saturates)
66g carbohydrate
0.4g salt

TECHNIQUES
see also bread basics (page 300)

1 Grease and baseline a deep, 20.5cm (8in) cake tin. Sift the flour, salt, spices and caster sugar into a bowl. Add the fast-action yeast, if using. Rub in the butter. If using fresh yeast, dissolve it in the milk. Add the yeast mixture, or the milk, to the flour to make a dough (if you find the dough is too dry, add a little more milk). Turn out the dough on to a lightly floured worksurface and knead for 10 minutes. For speed, put the dough in a food processor that has a dough hook and process for 2–3 minutes. Put the dough in a lightly oiled bowl, cover with oiled clingfilm and leave in a warm place for 2 hours or until doubled in size.

2 Turn out the dough on to a lightly floured worksurface and knead lightly. Shape into an oval, 60cm (24in) long. Scatter the almond paste and cherries over the surface and roll the dough up lengthways, then form a tight coil. Put in the cake tin, cover and leave in a warm place for 30 minutes or until doubled in size and spongy to the touch. Preheat the oven to 180°C (160°C fan oven) mark 4.

3 Bake for 40 minutes or until golden and the bread sounds hollow when tapped underneath. Transfer to a cooling rack. When cool, glaze with honey. To make the icing, mix the icing sugar with a few drops of water to form a paste. Drizzle over the bread.

Get ahead

Complete the recipe. Store the bread in an airtight container for up to two days.

Kugelhopf

SERVES 12

200g (7oz) raisins, black seedless if possible
3 tbsp light rum
2 tsp fast-action dried yeast
300g (11oz) plain white flour, plus extra to dust
4 large eggs
100ml (3½fl oz) milk
225g (8oz) unsalted butter, softened, plus extra to grease
75g (3oz) caster sugar
pinch of salt
zest of 1 lemon
100g (3½oz) split blanched almonds, lightly toasted
icing sugar to dust
whole glacé fruits, nuts and silver or gold dragées to decorate

PREPARATION TIME 45 minutes, plus overnight chilling and 3 hours rising
COOKING TIME 50–55 minutes

PER SERVING
382calories
22g fat (of which 11g saturates)
39g carbohydrate
0.4g salt

Cook's tip

- This cake is made with yeast, so it's best eaten within two days or it will go stale. If you have any left over, wrap and freeze in slices – it's tasty toasted or used for making bread and butter pudding.
- If you don't have a mixer with a beater attachment, use a food processor with a flat plastic blade.

1 Combine the raisins and rum, cover and soak overnight. Put the yeast and flour in a food mixer. Lightly whisk the eggs and milk then, with the machine running on a slow speed, pour in the egg mixture and mix for 10 minutes or until the dough is very smooth, shiny and elastic. In another bowl, beat the butter, caster sugar, salt and lemon zest then, with the mixer running, add to the dough, a spoonful at a time, until evenly incorporated. Turn the mixture into a large lightly floured bowl. Cover with clingfilm and chill overnight.

2 Generously butter a 2 litre (3½ pint) Kugelhopf ring mould. Press one-third of the almonds on to the sides of the mould. Chill. Roughly chop the remaining almonds. Mix by hand into the dough with the raisins and rum, then put in the mould, cover and leave for 3 hours in a warm place until it feels spongy and has risen to within 2cm (¾in) of the top of the mould.

3 Preheat the oven to 200°C (180°C fan oven) mark 6. Bake on a shelf below the centre of the oven for 10 minutes. Cover with greaseproof paper, reduce the temperature to 190°C (170°C fan oven) mark 5 and bake for 40–45 minutes until the Kugelhopf sounds hollow when you tap the mould. Cool in the tin for 15 minutes. Turn on to a wire rack to cool completely. Decorate and serve dusted with icing sugar.

Panettone Pudding

SERVES 4–6

50g (2oz) butter, at room temperature, plus extra to grease
500g (1lb 2oz) panettone, cut into slices about 5mm (¼in) thick
3 large eggs, beaten
150g (5oz) golden caster sugar
300ml (½ pint) full-fat milk
140ml (4½fl oz) double cream
zest of 1 orange

PREPARATION TIME 20 minutes, plus 20 minutes soaking
COOKING TIME 35–45 minutes

PER SERVING

872 calories per serving for 4
43g fat (of which 24g saturates)
109g carbohydrate
1.4g salt
581 calories per serving for 6
29g fat (of which 16g saturates)
73g carbohydrate
0.9g salt

TECHNIQUES

see also zesting citrus fruits (page 207)

1 Lightly butter the panettone slices. Tear them into pieces and arrange in a buttered 2 litre (3½ pint) ovenproof dish.

2 Mix the eggs with the sugar, then whisk in the milk, cream and orange zest. Pour the mixture over the buttered panettone and leave to soak for 20 minutes.

3 Put the dish in a roasting tin and pour in enough hot water to come halfway up the sides. Bake at 170°C (150°C fan oven) mark 3 for 35–45 minutes until the pudding is just set in the middle and golden.

Cook's tip

Panettone is a yeasted fruit cake that is a traditional Christmas treat in Italy and is most widely available around Christmas time.

Tuna Melt Pizza

SERVES 4
2 large pizza bases
4 tbsp sun-dried tomato pesto
2 × 185g cans tuna, drained
50g can anchovies, drained and chopped
125g (4oz) grated mature Cheddar cheese
rocket to serve

PREPARATION TIME 10 minutes
COOKING TIME 10–12 minutes

PER SERVING
670 calories
33g fat (of which 10g saturates)
51g carbohydrate
3.1g salt

TECHNIQUES
see also making pizzas (page 306)

1 Preheat the oven to 220°C (200°C fan oven) mark 7. Take the pizza bases and spread each base with 2 tbsp sun-dried tomato pesto. Top each with half the tuna, half the anchovies and half the grated cheese.

2 Put on to a baking sheet and cook for 10–12 minutes until the cheese has melted. Sprinkle with rocket to serve.

Cook's tip

You can make your own pizza base from scratch following the technique on page 306 or buy ready-made bases from the supermarket. You can buy fresh bases, vacuum-packed ones or packet mixes that you mix, knead and roll out yourself.

Garlic Cheese Pizza

SERVES 4

280g pack pizza-base mix
2 × 150g packs garlic and herb cheese
12 whole sun-dried tomatoes, drained of oil and cut into rough pieces
40g (1½oz) pinenuts
12 fresh basil leaves
3 tbsp olive oil

PREPARATION TIME 20 minutes
COOKING TIME 30 minutes

PER SERVING
698 calories
48g fat (of which 17g saturates)
54g carbohydrate
1.2g salt

TECHNIQUES
see also pizza toppings (page 306)

1 Put a pizza stone or large baking sheet in the oven and preheat to 220°C (200°C fan oven) mark 7.

2 Mix the pizza-base dough according to the pack instructions. On a lightly floured worksurface, knead for a few minutes or until smooth. Roll out to a 33cm (13in) round. Transfer the dough to the preheated pizza stone or baking sheet. Pinch a lip around the edge.

3 Crumble the cheese over the dough and flatten with a palette knife, then sprinkle on the sun-dried tomatoes, pinenuts and basil leaves.

4 Drizzle with the oil and bake for 20–30 minutes until pale golden and cooked to the centre.

Cook's tip

It's well worth buying a pizza stone to guarantee a crisp crust.

13 CAKES, COOKIES, BISCUITS AND TRAYBAKES

Learn the secrets of successful home baking with the easy-to-follow, step-by-step guide to preparation and cooking techniques – from lining tins and making cake and cookie mixtures to baking, filling and decorating. The chapter is packed with tips for success including testing cakes for doneness, cooling cakes and cookies and troubleshooting tips. The recipe collection is full of wonderful treats for children and adults alike including Almond cookies, Gingerbread houses, Nutty fudge shortbread, Apple madeleines, The ultimate chocolate brownie, Lime drizzle loaf, Apple and blueberry cake, Carrot tray bake or Sticky ginger ring.

Lining tins

Always line your cake tin with greaseproof paper – this will help to stop the cake sticking to the sides of the tin or burning. Lightly grease the tin first to help keep the paper in place.

Square tin

1 Cut out a square of greaseproof paper slightly smaller than the base of the tin. Cut four strips about 2cm (¾in) wider than the depth of the tin and fold up one of the longest edges of each strip by 1cm (½in).

2 Lightly grease the tin with butter, making sure it is coated on all sides and in the corners.

3 Cut one strip to the length of the side of the tin and press into place in one corner then along the length of the strip with the narrow folded section sitting on the base. Continue, cutting to fit into the corners, to cover all four sides.

4 Lay the square on the base of the tin, then grease the paper, taking care not to move the side strips.

Round tin

1 Put the tin on a sheet of greaseproof paper and draw a circle around its circumference. Cut out the circle just inside the drawn line.

2 Cut a strip or strips about 2cm (¾in) wider than the depth of the tin and fold up one long edge of each strip by 1cm (½in). Make cuts, about 2.5cm (1in) apart, through the folded edge of the strip(s) up to the fold line.

3 Lightly grease the tin with butter, making sure it is completely coated.

4 Press the strip(s) on to the sides of the tin so that the snipped edge sits on the base.

5 Lay the circle in the bottom of the tin and grease the paper.

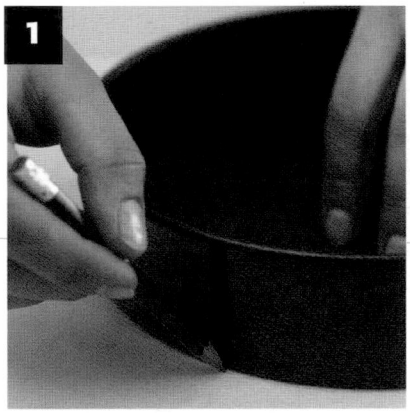

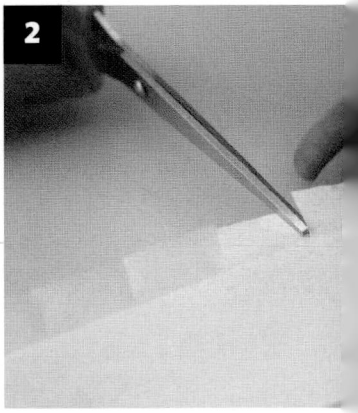

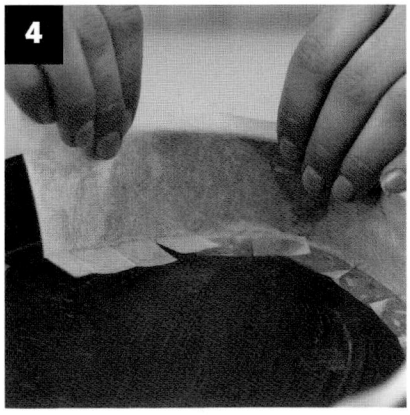

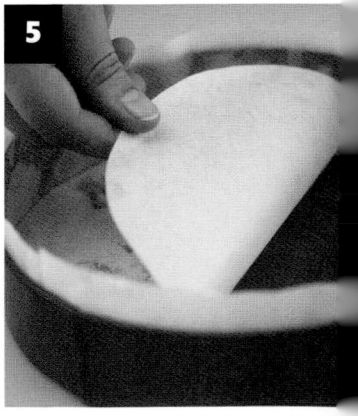

Swiss roll tin

Use this method for a Swiss roll or any other shallow baking tin.

1 Lightly grease the tin with butter, making sure it is completely coated.

2 Cut a piece of baking parchment into a rectangle 7.5cm (3in) wider and longer than the tin. Press it into the tin and cut at the corners, then fold to fit neatly. Grease all over.

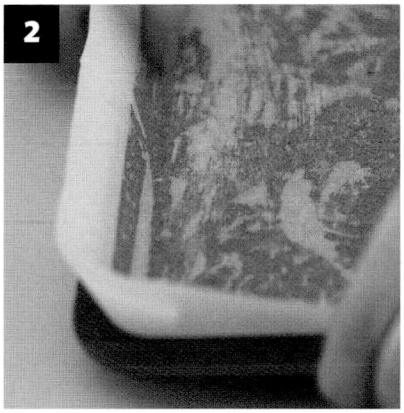

Perfect lining

- Use greaseproof paper for all cakes and baking parchment for roulades and meringues.
- Apply the butter with a small piece of greaseproof paper. Don't thickly grease the tin, as this would 'fry' the edges of the cake.

Loaf tin

1 Lightly grease the tin with butter, making sure it is completely coated.

2 Cut out a sheet of greaseproof paper to the same length as the base and wide enough to cover both the base and the long sides. Press it into position, making sure that it sits snugly in the corners.

3 Now cut another sheet to the same width as the base and long enough to cover both the base and the ends of the tin. Press into place. Grease the paper all over.

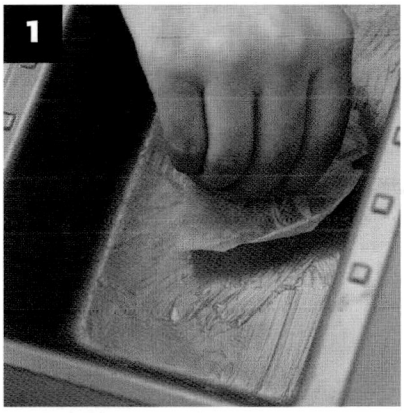

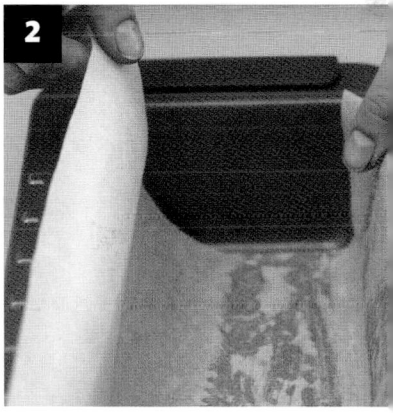

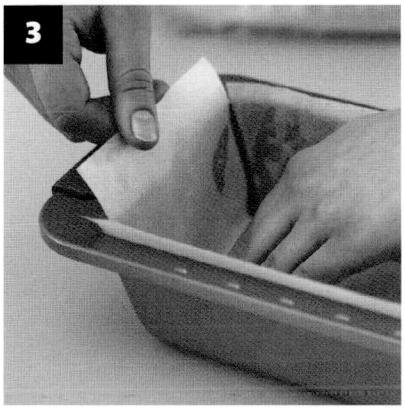

Making cakes

A wide variety of cakes can be prepared using just three basic techniques: creaming, all-in-one and whisking. These straightforward basic recipes can be adapted in several ways.

Creamed sponge

A classic Victoria sponge can be used to make many cakes, including chocolate or fruit.

You will need 175g (6oz) softened butter, 175g (6oz) caster sugar, 3 medium eggs, 175g (6oz) self-raising flour, 150g (5oz) mascarpone, 4 tbsp raspberry jam, icing sugar to dust.

1 Preheat the oven to 180°C (160°C fan oven) mark 4. Grease and line the base of two 18cm (7in) sandwich tins with greaseproof paper.

2 Put the butter and sugar in a bowl and beat with an electric whisk or wooden spoon until pale, soft and creamy.

3 Beat the eggs and gradually add to butter and sugar mixture, beating well until the mixture is thick and of dropping consistency. (If you like, add a spoonful of flour while adding the eggs to prevent curdling.)

4 Gently fold in the flour using a large metal spoon or spatula, then divide the mixture between the two tins and level the surface. Bake for 25–30 minutes until golden and firm to the touch. Cool slightly in the tins, then turn out on to a wire rack to cool completely.

5 When the cakes are cold, spread one with mascarpone and then the conserve. Place the other cake on top, and lightly press together. Put on a serving plate, and dust lightly with sifted icing sugar.

Cooling cakes

- Sponge cakes should be taken out of their tins soon after baking. Invert on to a wire rack, lined with sugar-dusted baking parchment.
- Leave fruit cakes to cool in the tin for 15 minutes before turning out.
- Allow rich fruit cakes to cool completely before turning out, there is a risk of breaking otherwise.

Testing sponges

1 Gently press the centre of the sponge. It should feel springy. If it's a whisked cake, it should be just shrinking away from the sides of the tin.

2 If you have to put it back into the oven, close the door gently so that the vibrations don't cause the cake to sink in the centre.

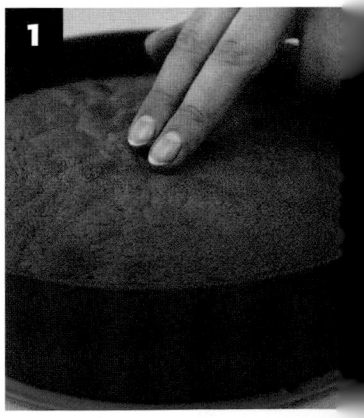

Whisked Genoese sponge

For this coffee cake you will need 1 tbsp instant espresso granules, 50g (2oz) butter, 4 large eggs, 125g (4oz) golden caster sugar, 125g (4oz) sifted plain flour. For the filling, you will need 1 tbsp instant coffee, 250g (9oz) mascarpone, 125g (4oz) sifted golden icing sugar, plus extra to dust.

1 Preheat the oven to 190°C (170°C fan oven) mark 5. Line two 18cm (7in) sandwich tins. Dissolve the coffee in 2 tsp boiling water.

2 Melt the butter in a small pan. Put the eggs and sugar in a large bowl set over a pan of simmering water. Whisk for about 5 minutes with an electric hand mixer until creamy and pale and the mixture leaves a trail when you lift the whisk.

3 Gently fold half the flour into the mixture. Mix the coffee into the butter and pour half around the edge of the mixture, then fold in the remaining flour, coffee and butter.

4 Pour into the tins and bake for 25 minutes or until risen, firm to the touch and shrinking away from the sides of the tin. Turn on to wire racks, remove the paper and leave to cool.

5 To make the filling, dissolve the coffee in 1 tbsp boiling water and beat with the mascarpone and sugar until smooth. Spread over one sponge, top with the other and dust with icing sugar.

All-in-one cherry cakes

To make 12 cupcakes, you will need 175g (6oz) butter, softened, 175g (6oz) golden caster sugar, 3 medium eggs, 175g (6oz) self-raising flour, sifted, pinch of baking powder, 75g (3oz) dried sour cherries, 2 tbsp milk.

1 Preheat the oven to 190°C (170°C fan oven) mark 5. Line a muffin tin with 12 muffin cases. Put the butter, sugar, eggs, flour and baking powder in a large bowl or mixer.

2 Mix slowly to start, then increase the speed slightly until well combined. Fold the cherries into the mixture with the milk. Spoon into the paper cases and bake for 15–20 minutes until pale golden, risen and springy to the touch. Remove and cool on a wire rack. Ice with buttercream (see page 330).

Marbled cake

You will need 175g (6oz) butter, softened, 175g (6oz) golden caster sugar, 3 medium eggs, 125g (4oz) self-raising flour, 50g (2oz) ground almonds, 1 tsp baking powder, finely grated zest of 1 orange, 1 tbsp brandy, 4 tbsp cocoa powder, sifted.

1 Preheat the oven to 190°C (fan oven 170°C) mark 5. Line a 900g (2lb) loaf tin.

2 Cream the butter and sugar until pale, then beat in the eggs, one at a time. Sift over the flour, almonds and baking powder, and fold in. Stir in the orange zest and brandy.

3 Divide the mixture between two bowls and stir the cocoa into one. Spoon the mixtures into the tin in two layers, then drag a skewer through. Bake for 45 minutes.

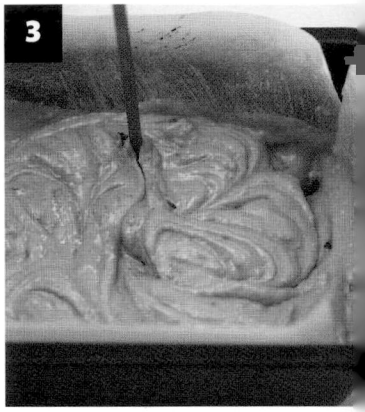

Fruity tea cake

You will need 75g (3oz) dried figs, 75g (3oz) stoned prunes, 150ml (¼ pint) hot Earl Grey tea, 200g (7oz) sultanas, 150g (5oz) dark muscovado sugar, 2 medium eggs, 225g (8oz) self-raising flour, 2 tsp ground mixed spice, vegetable oil to grease.

1 Chop the figs and prunes, then soak in the tea with the sultanas for 30 minutes.

2 Beat the sugar and eggs until creamy, then mix in the flour, spice, soaked fruit and tea.

3 Preheat oven to 190°C (fan oven 170°C) mark 5. Grease 900g (2lb) loaf tin and line with greaseproof paper. Pour in the mixture and bake for 1 hour or until a skewer inserted in the centre comes out clean. Cool on a wire rack. Serve sliced, with butter.

Testing fruit cakes

1 To test if a fruit cake is cooked, insert a skewer into the centre of the cake, leave for a few moments, then pull it out. If it comes away clean, the cake is ready.

2 If any mixture sticks to the skewer, the cake is not quite done so put the cake back in the oven for a few more minutes, then test again with a clean skewer.

Troubleshooting

A dense texture may be due to too little raising agent, or adding the eggs too quickly.
A peaked, cracked top appears if the oven is too hot or the cake is too near the top of the oven; the tin is too small; or too much raising agent was used.

Making roulades

A roulade is made from a very light cake mixture and does not contain flour. It remains very soft when baked, and can therefore be easily rolled around a layer of filling such as jam and cream.

Chocolate cherry roll

To serve eight, you will need 4 tbsp cocoa powder, 150ml (¼ pint) milk, 5 medium eggs, separated, 125g (4oz) golden caster sugar, 400g can pitted cherries, 1–2 tbsp cherry jam, sifted icing sugar to dust.

1 Preheat the oven to 180°C (160°C fan oven) mark 4 and line a 30.5 × 20.5cm (12 × 8in) Swiss roll tin with baking parchment.

2 Mix the cocoa with 3 tbsp milk in a bowl, then heat the remaining milk in a pan or in the microwave until almost boiling. Pour over the cocoa, stirring, then cool for 10 minutes.

3 Meanwhile, separate the eggs. Whisk the egg whites until soft peaks form. In another bowl, whisk the yolks with the sugar until pale and thick, then gradually whisk in the cooled milk.

4 Fold in the egg whites, spoon the mixture into the tin, and level. Bake for 25 minutes until just firm.

5 Turn out on to a board lined with baking parchment and peel off the lining paper. Cover with a damp teatowel.

6 Drain the cherries and chop. Spread the jam over the roulade and top with the chopped fruit.

7 Very carefully, roll up from the shortest end. Dust with cocoa and icing sugar and serve in slices.

Variation

You can add whipped cream to a roulade, but you will need to cool the roulade first. To do this, turn out the roulade on to baking parchment. Do not remove the lining paper but roll the roulade around it while still warm. Leave to cool, unroll and peel off the paper. Spread with cream, and jam if you wish, and re-roll.

Making cupcakes and muffins

Muffins and cupcakes are two members of the same family: individual cakes, usually based on a mixture made with self-raising flour, baked in bun tins or muffin pans so that it rises and sets to an airy texture.

Vanilla cupcakes

To make 12 cupcakes, you will need 125g (4oz) softened butter, 125g (4oz) golden caster sugar, 2 eggs, 125g (4oz) self-raising flour, 1 tbsp vanilla extract, 200g (7oz) white chocolate.

1 Preheat the oven to 190°C (170°C fan oven) mark 5. Line a bun tin or muffin pan with 12 paper cases.

2 Beat the butter, sugar, eggs, flour and vanilla until smooth and creamy. Half-fill the muffin cases with the mixture and bake for 15–20 minutes until pale golden, risen and springy to the touch. Transfer to a wire rack to cool.

3 When the cupcakes are cool, melt the chocolate (see page 356). Spoon over the cakes and leave to set.

Banana and pecan muffins

To make 12 muffins, you will need 275g (10oz) self-raising flour, 1 tbsp bicarbonate of soda, 1 tsp salt, 3 very ripe, large bananas, about 450g (1lb), peeled and mashed, 125g (4oz) golden caster sugar, 1 large egg, 50ml (2fl oz) milk, 75g (3oz) melted butter, 50g (2oz) chopped roasted pecans.

1 Preheat the oven to 180°C (160°C fan oven) mark 4. Line a muffin pan with 12 paper cases. Sift together the flour, bicarbonate of soda and salt. Set aside.

2 Combine the bananas, sugar, egg and milk, then pour in the melted butter and mix well. Add to the flour mixture with the nuts, stirring quickly and gently with just a few strokes.

3 Half-fill the muffin cases.

4 Bake for 20 minutes until golden and risen. Cool on a wire rack.

Perfect muffins

The secret to really light, fluffy muffins is a light hand.

- Be sure to sift the flour.
- Stir the mixture as little as possible; it's ok if it looks a little lumpy.
- Overmixing will give tough, chewy results.

Making cheesecakes

There are many ways to make this perennial favourite, which can be baked or simply chilled and set with gelatine. When baking cheeesecakes, watch the temperature as too high a heat can cause the top to crack.

Lemon cheesecake

You will need 125g (4oz) unsalted butter, 250g (9oz) digestive biscuits, 1 large lemon, 2 medium eggs, 500g (1lb 2oz) full-fat cream cheese, 140ml (4½fl oz) soured cream, 175g (6oz) golden caster sugar, 1½ tsp vanilla extract, 1 tsp cornflour, 50g (2oz) sultanas.

1 Grease base and sides of a 23cm (9in) springform tin. Melt the butter in a large pan. Chop biscuits in food processor, or put in a plastic bag and bash with a rolling pin. Stir into the butter, tip into tin and press down using back of spoon. Chill for 1 hour.

2 Preheat the oven to 180°C (fan 160°C) mark 4. Grate lemon zest into a large bowl and set aside. Halve the lemon, set aside 3 thin slices, and squeeze juice into bowl with zest.

3 Add the eggs, cream cheese, soured cream, sugar, vanilla and cornflour to the bowl. Using an electric mixer, whisk until smooth. Fold in the sultanas.

4 Pour the mixture into the tin and tap on the worktop to level it out.

5 Bake for 30 minutes, then arrange the lemon slices on top and bake for 20–25 minutes until just set but still a little wobbly in the centre. Turn off the oven, leave the door ajar and allow to cool for at least 2 hours.

6 Chill and remove from refrigerator 30 minutes before serving in slices.

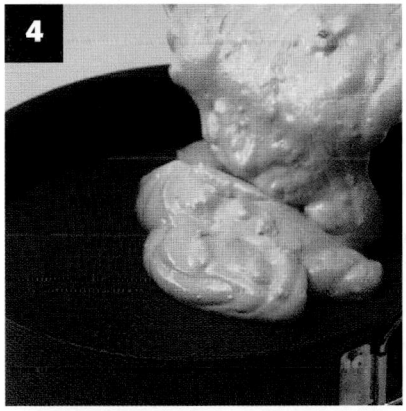

Chilled cheesecake

An uncooked cheesecake is usually set with gelatine and made with a mixture of cream cheese and perhaps some cottage cheese flavoured with lemon zest. The mixture is poured on to a biscuit crumb base (usually made with crushed biscuits mixed with melted butter) that has been pressed into a flan tin then chilled until firm. The whole cheesecake is then chilled to set. Fresh fruit or a fruit coulis can be added as a topping.

Filling and topping cakes

To make sponge cakes even tastier, they can be split and filled with jam, cream or buttercream. Icings complete a special-occasion cake and are especially good when covering home-made marzipan.

Splitting and filling a cake

1 Allow the cake to cool completely before splitting. Use a knife with a shallow thin blade such as a ham knife, a bread knife, or a carving knife. Cut a notch from top to bottom on one side so you will know where to line the pieces up.

2 Cut midway between top and bottom, about 30 per cent of the way through the cake. Turn the cake while cutting, taking care to keep the blade parallel with the base, until you have cut all the way around.

3 Cut through the central core and lift off the top of the cake.

4 Warm the filling slightly to make it easier to spread, then spread on top of the base, stopping 1cm (½in) from the edge.

5 Add the top layer of cake.

Buttercream icing

To cover the top of a 20.5cm (8in) cake, you will need 75g (3oz) unsalted butter, 175g (6oz) icing sugar, sifted, a few drops of vanilla extract, 1–2 tbsp milk.

1 Soften the butter in a mixing bowl, then beat until light and fluffy.

2 Gradually stir in the remaining ingredients and beat until smooth.

Variations

- **Citrus** Replace the vanilla with a little orange, lemon or lime zest, and use some of the fruit's juice in place of the milk.
- **Chocolate** Blend 1 tbsp cocoa powder with 2 tbsp boiling water. Cool, then add to the mixture.

Marzipan

A versatile and attractive cake topping, marzipan can be used in a number of ways. Home-made marzipan has a good flavour and is not difficult to make.

To make 450g (1lb) marzipan, you will need 225g (8oz) ground almonds, 125g (4oz) golden caster sugar, 125g (4oz) sifted golden icing sugar, 1 large egg, 2 tsp lemon juice, 1 tsp sherry, 1–2 drops vanilla extract.

1 Put the ground almonds and sugars in a bowl and stir to combine. In another bowl, whisk together the remaining ingredients then add to the dry ingredients.

2 Stir well to mix, pounding gently to release some of the oil from the almonds. Knead with your hands until smooth, then cover until ready to use.

Covering a cake with marzipan

For a completely flat-topped cake, invert the cake on to a sheet of greaseproof paper. The base will then become the top of the cake. Lightly brush melted apricot jam over the top and sides to help stick the marzipan to the cake. Make a long narrow sausage of marzipan and place it around the base of the cake. Press to fit. Fill any holes in the cake with small pieces of marzipan. Roll out the marzipan to about 5mm (¼in) thick. Lift it over a rolling pin and place over the cake. Using the palm of your hand, smooth and ease the marzipan over the top and sides of the cake. Trim away the marzipan at the base edge. Leave to harden for about two days before icing.

Easiest icing

To cover a 20.5cm (8in) marzipan-covered cake. You will need 3 egg medium whites, 2 tbsp lemon juice, 2 tsp glycerine, 675g (1½lb) icing sugar, sifted.

1 Put the egg whites in a large bowl, and whisk until frothy. There should be just a layer of bubbles across the top. Add the lemon juice, glycerine and 2 tbsp of icing sugar and whisk until smooth.

2 Whisk in the rest of the sugar, a little at a time, until the mixture is smooth and thick, forming soft peaks.

3 Using a palette knife, smooth half the icing over the top and sides of the cake, then repeat using the remaining icing to cover. Run the knife around the sides to neaten, then use the tip to make peaks all over the top. Leave to dry in a cool place for at least 48 hours.

Making biscuits

Each recipe in this section covers one of the main techniques in biscuit making: creamed, the all-in-one method, rolled, refrigerator biscuits, whisked, melted, moulded and piped.

Creamed choc-oat cookies

Biscuits using this creaming method firm up when cooled.

To make 18 cookies, you will need 125g (4oz) white chocolate, 125g (4oz) plain chocolate, 125g (4oz) unsalted butter, softened, 125g (4oz) caster sugar, 1 medium egg, 1 tsp vanilla extract, 125g (4oz) porridge oats, 150g (5oz) plain flour, ½ tsp baking powder.

1 Preheat the oven to 180°C (160°C fan oven) mark 4 and lightly grease two baking sheets. Using a sharp knife, chop the white and plain chocolate into small chunks, no larger than 1cm (½in).

2 Cream the butter and sugar together in a bowl until pale. Add the egg, vanilla and oats. Sift in the flour and baking powder, and mix until evenly combined. Stir in the chocolate chunks.

3 Place dessertspoonfuls of the mixture on to the baking sheets, spacing them apart to allow room for spreading. Flatten each one slightly with the back of a fork.

4 Bake for 12–15 minutes until risen and turning golden. Leave on the baking sheets for 5 minutes, then transfer to a wire rack to cool completely. Store in an airtight tin for up to one week.

All-in-one peanut cookies

Softened butter is essential for making all-in-one cookies.

To make 30 cookies, you will need 125g (4oz) butter, softened, 150g (5oz) caster sugar, 1 medium egg, 150g (5oz) plain white flour, ½ tsp baking powder, pinch of salt, 125g (4oz) crunchy peanut butter, 175g (6oz) raisins.

1 Preheat the oven to 190°C (170°C fan oven) mark 5 and lightly grease two baking sheets.

2 Put all the ingredients except the raisins into a bowl and beat together until well blended. Stir in the raisins.

3 Spoon large teaspoonfuls of the mixture on to the baking sheets, spacing them apart to leave room for spreading.

4 Bake for 15 minutes or until golden brown around the edges. Allow to cool slightly before lifting on to a wire rack to cool completely.

Rolled vanilla biscuits

The quickest and easiest way to make biscuits of consistent thickness is by rolling and then cutting using a biscuit cutter. The dough must be firm enough to roll to a thickness of 3mm (⅛in).

You will need 175g (6oz) softened unsalted butter, 200g (7oz) golden caster sugar, 350g (12oz) plain flour, 1 medium egg, 2 tsp vanilla bean paste, 2 tbsp golden icing sugar.

1 Preheat the oven to 200°C (180°C fan oven) mark 6. Put the butter, sugar, flour, egg and vanilla bean paste into a food processor and whiz to combine. Alternatively, cream the butter and sugar, and then stir in the flour, egg and vanilla.

2 Put the dough on a large sheet of baking parchment. Press the dough gently but firmly with the palm of your hand to flatten it slightly, then put another sheet of baking parchment on top – this will prevent the dough from sticking.

3 Use a rolling pin to roll out the dough to 3mm (⅛in) thick, and then remove the top sheet of baking parchment.

4 Using 6.5cm (2½in) cutters, stamp out biscuits, leaving a 3mm (⅛in) gap between each one.

5 Peel off the trimmings around the shapes, then slide the baking parchment and biscuits on to a flat baking sheet.

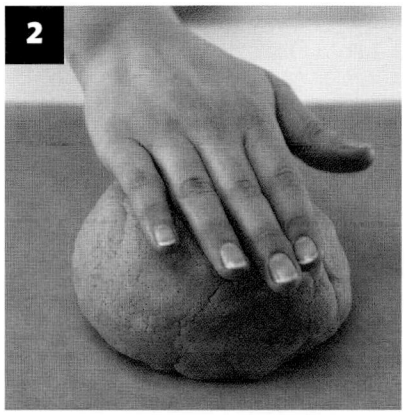

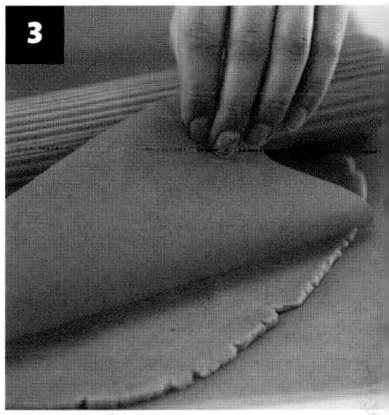

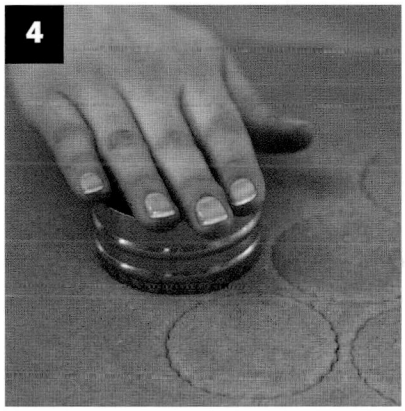

6 Re-roll the trimmings between two new sheets of baking parchment, then stamp out shapes as before and slide on to another baking sheet.

7 Bake the biscuits for 10–12 minutes until pale golden. Cool for a few minutes, then transfer to a wire rack to cool completely.

8 Dust the biscuits with sifted icing sugar. Store in an airtight container for up to five days.

Chocolate refrigerator roll

There is no baking required for refrigerator biscuits.

To make 14 slices, you will need 75g (3oz) digestive biscuits, 50g (2oz) flaked almonds, lightly toasted, 50g (2oz) ready-to-eat dried apricots, finely chopped, 1 piece preserved stem ginger in syrup, drained and finely chopped, 75g (3oz) white chocolate, roughly chopped, 175g (6oz) plain chocolate, in pieces, 65g (2½oz) unsalted butter, 50g (2oz) white chocolate, melted, to decorate.

1 Break the biscuits into chunky pieces and mix with the almonds, apricots, ginger and white chocolate.

2 Melt the plain chocolate with the butter in a heatproof bowl over a pan of gently simmering water, stirring occasionally, until smooth. Remove from the heat and leave until cool, but not beginning to set.

3 Pour the chocolate on to the biscuit mixture and stir gently to mix.

4 Spoon on to greaseproof paper and wrap this around the mixture, making a sausage about 20.5cm (8in) long. Chill for 1–2 hours till firm.

5 Cut the roll into 1cm (½in) slices.

6 Place on a clean sheet of greaseproof paper. Using a teaspoon, drizzle lines of melted white chocolate over the slices to decorate. Chill until ready to serve.

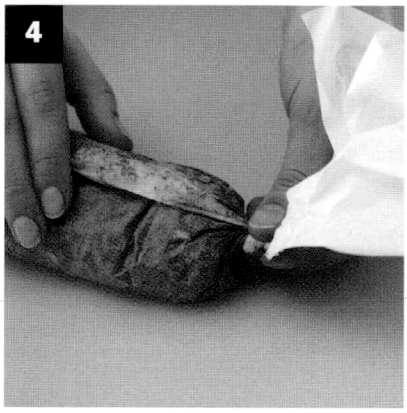

Cook's tip

Always make sure that the melted chocolate is quite cool before you mix it with the other ingredients, or the white chocolate will melt.

Melted ginger biscuits

Some biscuits using the melted method are soft, others brittle.

To make 24 biscuits, you will need 125g (4oz) golden syrup, 50g (2oz) butter, 50g (2oz) dark muscovado sugar, grated zest of 1 orange, 2 tbsp orange juice, 175g (6oz) self-raising flour, 1 tsp ground ginger.

1 Preheat the oven to 180°C (160°C fan oven) mark 4 and lightly grease two large baking sheets.

2 Put the syrup, butter, sugar, orange zest and juice in a pan and heat gently until melted. Mix. Leave the mixture to cool slightly, then sift in the flour with the ginger. Mix thoroughly until smooth.

3 Space spoonfuls well apart on baking sheets, to allow for spreading. Bake for 12 minutes or until golden brown. Leave for 1 minute, then transfer to a wire rack to cool.

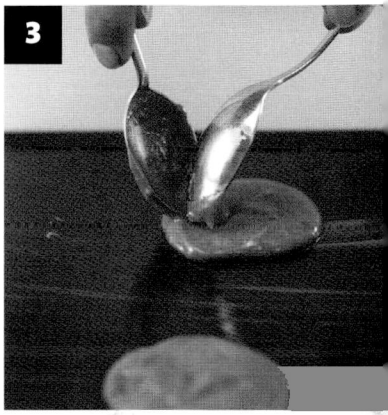

Coconut macaroons

Biscuits using the whisked method are light with very little fat.
To make 24 macaroons, you will need 2 medium egg whites, 125g (4oz) icing sugar, sifted, 125g (4oz) ground almonds, few drops almond extract, 125g (4oz) desiccated coconut, 2 tbsp shredded coconut.

1 Preheat the oven to 150°C (130°C fan oven) mark 2. Whisk the egg whites until stiff and fold in the icing sugar. Stir in the ground almonds, almond extract and coconut to make a sticky dough.

2 Spoon walnut-sized pieces of mixture on to two baking sheets lined with non-stick baking parchment, spacing well apart. Add a few strands of shredded coconut.

3 Bake for 25 minutes or until the outer crust is golden and the inside soft and chewy. Cool on a wire rack.

Chocolate chip cookies

The mixture for moulded biscuits is fairly soft but firm enough to shape into balls. It needs to be handled lightly and gently.

To make about 15 cookies, you will need 75g (3oz) butter, softened, 75g (3oz) granulated sugar, 75g (3oz) soft light brown sugar, 1 tsp vanilla extract, 1 egg, beaten, 175g (6oz) self-raising flour, pinch of salt, 125g (4oz) chocolate drops, 75g (3oz) macadamia nuts, roughly chopped.

1 Preheat the oven to 180°C (160°C fan oven) mark 4 and grease two baking sheets. Cream the butter until soft, then beat in the sugars and vanilla extract. Mix in the egg.

2 Sift the flour and salt into a bowl. Fold into the creamed mixture. Add the chocolate drops and 50g (2oz) macadamia nuts. Stir together until thoroughly combined.

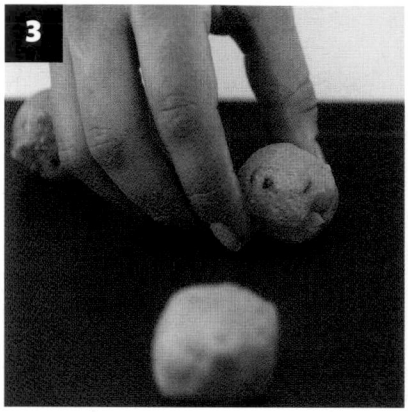

3 Roll the mixture into about 15 balls and arrange on the prepared baking sheets, leaving space for the cookies to spread.

4 Flatten lightly with a wet fork. Sprinkle the remaining nuts on top, pressing them down lightly.

5 Bake for 10 minutes, or until golden. Leave to cool slightly on wire racks. Eat warm.

Viennese fingers

To make 20 fingers, you will need 125g (4oz) softened butter, 25g (1oz) icing sugar, 25g (1oz) plain chocolate, 125g (4oz) plain flour, ¼ tsp baking powder, 1 tbsp drinking chocolate, a few drops of vanilla extract, 50g (2oz) plain, milk or white chocolate, melted, to decorate.

1 Preheat the oven to 190°C (170°C fan oven) mark 5 and grease two baking sheets. Beat the butter and icing sugar until creamy.

2 Melt the plain chocolate in a bowl set over a pan of hot water. Cool for 10 minutes, then beat into the creamed mixture. Sift in the flour, baking powder and drinking chocolate. Fold in, then add the vanilla. Spoon into a piping bag with a star-shaped nozzle and pipe finger shapes about 7.5cm (3in) long on to baking sheets.

3 Bake for 15–20 minutes until golden. Cool on wire rack, then dip in melted chocolate and leave to set.

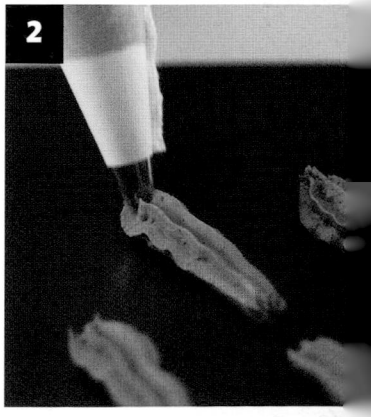

Muesli bars

Some of the simplest biscuits to make are traybakes, which are cooked in one piece and then cut into bars. The mixtures often contain fruit, nuts and sometimes oats.

To make 12 bars, you will need 175g (6oz) unsalted butter, cut into pieces, 150g (5oz) light muscovado sugar, 2 tbsp golden syrup, 375g (13oz) porridge oats, 100g (3½oz) ready-to-eat dried papaya, roughly chopped, 50g (2oz) sultanas, 50g (2oz) pecan nuts, roughly chopped, 25g (1oz) pinenuts, 25g (1oz) pumpkin seeds, 1 tbsp plain flour, 1 tsp ground cinnamon.

1 Preheat the oven to 180°C (160°C fan oven) mark 4. Melt the butter, sugar and golden syrup together in a heavy-based pan over a low heat.

2 Meanwhile put the oats, dried fruit, nuts, seeds, flour and cinnamon into a large bowl and stir to mix. Pour in the melted mixture and mix together until combined.

3 Spoon the mixture into a 30.5 × 20.5cm (12 × 8in) non-stick baking tin and press down into the corners.

4 Bake for 25–30 minutes or until golden. Press the mixture down again if necessary, then use a palette knife to mark into 12 bars.

5 Leave to cool completely. Use a palette knife to lift the bars out of the tin and store in an airtight container.

Perfect traybakes

- Be careful not to overcook traybakes. They are ready when they are golden brown, but will not be set firm when they come out of the oven.
- Some traybakes (such as flapjacks) are soft mixtures when hot and firm up when cold (especially when made with golden syrup or honey), so it is essential to mark the cooked bake into squares or bars while hot. Leave to cool completely in the baking tray before turning out of the tin.
- Remove carefully, using a spatula or palette knife, as some bakes can be a little crumbly.
- Some traybakes have a more 'cakey' mixture (containing a larger amount of flour and some eggs) and can be made with two different layers of mixture or an iced topping. These bakes are usually allowed to cool before they are cut into squares.

Decorating and filling biscuits

The simplest way to decorate a biscuit, and one of the best, is to dust it with icing sugar, but you can take other options for more elaborate effects and these are worth the effort.

Unbaked biscuits

A simple decoration for a plain biscuit is to add a glacé cherry or whole nut, such as an almond, or a half-walnut on the raw biscuit dough before it is cooked.

1 Just press the decoration gently into the surface. This technique is suitable for firmer biscuit and cookie mixtures, such as moulded and rolled biscuits.

Kid's cookies

Small children can have fun decorating cut-out shapes from a rolled cookie mixture. Coloured sweets look pretty, but for a healthier option, try using nuts, seeds and dried fruit, such as raisins.

Icing biscuits

1 Mix 125g (4oz) icing sugar with a little water, or lemon or orange juice, until it is smooth and runny.

2 To drizzle, spoon thin trails of icing over the cooled biscuits.

3 To spread, make the icing a little thicker. If making the biscuits for children they can be decorated with brightly coloured sweets.

Filling biscuits

1 Cream filling To sandwich about 18 biscuits, cream 50g (2oz) butter until soft then beat in 75g (3oz) sifted icing sugar. Mix well and soften by adding a few drops of orange juice or vanilla extract until the mixture is of a firm, spreadable consistency. Spread the mixture on to the flat side of a biscuit and gently press a second biscuit on top to make a sandwich.

2 Chocolate filling Cream 50g (2oz) butter until soft then add 75g (3oz) icing sugar and 2 tsp cocoa powder. Mix well and add a few drops of milk to soften if necessary. (Makes enough to fill 18 biscuits.)

3 Toffee filling Spread dulce de leche (see page 373) over one biscuit and top with another. Roll the edges in desiccated coconut if you like.

Decorating with chocolate

1 Drizzling chocolate Melt some chocolate (see pages 356 and 445) and drizzle over cooled biscuits. If you like, use a dark chocolate, leave it to set and then drizzle white or milk chocolate over the top. Alternatively, spoon melted chocolate into a piping bag with a narrow nozzle and pipe lines on to the biscuit. Leave to cool, then pipe a contrasting colour over the top.

2 Dipped chocolate Biscuits can be dipped in melted chocolate once they are cooked and completely cooled. To do this, dip half the biscuit into melted chocolate and rest it on the edge of a wire rack, so that the chocolate-covered area hangs over the edge while the chocolate cools and firms up.

Cookie troubleshooting

Although very simple in their composition, biscuits can be surprisingly prone to baking problems because they cook so quickly. It's as well to be aware of the possible problems and to know what can cause them. Following a few key points should minimise most of the risks and potential pitfalls.

- Use a shiny-based baking sheet; a darker-coloured sheet will absorb a greater amount of heat and can therefore burn the underside of the biscuits.
- Don't overcrowd the biscuits on the baking sheet or in the oven – air needs to circulate all around them. If you are baking more than one sheet, make sure they are on shelves at least 20.5cm (8in) apart.
- Turn the baking sheet(s) around once or twice during baking. Most ovens get hotter in some places than in others, and this can cause uneven cooking.
- If you are cooking more than one sheet, be prepared to have them bake at different speeds. Watch them closely for uneven cooking.
- Start testing biscuits slightly before you expect them to be cooked. And watch them very closely during the final minutes, as they can go from perfect to overcooked in a matter of only a few seconds.
- Like cakes, biscuits must be transfered to a wire rack while they are still hot. The hot baking sheet will continue to cook them, and steam will build up underneath, which can make the bases soggy. As soon as they are cooked, lift the biscuits from the baking sheet and transfer to a wire rack to cool. Some biscuits, however (particularly those made with syrup), need to be left on the baking sheet to firm up a little before they are transferred to a rack.
- Put the biscuits on a fairly fine-meshed rack if at all possible.
- If possible, raise the rack by putting it on supports so that it is at least a few centimetres higher than the worksurface underneath: the more air circulating underneath, the crisper the bases will be.
- If the biscuits are tough or dry, the dough may have been overworked or too much flour may have been added.
- Biscuits that spread too much during baking contain too much butter or sugar, or the mixture may have been overbeaten.
- A cake-like texture indicates that too much flour was used or the biscuits were baked at too high a temperature.

Cranberry Biscuits

MAKES 24 BISCUITS
125g (4oz) butter, chilled
50g (2oz) caster sugar
25g (1oz) dried cranberries
125g (4oz) plain flour, sifted, plus extra to dust
75g (3oz) ground rice

PREPARATION TIME 15 minutes, plus 30 minutes chilling
COOKING TIME 8–10 minutes

PER BISCUIT
79 calories
4g fat (of which 3g saturates)
10g carbohydrate
0.1g salt

1 Whiz the butter and sugar in a food processor, or use an electric hand mixer. Add the cranberries, flour and ground rice, and pulse or mix until the mixture comes together. Turn out on to a lightly floured worksurface and shape into a rectangle about 12.5 × 7.5 × 2cm (5 × 3 × ¾in). Wrap and chill for 30 minutes. Preheat the oven to 200°C (180°C fan oven) mark 6.

2 Cut the dough into 3mm (⅛in) slices and put on a non-stick baking sheet. Bake for 8–10 minutes until golden. Cool before removing from the sheet. The cookies can be stored in an airtight container for up to one week.

Variations

You can use dried cherries or dried blueberries in place of the cranberries.

Almond Cookies

MAKES 12 COOKIES
2 medium egg whites
200g (7oz) caster sugar
200g (7oz) ground almonds
zest of 1 orange
½ tsp ground ginger
40g (1½oz) stem ginger in syrup, drained and roughly chopped
2 tbsp plain flour, sifted to dust
12 natural glacé cherries
rice paper for lining

PREPARATION TIME 15 minutes
COOKING TIME 20 minutes

PER COOKIE
204 calories
10g fat (of which 1g saturates)
27g carbohydrate
0g salt

TECHNIQUES
see also separating eggs (page 52), zesting citrus fruits (page 207)

1 Preheat the oven to 180°C (160°C fan oven) mark 4. Line two baking sheets with rice paper. Put the egg whites in a large bowl and whisk until they form stiff peaks. In another large bowl, stir together the sugar, ground almonds, orange zest, ¼ tsp ground ginger. With a wooden spoon, mix in the egg whites to form a sticky dough.

2 Roll the dough into 12 equal-sized balls. Mix together the flour and remaining ground ginger in a bowl. Lightly coat each ball in the flour and shake off the excess. Put the balls, spaced well apart, on to the prepared baking sheets. Flatten each one into rounds.

3 Push a glacé cherry in the middle of each cookie and bake for 15–20 minutes until lightly golden. Cool on a wire rack then trim away the excess rice paper.

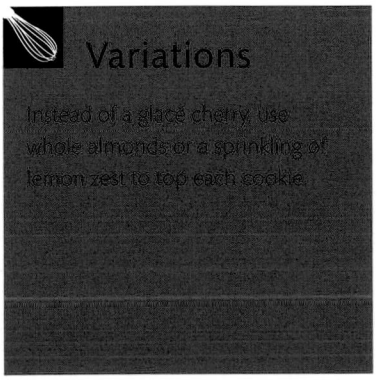

Variations

Instead of a glacé cherry, use whole almonds or a sprinkling of lemon zest to top each cookie.

Gingerbread House

MAKES 4 HOUSES

350g (12oz) plain white flour, sifted
1 tsp bicarbonate of soda
2 tbsp ground ginger
150g (5oz) butter
200g (7oz) light muscovado sugar
2 tbsp golden syrup
1 medium egg, beaten

For the decoration

200g (7oz) icing sugar, sifted
1 medium egg white
75g (3oz) assorted sweets

Materials

Card to make the three templates:
roof: 10 × 6.5cm (4 x 2½in)
end wall: 10 × 6cm (4 x 2¼in)
side wall: 6 × 8cm 2¼ x 3¼in)
four 15cm (6in) cake boards covered in paper
ribbon and cellophane

PREPARATION TIME 4 hours, plus 30 minutes chilling and 5 hours drying
COOKING TIME 10 minutes

PER HOUSE

1000 calories
34g fat (of which 20g saturates)
172g carbohydrate
0.7g salt

Finishing touches

Pipe names on the gift tags and leave the house and tags to set for at least 2 hours. Wrap each gingerbread house in cellophane and tie with ribbon. Attach the gift tags with ribbon.

1 Grease two baking sheets. Cut the card into templates for the roof and walls. Put the flour, bicarbonate of soda and ginger into a bowl. Rub in the butter until the mixture resembles breadcrumbs. Stir in the sugar. Warm the syrup in a pan, pour on to the flour with the beaten egg and stir. Bring together into a soft dough and knead until smooth. Divide into four pieces, wrap in clingfilm and chill for 15 minutes.

2 Roll out one piece of dough to 3mm (⅛in) thick. Cut out two of each template. Put on the baking sheets. Repeat with the remaining dough. Stamp out four hearts from the trimmings and skewer a hole in the top of each. Put on the baking sheets. Chill for 15 minutes. Preheat the oven to 190°C (170°C fan oven) mark 5. Bake for 8–10 minutes until golden. While still warm, push a skewer through the holes. Leave on the trays for 5 minutes, then transfer to a wire rack to cool.

3 To decorate, beat the icing sugar into the egg white until the mixture stands in peaks. Spoon into a piping bag and pipe windows and doors on the walls and squiggly lines on the roof. Leave to dry for 2 hours. Pipe icing along the edge of the side walls and stick to the end walls. Leave to dry for 1 hour, then place on a board and fill with sweets. Pipe icing along the top of each house and the roof pieces and press gently in position; hold for 1–2 minutes until secure.

Nutty Fudge Shortbread

MAKES 16 WEDGES

225g (8oz) unsalted butter, softened, plus extra to grease
300g (11oz) plain flour, sifted
pinch of salt
125g (4oz) caster sugar
125g (4oz) light muscovado sugar, sifted
2 tbsp golden syrup
170g can condensed milk
300g (11oz) plain chocolate, such as Bournville
100g (3½oz) walnut halves
100g (3½oz) hazelnuts, lightly toasted

PREPARATION TIME 40 minutes, plus 3 hours chilling
COOKING TIME 40 minutes

PER WEDGE

450 calories
26g fat (of which 12g saturates)
51g carbohydrate
0.3g salt

TECHNIQUES

see also toasting nuts (page 218)

1 Preheat the oven to 180°C (160°C fan oven) mark 4. Grease a 20.5 × 30.5cm (8 × 12in) Swiss roll tin. Whiz the flour, salt, caster sugar and 140g (4½oz) butter in a processor until it begins to come together. (Alternatively, use a food mixer.) Press the mixture into the prepared tin and smooth over with the back of a spoon. Bake for 20–30 minutes until golden. Cool.

2 Put the remaining butter, the muscovado sugar, syrup and condensed milk in a pan and heat gently but don't boil. Whisk together until combined. Pour over the shortbread, smooth the surface and chill for 3 hours.

3 Melt the chocolate in a heatproof bowl over a pan of gently simmering water. Mix with the nuts and pour over the fudge mixture. Smooth the top and leave to set. Cut into wedges to serve.

Chocolate and Hazelnut Biscotti

MAKES ABOUT 20

125g (4oz) plain flour, sifted, plus extra to dust
75g (3oz) golden caster sugar
¼ tsp baking powder
pinch of cinnamon
pinch of salt
1 large egg, beaten
1 tbsp milk
¼ tsp vanilla extract
25g (1oz) hazelnuts
25g (1oz) plain chocolate chips

PREPARATION TIME 10 minutes
COOKING TIME 40 minutes

PER BISCUIT
50 calories
1g fat (of which trace saturates)
9g carbohydrate
0g salt

1 Preheat the oven to 200°C (180°C fan oven) mark 6. Put the flour into a large bowl. Stir in the sugar, baking powder and salt. Make a well in the centre and stir in the beaten eggs, milk, vanilla extract, hazelnuts and chocolate chips with a fork to form a sticky dough.

2 On a lightly floured surface, gently knead the mixture into a ball. Roll into a 28cm (11in) sausage shape. Put on a baking sheet and flatten slightly. Bake for 20–25 minutes or until pale golden.

3 Turn down the oven temperature to 150°C (130°C fan oven) mark 2. Put the biscotti log on to a chopping board and slice diagonally with a bread knife at 1cm (½in) intervals. Arrange the slices on the baking sheet and put back in the oven for 15 minutes or until golden and dry. Transfer to a wire rack to cool. To enjoy Italian-style, dunk into coffee or dessert wine.

Finishing touches

To make as gifts, divide the biscuits among four large squares of cellophane, then draw up the edges and tie with ribbon. Label the packages with storage information and an eat-by date.

Apple Madeleines

MAKES 24

150g (5oz) unsalted butter, melted and cooled, plus extra to grease
3 large eggs
150g (5oz) caster sugar
1 tsp vanilla extract
150g (5oz) plain flour, sifted
½ tsp baking powder
2 apples such as Cox's, peeled, cored and finely chopped
icing sugar to dust

PREPARATION TIME 15 minutes
COOKING TIME 8–10 minutes

PER MADELEINE
106 calories
6g fat (of which 4g saturates)
13g carbohydrate
0.1g salt

TECHNIQUES
see also preparing apples (page 206)

1 Preheat the oven to 200°C (180°C fan oven) mark 6. Grease the Madeleine tins. Using an electric whisk, beat the eggs and caster sugar together until thick (this should take about 8 minutes), then add the vanilla extract. Quickly but gently, fold in the flour, baking powder and apples followed by the melted butter, making sure the butter doesn't settle at the bottom of the bowl.

2 Spoon the mixture into the Madeleine tins. Bake for 8–10 minutes until golden, then remove from the tins and cool on wire racks. Dust with icing sugar before serving.

Get ahead

You can make these madeleines up to two days ahead. Complete the recipe, then cool, cover and store in an airtight container.

Sticky Ginger Flapjacks

MAKES 12 LARGE SQUARES OR 24 SMALL TRIANGLES

350g (12oz) unsalted butter, plus extra to grease
275g (10oz) caster sugar
225g (8oz) golden syrup
450g (1lb) rolled oats
1 tbsp ground ginger

PREPARATION TIME 10 minutes
COOKING TIME 40 minutes

PER SERVING
517 calories per large square
27g fat (of which 15g saturates)
67g carbohydrate
0.6g salt
259 calories per small triangle
14g fat (of which 8g saturates)
33g carbohydrate
0.3g salt

TECHNIQUES
see also lining tins (page 322)

1 Preheat the oven to 180°C (160°C fan oven) mark 4. Grease and baseline an 18 × 28cm (7 × 11in), 5cm (2in) deep cake tin with non-stick baking parchment. Put the butter, sugar and golden syrup in a large pan and heat them together gently until melted. Mix in the rolled oats and ground ginger until they are thoroughly combined.

2 Pour the mixture into the tin, level the surface and bake for 30–35 minutes until golden brown around the edges (see Cook's tip).

3 Leave to cool in the tin for 15 minutes. While still warm, score into squares or triangles with a sharp knife. Leave in the tin to cool completely, then turn out and cut into the required shape.

Cook's tip

Don't overcook the flapjacks or they will be hard and dry. When they are cooked, they should still be sticky and slightly soft when you press them in the middle.

The Ultimate Chocolate Brownie

MAKES 16

200g (7oz) salted butter, plus extra to grease
400g (14oz) good-quality plain chocolate
225g (8oz) light muscovado sugar
1 tsp vanilla extract
150g (5oz) pecan nuts, roughly chopped
25g (1oz) cocoa powder, sifted
75g (3oz) self-raising flour, sifted
3 large eggs, beaten
sifted cocoa powder to dust

PREPARATION TIME 15 minutes, plus 2 hours cooling
COOKING TIME 1 hour 20 minutes

PER BROWNIE
257 calories
11g fat (of which 6g saturates)
38g carbohydrate
0.2g salt

TECHNIQUES
see also which chocolate to choose? (page 357), chopping nuts (page 218), lining tins (page 322), melting chocolate (page 356)

1 Preheat the oven to 170°C (150°C fan oven) mark 3. Grease and baseline a 20.5cm (8in) square, 5cm (2in) deep baking tin with non-stick baking parchment. Put the butter and chocolate in a heatproof bowl over a pan of gently simmering water and stir until melted. Remove from the heat and stir in the sugar, vanilla extract, pecan nuts, cocoa, flour and eggs.

2 Turn the mixture into the prepared tin and level with the back of a spoon. Bake for about 1 hour 15 minutes or until set to the centre on the surface but still soft underneath.

3 Leave to cool in the tin for 2 hours. Turn out, dust with sifted cocoa powder and cut into squares. Eat cold or serve warm with ice cream.

Cook's tip

The secret to really moist, squidgy brownies is all in the timing. A few minutes too long in the oven will produce a dry texture so be careful not to bake them for too long.

Lime Drizzle Loaf

SERVES 12

175g (6oz) self-raising flour, sifted with a pinch of salt
175g (6oz) butter, diced
175g (6oz) golden caster sugar
3 medium eggs, beaten
50g (2oz) sweetened and tenderised coconut
zest and juice of 2 limes
1 tsp baking powder

For the icing

1 lime
125g (4oz) golden icing sugar, sifted
1 tbsp sweetened and tenderised coconut to decorate

PREPARATION TIME 15 minutes
COOKING TIME 45–55 minutes

PER SERVING

306 calories
17g fat (of which 11g saturates)
38g carbohydrate
0.4g salt

TECHNIQUES

see also zesting citrus fruits (page 207), lining a loaf tin (page 323)

1 Preheat the oven to 180°C (160°C fan oven) mark 4. Line a 900g (2lb) loaf tin with a greaseproof loaf liner.

2 Put the flour, salt, butter, caster sugar, eggs, coconut, lime zest and juice and baking powder in the bowl of a freestanding mixer, fitted with a K beater. Mix together slowly, gradually increasing the speed and mixing for 2 minutes. (Alternatively, use a hand mixer.)

3 Pour the mixture (it'll be quite runny) into the tin and bake in the oven for 45–55 minutes or until golden, well risen and cooked through – a skewer inserted into the centre should come out clean. Leave to cool for 10 minutes, then lift out the cake, keeping it in the liner.

4 To make the icing, finely grate the zest from the lime and cut away the white pith. Chop the lime flesh, then put in a mini processor or blender with the zest and whiz for 1–2 minutes or until finely chopped. Add the icing sugar and blend until smooth. Pour over the cake, then sprinkle the coconut on top to decorate.

Almond and Orange Torte

SERVES 12
oil to grease
flour to dust
1 medium orange
3 medium eggs
225g (8oz) golden caster sugar
250g (9oz) ground almonds
½ tsp baking powder
golden icing sugar to dust
crème fraîche to serve

PREPARATION TIME 30 minutes
COOKING TIME 1 hour 50 minutes

PER SERVING
223 calories
13g fat (of which 1g saturates)
22g carbohydrate
0.1g salt

TECHNIQUES
see also lining a loaf tin (page 323)

1 Grease and line, then oil and flour a 20.5cm (8in) springform cake tin. Put the whole orange in a small pan and cover with water. Bring to the boil, then cover and simmer for at least 1 hour until tender. Remove from the water and cool.

2 Cut the orange in half and remove the pips. Whiz in a food processor or blender to make a smooth purée.

3 Preheat the oven to 180°C (160°C fan oven) mark 4. Put the eggs and caster sugar in a bowl and whisk together until thick and pale. Fold in the almonds, baking powder and orange purée.

4 Pour the mixture into the prepared tin. Bake for 40–50 minutes until a skewer inserted into the centre comes out clean. Leave to cool in the tin.

5 Release the clasp on the tin and remove the cake. Carefully peel off the parchment and put the cake on a serving plate. Dust with icing sugar, then cut into 12 wedges. Serve with crème fraîche.

Cook's tip

To save time, you can microwave the orange. Put it in a small bowl, cover with 100ml (3½fl oz) water and cook in a 900W microwave oven on High for 10–12 minutes until soft.

Apple and Blueberry Cake

SERVES 8

125g (4oz) butter, diced, plus extra to grease
225g (8oz) self-raising flour, sifted
½ tsp salt
175g (6oz) granulated sugar, golden if possible
2 large eggs, beaten
2 large Granny Smith apples, peeled, cored and sliced
140g (4½oz) punnet blueberries
175g (6oz) apricot jam
1 tbsp lemon juice

PREPARATION TIME 20 minutes, plus cooling
COOKING TIME 1 hour

PER SERVING
394 calories
15g fat (of which 9g saturates)
65g carbohydrate
0.6g salt

TECHNIQUES
see also preparing apples (page 206), lining a loaf tin (page 323)

1 Preheat the oven to 190°C (170°C fan oven) mark 5, then grease and baseline a 20.5cm (8in) springform tin with non-stick baking parchment. Put the flour and salt in a large mixing bowl, add the diced butter and rub in the flour until the mixture looks like fine breadcrumbs. Add 140g (4½oz) sugar with the beaten eggs and stir well.

2 Spread half the mixture in a thin layer in the tin, then layer the sliced apples and the blueberries evenly over the surface, setting aside a little of the fruit for the top of the cake. Sprinkle with the remaining sugar, then spoon in the rest of the cake mixture. Add the remaining apple slices and blueberries, pressing them down slightly into the mixture.

3 Bake for 45–55 minutes until risen and firm to the touch – a skewer inserted into the centre of the cake should come out clean. Cool in the tin for 10 minutes, then unmould and put on a wire rack to cool.

4 Warm the jam and lemon juice in a small pan until evenly combined. Sieve the mixture and, while it's still warm, brush it over the top of the cake. Serve immediately.

Freezing tip

Wrap the cake in a freezer bag and freeze for up to one month.
To use Thaw for 3 hours at cool room temperature. Heat individual cake slices in the microwave set on High for 1 minute per slice.

Carrot Tray Bake

SERVES 15

100g (3½oz) butter, chopped, plus extra for greasing
140g (4½oz) carrots, grated
100g (3½oz) sultanas
100g (3½oz) chopped dried dates
50g (2oz) tenderised coconut
1 tsp ground cinnamon
½ tsp freshly grated nutmeg
330g bottle maple syrup
150ml (¼ pint) apple juice
zest and juice of 2 oranges
225g (8oz) wholemeal self-raising flour, sifted
2 tsp bicarbonate of soda
125g (4oz) walnut pieces

For the topping

pared zest from ½–1 orange
200g (7oz) cream cheese
200g (7oz) crème fraîche
2 tbsp icing sugar
1 tsp vanilla extract

PREPARATION TIME 30 minutes
COOKING TIME 50 minutes–1 hour 5 minutes

PER SERVING

399 calories
25g fat (of which 13g saturates)
41g carbohydrate
0.4g salt

TECHNIQUES

see also preparing root vegetables (page 181), zesting citrus fruits (page 207)

1 Preheat the oven to 190°C (170°C fan oven) mark 5. Grease a 23 × 23cm (9 × 9in) cake tin and line with greaseproof paper.

2 Put the butter, carrots, sultanas, dates, coconut, spices, maple syrup, apple juice and orange zest and juice into a large pan. Cover and bring to the boil, then cook for ?? minutes. Tip into a bowl and leave to cool.

3 Put the flour, bicarbonate of soda and walnuts in a large bowl and stir together. Add the cooled carrot mixture and stir well.

4 Spoon the mixture into the tin and bake for 45 minutes–1 hour until firm. Leave in the tin for 10 minutes, then remove and cool on a wire rack.

5 To make the topping, finely slice the orange zest. Put the cream cheese, crème fraîche, icing sugar and vanilla in a bowl and stir with a spatula. Spread over the cake and top with the zest.

Banana and Butterscotch Loaf

MAKES 1 LOAF (15 SLICES)
butter to grease
175g (6oz) plain flour, sifted
2 tsp baking powder
½ tsp bicarbonate of soda
½ tsp salt
175g (6oz) light muscovado sugar
2 large eggs
3 medium ripe bananas, mashed
150g carton natural yogurt
150g bar butterscotch chocolate, roughly chopped
100g (3½oz) pecan nuts, chopped
1–2 tbsp demerara sugar

PREPARATION TIME 20 minutes
COOKING TIME 1hour

PER SERVING
221cals
9g fat (of which 2g saturates)
34g carbohydrate
0.2g salt

TECHNIQUES
see also chopping nuts (page 218), lining a loaf tin (page 323)

1 Preheat the oven to 170°C (150°C fan oven) mark 3. Grease and line a 1.4kg (3lb) loaf tin with greaseproof paper.

2 Put the flour, baking powder, bicarbonate of soda and salt in a large bowl and mix together.

3 In a separate bowl, beat together the mucovado sugar and eggs with an electric hand whisk until pale and fluffy. Carefully stir in the bananas, yogurt, chocolate and 50g (2oz) pecan nuts, followed by the flour mixture.

4 Spoon into the loaf tin and sprinkle over the remaining chopped pecan nuts and the demerara sugar. Bake for 1 hour or until a skewer inserted into the centre comes out clean. Cool in the tin on a wire rack, then turn out and slice.

Variation

If you can't find butterscotch chocolate, use a bar of plain dark chocolate instead.

Sticky Ginger Ring

MAKES 8 SLICES

100g (3½oz) butter, diced, plus extra to grease
100g (3½oz) soft brown sugar
3 tbsp black treacle
100ml (3½fl oz) milk
2 tbsp brandy
1 large egg, beaten
150g (5oz) plain flour
2 tsp ground ginger
2 tsp ground cinnamon
1 tsp bicarbonate of soda
75g (3oz) ready-to-eat pitted prunes, chopped coarsely

For the topping

225g (8oz) icing sugar, sifted
2 pieces stem ginger, drained from syrup and roughly chopped

PREPARATION TIME 15 minutes, plus cooling
COOKING TIME 1 hour

PER SLICE

375 calories
12g fat (of which 7g saturates)
64g carbohydrate
0.3g salt

1 Preheat the oven to 150°C (130°C fan oven) mark 4. Using your hands, generously grease a 21cm (8½in), 600ml (1 pint) capacity round ring mould with butter.

2 Put the butter, brown sugar and treacle in a pan and heat gently until melted, stirring all the time. Add the milk and brandy. Cool, then beat in the egg.

3 Sift the flour, spices and bicarbonate of soda into a large mixing bowl. Make a well in the centre, pour in the treacle mixture and stir together until all the flour has been combined – it should have a soft dropping consistency. Then, stir in the chopped prunes.

4 Pour the mixture into the greased ring mould and bake in the oven for 1 hour or until the cake is firm to the touch and a skewer inserted in the centre comes out clean. Leave to cool in the tin for 10 minutes, then loosen the sides of the cake and turn out on to a wire rack.

5 To make the icing, mix the icing sugar with about 2 tbsp hot water to create a coating consistency. Drizzle over the cake and down the sides, then decorate with the stem ginger.

Freezing tip

Complete to step 4, wrap the cake in clingfilm and foil. Freeze for up to one month.
To use Thaw for 3 hours and complete the cake.

CHOCOLATE

Everyone's favourite – whether you're eating it on its own or turning it into an indulgent treat! This chapter is dedicated to cooking with and using chocolate. It guides you through all the basics from melting chocolate to making chocolate decorations, dipping fruit and making sauces, plus invaluable tips on choosing the right chocolate for the job and tips for ensuring perfect results. The recipe section builds on these skills with fabulous recipes including White chocolate mousse cake, Decadent chocolate cake, Chocolate-chunk bread pudding, Warm chocolate fondant, White chocolate mousse and Nutty chocolate truffles.

Using chocolate

Chocolate is delicious to eat, and is fabulous used with other ingredients in recipes. However, it has many other wonderful uses in the kitchen too, and can be turned into stunning decorations.

Melting

For cooking or making decorations, chocolate is usually melted first.

1 Break the chocolate into pieces and put in a heatproof bowl or in the top of a double boiler. Set over a pan of gently simmering water.

2 Heat very gently until the chocolate starts to melt, then stir regularly until completely melted.

Shaving

This is the easiest decoration of all because it doesn't call for melting the chocolate.

1 Hold a chocolate bar upright on the work surface and shave pieces off the edge with a swivel peeler.

2 Alternatively, grate the chocolate, against a coarse or medium-coarse grater, to make very fine shavings.

Chocolate curls

1 Melt the chocolate, as above, and spread it out in a thin layer on a marble slab or clean worksurface. Leave to firm up.

2 Use a sharp, flat-ended blade (such as a pastry scraper or a very stiff spatula) to scrape through the chocolate at a 45 degree angle. The size of the curls will be determined by the width of the blade.

Cook's tips

- When melting chocolate, use a gentle heat.
- Don't let water or steam touch the chocolate or it will 'seize' – become hard and unworkable. If it has siezed, you can try saving it by stirring in a few drops of flavourless vegetable oil.

Chocolate leaves

1 Wash and dry some rose or bay leaves for coating. Spread slightly cooled melted chocolate in a thin, even layer over the shiny side of the leaf. Spread it right out to the edge using a paintbrush, but wipe off any chocolate that drips over the edge.

2 Leave to cool completely. Then, working very gently and carefully, peel the leaf off the chocolate.

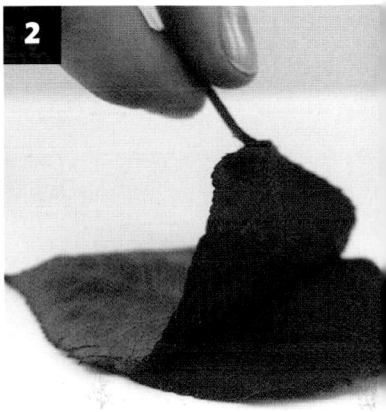

Chocolate wafers

1 You can make flat or curved wafers in any shape you like. Cut a piece of greaseproof paper to the required width.

2 Brush the paper evenly with melted chocolate and leave until the chocolate has almost set.

3 Using a knife, cut the chocolate (while still on the paper) into pieces of the desired size and shape (straight or curved, square or triangular, narrow or wide). You can also cut out chocolate shapes using small cutters.

4 Leave to cool and harden completely, either on the work surface (for flat wafers) or draped over a rolling pin (for curled).

5 Carefully peel the wafers off the paper, handling them as little as possible, and store in the refrigerator for up to 24 hours.

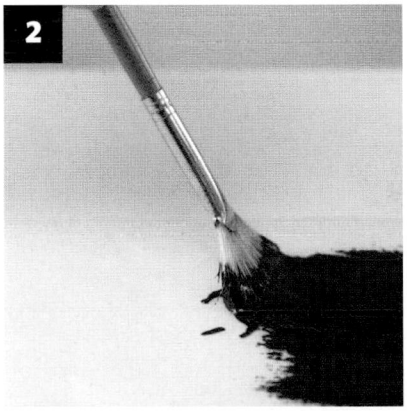

Which chocolate to choose?

The type of chocolate you choose will have a dramatic effect on the end product. For the best results, buy chocolate that has a high proportion of cocoa solids, preferably at least 70 per cent. Most supermarkets stock a selection. Chocolate with a high percentage of cocoa solids has a rich flavour and is perfect for sauces, ganache (see page 359), most sweets, cakes and desserts. At the top end of the scale, couverture chocolate is the one preferred by chefs for confectionery work and gives an intense chocolate flavour that is probably best reserved for special mousses and gâteaux. It is available in milk, plain and white varieties from specialist chocolate shops. For most purposes, a good-quality couverture with a high proportion of cocoa solids will usually give great results.

Chocolate moulds

You can make almost any hollow container – such as an espresso cup or petit four case – into a mould.

1 Pour the melted chocolate into the mould, turning it to coat it evenly, and then pour out the excess. Chill until set.

2 Repeat the process until you have achieved the required thickness that you want (see Cook's tips). Leave to set, and then turn out, remembering to handle very gently.

3 Alternatively, you can use a small paintbrush to layer the chocolate. Simply dip the brush – scrupulously clean, of course – into the melted chocolate and paint the inside of the mould with it. Chill until set, then repeat layering with chocolate until you have achieved the thickness required for your particular purpose.

Cook's tips

- Your mould should not have any awkward curves or angles, or you will not be able to release the chocolate from the mould. A simple bowl or straight-sided shape is best.
- The larger the mould, the thicker the chocolate layer should be. For something small like a teacup, the thickness can be just a few coatings of chocolate; while for larger moulds, it should be around 6mm (¼ inch).
- Make sure that your mould is spotlessly clean, completely dry and free of lint or fibres (if you have dried it with a teatowel).

Piping

1 Draw your designs on a sheet of white paper, then lay a sheet of greaseproof paper on top.

2 Take a piping cone or piping bag fitted with a fine nozzle and fill with melted chocolate.

3 Using light, even pressure, pipe chocolate on to the paper following the outline of the drawing. Leave to set, then carefully remove the piped lines using a fine-bladed knife.

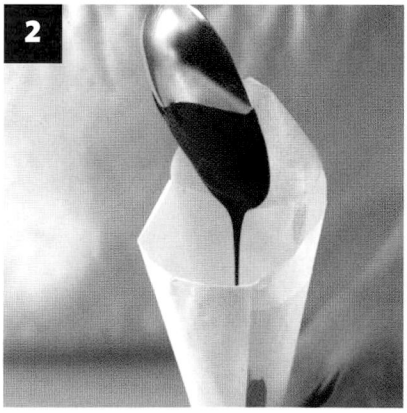

Chocolate-dipped fruit

1 Melt the chocolate in a bowl set over a pan of hot water. Lay a sheet of greaseproof paper on the work surface next to the hob.

2 Ensure the fruit is dry. If using whole fruit such as strawberries, hold them by the stem and dip into the chocolate. Allow excess to drain off. Leave to cool on the greaseproof paper, then chill.

3 If using pieces of fruit or dried fruit, hold them individually with tongs or tweezers and dip in the chocolate. (You can do this faster by putting a handful of fruits on a skimmer or slotted spoon and dipping them together.) Allow the excess to drain, then put on greaseproof paper. Leave to cool and chill until needed (for a maximum of one day).

Chocolate sauce

1 Chop the best-quality dark chocolate (with a minimum of 70 per cent cocoa solids) and put it into a saucepan with 50ml (2fl oz) water per 100g (3½ oz) chocolate.

2 Heat slowly, allowing the chocolate to melt, then stir until the sauce is smooth. To liven up this simple chocolate sauce, see the variations below right.

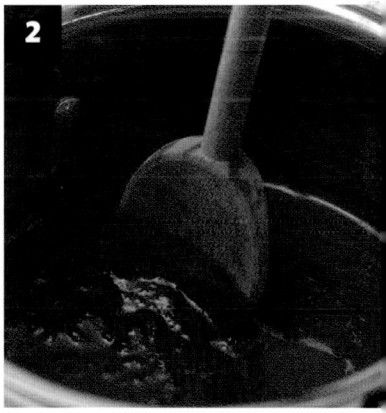

Ganache

This topping is made from good-quality chocolate mixed with cream and butter. Increasing the ratio of cream to chocolate will make the ganache lighter, and sometimes the butter is left out so that the ganache won't be too rich. The recipe on page 361 (step 2 of Nutty Chocolate Truffles) is very versatile.

Variations

These are all suitable for a sauce made with 200g (7oz) chocolate:

- **Milk or single cream** Substituted in whole or in part for the water.
- **Coffee** Stir in a teaspoon of instant coffee or a shot of espresso when melting the chocolate.
- **Spices** Add a pinch of ground cinnamon, crushed cardamom seeds or freshly grated nutmeg to the melting chocolate.
- **Vanilla extract** Stir in ¼ tsp vanilla when melting the chocolate.
- **Rum, whisky or cognac** Stir in about 1 tsp alcohol when melting the chocolate.
- **Butter** Stir in 25g (1oz) towards the end of heating.

Chocolate and Cherry Gateau

SERVES 12

350g (12oz) cherries, pitted, (or 400g can pitted cherries, drained), plus extra fresh cherries for decoration
3 tbsp dark rum
50g (2oz) almonds, toasted
50g (2oz) plain flour, sifted
350g (12oz) plain chocolate (70 per cent cocoa solids, if possible)
3 large eggs, separated
125g (4oz) butter, softened, plus extra to grease
125g (4oz) caster sugar
450ml (¾ pint) double cream
chocolate curls and cocoa powder to decorate
single cream to serve (optional)

PREPARATION TIME 1 hour, plus 8 hours marinating and chilling
COOKING TIME 45 minutes

PER SERVING

537 calories
41g fat (of which 23g saturates)
38g carbohydrate
0.2g salt

TECHNIQUES

see also pitting cherries (page 208), toasting nuts (page 218), separating eggs (page 52), lining tins (page 322), making chocolate curls (page 356)

Freezing tip

Complete step 2, but don't decorate the cake, then pack and freeze.
To use Thaw overnight at cool room temperature. Complete the recipe.

1 Put the cherries in a bowl with 2 tbsp rum. Cover and soak for at least 6 hours. Whiz the almonds and flour in a food processor until finely ground. Preheat the oven to 180°C (160°C fan oven) mark 4. Grease and baseline a 23cm (9in) diameter deep cake tin. Melt 140g (4½oz) chocolate with 3 tbsp water in a bowl over a pan of gently simmering water. Remove from the heat, add the remaining rum and the egg yolks and beat until smooth. Beat the butter and sugar together until light and fluffy. Stir in the chocolate mixture and fold in the flour and almonds. Whisk the egg whites until soft peaks form, then fold into the chocolate mixture. Pour into the tin and bake for 30–35 minutes until a skewer comes out clean with a few crumbs on it. Cool in the tin for 10 minutes, then turn out on to a wire rack to cool.

2 Roughly chop the remaining chocolate. Bring the cream to the boil, pour over the chocolate, leave for 5 minutes, then stir until melted. Allow to cool, then, using an electric whisk, beat the mixture until thick and lighter in colour. Clean the cake tin and return the cake to the tin. Spoon the cherries and any juice over the cake. Spread the chocolate cream on top, smooth the surface, cover and chill for at least 2 hours. Decorate with chocolate curls, dust with cocoa and serve with cherries and cream, if you like.

White Chocolate Mousse Cake

SERVES 10
vegetable oil to grease
450g (1lb) white chocolate
285ml (9½fl oz) double cream
finely grated zest of 1 large orange
2 tsp orange liqueur, such as Grand Marnier
300ml (½ pint) full-fat Greek yogurt

PREPARATION TIME 30 minutes, plus overnight freezing
COOKING TIME 20–30 minutes

PER SERVING
416 calories
32g fat (of which 19g saturates)
27g carbohydrate
0.2g salt

TECHNIQUES
see also melting chocolate (page 356), zesting citrus fruits (page 207)

1 Lightly oil a shallow 20cm (8in) round cake tin and line with baking parchment.

2 Break the chocolate into pieces and put into a large bowl with half the cream. Bring a large pan of water to the boil, remove from the heat and sit the bowl of chocolate and cream on top, making sure the base of the bowl doesn't touch the water. Leave for 20–30 minutes until the chocolate has melted. Don't stir; just leave it to melt.

3 Meanwhile, put the orange zest and liqueur into a small bowl. Set aside to soak. Whip the remaining cream until it just holds its shape.

4 Remove the bowl of melted chocolate from the pan and beat in the yogurt. Fold in the cream with the zest and liqueur mix.

5 Spoon the mixture into the prepared tin, cover with clingfilm and freeze overnight or for up to one month. One hour before serving, transfer from the freezer to the refrigerator. Unwrap and put on a serving plate.

Cook's tip

If you like, you can decorate the mousse with a few halved strawberries, some blueberries and a handful of unsprayed rose petals, then dust with icing sugar.

Chocolate Amaretti Tart

SERVES 8

400g (14oz) pitted morello cherries (bottled or canned), drained
3 tbsp brandy, sloe gin or almond-flavoured liqueur
150g (5oz) butter, softened
50g (2oz) icing sugar, plus extra to dust
1 small egg, beaten
225g (8oz) plain white flour, plus extra to dust

For the filling

100g (3½oz) plain chocolate
125g (4oz) butter, softened
125g (4oz) caster sugar
3 large eggs, beaten
125g (4oz) ground almonds
25g (1oz) self-raising flour
50g (2oz) amaretti biscuits, crushed
75g (3oz) slivered or flaked almonds

PREPARATION TIME 30 minutes, plus 50 minutes chilling
COOKING TIME 1½ hours, plus 10–15 minutes cooling

PER SERVING

777calories
50g fat (of which 22g saturates)
71g carbohydrate
0.7g salt

Freezing tip

Complete the recipe up to baking the cake at step 2, then cool, wrap and freeze.
To use Thaw at cool room temperature overnight. Warm through as above and dust with icing sugar before serving.

1 Put the cherries in a bowl with the brandy, gin or liqueur and leave for 30 minutes. Put the butter, icing sugar and egg in a food processor and whiz until almost smooth. Add the flour and whiz until the mixture begins to form a dough. (Alternatively, rub the fat into the flour by hand or using a pastry cutter and stir in the icing sugar and egg.) Lightly knead the pastry on a floured worksurface, then wrap and chill for 30 minutes. Roll out the pastry on a lightly floured worksurface and line a 24cm (9½in) fluted loose-based flan tin. Chill for 20 minutes. Preheat the oven to 200°C (180°C fan oven) mark 6. Line the pastry base with greaseproof paper and baking beans and cook for 15 minutes. Remove the weighted paper and put back in the oven for a further 5 minutes. Reduce the oven temperature to 150°C (130°C fan oven) mark 2.

2 For the filling, put the chocolate in a heatproof bowl over a pan of gently simmering water. Stir until melted and smooth. Cool. In a bowl, beat the butter with the sugar until pale and fluffy. Gradually beat in the eggs alternately with the almonds and flour. Fold in the chocolate and amaretti biscuits. Spoon one-third of the mixture over the base of the pastry case. Spoon the cherries over. Spread the remaining filling mixture to cover the cherries. Sprinkle on the almonds and bake for about 1 hour. The tart will have a thin top crust but be soft underneath. Cool in the tin for 10–15 minutes, then unmould, dust with icing sugar and serve.

Decadent Chocolate Cake

SERVES 12

225g (8oz) unsalted butter, softened, plus extra to grease
300g (11oz) plain chocolate, broken into pieces
225g (8oz) golden caster sugar
225g (8oz) ground almonds
8 large eggs, separated
125g (4oz) fresh brown breadcrumbs
4 tbsp apricot jam (optional)

For the ganache

175g (6oz) plain chocolate, broken into pieces
75g (3oz) butter, softened
4 tbsp double cream

PREPARATION TIME 30 minutes
COOKING TIME 1½ hours, plus 2–3 hours cooling

PER SERVING

687 calories
49g fat (of which 23g saturates)
54g carbohydrate
0.7g salt

TECHNIQUES

see also separating eggs (page 52), making breadcrumbs (page 308), lining tins (page 322), melting chocolate (page 356), whisking egg whites (page 52), testing sponges (page 324), cooling cakes (page 324)

1 Preheat the oven to 180°C (160°C fan oven) mark 4. Grease and line a 23cm (9in) springform cake tin. Melt the chocolate in a heatproof bowl over a pan of gently simmering water. Remove from the heat. Put the butter and sugar into a large bowl and beat until light and creamy. Add the almonds, egg yolks and breadcrumbs. Beat well until thoroughly mixed. Slowly add the chocolate and carefully stir it in. Do not over-mix as the chocolate may seize up. Put the egg whites into a clean grease-free bowl and whisk until stiff peaks form. Add half the whites to the chocolate mixture and fold in lightly using a large metal spoon. Carefully fold in the remainder. Pour into the tin and level the surface. Bake for 1 hour 20 minutes or until the cake is firm to the touch and a skewer inserted into the centre comes out clean. Cool in the tin for 5 minutes, then transfer to a rack for 2–3 hours to cool completely.

2 Put the jam, if using, into a pan and melt over a low heat. Brush jam over the top and sides of the cooled cake.

3 Melt the chocolate, butter and cream in a heatproof bowl over a pan of gently simmering water. Stir just once until smooth. Either raise the cake off the worktop on the upturned tin or put it (still on the rack) on to a tray to catch the drips. Pour the ganache over the centre and tip the cake to let it run down the sides evenly, or spread it with a palette knife.

Chocolate-chunk Bread Pudding

SERVES 6

200g (7oz) baguette
100g (3½oz) milk chocolate, roughly chopped
500g carton fresh vanilla custard
150ml (¼ pint) milk
1 large egg, beaten
1 tbsp demerara sugar
50g (2oz) walnuts, finely chopped
50g (2oz) plain or milk chocolate, in chunks
icing sugar to dust
single cream to serve (optional)

PREPARATION TIME 20 minutes, plus minimum 4 hours chilling
COOKING TIME 55 minutes–1 hour 15 minutes

PER SERVING
390 calories
17g fat (of which 6g saturates)
51g carbohydrate
0.7g salt

TECHNIQUES
see also chopping nuts (page 218)

1 Roughly chop the baguette and put it into a large bowl. Put the milk chocolate in a pan with the custard and milk over a low heat. Stir gently until the chocolate has melted. Beat in the egg.

2 Pour the chocolate mixture over the bread, stir well to coat, then cover and chill for at least 4 hours.

3 Preheat the oven to 180°C (160°C fan oven) mark 4. Spoon the soaked bread into a buttered 1.4 litre (2½ pint), 7.5cm (3in) deep ovenproof dish, then bake for 30–40 minutes.

4 Sprinkle over the demerara sugar, walnuts and chocolate chunks. Return to the oven to cook for 20–30 minutes until lightly set. Dust with icing sugar. Serve the pudding warm, with single cream, if you like.

Warm Chocolate Fondant

SERVES 6

3 whole medium eggs, plus 3 egg yolks
50g (2oz) golden caster sugar
175g (6oz) plain chocolate
150g (5oz) unsalted butter
50g (2oz) plain flour, sifted
6 chocolate truffles
good-quality vanilla ice cream to serve

PREPARATION TIME 10 minutes
COOKING TIME about 25 minutes

PER SERVING
502 calories
37g fat (of which 21g saturates)
39g carbohydrate
0.5g salt

TECHNIQUES
see also separating eggs (page 52), melting chocolate (page 356), making vanilla ice cream (page 388)

1 Preheat the oven to 200°C (180°C fan oven) mark 6. Put the eggs, egg yolks and sugar into a large bowl and beat with an electric whisk for 8–10 minutes until light and fluffy. You can do this by hand but it will take a little longer.

2 Melt the chocolate and butter in a heatproof bowl over a pan of gently simmering water, taking care not to let the bowl touch the water.

3 Gently fold the flour into the egg mixture. Stir a spoonful of egg mixture into the melted chocolate, then gently fold the chocolate mixture into the remaining egg mixture.

4 Put a large spoonful of mixture into each of six 200ml (7fl oz) ramekins. Put a chocolate truffle into the centre of each, taking care not to push it down. Divide the remainder of the mixture among the ramekins to cover the truffle. Each ramekin should be about three-quarters full.

5 Bake for 10–12 minutes until the top is firm and starting to rise and crack. Serve with ice cream.

Cook's tip

Be sure to choose a good quality chocolate with minimum 70 per cent cocoa solids. It will give the rich, intense chocolate flavour that you need in these indulgent fondants.

White Chocolate Mousse

SERVES 6
100ml (3½fl oz) full-fat milk
1 cinnamon stick
250g (9oz) good-quality white chocolate
285ml (9½fl oz) double cream
3 large egg whites
50g (2oz) plain chocolate
a little cocoa powder and ground cinnamon to decorate

PREPARATION TIME 15 minutes, plus minimum 4 hours chilling
COOKING TIME 15 minutes

PER SERVING
515 calories
41g fat (of which 25g saturates)
31g carbohydrate
0.2g salt

TECHNIQUES
see also separating eggs (page 52), melting chocolate (page 356), whisking egg whites (page 52)

1 Put the milk and cinnamon stick in a small pan and warm over a medium heat until the milk is almost boiling. Take the pan off the heat and set aside.

2 Melt the white chocolate in a heatproof bowl over a pan of gently simmering water. Take the bowl off the pan and leave to cool a little.

3 Strain the warm milk on to the melted chocolate and stir together until completely smooth. Leave to cool for 10 minutes.

4 Whip the cream in a bowl until it just begins to hold its shape – it should still be a bit floppy. Whisk the egg whites until soft peaks form. Fold the whipped cream into the chocolate mixture with a large metal spoon, then carefully fold in the egg whites. Spoon the mixture into six small bowls or glasses – each measuring about 150ml (¼ pint) – and chill for 4 hours or overnight.

5 Pull a vegetable peeler across the edge of the plain chocolate to make rough curls. Sprinkle over the mousse. Dust with cocoa powder and a pinch of cinnamon.

Get ahead

Make up to the end of step 4 up to one day ahead. Cover and chill until needed.
To use Complete the recipe.

Chilled Chocolate Biscuit Cake

MAKES 21

125g (4oz) butter, chopped, plus extra to grease
150g (5oz) plain chocolate, broken into pieces
250g (9oz) paneforte, finely chopped
100g (3½oz) cantuccini biscuits or Rich Tea biscuits, finely chopped
2–3 tbsp Amaretto, rum or brandy
ice cream to serve

PREPARATION TIME 15 minutes, plus 2 hours chilling
COOKING TIME 5 minutes

PER SLICE
157 calories
9g fat (of which 5g saturates)
17g carbohydrate
0.3g salt

TECHNIQUES
see also lining tins (page 322), melting chocolate (page 356)

1 Grease an 18cm (7in) square cake tin and baseline with baking parchment. Put the butter and chocolate in a heatproof bowl over a pan of gently simmering water. Stir until melted and set aside.

2 In a large bowl, mix the paneforte, cantuccini or Rich Tea biscuits and liqueur, rum or brandy. Add in the chocolate mixture and stir to coat.

3 Pour the mixture into the cake tin and chill for at least 2 hours. Cut into wedges and serve with ice cream.

Freezing tip

Complete the recipe but don't cut into wedges. Wrap and freeze.
To use Thaw at cool room temperature]erve.

Nutty Chocolate Truffles

MAKES ABOUT 30

100g pack hazelnuts
200g (7oz) plain chocolate (minimum 50 per cent cocoa solids), broken into pieces
25g (1oz) butter
140ml (4½fl oz) double cream
3 tbsp cocoa powder, sifted
3 tbsp golden icing sugar, sifted

PREPARATION TIME 15–20 minutes
COOKING TIME 12 minutes, plus 1–2 hours chilling

PER SERVING
96 calories
8g fat (of which 4g saturates)
6g carbohydrate
0.1g salt

TECHNIQUES
see also melting chocolate (page 356)

1 Put the hazelnuts into a frying pan and heat gently for 3–4 minutes, shaking the pan occasionally, to toast all over. Put 30 nuts into a bowl and leave to cool. Whiz the remaining nuts in a food processor until finely chopped. Put the chopped nuts into a shallow dish.

2 Melt the chocolate in a heatproof bowl over a pan of gently simmering water, taking care not to let the bowl touch the water. In a separate pan, melt the butter and cream together. Bring just to the boil, then remove from the heat. Carefully stir into the chocolate. Whisk until cool and thick, then chill for 1–2 hours.

3 Put the cocoa powder and icing sugar into separate shallow dishes. Scoop up a teaspoonful of truffle mix and push a hazelnut into the centre. Working quickly, shape into a ball, then roll in cocoa powder, icing sugar or chopped nuts. Repeat with remaining mix, then chill.

Get ahead

Store in an airtight container in the refrigerator for up to two weeks.

Hot Chocolate

SERVES 6
125g (4oz) plain chocolate, grated
450ml (¾ pint) milk
1 tbsp cornflour
4 tbsp golden caster sugar
140ml (4½fl oz) double cream

PREPARATION TIME 10 minutes
COOKING TIME 8–10 minutes

PER SERVING
306 calories
20g fat (of which 12g saturates)
30g carbohydrate
0.1g salt

TECHNIQUES
see also melting chocolate (page 356), shaving chocolate (page 356)

1 Put the grated chocolate and half the milk into a pan and heat gently until the chocolate has melted. Put the cornflour into a bowl and slowly add the remaining milk, stirring well to mix thoroughly. Add the cornflour mix to the pan and whisk it into the melted chocolate, then stir in the sugar. Cook on a low heat for 3 minutes, whisking constantly, until the hot chocolate thickens. Remove the pan from the heat and continue to whisk the chocolate until smooth.

2 Whisk the cream until thick. Pour the hot chocolate into six cups, top with cream and serve.

15 SUGAR

Incredibly versatile, sugar can be heated and transformed into all kinds of sweet treats such as caramel, toffee, fudge and praline, which can be eaten on their own, or used in sweet recipes. This chapter provides a guide to all the basic techniques including how to make caramel decorations, toffee, dulce de leche, fudge, praline, sugar syrup and spun sugar. The recipe section then puts these techniques into practice in indulgent recipes such as Cookies and cream fudge, Caramelised pineapple, Strawberry brûlée, Toffee cheesecake, Sticky banoffee pies and Apples with butterscotch sauce.

Working with sugar

Sugar is a wonderfully versatile ingredient. When heated it can be transformed entirely – into crisp caramel and praline, chewy toffee, creamy fudge and delicate spun sugar, to name but a few.

Dry caramel

Use to make decorations. They can be made up to 24 hours in advance and stored in airtight container.

1 Line a baking sheet with oiled greaseproof paper. Put 200g (7oz) caster sugar in a heavy-based pan with 4 tbsp water. Heat gently until the sugar dissolves.

2 Bring to the boil, then cook until it turns a medium caramel colour. Dip base of the pan in cold water. Use immediately before the caramel begins to harden.

3 For caramel flowers, make abstract shapes with a fork 4cm (1½in) in diameter on oiled greaseproof paper.

4 For caramel cages, lightly oil the back of a ladle. Drizzle caramel threads in a crisscross pattern, finishing with thread around the rim.

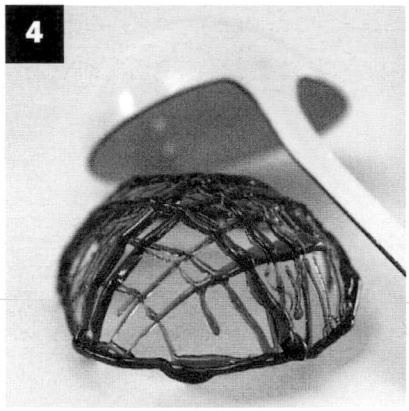

Cook's tips

- Once the syrup starts to colour, watch it closely – the colour can deepen rapidly, and very dark caramel tastes bitter.
- Have a pan of cold water ready to dip the base of the pan into to stop the caramel cooking further.

Wet caramel

A good sauce to use with fruit such as oranges, peaches and pineapple.

1 Put 200g (7oz) sugar in a heavy pan with 150ml (¼ pint) water. Heat gently to dissolve. Bring to boil and cook until a medium caramel colour.

2 Remove from heat, stand away and pour in 150ml (¼ pint) water. Heat and stir to dissolve, then cool.

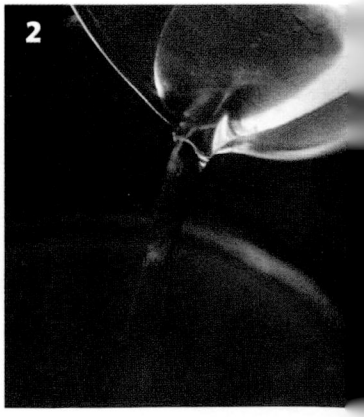

Toffee

To make 500g (1lb 2oz) toffee, you will need 250g (9oz) butter, 250g (9oz) sugar.

1 Line a shallow roasting tin with oiled baking parchment. Put the butter and sugar in a heavy-based pan and cook gently to dissolve the sugar.

2 Turn the heat up to medium and continue cooking, stirring frequently, until the mixture is a deep brown. On a sugar thermometer it should give a reading of around 150°C (300°F). (Test by putting a little of the syrup into a cup of cold water, it should form thick threads that bend a little but then break up.)

3 Pour the mixture into the roasting tin and smooth the top with a knife. Leave to set, then cut into squares or bite-sized pieces.

Nutty toffee

While the toffee is cooking, sprinkle the roasting tin with some coarsely chopped nuts, such as pecan nuts, almonds or walnuts. When the toffee is ready, pour it over the nuts and leave to set, as before. The mixture gives a really successful combination of flavours.

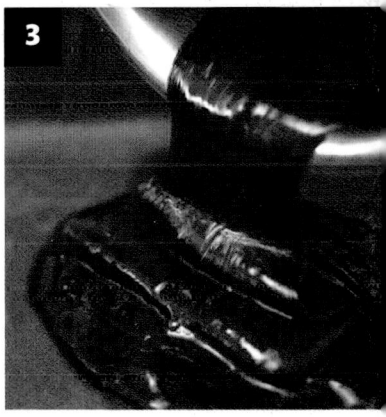

Dulce de leche

This soft toffee sauce is good with desserts such as crêpes, ice cream and banofee pie.

1 Pierce two holes in a can of condensed milk. Place in a pan. Pour water three-quarters up the can.

2 Simmer for 2 hours (for a runny sauce) to 4 hours (for a thick spread), topping up the water as needed.

Cookies and Cream Fudge

MAKES 36 PIECES
sunflower oil to grease
125g (4oz) unsalted butter
200ml (7fl oz) evaporated milk
450g (1lb) golden caster sugar
1 tsp vanilla extract
75g (3oz) plain chocolate, chopped
25g (1oz) hazelnuts, toasted and roughly chopped
6 Oreo cookies or bourbon biscuits, roughly chopped

PREPARATION TIME 10 minutes
COOKING TIME 15 minutes

PER PIECE
81 calories
2g fat (of which 1g saturates)
17g carbohydrate
0.1g salt

TECHNIQUES
see also toasting nuts (page 218), vanilla fudge (page 374)

1 Lightly grease a 450g (1lb) loaf tin with a little oil.

2 Put the butter, evaporated milk, sugar, vanilla extract and 50ml (2fl oz) water in a large heavy-based pan, set over a low heat, and stir until the butter has melted and the sugar dissolved. Increase the heat to a gentle boil and cook for about 10 minutes, stirring all the time, until the fudge forms a soft ball when half a teaspoonful is dropped into a cup of cold water. Remove the pan from the heat and, working quickly, divide the fudge mixture between two bowls. Add the chocolate to one of the bowls, and allow it to melt into the fudge. Stir the mixture gently until smooth.

3 Pour half the chocolate fudge into the tin and smooth the surface, then scatter over half the hazelnuts and half the biscuits.

4 Pour the vanilla fudge into the tin on top of the nuts and biscuits, then top with the remaining nuts and biscuits.

5 Finish with a final layer of the chocolate fudge and set aside to cool. Cover with clingfilm and leave in the refrigerator overnight to set firm. Once the fudge has set, remove it from the loaf tin and cut into slices, then chop up each slice.

Finishing touches

To make a gift, wrap pieces of the fudge in clear cellophane and tie with a pretty ribbon, then attach a label to each parcel with an eat-by date and a note that the fudge should be stored in the refrigerator.

Caramelised Pineapple

SERVES 6
1 large ripe pineapple, peeled and sliced into rounds
6 tbsp brown sugar
6 tbsp rum
2 tbsp olive oil

PREPARATION TIME 10 minutes
COOKING TIME about 20 minutes

PER SERVING
187 calories
4g fat (of which trace saturates)
31g carbohydrate
0g salt

TECHNIQUES
see also preparing pineapple (page 210)

1 Cut each pineapple round in half and remove the core. Put the sugar and rum into a bowl with the pineapple and toss to coat.

2 Heat the oil in a non-stick frying pan until hot. Add the pineapple, keeping the liquid to one side, and fry on each side over a medium heat for 4–5 minutes until golden and caramelised.

3 Divide the pineapple among six plates. Add the rum and sugar to the pan and bubble for 1 minute. Drizzle this sauce over the pineapple to serve.

Cook's tip

To check whether a pineapple is ripe, pull on one of the leaves. If it pulls out easily, the fruit is ripe.

Strawberry Brûlée

SERVES 4

250g (9oz) strawberries, washed, hulled and sliced
2 tsp golden icing sugar
1 vanilla pod
400ml (14fl oz) Greek yogurt
100g (3½oz) golden caster sugar

PREPARATION TIME 15 minutes
COOKING TIME 5 minutes, plus 15 minutes cooling or 2 hours chilling

PER SERVING
240 calories
10g fat (of which 5g saturates)
35g carbohydrate
0.2g salt

TECHNIQUES
see also preparing berries (page 209)

1 Arrange the strawberries in the base of four ramekins and sprinkle with icing sugar.

2 Scrape the seeds from the vanilla pod and stir into the yogurt, then spread the mixture evenly over the fruit.

3 Preheat the grill to high. Sprinkle the caster sugar evenly over the top of the yogurt until it's well covered.

4 Put the ramekins on to a baking sheet or into the grill pan and grill until the sugar turns dark brown and caramelises. Cool for 15 minutes or until the caramel is cool enough to eat, or chill for up to 2 hours before serving.

Variations

Use raspberries or blueberries in place of the strawberries.

Caramel Custard Squares

SERVES 4
vegetable oil to grease
50g (2oz) white granulated sugar
75g (3oz) golden caster sugar
1 tsp vanilla extract
6 large egg yolks

PREPARATION TIME 20 minutes
COOKING TIME 30 minutes, plus cooling

PER SERVING
210 calories
8g fat (of which 2g saturates)
31g carbohydrate
0g salt

TECHNIQUES
see also separating eggs (page 52), lining a loaf tin (page 323), making caramel (page 372)

1 Preheat the oven to 170°C (150°C fan oven) mark 3. Lightly oil a 450g (1lb) loaf tin and line the base with baking parchment.

2 Put the granulated sugar into a small pan and heat gently until dissolved. Bring to the boil and cook for 2–3 minutes, tilting the pan but not stirring until the syrup turns a golden caramel. Pour into the prepared tin. Put the caster sugar into a pan with 75ml (2½fl oz) cold water and the vanilla extract. Heat gently until the sugar has dissolved. Increase the heat and boil for 3 minutes or until syrupy. Cool for 5 minutes.

3 Put the egg yolks into a large bowl and gradually stir in the cooled sugar syrup with a wooden spoon. Strain through a metal sieve into the loaf tin on to the caramel. Pour 2.5cm (1in) boiling water into a roasting tin, then rest a wire rack on top. Sit the loaf tin on the rack and cover the whole roasting tin with foil. Bake for 25 minutes until just firm and a skewer inserted into the centre comes out clean. Cool and chill.

4 To serve, dip the base of the tin into a shallow dish of boiling water for 10 seconds. Run a sharp knife around the custard to loosen, then upturn on to a serving dish – there may be some caramel left in the tin but don't worry. Cut into eight squares and put in petit four cases.

Cook's tip

Serve these sweet squares with a coffee after dinner.

Toffee Cheesecake

SERVES 10
300g pack digestive biscuits, broken
125g (4oz) butter, melted

For the filling
450g (1lb) curd cheese
140ml (4½fl oz) double cream
juice of ½ lemon
3 medium eggs, beaten
50g (2oz) golden caster sugar
6 tbsp dulce de leche toffee sauce, plus extra to drizzle

PREPARATION TIME 15 minutes, plus chilling
COOKING TIME 45 minutes–1 hour

PER SERVING
379g calories
24g fat (of which 13g saturates)
34g carbohydrate
1.1g salt

TECHNIQUES
see also making dulce de leche (page 373)

1 Preheat the oven to 200°C (180°C fan oven) gas mark 6. To make the crust, put the biscuits into a food processor and grind until fine. (Alternatively, put them in a plastic bag and crush with a rolling pin. Transfer to a bowl.) Add the butter and blend briefly, or stir in, to combine. Press the mixture evenly into the base and up the sides of a 20.5cm (8in) springform cake tin. Chill in the refrigerator.

2 To make the filling, put the curd cheese and cream in a food processor or blender and blend until smooth. Add the lemon juice, eggs, sugar and toffee sauce, then blend again until smooth. Pour into the chilled biscuit case and bake for 10 minutes. Reduce the oven temperature to 180°C (160°C fan oven) mark 4, then bake for 45 minutes or until set and golden brown.

3 Turn off the oven, leave the door ajar and let the cheesecake cool. When completely cool, chill to firm up the crust.

4 Remove the cheesecake from the tin by running a knife around the edge. Open the tin carefully, then use a palette knife to ease the cheesecake out. Cut into wedges, put on a serving plate, then drizzle with toffee sauce.

Cook's tip

To slice the cheesecake easily, use a sharp knife dipped into a jug of boiling water and then wiped dry.

Almond Toffee Meringues

SERVES 4

oil to grease
25g (1oz) light muscovado sugar
100g (3½oz) egg whites (about 3 medium eggs)
225g (8oz) caster sugar
25g (1oz) flaked almonds
lightly whipped cream to serve

For the marinated summer fruit

125ml (4fl oz) crème de cassis
juice of 1 orange
2 tbsp redcurrant jelly
200g (7oz) raspberries
4 nectarines, halved, stoned and sliced

PREPARATION TIME 35 minutes
COOKING TIME 22–25 minutes, plus 15 minutes sugar cooling and overnight cooling in the oven

PER SERVING

458 calories
4g fat (of which trace saturates)
95g carbohydrate
0.2g salt

TECHNIQUES

see also separating eggs (page 52), slivering nuts (page 219), stoning fruits (page 208), making meringues (pages 58–59)

1 To make the marinated fruit, put the crème de cassis, orange juice and redcurrant jelly in a small pan. Heat gently to melt, then bubble for 2–3 minutes until syrupy. Pour into a large bowl to cool. Add the raspberries and nectarines, and stir gently. Cover and chill.

2 Preheat the oven to 170°C (150°C fan oven) mark 3 and preheat the grill. Lightly oil a baking sheet and sprinkle over the muscovado sugar. Grill for 2–3 minutes until the sugar begins to bubble and caramelise. Cool for about 15 minutes, then break the sugar into a food processor and whiz to a coarse powder.

3 Put the egg whites and caster sugar in a large clean bowl over a pan of gently simmering water. Stir until the sugar has dissolved and the egg white is warm, about 10 minutes. Remove from the heat and place on a teatowel. Beat with an electric whisk for at least 15 minutes or until cold and glossy and standing in stiff shiny peaks when the whisk is lifted. Cover two baking sheets with non-stick baking parchment. Fold half the powdered sugar into the meringue mixture. Spoon four oval mounds on to the baking sheets, leaving plenty of space between each. Sprinkle with flaked almonds and the remaining powdered sugar. Bake for 20 minutes, then turn off the heat and leave in the oven to dry out overnight. Serve with the marinated fruit and lightly whipped cream.

Cook's tips

- Make sure the bowl does not touch the hot water while you make the meringues.
- The flavour of the marinated fruit will be even better if you chill it overnight. (If the syrup thickens during chilling, stir in 1–2 tbsp orange juice.)

Sticky Banoffee Pies

SERVES 6

150g (5oz) digestive biscuits
75g (3oz) unsalted butter, melted, plus butter to grease
1 tsp ground ginger (optional)
450g (1lb) dulce de leche toffee sauce
4 medium-sized bananas, peeled, sliced and tossed in the juice of 1 lemon
285ml (9½fl oz) double cream, softly whipped
plain chocolate shavings

PREPARATION TIME 15 minutes

PER SERVING

827 calories
55g fat (of which 32g saturates)
84g carbohydrate
1.2g salt

TECHNIQUES

see also making dulce de leche (page 373), shaving chocolate (page 356)

1 Put the biscuits in a food processor and whiz to a crumb. (Alternatively, put them in a plastic bag and crush with a rolling pin. Transfer to a bowl.) Add the melted butter and ginger, and process, or stir well, for 1 minute to combine.

2 Butter six 10cm (4in) rings or tartlet tins and line with greaseproof paper. Press the biscuit mixture into each ring. Divide the toffee sauce equally among the rings and top with the bananas. Pipe or spoon on the cream, sprinkle with chocolate shavings and chill. Remove from the rings or tins to serve.

Finishing touches

Finish the banoffee pie with any kind of chocolate: dark, milk, white, flake, grated, whole, curled, shaving, and chips or buttons. Check out the techniques on page 356.

Caramelised Orange Trifle

SERVES 16

125g (4oz) light muscovado sugar
2 × 135g packs orange jelly, broken into cubes
100ml (3½fl oz) brandy
10 oranges, peeled and all pith removed
150g pack ratafia biscuits
4 tbsp sweet sherry
500g carton fresh custard sauce
284ml carton double cream
2 × 250g cartons mascarpone cheese
¼ tsp vanilla extract
125g (4oz) granulated sugar

PREPARATION TIME 45 minutes, plus 4 hours setting
COOKING TIME 5 minutes

PER SERVING

358 calories
15g fat (of which 9g saturates)
48g carbohydrate
0.1g salt

TECHNIQUES

see also preparing citrus fruit (page 207), making spun sugar (page 375)

1 Put the muscovado sugar in a large heavy-based pan. Add 100ml (3½fl oz) water. Dissolve the sugar over a low heat. Increase the heat and cook for 5 minutes or until the sugar is syrupy and thick. Remove from the heat and add 450ml (¾ pint) boiling water (the sugar will splutter). Add the jelly and stir until dissolved. Add the brandy and set aside.

2 Slice the orange flesh into rounds, putting any juice to one side. Add the juice – about 125ml (4fl oz) – to the jelly. Cool. Tip the ratafia biscuits into the base of a 3.5 litre (6¼ pint) bowl and drizzle with sherry. Arrange the orange rounds on top, then pour the jelly over. Chill for 4 hours until set. Pour the custard over the top and smooth over. Put the cream, mascarpone and vanilla extract in a bowl and combine with an electric hand mixer. Spoon three-quarters of the mixture on to the custard. Smooth the surface. Put the remainder in a piping bag and pipe 10 swirls around the edge. Chill.

3 Line a large baking sheet with baking parchment. Half-fill the sink with cold water. Heat the granulated sugar in a heavy-based pan until dissolved. Increase the heat and cook to a golden caramel, then plunge the base of the pan into the sink. Dip in a fork and pick up the caramel, then flick it back and forth over the parchment to form fine strands. Put the sugar strands on top of the trifle.

Finishing touches

For an alternative, try sprinkling over silver dragees, toasted flaked almonds or grated chocolate (page 354) instead.

Sticky Toffee Puddings

SERVES 4
1 tbsp golden syrup
1 tbsp black treacle
150g (5oz) butter, softened
25g (1oz) pecan nuts or walnuts
75g (3oz) self-raising flour
125g (4oz) caster sugar
2 large eggs, beaten
custard or cream to serve

PREPARATION TIME 20 minutes, plus 5 minutes resting
COOKING TIME 25–30 minutes

PER SERVING
565 calories
38g fat (of which 21g saturates)
53g carbohydrate
0.9g salt

TECHNIQUES
see also making vanilla custard (page 26)

1 Preheat the oven to 180°C (160°C fan oven) mark 4. Put the syrup, treacle and 25g (1oz) butter into a bowl and beat until smooth. Divide the mixture among four 150ml (¼ pint) timbales or ramekins and set aside.

2 Finely process the nuts in a food processor. Put the nuts in a bowl, sift in the flour and mix together well.

3 Put the remaining butter and the sugar into a food processor and blend briefly. (Alternatively, use an electric hand mixer.) Add the beaten eggs and the flour mixture and blend or mix again for 30 seconds.

4 Spoon the sponge mixture into the timbales or ramekins, covering the syrup mixture on the bottom. Bake for 25–30 minutes until risen and golden.

5 Remove the puddings from the oven and leave to rest for 5 minutes, then unmould on to warmed serving plates. Serve immediately with custard or cream.

Apples with Butterscotch Sauce

SERVES 6
125g (4oz) sultanas
2 tbsp brandy
6 large Bramley apples, cored
4 tbsp soft brown sugar
2 tbsp apple juice
125g (4oz) chopped and toasted hazelnuts
ricotta cheese to serve

For the butterscotch sauce
125g (4oz) butter
125g (4oz) soft brown sugar
2 tbsp golden syrup
2 tbsp black treacle
4 tbsp brandy
285ml (9½fl oz) double cream

PREPARATION TIME 5 minutes, plus 10 minutes soaking
COOKING TIME 15–20 minutes

PER SERVING
694 calories
45g fat (of which 27g saturates)
65g carbohydrate
3.5g salt

TECHNIQUES
see also preparing apples (page 206)

1 Soak the sultanas in the brandy and set aside for 10 minutes, then stuff each apple with equal amounts.

2 Preheat the oven to 220°C (200°C fan oven) mark 7. Put the apples in a roasting tin, sprinkle over the brown sugar and apple juice. Cook for 15–20 minutes until soft.

3 Meanwhile, make the sauce. Melt the butter, brown sugar, golden syrup and treacle in a heavy-based pan, stirring continuously. When the sugar has dissolved and the mixture is bubbling, stir in the brandy and cream. Bring back to the boil and set aside. Remove the apples from the oven.

4 Serve the apples with the butterscotch sauce, hazelnuts and a dollop of ricotta cheese.

Get ahead

Complete step 3 of the recipe, then cool, cover and chill for up to one day. Complete step 1 up to 4 hours in advance.
To use Complete the recipe and bring the sauce back to the boil to serve.

16 ICE CREAMS, SORBETS AND ICED DESSERTS

Rich and creamy, fresh and fruity or sweet and indulgent, ice creams and iced desserts are easy to make yourself. With easy-to-follow step-by-step instructions, the techniques sections guides you through the basics of making ice creams and sorbets – in a machine and by hand – as well as making parfaits, layering, rippling and making ice cream bombes. The recipe collection builds on these skills with stunning desserts including Nougat ice cream, Frozen yogurt sorbet, Cinnamon and nutmeg ice cream, Iced lemon meringue, Cranberry Christmas bombe and Iced raspberry soufflés.

Making ice cream

Good ice cream needs a smooth, creamy texture. Using an ice-cream maker is the best way to achieve it, but freezing and breaking up the ice crystals by hand works well, too.

Vanilla ice cream

To serve four to six, you will need 300ml (½ pint) milk, 1 vanilla pod, split lengthways, 3 medium egg yolks, 75g (3oz) golden caster sugar, 300ml (½ pint) double cream.

1 Put the milk and vanilla in a pan. Heat slowly until almost boiling. Cool for 20 minutes and remove the vanilla. In a large bowl, whisk the egg yolks and sugar until thick and creamy. Gradually whisk in the milk, then strain back into the pan.

2 Cook over a low heat, stirring, until thick enough to coat the back of the spoon. (Do not boil.) Pour into a chilled bowl and leave to cool.

3 Whisk the cream into the custard

4 Pour into an ice-cream maker and freeze or churn according to the manufacturer's instructions.

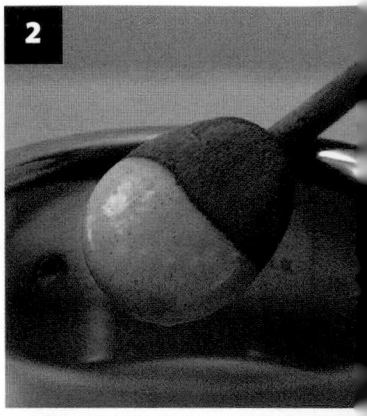

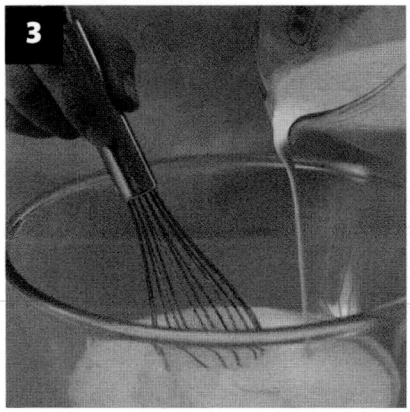

Variations

- **Fruit ice cream** Sweeten 300ml (½ pint) fruit purée (such as rhubarb, gooseberry, raspberry or strawberry) to taste; then stir into the cooked custard and churn.
- **Chocolate ice cream** Omit the vanilla and add 125g (4oz) dark chocolate to the milk. Heat gently until melted, then bring almost to the boil and proceed as above.
- **Coffee ice cream** Omit the vanilla and add 150ml (¼ pint) cooled strong coffee to the cooked custard.

Making by hand

1 If possible, set the freezer to fast freeze 1 hour ahead. Pour the ice-cream mixture into a shallow freezer-proof container, cover and freeze until it's partially frozen.

2 Spoon into a bowl and mash with a fork to break up the ice crystals. Return to the container and freeze for another 2 hours.

3 Repeat and freeze for another 3 hours.

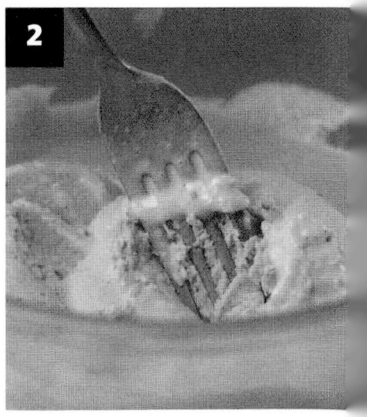

Layering, shaping and rippling

Freshly made ice cream is soft enough to shape into moulds, layer and ripple for a more elegant presentation. You can buy a bombe or ice-cream mould, or just use a bowl or loaf tin.

Layering

1 For a layered effect, make two or more flavoured ice creams of distinct colours. While the first ice cream is still soft, pack it into a mould lined with clingfilm. Freeze until firm, then layer the second ice cream on top and freeze until firm.

2 Continue in the same way with the remaining flavour(s) and serve cut into slices.

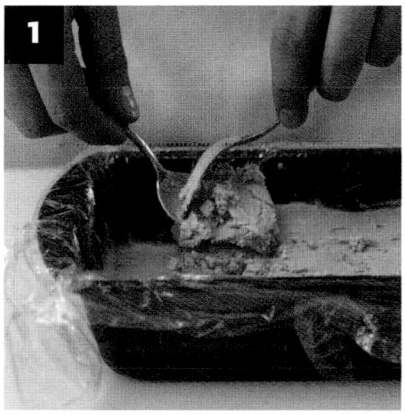

Ice cream bombes

1 First make two flavours of ice cream. While the first ice cream is still soft, press it against the sides and base of a large mould or bowl, making a hollow in the centre. Freeze until firm.

2 Fill the hollow with the soft second ice cream and cover with clingfilm. Freeze until firm, then unmould and serve in slices.

Rippling and marbling

1 Make vanilla ice cream and churn in an ice-cream maker (or make by hand) until thick, but soft. Spoon a layer into a freezerproof container, then drizzle with fruit purée. Top with more ice cream and purée.

2 Pass a wooden spoon handle through the ice cream five or six times to ripple the ice cream. Freeze for 4–5 hours until firm.

Making parfaits

Ice-cream parfait is a kind of frozen, sweet mousse, which doesn't require an ice-cream maker. The mixture can be frozen as it is, with no need for churning.

Pistachio parfait

To serve six, you will need 75g (3oz) shelled pistachio nuts, plus extra to decorate, oil to grease, 200ml (7fl oz) double cream, 4 large egg whites, 75g (3oz) icing sugar, 2 tbsp orange-flavoured liqueur, such as Grand Marnier, 75g (3oz) white chocolate.

1 Toast the pistachios in a dry frying pan and chop finely. Lightly oil and line six 150ml (¼ pint) ramekins with greaseproof paper. Sprinkle lightly with 25g (1oz) nuts. Cut six strips of greaseproof paper, each 5 × 25.5cm (2 × 10in), and lightly oil one side of each strip. Sprinkle with 25g (1oz) nuts and line each ramekin with a strip, nut side inwards.

2 Lightly whip the cream.

3 Whisk the egg whites until just soft, then whisk in the icing sugar.

4 Fold the remaining nuts into the egg whites with the liqueur and whipped cream. Do not over-mix.

5 Divide the mixture between the ramekins and freeze overnight.

6 Melt chocolate in a bowl over hot water. Cut six strips of baking parchment measuring 5 × 25.5cm (2 × 10in), and spread each one with chocolate. Leave to firm up slightly. Unmould the parfaits and remove the lining papers. Lift the chocolate-covered strips and wrap each one around a parfait, with the chocolate side inside. Freeze for 30 minutes. To serve, remove the paper strips.

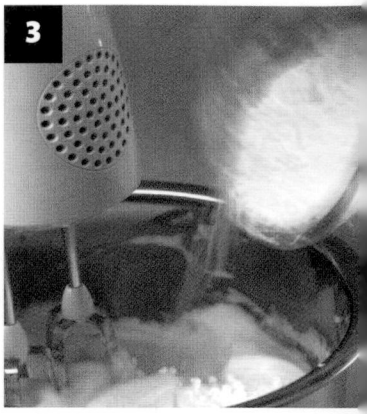

Cook's tips

- For a much simpler dessert, you could omit the chocolate and just make the recipe up to step 5, then unmould the parfaits and serve.
- To decorate, use 75g white chocolate and make chocolate curls following the instructions on page 356.

Making sorbet

Sorbets have a fine, smooth texture and are most frequently fruit-flavoured. Fruits vary in sweetness, so taste the mixture before freezing. Remove the sorbet from the freezer 20 minutes before serving.

Simple orange sorbet

To serve six, you will need the zest of 3 oranges and the juice of 6 oranges, about 600ml (1 pint), 200g (7oz) granulated sugar, 1 tbsp orange flower water, 1 medium egg white.

1 Put the orange zest and sugar in a pan with 300ml (½ pint) water. Bring slowly to the boil, stirring. Simmer for 5 minutes, leave to cool for 2 minutes, then strain and leave to cool completely.

2 Strain the orange juice into the syrup and add the orange flower water. Chill for 30 minutes.

3 Using an ice-cream maker, follow the manufacturer's instructions but remove the sorbet halfway through.

4 Whisk the egg white, add to the bowl, and continue churning until the sorbet is firm enough to scoop.

3

Granitas

Granita is an Italian water ice with larger crystals than a sorbet. It isn't churned but is broken up with a fork, which makes it more like a frozen fruit slush. Quick to melt, it must be served and eaten quickly and makes a wonderful refresher in summer. Fruit-flavoured, granitas are frequently also popularly flavoured with coffee.

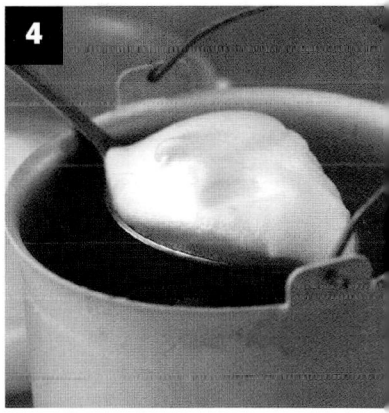

Making by hand

1 Pour the mixture into a shallow container, cover and freeze for about 3 hours, until partially frozen to a slushy consistency. Beat the sorbet with a whisk or fork until smooth.

2 Whisk the egg white and fold into the mixture, then return to the freezer and freeze until firm enough to scoop, 2–4 hours.

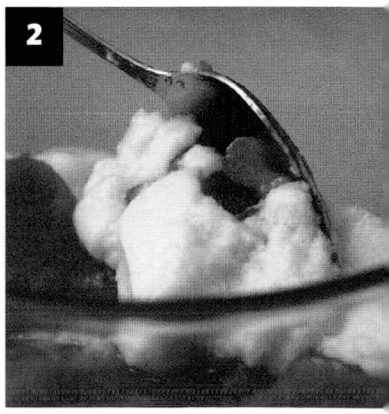

Spicy Ginger Ice Cream

SERVES 8

575ml (19½fl oz) double cream
125g (4oz) golden caster sugar, plus 1 tbsp
4 medium eggs, separated
2 tsp ground ginger
4 pieces stem ginger, roughly chopped
brandy snaps to serve

For the sauce

50g (2oz) unsalted butter
50g (2oz) golden caster sugar
2 tbsp whisky
2 tbsp ginger syrup (from the jar of stem ginger)

PREPARATION TIME 30 minutes, plus 8 hours freezing
COOKING TIME 5 minutes

PER SERVING

541 calories
46g fat (of which 28g saturates)
27g carbohydrate
0.2g salt

TECHNIQUES

see also separating eggs (page 52), rippling ice cream (page 389)

1 Whisk the cream until just thickened. Chill. Whisk the 125g (4oz) caster sugar with the egg yolks until pale and creamy.

2 Beat the egg whites in a clean grease-free bowl until stiff. Beat in the 1 tbsp caster sugar.

3 Fold the cream into the egg yolk and sugar mixture with the ground ginger, then quickly fold in the beaten egg whites. Pour into a freezerproof container and freeze for 4 hours.

4 To make the sauce, put the butter, sugar, whisky and ginger syrup in a pan and heat gently. Bring to the boil and simmer for 5 minutes or until thick. Cool.

5 Fold the stem ginger through the ice cream and drizzle the sauce over. Stir once or twice to create a ripple effect and continue to freeze for 4 hours or overnight. Serve with brandy snaps.

Nougat Ice Cream

SERVES 6
900ml (1½ pints) full-fat milk
285ml (9½fl oz) single cream
200g (7oz) white nougat, broken or chopped into chunks
8 medium egg yolks
125g (4oz) golden caster sugar
chopped pistachio nuts, almonds and golden icing sugar to decorate

PREPARATION TIME 20 minutes, plus chilling and freezing
COOKING TIME 20 minutes

PER SERVING
520 calories
32g fat (of which 15g saturates)
48g carbohydrate
0.5g salt

TECHNIQUES
see also separating eggs (page 52), chopping nuts (page 218), making ice cream (page 388)

1 Pour the milk into a pan and add the cream. Gently bring to the boil. Remove the pan from the heat and add the nougat. Set aside until the nougat has melted, stirring occasionally.

2 Meanwhile, whisk the egg yolks and sugar together in a bowl. Pour the warm milk and nougat mixture into the bowl, stir well, then pour back into the pan. Cook over a gentle heat, stirring constantly, for about 15 minutes or until the mixture coats the back of a wooden spoon. Pour into a bowl, cool and chill until cold.

3 When cold, tip the mixture into an ice-cream machine and churn according to the manufacturer's instructions until thick. Spoon it into a chilled 2 litre (3½ pint) freezerproof container, level off and put a piece of greaseproof paper over the surface. (Alternatively, to make the ice cream by hand, transfer the mixture to the freezerproof container. Freeze for 4 hours, then whisk to break up the ice crystals. Freeze for another 4 hours, then whisk again. Cover with greaseproof paper.) Cover and freeze until ready to serve.

4 Soften in the refrigerator for 20 minutes before serving. Scoop into balls, put into individual bowls, scatter with chopped pistachio nuts and almonds, and dust with icing sugar.

Instant Banana Ice Cream

SERVES 4

6 ripe bananas, about 700g (1lb 9oz), peeled, cut into thin slices and frozen (see Cook's tip)
1–2 tbsp virtually fat-free fromage frais
1–2 tbsp orange juice
1 tsp vanilla extract
splash of rum or Cointreau (optional)
a few drops of lime juice to taste

PREPARATION TIME 5 minutes, plus 30 minutes freezing

PER SERVING

178 calories
1g fat (of whether 0g saturates)
42g carbohydrate
0.3g salt

1 Leave the frozen banana to stand at room temperature for 2–3 minutes. Put the still frozen pieces in a food processor or blender with 1 tbsp fromage frais, 1 tbsp orange juice, the vanilla extract and the liqueur, if you like.

2 Whiz until smooth, scraping down the sides of the bowl and adding more fromage frais and orange juice as necessary to give a creamy consistency. Add lime juice to taste and serve at once or turn into a freezer container and freeze for up to one month.

Cook's tip

To freeze bananas, peel and slice them thinly, then put the banana slices on a large non-stick baking tray and put into the freezer for 30 minutes or until frozen. Transfer to a plastic bag and store in the freezer until needed.

Frozen Yogurt Sorbet

SERVES 8

450g (1lb) thawed frozen mixed fruit, plus extra to serve
100g (3½oz) clear honey
3 medium egg whites
450g (1lb) low-fat natural Greek yogurt

PREPARATION TIME 15 minutes, plus 8 hours freezing

PER SERVING

120 calories
6g fat (of which 3g saturates)
14g carbohydrate
0.2g salt

TECHNIQUES

see also separating eggs (page 52)

1 Line a 750ml (1¼ pint) loaf tin with clingfilm. Whiz the thawed frozen mixed fruit in a food processor or blender to make a purée. Sieve into a bowl, pressing all the juice through with the back of a spoon. Stir the honey into the juice.

2 Whisk the egg whites in a clean grease-free bowl until soft peaks form, then fold into the fruit with the yogurt. Pour the mixture into the prepared tin and freeze for 4 hours. Stir to break up the ice crystals, then freeze again for 4 hours. Stir again, then freeze for a further 4 hours or until firm.

3 Transfer to the refrigerator for 20 minutes, then turn out of the tin and remove the clingfilm. Slice and serve with a spoonful of thawed frozen berries.

Cook's tip

Use any selection of frozen mixed berries that you like. Summer berries and forest fruits work well.

Cinnamon and Nutmeg Ice Cream

SERVES 8

½ tsp ground cinnamon, plus extra to dust
½ tsp freshly grated nutmeg
50g (2oz) golden caster sugar
140ml (4½fl oz) double cream
250g (9oz) mascarpone cheese
400g carton fresh custard

PREPARATION TIME 10 minutes, plus 6 hours freezing
COOKING TIME 5 minutes

PER SERVING
221g calories
15g fat (of which 9g saturates)
16g carbohydrate
0.1g salt

TECHNIQUES
see also making ice cream by hand (page 388)

1 Put the cinnamon, nutmeg, sugar and cream in a small pan, bring slowly to the boil, then put to one side to cool.

2 Put the mascarpone in a large bowl and beat until smooth. Stir in the custard and the cooled spiced cream. Pour the mixture into a shallow freezerproof container and freeze for 2–3 hours.

3 Whisk to break up the ice crystals and freeze for a further 2–3 hours before serving, dusted with cinnamon.

Cook's tip

The ice cream will keep in the freezer for up to one month.

Iced Lemon Meringue

SERVES 8
4 large egg whites, at room temperature
1 tsp lemon juice
100g (3½oz) golden caster sugar
100g (3½oz) light muscovado sugar
1 tbsp cornflour, sifted
½ tsp almond extract
25g (1oz) flaked almonds

For the lemon filling
2 tbsp cornflour, sifted
4 large egg yolks
100g (3½oz) golden caster sugar
zest and juice of 1 lemon
zest and juice of 1 lime
125ml (4fl oz) milk
285ml (9½fl oz) double cream

For the raspberry coulis
200g (7oz) frozen raspberries
1 tbsp golden icing sugar

PREPARATION TIME 30 minutes, plus drying
COOKING TIME 1 hour 35 minutes

PER SERVING
420 calories
24g fat (of which 13g saturates)
49g carbohydrate
0.1g salt

TECHNIQUES
see also separating eggs (page 52), slivering nuts (page 219), zesting citrus fruits (page 207), freezing fruit (page 435), whisking egg whites (page 52), making meringues (pages 58–59), toasting nuts (page 218)

1 Preheat the oven to 140°C (120°C fan oven) mark 1. Draw three 25.5 × 10cm (10 × 4in) rectangles on baking parchment. Cut around each, leaving a 10cm (4in) border. Turn over and put on a baking sheet. Whisk the egg whites to soft peaks. Add the lemon juice and whisk until stiff. Whisk in the sugars, 1 tbsp at a time, until glossy and soft peaks form. Beat in 1 tbsp boiling water, then fold in the cornflour and almond extract. Divide among the rectangles and lift into peaks. Reserve 1 tbsp almonds and sprinkle the rest over the meringues. Bake for 20 minutes, reduce the temperature to 110°C (90°C fan oven) mark ¼ and bake for 1¼ hours. Turn off the oven and leave for 30 minutes–1 hour to dry.

2 To make the filling, mix the cornflour with 1 tbsp water, then stir in the egg yolks, sugar, citrus zest and juice. Bring the milk to the boil, stir in the cornflour and stir over a gentle heat until thick. Tip into a bowl, cover with wet greaseproof paper and cool. Whip the cream to soft peaks, then fold into the filling. Sandwich the meringues with the filling. Put on a baking sheet and open freeze until firm. Wrap and refreeze.

3 Reserve eight raspberries and gently heat the remainder with the icing sugar and 1 tbsp water for 5 minutes. Cool, then sieve. To serve, transfer the meringue to the refrigerator for 5 minutes. Toast the reserved almonds, sprinkle over the top with the reserved frozen raspberries and serve in slices with the coulis.

Mango Ice Cream Terrine

SERVES 8

vegetable oil to grease
2 small mangoes, peeled and chopped
2 medium eggs
125g (4oz) golden caster sugar
285ml (9½fl oz) double cream, whipped
1½ tsp Malibu
4 ratafia biscuits, roughly crushed

PREPARATION TIME 20–25 minutes, plus overnight freezing

PER SERVING

306calories
21g fat (of which 13g saturates)
26g carbohydrate
0.1g salt

TECHNIQUES

see also preparing mangoes (page 210), layering ice cream (page 389)

1 Lightly oil a 900g (2lb) loaf tin, then line with clingfilm, leaving enough to hang over the edges and smoothing any creases.

2 Whiz the mangoes in a food processor or blender until smooth. Set aside. Put the eggs and sugar into a large bowl. Using an electric hand whisk, mix together until thick – this should take 5 minutes.

3 Add the whipped cream to the mixture and fold together with a large metal spoon. Fold in three-quarters of the puréed mango and the Malibu. Spoon the remaining mango purée into the lined tin to cover the base, then pour in the ice cream mixture. Cover with the overhanging clingfilm and freeze overnight or for up to one month.

4 Remove the ice cream from the freezer 5 minutes before serving. Unwrap the clingfilm. Turn out on to a serving dish, cover with the biscuits, slice and serve.

Cranberry Christmas Bombe

SERVES 8–10
125g (4oz) granulated sugar
300ml (½ pint) cranberry juice
225g (8oz) each cranberries and raspberries, fresh or frozen
2 large egg whites
75g (3oz) caster sugar
groundnut oil to grease
500ml tub good-quality vanilla ice cream

For the sugared redcurrants
a few sprigs of redcurrants
1 large egg white, lightly beaten
a little caster sugar

PREPARATION TIME 30 minutes, plus 6½ hours hours chilling and freezing
COOKING TIME 15 minutes

PER SERVING
236 calories per serving for 8
6g fat (of which 4g saturates)
44g carbohydrate
0.1g salt
189 calories per serving for 10
5g fat (of which 3g saturates)
35g carbohydrate
0.1g salt

TECHNIQUES
see also separating eggs (page 52), whisking egg whites (page 52), making ice cream bombes (page 389)

1 Put the granulated sugar and cranberry juice in a pan and heat gently until the sugar has dissolved. Bring to the boil, then add the cranberries. Cover and simmer for 15 minutes until very soft. Leave to cool. Blend with the raspberries in a food processor or blender, press through a nylon sieve, then chill. Whisk the egg whites until soft peaks form. Whisk in the sugar a spoonful at a time until stiff and glossy. Fold into the fruit purée. Pour into an ice-cream maker and churn until stiff.

2 Meanwhile, lightly grease a 1.4 litre (2½ pint) pudding basin with a little oil, then put a disc of foil in the base. Put in the freezer for 30 minutes. Spoon the sorbet into the basin (reserving 3–4 tbsp), creating a hollow in the centre, and return to the freezer. Leave the ice cream at room temperature for 10 minutes. Spoon the ice cream into the centre of the sorbet and press down well. Spread the reserved sorbet on top. Freeze for 4 hours or until firm.

3 To make the sugared redcurrants, dip the sprigs in the beaten egg white, then in the sugar. Allow to harden on a baking sheet lined with greaseproof paper. To unmould the bombe, dip the basin in hot water for 10 seconds, then loosen the edges with a round-bladed knife, invert on to a plate, shake firmly and remove the foil. Decorate with redcurrants, then use a warm knife to cut the bombe into wedges.

Italian Ice Cream Cake

SERVES 10

400g (14oz) fresh cherries, pitted and quartered
4 tbsp amaretto liqueur
10 tbsp crème de cacao liqueur
200g (7oz) Savoiardi biscuits or sponge fingers
5 medium egg yolks
150g (5oz) golden caster sugar
450ml (¾ pint) double cream, lightly whipped
1 tbsp vanilla extract
75g (3oz) pistachio nuts or hazelnuts, roughly chopped in a food processor
75g (3oz) plain chocolate, roughly chopped in a food processor
2–3 tbsp cocoa powder
2–3 tbsp golden icing sugar

PREPARATION TIME 40 minutes, plus 5 hours freezing

PER SERVING

522 calories
33g fat (of which 15g saturates)
46g carbohydrate
0.2g salt

TECHNIQUES

see also pitting cherries (page 208), separating eggs (page 52), chopping nuts (page 218)

1 Put the cherries and amaretto in a bowl, stir, cover with clingfilm and put to one side. Pour the crème de cacao into a shallow dish and take out a large chopping board. Quickly dip a sponge finger into the liqueur – on one side only, so that it doesn't go soggy and fall apart – then put on to the board and cut in half lengthways to separate the sugary side from the base. Repeat with each biscuit.

2 Double line a 24 × 4cm (9½ × 1½in) round tin with clingfilm. Arrange the sugar-coated sponge finger halves, sugar side down, on the base of the tin. Drizzle with any remaining crème de cacao.

3 Put the yolks and caster sugar into a bowl and whisk until pale, light and fluffy. Fold in the cream, vanilla extract, nuts, chocolate and cherries, plus any remaining amaretto. Spoon on top of the sponge fingers in the tin and cover with the remaining sponge finger halves, cut side down. Cover with clingfilm and freeze for at least 5 hours.

4 To serve, upturn the cake on to a serving plate and remove the clingfilm. Sift cocoa and icing sugar over the cake and cut into wedges. Leave at room temperature for 20 minutes if the weather is warm, 40 minutes at cool room temperature, or 1 hour in the refrigerator, to allow the cherries to thaw and the ice cream to become moussey.

Finishing touches

Use the lid to cut a circle of greaseproof paper then fold it into eight triangles. Cut these out and put four on the cake and dust with cocoa powder. Remove the triangles, cover the cocoa with four triangles and dust with the icing sugar.

Iced Raspberry Soufflés

SERVES 8

juice of 1 orange
juice of 1 lemon
700g (1lb 9oz) raspberries
225g (8oz) caster sugar
450ml (¾ pint) double cream
2 large egg whites
400g (14oz) plain chocolate
350g (12oz) mixed berries, such as redcurrants, blueberries and blackberries

PREPARATION TIME 1¼ hours, plus about 9 hours freezing

PER SERVING

683 calories
45g fat (of which 27g saturates)
69g carbohydrate
0.1g salt

TECHNIQUES

see also separating eggs (page 52)

1 Wrap eight 100ml (3½fl oz) glasses with non-stick baking parchment, 6.5 × 25.5cm (2½ × 10in), to form a collar above the rim. Put 2 tbsp each of the citrus juices in a food processor or blender with the raspberries and sugar. Process until smooth, then sieve. Set aside 150ml (¼ pint), then cover and chill. Put the remaining sauce in a large bowl. Whip the cream until it just holds its shape, then fold the cream into the sauce. Whisk the egg whites until soft peaks form. Fold into the raspberry cream and spoon into the prepared glasses and freeze overnight.

2 Cut eight strips of non-stick baking parchment. Melt 225g (8oz) chocolate in a heatproof bowl over a pan of gently simmering water. Cool slightly, then brush over the parchment strips to cover completely. Remove the soufflés from the freezer and peel off the parchment. Carefully wrap the chocolate-covered strips around the tops of the soufflés and return to the freezer for 5 minutes. Peel the baking parchment away from the chocolate and return the soufflés to the freezer.

3 Melt the remaining chocolate as before, then spread it over a marble slab or worksurface. When it has just set, push the blade of a knife at a 25 degree angle across the chocolate to form the curls. Put the soufflés in the refrigerator for 20 minutes before serving. Serve decorated with mixed berries, chocolate curls and the reserved sauce.

Cook's tips

- Don't over-whip the cream, as the acidity of the raspberries will help to thicken it – aim for a soft dropping consistency.
- If the chocolate doesn't form curls easily and breaks up, it has set too much. Melt it again and reuse.
- To make one large soufflé, line the outside of a 1.3 litre (2¼ pint) soufflé dish with a collar of non-stick baking parchment, deep enough to come about 5cm (2in) above the rim of the dish. Omit the chocolate collar (steps 2) and don't turn the soufflé out of its dish for serving.

17 PRESERVES

Very little beats a storecupboard full of homemade jams, jellies, marmalades, chutneys, pickles and relishes and other delicious preserves. Follow the step-by-step techniques to learn how to sterilise jars, test for a set and pot preserves, as well as how to make all the basic types of preserve. There are invaluable cook's tips to ensure perfect results and advice on avoiding the pitfalls, as well as a handy table showing the pectin content and setting properties of different fruits. The recipe collection includes recipes for every type of preserve so try your hand at making Strawberry and redcurrant jam, Quick marmalade, Spiced Clementines in brandy, Plum chutney, Sweetcorn relish, Sweet-and-sour figs or The Ultimate barbecue sauce to name but a few.

Preparing jars

A completely sterile jar is essential for making preserves to ensure the jam, jelly, chutney, relish or pickle keeps properly and does not become mouldy. There are various ways of sterilising jars.

Sterilising methods

Prepare the jars in advance so that they are ready to fill.

1 Thoroughly wash new and used jars (soak them in hot water first if necessary to remove old labels).

2 Oven method Preheat the oven to 140°C (120°C fan oven) gas 1. Put the jars on a clean baking sheet or roasting tin in the oven for 10–15 minutes or until completely dry.

3 Microwave method First ensure there are no metal parts on the jars. Quarter fill the jars with water and arrange in a circle in the microwave. Bring to the boil on full power. Remove the jars with oven gloves, pour out the water and invert on to a clean teatowel or some kitchen paper.

4 Dishwasher method Run the upturned jars through a hot dishwasher cycle.

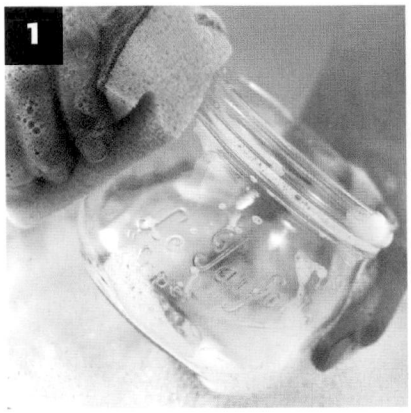

Food safety

When making jams and preserves in larger quantities that are likely to take longer to finish, sterilising is essential to ensure that there is no bacteria in the jar that might later cause the preserve to beccome mouldy.

Packing preserves

Everything you need to cover, seal and label preserves can be bought in small cellophane packs. These will usually contain wax discs to cover the jam, cellophane to go over the top of the jar, and elastic bands to secure it. Use metal lids on top of this, which can still be covered attractively with paper or fabric, if you want an extra seal.

Labelling

A sticky white label is the best way of guaranteeing that you know what's inside your jars. Write the preserve and date with a pen. When the jars have been filled, sealed and are completely cool, stick on the label, then store in a cool dry place.

Potting preserves

Correct potting of your home-made preserves, by sealing the surface and making the jars airtight, will ensure that they keep well. Label each jar so that you know when it was made.

Filling and covering

All preserves should go into their storage jars as soon as they have been made, and then sealed quickly. Cut rounds of greaseproof or waxed paper to fit exactly the diameter of the rim of your preserving jars.

1 When the preserve has reached setting point (see below), leave it to cool for a few minutes while you get the jars ready.

2 Pour the preserve into the jars using a jam funnel, filling them to within 5mm (¼in) of the rim.

3 Put a piece of wax paper (wax side down) on top of the preserve.

4 Wet a cellophane disc and put on the top of the jar, then secure with a rubber band.

Screw-top lids

If you want to use lids to cover your jars, sterilise them with the jars. Fill the jars to within 1cm (½in) of the rim, and then proceed from step 3. Use the screw-top lids instead of the cellophane discs at step 4. The end result will be a little more professional-looking, but some people prefer the home-made look.

Testing for a set

There are three methods for doing this:

1. **Thermometer test** Dip a sugar thermometer or an instant-read thermometer into the centre of the pan shortly before the cooking time is complete. Keep it away from the base and sides of the pan, and leave it for a few moments. Jams and jellies set when the temperature reaches 105°C (220°F). If you have to take a second reading, wash the probe before using it again.
2. **Saucer test** Put two or three saucers in the freezer to chill. When the preserve is nearly ready, take the pan off the heat and spoon a blob of preserve on to a plate and chill for a few minutes. When the preserve has cooled, push the surface with your finger. If the surface wrinkles and doesn't break to reveal liquid jam, it is set.
3. **Flake test** Using a large wooden spoon, lift a little of the jam out of the pan. Let it cool slightly, then tip the spoon so that the jam drops back into the pan. If setting point has been reached, it will run together along the edge of the spoon and form flakes that will break off.

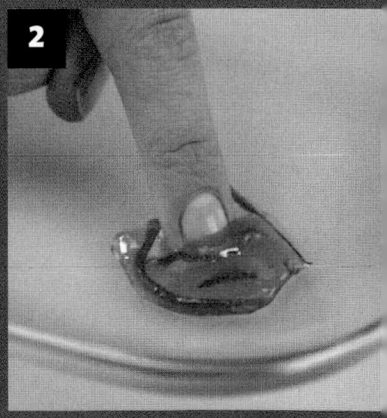

Making jams

You can use a special preserving pan, but a large stainless steel pan with a thick base will do. It should have a capacity of at least 9 litres (15¾ pints).

Summer jam

To make 3.2kg (7lb) jam, you will need 900g (2lb) prepared summer fruits (raspberries, blackcurrants, loganberries, blackberries or blueberries), 900g (2lb) granulated or preserving sugar, 2 lemons, pinch of salt.

1 Prepare the fruits and layer them, being careful not to bruise them, with the sugar in a non-metallic bowl. Halve the lemons and strain their juice on to the fruit and sugar. Then cover the bowl and set aside for at least 8 hours, until the sugar has dissolved.

2 Put the fruit and juices in a preserving pan and bring slowly to the boil. Boil as rapidly as possible, without letting the jam boil over, until setting point has been reached (see page 405). Then add the salt and cool slightly.

3 Pour into warm, sterilised jars (see page 404). Seal and label, and store in a cool dark place for up to one year.

Perfect jams

- Just-ripe fruits have the highest level of pectin. Make sure they are in perfect condition and don't use over-ripe fruits.
- Don't wash the fruit unless absolutely necessary, as any water that remains will dilute the juice.
- Leave summer fruits whole but remove the stalks. Halve and stone apricots and plums.
- Apricots gel quickly, but for a better flavour cook to a deep terracotta.
- If making a jam containing whole strawberries or other pieces of fruit, leave to stand for 15 minutes before potting, to prevent the fruit rising.

Pectin

Naturally found in fruit, pectin combines with sugar to make cooked fruits gel. Low pectin fruits are usually cooked with high pectin fruits or with commercial pectin, citric acid or tartaric acid to help them set.

Pectin content	Fruit
High	Cooking apples, crab apples, cranberries, citrus fruit, damsons, gooseberries, redcurrants, blackcurrants, some plums, quince.
Medium	Apricots, blackberries, dessert apples, greengages, loganberries, mulberries, raspberries, some plums.
Low	Bananas, cherries, figs, grapes, japonicas, marrows, medlars, melons, nectarines, peaches, pears, pineapples, rhubarb, strawberries.

Making marmalade

Orange marmalade is the best-known type of marmalade but you can also make it from other citrus fruits – or from a combination of two or more, such as lemon, grapefuit or lime.

Seville orange marmalade

To make 1.4kg (3lb) marmalade, you will need 450g (1lb) Seville oranges, 1 lemon, 900g (2lb) granulated sugar.

1 Wash the oranges and halve them. Squeeze out the juice and pips into a bowl. Squeeze the lemon into the same bowl and discard the peel. Collect the pips – plus any membranes that come away in squeezing – and tie them up in a piece of muslin.

2 Slice the orange peel thickly or thinly, as you prefer, and put it into a preserving pan with the fruit juices, muslin bag and 1.1 litres (2 pints) water. Simmer gently for about 2 hours or until the peel is really soft and the liquid has reduced by about half.

3 Remove the bag and squeeze it over the pan so that the juices run back. Add the sugar.

4 Heat gently and stir until the sugar has dissolved, then bring back to the boil and boil rapidly for about 15 minutes or until setting point has been reached (page see 405). Remove any scum from the surface with a slotted spoon.

5 Pour into warm, sterilised jars (see page 404). Seal and label, and store in a cool dark place for up to one year.

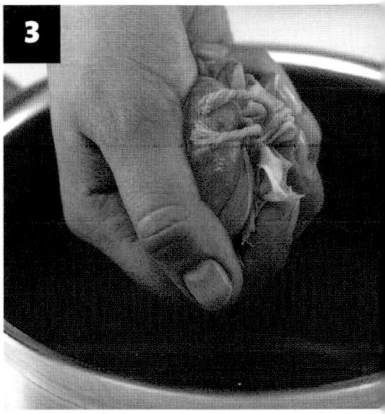

Perfect marmalade

- Citrus peel gives marmalade its distinctive flavour and texture, but it is tough and needs lengthy cooking. Citrus fruits are high in pectin so marmalades tend to set well.
- Seville oranges are by far the best choice because of their tart flavour.
- Wash citrus fruits well to remove their waxy coating.
- The pith and pips of citrus fruit contain pectin, which makes the marmalade set. Collect all the pips and put them into a muslin bag to be cooked with the fruit and then discarded.
- Squeeze the citrus juice into the pan and slice the peel thinly or thickly according to your preference.
- Make sure the peel is very soft and tender before adding the sugar, as it will not soften any more once the sugar is added.

Making jellies

Clear fruit jellies made from summer berries, plums and currants make delicate preserves to serve with scones or to use in cake making and desserts.

Mixed berry jelly

The recipe here uses a mixture of fruits, but you can substitute others – or use just a single fruit.

To make 3.2kg (7lb) jelly, you will need 450g (1lb) redcurrants, 450g (1lb) raspberries, 450g (1lb) Morello or May Duke cherries, 450g (1lb) strawberries, 4 tbsp lemon juice, granulated sugar.

1 Put all the fruits in a preserving pan with the lemon juice and 600ml (1 pint) water. Simmer gently for about 1 hour, or until the fruit is really soft and pulpy. Stir from time to time to prevent sticking.

2 Tie a jelly bag or heavy cloth to the legs of an upturned stool, and place a large bowl on the underside of the seat. Spoon the pulp into the bag and leave to strain for at least 12 hours.

3 Discard the pulp remaining in the bag. Measure the extract by volume of juice and return it to a preserving pan. Add 450g (1lb) sugar for every 600ml (1 pint) of extract.

4 Heat gently, stirring, until the sugar has dissolved. Bring to the boil and boil rapidly for about 10 minutes or until setting point has been reached (see page 405). Remove any scum with a slotted spoon.

5 Leave to cool slightly, then pour into warm, sterilised jars (see page 404). Seal and label, and store in a cool dark place for up to two years.

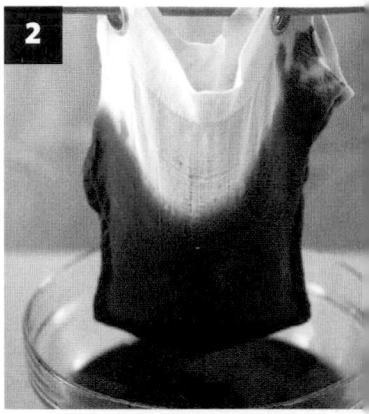

Perfect jellies

- Home-made jellies take longer to make than jams and marmalades because the fruit pulp needs to be left to strain in a jelly bag to ensure a clear juice. The fruit is not peeled, cored or stoned, as this will be discarded after straining, although you will need to roughly chop larger fruits such as apples or pears. After cooking the fruit is strained very slowly (overnight is best). Sugar is added to the fruit juice after the initial cooking.
- Choose fruits with a high level of pectin (see page 406).
- The fruit should be simmered very gently until tender; this can take from 30 minutes to 1½ hours.
- Scald the jelly bag in boiling water before adding the fruit for straining.
- The jelly should be bright and clear, so do not squeeze the jelly bag used for straining the juice, as this will make the jelly cloudy.

Making fruit curds and cheeses

Eggs are used for making fruit curds, and the ever-popular lemon curd is especially good when home-made. If you have a glut of home-grown stone fruits, a fruit cheese is well worth considering.

Lemon curd

To make 700g (1lb 9oz), you will need 4 lemons, 100g (3½oz) butter, 4 eggs, 350g (12oz) caster sugar.

1 Put the lemon zest and juice in a double boiler. Cut the butter into small pieces. Add the butter, eggs and sugar. Place over simmering water. Stir until the sugar dissolves and heat gently, without boiling, for 20 minutes. Strain into jars, cover and refrigerate.

Variations

Both lime and orange curd can be made in the same way. In place of the lemons, use:

- 5–8 limes depending on size.
- 2–3 oranges.

Damson cheese

To make 1.4kg (3lb), you will need 1.4kg (3lb) damsons or plums, sugar.

1 Wash the fruit and put into a pan. Cover with water and simmer gently for 15–20 minutes until the fruit is soft. As the fruit cooks, scoop out any stones that float to the surface.

2 Using a wooden spoon, press the fruit pulp through a nylon or stainless steel sieve into a large bowl. Measure the purée by volume and return it to the pan.

3 Add 350g (12oz) sugar for each 600ml (1 pint) of purée. Heat gently, stirring, until the sugar has dissolved, then bring to the boil and boil gently, stirring, for 30–40 minutes until the mixture is so thick that a spoon leaves a clean line when drawn along the bottom of the pan.

4 Pot and cover the cheese or, if you prefer, set in several dishes or moulds.

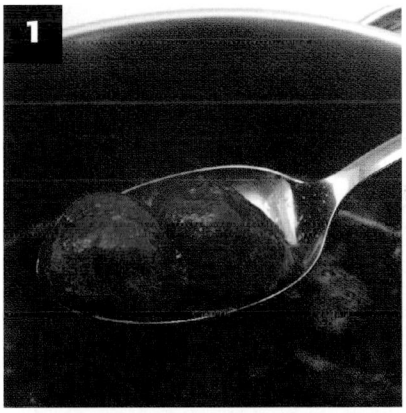

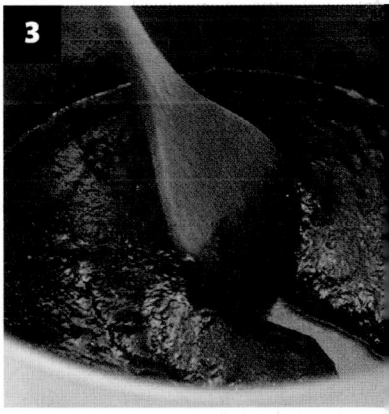

Perfect curds and cheeses

- In fruit curd, the juice of the fruit is set using egg as the thickener. Because of the eggs, these differ from jams, jellies and marmalades in being unsuitable for long storage. Store in the refrigerator, and keep for no more than two weeks.
- Fruit cheeses are made with stone fruits, such as plums and damsons, and are a good thing to make if the fruits are plentiful and cheap, as you need a large quantity of fruit to make a purée.
- As with any dish containing eggs, heat control is vital. Don't let the bottom of the bowl touch the simmering water, and take it off the heat for a minute or so if it shows signs of coming to the boil.
- Make only as much as you can eat in two weeks.

Making bottled fruits

Fruit preserved in this way can be steeped in water or, better still, in a full-flavoured syrup. Here, peaches are bottled in a sweet brandy syrup.

Brandied peaches

To make 450g (1lb), you will need 225g (8oz) sugar, 450g (1lb) fresh peaches, about 150ml (¼ pint) brandy or orange-flavoured liqueur.

1 Make a light syrup by dissolving 100g (3½oz) sugar in 300ml (½ pint) water. Skin the peaches by plunging them into boiling water, then gently peeling off the skins. Halve and remove the stones, then gently poach the fruit in the syrup for 4–5 minutes.

2 Remove the pan from the heat, drain the peaches, reserving the syrup, and leave to cool. Arrange the fruit in wide-necked sterilised jars (see page 404).

3 Add the remaining sugar to the syrup and dissolve it slowly. Bring it to the boil and boil to a temperature of 110°C, then allow to cool.

4 Measure the syrup and add an equal quantity of brandy or liqueur. Pour over the peaches and cover with the lids. Label and leave for two to three months before eating.

Perfect bottled fruit

- In this method of preserving, fruit is kept whole or halved and is surrounded by a boiled sugar syrup. It is essential to use fresh, ripe fruit of the best quality. Make sure it is properly cleaned and prepared so that no stalks or stems remain.
- Bottling is appropriate for a wide variety of fruits, such as berries, rhubarb, apples, peaches and plums.
- It's best to use a sugar thermometer or an instant-read thermometer while making the syrup. If you don't have one, boiling the syrup for a minute or two should be enough to bring it to the correct temperature.

Making pickles

Vegetables pickled in a good, spicy vinegar go well with cold meats and savouries and none is more popular than pickled onions.

Pickled onions

To make 1.8kg (4lb), you will need 1.8kg (4lb) pickling onions, unpeeled and roots trimmed, 450g (1lb) salt, 1.1 litres (2 pints) spiced vinegar (page 430).

1 Put the unpeeled onions into a large bowl. Dissolve half the salt in 2.3 litres (4 pints) water, pour it over the onions, and leave for 12 hours.

2 Drain the onions, then carefully slit the skins and peel off. Put the onions in a bowl.

3 Cover the onions with a fresh brine made from the remaining salt and a further 2.3 litres (4 pints) water. Leave for 24–36 hours.

4 Drain the onions and rinse well, then pack into sterilised jars (see page 404) and cover with the spiced vinegar. It is worth noting that a 450g (1lb) jar will usually hold about 450g (1lb) of prepared vegetables. Cover and seal the jars, label and leave for three months before using.

Perfect pickles

- Pickling uses vinegar to preserve fresh or lightly cooked vegetables and fruits, but first they have to be soaked in brine (salted water) to draw out their juices. A good-flavoured vinegar with herbs and spices is essential for the best taste, and the bottled pickles need to be left for at least one month before eating.
- Choose young, fresh vegetables and firm, ripe fruits for the best flavour and texture.
- Wash the vegetables well, removing any damaged parts, then peel and trim as required in the recipe.
- Vegetables such as onions are wet brined (submerged in a brine solution), whereas those containing large amounts of water are dry brined (layered with plenty of salt in a large bowl) to draw out excess water, which would dilute the flavour and reduce the storage time.

Making chutneys

Chutneys differ from other preserves in that they can be eaten soon after making them, if you like. But they can also be stored for long periods as long as they are bottled in sterilised containers.

Tomato chutney

Make this chutney when tomatoes are in season and are both plentiful and have a good flavour.

To make 3kg (6½lb), you will need 700g (1lb 9oz) tomatoes, 1 apple, 50g (2oz) onion, finely chopped, 1 garlic clove, crushed, 1 tsp finely chopped fresh root ginger, 125g (4oz) light soft brown sugar, ½ tsp turmeric, 125g (4oz) sultanas, 50ml (2fl oz) white wine vinegar.

1 Peel, deseed and chop the tomatoes. Peel, core and roughly chop the apple.

2 Put all the ingredients in a pan and bring to the boil. Simmer for 30 minutes or until reduced and thick – there should be hardly any liquid left. Cool and use the chutney immediately, or pack into sterilised jars, seal and label (see page 404).

Plum chutney

You will need 2kg (4½lb) plums, 2 cooking apples, 2 red onions, finely chopped, 600ml (1 pint) red wine vinegar, 600g (1lb 5oz) light muscovado sugar, 1 tsp cloves, 1 tsp salt, 1 tbsp mustard. Makes 3kg (6½lb).

1 Halve, stone and roughly chop the plums. Peel, core and roughly chop the apples.

2 Put all the ingredients in a large pan and cook over a low heat, stirring until the sugar dissolves.

3 Bring to the boil and simmer, uncovered, over a low heat for about 3 hours – until the mixture is thick and pulpy. There should be hardly any liquid left.

4 Cool and use the chutney immediately, or pack into six sterilised 300ml (½ pint) jars, and seal and label (see page 404).

Perfect chutney

- When you make chutney for use immediately, always make extra for the storecupboard.
- The flavour of chutney improves with keeping.
- Use jars with plastic or coated-metal lids – vinegar corrodes metal so chutneys must be covered with airtight, vinegar-proof lids. Vinegar will also evaporate through jam pot discs and covers.

Making refrigerator preserves

Some preserves are designed to be kept for a matter of weeks rather than months. The good thing is that they start to taste really good within only a day of making.

Marinated olives

These can be made with green or black olives, or both.

To make 1kg (2¼lb), you will need 750g (1lb 10oz) plain olives with the pits still in, a small pinch each of dried oregano and thyme, 2 bay leaves, 3 large garlic cloves, 1 small chilli, halved and seeded, 100ml (3½fl oz) red wine vinegar, 2 tbsp whole black peppercorns, 200ml (7fl oz) extra-virgin olive oil.

1 Peel the garlic and smash with a knife blade but leave whole.

2 Put all the ingredients in a glass bowl. Cover with a lid or clingfilm and chill in the refrigerator for at least a day, stirring occasionally.

3 Spoon into two jars and chill for two days before using, shaking now and then. Store for up to one month.

Chilli sauce

You can make this sauce hotter by leaving some or all of the seeds in the chillies, and vary the seasonings.

To make about 600ml (1 pint), you will need 100g (3½oz) fresh chillies, deseeded and chopped, 50g (2oz) pinenuts, 15 garlic cloves, chopped, 1 small onion, chopped, 1 tsp ground cumin, 1 tsp ground coriander, ½ tsp paprika, ½ tsp dried oregano, 2 tbsp tomato paste, 300ml (½ pint) red wine vinegar, salt and ground black pepper.

1 Place the chopped chillies in the bowl of the blender.

2 Toast the pinenuts in a dry frying pan until golden brown, then add to the blender with the remaining ingredients. Blend until smooth, then add 300ml (½ pint) water.

3 Pour into two or three clean glass bottles and refrigerate for up to two months.

Cook's tips

- Refrigerated preserves will keep better if they contain no animal products of any kind, including fat, meat or dairy products.
- Although they are not destined for long storage, they will keep for longer in a sterilised jar or bottle (see page 404).

Making relishes

Relishes are a type of pickle, but whereas pickles can be either cooked or uncooked, relishes are always cooked.

Mustard relish

To make 1.4kg (3lb), you will need 225g (8oz) cauliflower, 100g (3½oz) tomatoes, 1 red and 1 green pepper, 175g (6oz) cucumber, finely chopped, 175g (6oz) onion, finely chopped, 225g (8oz) fresh gherkins, thickly sliced, 25g (1oz) salt, 1 tbsp mustard seeds, 250g (9oz) sugar, 25g (1oz) plain flour, ½ tsp mustard powder, ½ tsp turmeric, 450ml (¾ pint) malt vinegar.

1 Break the cauliflower into florets. Core and roughly chop the tomatoes. Deseed and finely chop the peppers. Put all the vegetables in a large bowl. Dissolve the salt in 1.1 litres (2 pints) water and pour over the vegetables, then cover and leave to stand overnight.

2 Drain the vegetables and rinse well. Blend the remaining ingredients except the vinegar in a large heavy pan, then gradually stir in the vinegar. Bring to the boil, stirring.

3 Add all the vegetables to the pan and bring to the boil.

4 Reduce the heat and simmer gently, uncovered, for about 30 minutes or until all the vegetables are soft. Stir gently from time to time to prevent sticking.

5 Pour into warm, sterilised jars (see page 404). Seal, label when cold, and store in a cool dark place for up to one year.

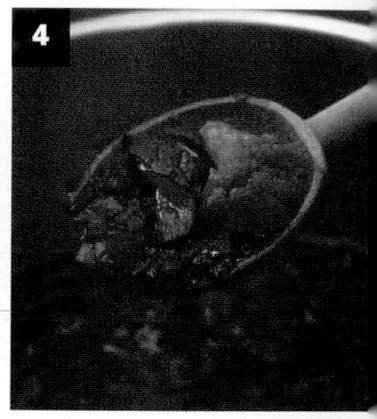

Cook's tips

- Don't be tempted to use less sugar than a recipe requires. The sugar is a preservative, and the relish may ferment if there isn't enough of it.
- Relishes, like chutneys, must be covered with airtight, vinegar-proof lids. Use jars with plastic or coated-metal lids.
- Add a slice of chilli pepper to the mixture at step 4 for a mild touch of heat.

Variations

Instead of making relish with a combination of vegetables, you can adapt this recipe to include just one or two. Use vegetables with a total weight comparable to that in the recipe. Other good vegetables to use include: sweetcorn, green tomatoes, French beans, courgettes, marrow, yellow squash, celery.

Making sauces

Preserved sauces are worth making when you can buy the main ingredient very fresh and of the highest quality, at a reasonable price. With tomatoes, this means making ketchup in summertime.

Tomato ketchup

To make 1.1 litres (2 pints), you will need 2.7kg (6lb) ripe tomatoes, 225g (8oz) sugar, 300ml (½ pint) spiced vinegar (page 430), 1 tbsp tarragon vinegar (optional), pinch of cayenne pepper, 1 tsp paprika, 1 tsp salt.

1 Slice the tomatoes and cook over a very low heat, stirring frequently, until they cook down to a pulp, about 45 minutes. Bring to the boil and cook rapidly, stirring frequently, until the pulp thickens.

2 Press the pulp through a nylon or stainless steel sieve, then return to the pan and stir in the remaining ingredients. Simmer gently until the mixture thickens.

3 Pour the ketchup into warm, sterilised bottles. Seal and label, and store in a cool dark place for up to one year.

Tomato sauce

This contains no oil or butter, so stir some in just before serving.

To make 2.5kg (5½lb), you will need 2.7kg (6lb) ripe tomatoes, 3 onions, finely chopped, 6 garlic cloves, finely chopped, 150ml (¼ pint) sun-dried tomato paste, 1 tbsp freshly chopped oregano, salt and ground black pepper.

1 Skin, deseed and quarter the tomatoes, then chop the flesh.

2 Put all the ingredients in a large pan and bring to the boil. Simmer, uncovered, over a low heat for 25–30 minutes, stirring occasionally, until the sauce is thick and pulpy. Season with salt and pepper to taste, and cook for a few minutes more.

3 Pour into warm, sterilised jars (see page 404). Seal and label, and store in a cool dark place for up to six months.

Strawberry and Redcurrant Jam

MAKES ABOUT 1.4KG (3LB)
700g (1lb 9oz) granulated or preserving sugar
1kg (2¼lb) strawberries, hulled and halved if large
225g (8oz) redcurrants, stripped from their stalks
juice of 1 lemon

PREPARATION TIME 20 minutes
COOKING TIME 30 minutes

PER TSP
11 calories
0g fat (of which 0g saturates)
3g carbohydrate
0g salt

TECHNIQUES
see also preparing berries and currants (page 209), sterilising jars (page 404), testing for a set (page 405), potting preserves (page 405), labelling (page 404), making jams (page 406)

1 Put the sugar in a roasting tin and warm at 180°C (160°C fan oven) mark 4 for 10 minutes. Put half the strawberries and all the redcurrants in a preserving pan over a low heat and cook until soft and the juice runs.

2 Add the remaining strawberries to the pan and bring to the boil. Add the lemon juice and warmed sugar to the pan, bring to the boil, then simmer until the sugar dissolves. Bubble for 25 minutes, or until setting point has been reached (see page 405). Cool and pot, then cover and label the jars. Store in a cool, dry place for up to six months.

Cook's tip

Strawberry jam can be quite runny, so adding redcurrants and lemon juice, which are both high in pectin, wil give the jam a firmer set.

Quick Marmalade

MAKES 4.5KG (10LB)
900g (2lb) Seville oranges, scrubbed and chopped, pips discarded
2kg (4½lb) preserving sugar

PREPARATION TIME 25 minutes
COOKING TIME 1 hour 10 minutes

PER TSP
9 calories
0g fat (of which 0g saturates)
2g carbohydrate
0g salt

TECHNIQUES
see also sterilising jars (page 404), testing for a set (page 405), potting preserves (page 405), labelling (page 404), making marmalade (page 407)

1 Whiz the chopped oranges briefly in a food processor or blender, then put in a preserving pan with 1.6 litres (2¾ pints) water. Bring to the boil and simmer for 1 hour.

2 Add the sugar and stir over a gentle heat until dissolved. Bubble rapidly for 4 minutes or until setting point has been reached (see page 405). Leave to cool for 5 minutes, stirring once or twice, then pot and seal. Label when cold and store the jars in a cool, dry place for up to six months.

Cook's tip

Seville oranges are the traditional marmalade orange due to their unique bitter flavour. They are only available and in season for a very short time – usually mid–late winter.

Cranberry and Apple Jelly

MAKES ABOUT 1.4KG (3LB)
1.4kg (3lb) cooking apples, washed
900g (2lb) cranberries, washed
granulated sugar

PREPARATION TIME 25 minutes, plus minimum 12 hours standing
COOKING TIME 1 hour 20 minutes

PER TSP
10 calories
0g fat (of which 0g saturates)
2.7g carbohydrate
0g salt

TECHNIQUES
see also sterilising jars (page 404), testing for a set (page 405), potting preserves (page 405), labelling (page 404), making jellies (page 408)

1 Remove any bruised or damaged portions from the apples, then roughly chop them without peeling or coring.

2 Put the apples and cranberries in a preserving pan with sufficient water to cover them, and simmer gently for 45 minutes–1 hour until the fruit is really soft and pulpy. Stir from time to time to prevent sticking.

3 Spoon the pulp into a jelly bag or cloth attached to the legs of an upturned stool, and leave to strain into a large bowl for at least 12 hours.

4 Discard the pulp remaining in the jelly bag. Measure the extract and return it to the preserving pan with 450g (1lb) sugar for each 600ml (1 pint) of extract. Bring slowly to the boil, stirring, until the sugar has dissolved, then boil rapidly for about 10 minutes or until setting point has been reached (see page 405).

5 Remove any scum with a slotted spoon, then pot and cover. Label when cold and store in a cool, dark place for up to six months.

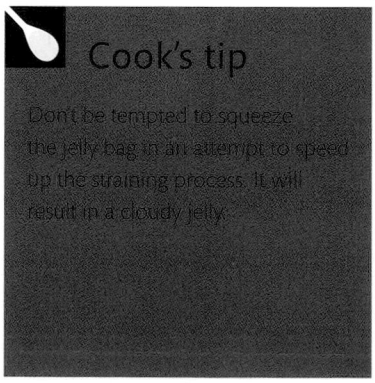

Cook's tip

Don't be tempted to squeeze the jelly bag in an attempt to speed up the straining process. It will result in a cloudy jelly.

Spiced Clementines in Brandy

MAKES TWO 500ML (18FL OZ) JARS

350g (12oz) caster sugar
14 kumquats, halved lengthways, seeds removed
5cm (2in) piece fresh root ginger, peeled and finely sliced
1 tsp allspice berries
8 clementines, peel and pith removed
6 fresh bay leaves
225ml (8fl oz) brandy

PREPARATION TIME 25 minutes
COOKING TIME 13 minutes

PER JAR
999 calories
0g fat (of which 0g saturates)
197g carbohydrate
0g salt

TECHNIQUES
see also preparing fresh spices (page 429), sterilising jars (page 404), potting preserves (page 405), labelling (page 404)

1 Put 175g (6oz) sugar with 300ml (½ pint) water in a wide pan and heat gently to dissolve the sugar. Add the kumquats, ginger and allspice. Bring to a simmer and poach with the lid on for 8 minutes or until softened.

2 Lift the kumquats and spices out of the pan with a slotted spoon and put to one side. Add the remaining sugar and dissolve, stirring, over a low heat. Increase the heat and boil uncovered for about 5 minutes or until the liquid measures about 250ml (9fl oz). Cool slightly.

3 Pierce the clementines all over with a skewer and arrange in sterilised jars with the kumquats, spices and bay leaves. Add the brandy to the syrup and pour over the fruit, making sure the fruit is submerged. Seal, label when cold and store in the refrigerator for up to 1 month.

Plum Chutney

MAKES SIX 300ML (½ PINT) JARS

2kg (4½lb) plums, halved, stoned and roughly chopped
2 red onions, finely chopped
2 cooking apples, peeled, cored and roughly chopped
600ml (1 pint) red wine vinegar
600g (1lb 5oz) light muscovado sugar
1 tsp each cloves and salt
1 tbsp mustard seeds

PREPARATION TIME 20 minutes
COOKING TIME 3–3½ hours

PER TSP
30 calories
0g fat (of which 0g saturates)
2g carbohydrate
0g salt

TECHNIQUES
see also stoning fruits (page 208), sterilising jars (page 404), potting preserves (page 405), making chutneys (page 412)

1 Put all the ingredients in a large pan and cook over a low heat, stirring until the sugar dissolves.

2 Bring to the boil and simmer, uncovered, over a low heat for 3–3½ hours until the mixture is thick and pulpy. There should be hardly any liquid left.

3 Spoon the chutney into six 300ml (1/2 pint) jars, then cover with a waxed disc and a larger circle of dampened clear wrap. Secure around the rim with an elastic band. Label when cold, and keep in a cool, dark place for one month to mature. Store for up to six months.

Rhubarb and Ginger Chutney

MAKES ABOUT 1.6KG (3½LB)

1kg (2¼lb) thick rhubarb stems, trimmed and cut into 5cm (2in) pieces
4 tsp salt
225g (8oz) red onions, cut into thick slices
700g (1lb 9oz) dark muscovado sugar
450ml (¾ pint) white wine vinegar
25g (1oz) fresh root ginger, peeled and coarsely grated
¼ tsp ground allspice
125g (4oz) raisins

PREPARATION TIME 15 minutes, plus 12 hours standing
COOKING TIME 1¼ hours

PER TSP
10cals
0g fat (of which 0g saturates)
3g carbs
0.1g salt

TECHNIQUES
see also preparing onions (page 170), preparing fresh spices (page 429), sterilising jars (page 404), potting preserves (page 405), labelling (page 404), making chutneys (page 412)

1 Put the rhubarb in a non-metallic bowl, mix with 1 tsp salt, then cover and leave in a cool place for 12 hours.

2 Drain and rinse the rhubarb, then put in a preserving pan with all the other ingredients except the raisins. Cook over a gentle heat until the sugar has dissolved, then increase the heat and bubble for 45 minutes–1 hour until well reduced and pulpy. Add the raisins and bubble for 5 minutes.

3 Pot hot or cool (not warm), then cover, and label the jars when cold. Store in a cool, dark place for up to six months.

Cook's tip

This spiced chutney is a useful preserve to have in the store-cupboard and tastes especially good with mature cheeses and cold meats.

Sweetcorn Relish

MAKES 2.3KG (5LB)

6 corn cobs, trimmed, and leaves and silk removed
½ small white cabbage, trimmed and roughly chopped
2 medium onions, skinned and halved
1½ red peppers, washed, deseeded and quartered
2 tsp salt
2 tbsp plain flour
½ tsp ground turmeric
175g (6oz) sugar
2 tsp mustard powder
600ml (1 pint) distilled vinegar

PREPARATION TIME 25 minutes
COOKING TIME 40 minutes

PER TSP

5 calories
trace fat (of which 0g saturates)
1g carbohydrate
0g salt

TECHNIQUES

see also preparing vegetables (pages 170–182), sterilising jars (page 404)

1 Cook the corn cobs in boiling salted water for 3 minutes, then drain. Using a sharp knife, cut the corn from the cobs. Coarsely mince the cabbage, onions and red peppers, and combine with the corn.

2 Blend the salt, flour, turmeric, sugar and mustard powder together in a preserving pan, then gradually stir in the vinegar. Heat gently, stirring, until the sugar has dissolved, then bring to the boil. Reduce the heat, add the vegetables, and simmer for 25–30 minutes, stirring occasionally.

3 Spoon the relish into jars, cover and seal. Label when cold and store in a cool, dark place for up to three months.

Sweet and sour Figs

MAKES ABOUT 700G (1LB 9OZ)
SERVES 10
450ml (¾ pint) distilled malt vinegar
small piece of fresh root ginger, peeled and thinly sliced
3 allspice berries
6 black peppercorns
3 whole cloves
2 cinnamon sticks
pared zest of 1 lemon
2 tbsp honey
250g (9oz) sugar
700g (1lb 9oz) firm green figs, stalks trimmed

PREPARATION TIME 20 minutes, plus overnight standing
COOKING TIME 15 minutes

PER SERVING
198 calories
1g fat (of which 0g saturates)
50g carbohydrate
0.1g salt

TECHNIQUES
see also using spices (page 429), zesting citrus fruits (page 207), sterilising jars (page 404)

1 Put the vinegar in a large shallow pan with the ginger, allspice, peppercorns, cloves, cinnamon, lemon zest, honey and sugar. Heat gently, stirring, until the sugar has dissolved.

2 Bring to the boil, boil for 1 minute, then remove from the heat. Thickly slice the figs into the warm vinegar. Bring to the boil, then simmer, uncovered, for 1 minute, gently pushing the fig slices under the vinegar. Carefully transfer the figs and vinegar to a large non-metallic bowl. Cover tightly with clingfilm and leave overnight.

3 Remove the fig slices from the vinegar with a slotted spoon. Tightly pack into clean preheated jars. Return the vinegar mixture to a clean pan and bring to the boil. Boil rapidly until reduced to 150ml (¼ pint).

4 Pour the hot vinegar into the jars. Cover and seal. Label when cold and store for at least one week before using.

Cook's tip

Serve these pickled figs with cheese or cold roast meats.

Mixed Dill Pickle

MAKES 1.5–2KG (3LB 5OZ–4LB 8OZ)

1 cauliflower, about 550g (1¼lb), divided into small florets
175g (6oz) courgettes, cut into 5mm (¼in) diagonal slices
1 green pepper, about 225g (8oz), cut into 5mm (¼in) strips
175g (6oz) fine green beans, trimmed and halved
100g (3½oz) pickling or button onions, peeled with roots intact
1 cucumber, halved lengthways and sliced
225g (8oz) coarse salt
1.1–1.3 litres (2–2¼ pints) white wine vinegar
2 tbsp pickling spice
1 tbsp salt
100g (3½oz) sugar
2 garlic cloves
2 good stalks of fresh dill
1 tsp dried dill
2 stalks of tarragon

PREPARATION TIME 30 minutes, plus 25 hours standing
COOKING TIME 15 minutes

PER TBSP WITHOUT LIQUID
13 calories
0g fat
2g carbohydrate
0.1g salt

TECHNIQUES
see also preparing vegetables (pages 170–182), sterilising jars (page 404), making pickles (page 411)

1 Put all the prepared vegetables in a large bowl. Cover with the coarse salt. Mix, cover and leave in a cold place for 24 hours.

2 Put the remaining ingredients in a preserving pan. Heat gently to simmering point. Remove from the heat and leave to cool completely.

3 Drain the vegetables, rinse well and drain again. Bring two large pans of water to the boil. Add the vegetables and bring back to the boil. Drain the vegetables and refresh under cold water to stop the cooking process and preserve the colour. Leave to drain well.

4 Pack the vegetables into preheated jars. Leave to stand for 1 hour, then drain off the excess liquid. Pour over the cooled pickling vinegar to cover completely. Cover and seal the jars, then label. The pickle will darken a little on storing but it will remain clear if stored in the refrigerator for up to one month.

The Ultimate Barbecue Sauce

MAKES ABOUT 300ML (½ PINT)

3 tbsp olive oil
3 garlic cloves, finely chopped
3 tbsp balsamic vinegar
4 tbsp dry sherry
3 tbsp sun-dried tomato paste or tomato purée
3 tbsp sweet chilli sauce
300ml (½ pint) passata
5 tbsp clear honey

PREPARATION TIME 5 minutes
COOKING TIME 15 minutes

PER TSP
12 calories
1g fat (of which 0g saturates)
2g carbohydrate
0.1g salt

TECHNIQUES
see also preparing garlic (page 171), sterilising jars (page 404)

1 Mix together the oil, garlic, vinegar, sherry, sun-dried tomato paste or tomato purée and chilli sauce.

2 Turn into a small pan and add the passata and honey. Bring to the boil, reduce the heat and simmer gently for 10–15 minutes or until thickened and glossy. Bottle in sterilised jars and store in the refrigerator for up to one month.

Cook's tip

Quick to make, this sauce goes well with chicken, pork, burgers or pork sausages.

18 HERBS, SPICES AND FLAVOURINGS

Flavourings are an essential in every kitchen and will make the difference between a good dish and a really delicious one – and this chapter shows you how to make the most of them. As well as preparing fresh herbs and fresh and dried spices, the step-by-step techniques show you how to make flavoured vinegars that can be used in dressings and sauces, flavoured sugars that can be used in desserts and baking, and flavoured salts that can be used to add extra flavour to savoury dishes.

Using herbs

Most herbs are the leaf of a flowering plant, and are usually sold with much of the stalk intact. They have to be washed, trimmed and then chopped or torn into pieces suitable for your recipe.

Washing

1 Trim the roots and part of the stalks from the herbs. Immerse in cold water and shake briskly. Leave in the water for a few minutes.

2 Lift out of the water and put in a colander or sieve, then rinse again under the cold tap. Leave to drain for a few minutes, then dry thoroughly on kitchen paper or teatowels, or use a salad spinner.

Chopping

1 Trim the herbs by pinching off all but the smallest, most tender stalks. If the herb is one with a woody stalk, such as rosemary or thyme, it may be easier to remove the leaves by rubbing the whole bunch between your hands; the leaves should simply pull off the stems.

2 If you are chopping the leaves, gather them into a compact ball in one hand, keeping your fist around the ball (but being careful not to crush them).

3 Chop with a large knife, using a rocking motion and letting just a little of the ball out of your fingers at a time.

4 When the herbs are roughly chopped, continue chopping until the pieces are in small shreds or flakes.

Perfect herbs

- Don't pour the herbs and their water into the sieve, because dirt in the water might get caught in the leaves.
- If the herb has fleshy stalks, such as parsley or coriander, the stalks can be saved to flavour stock or soup. Tie them in a bundle with string for easy removal.

Using spices

The flavour of spices is most pronounced when they are first roasted and then ground for use in recipes. Fresh root ginger is one of the most frequently used wet spices and is easy to prepare.

Roasting spices

Whole spices are roasted in a dry frying pan to bring out their flavour.

1 Place a small frying pan over a high heat. When it's very hot, pour in the spices and cook until they take on a darker colour and just begin to pop and they release their fragrance. Don't let them burn.

2 Remove to a bowl and cool.

Grinding

The traditional method uses a mortar and pestle. The alternative, quicker method is to buy a hand-cranked spice mill or use a coffee grinder. If you use a coffee grinder, use it only for spices or they will flavour your coffee!

Preparing fresh spices

Ginger, galangal and turmeric are the most common fresh spices. They are prepared in the same way.

1 Grating Peel a large section of the spice with a vegetable peeler and cut off any soft brown spots.

2 Using a wooden or fine metal grater resting on a small plate or bowl, grate the spice. Discard any large fibres adhering to the pulp.

3 Chopping Cut slices off the spice and cut off the skin carefully and remove any soft brown spots. If you need very large quantities, you can peel a large section with a vegetable peeler before slicing.

4 Stack the slices and cut into shreds of the required thickness. To make dice, stack the shreds and cut to the required size.

5 Pressing If you need just the juice, cut thick slices off the ginger or galangal root and cut off the skin carefully, taking care to remove any soft brown spots under the skin. If you need very large quantities, you can peel a large section with a vegetable peeler. Cut the slices into chunks, and press them with a garlic press into a small bowl.

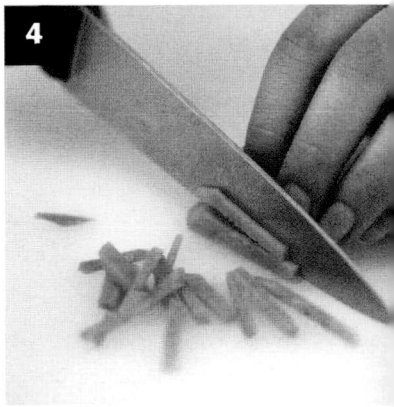

Making flavoured vinegars

These are easy to make using tarragon, thyme or rosemary, and can be stored in a cool dark place for one month. Use sterilised storage bottles, wash all the ingredients well and dry before adding to the vinegar.

Herb vinegar

You will need 25g (1oz) fresh herbs, plus extra sprigs for bottling, 600ml (1 pint) red or white wine vinegar.

1 Put the herbs and vinegar in a pan and bring to the boil. Pour into a bowl, cover and leave overnight.

2 Strain through a muslin-lined sieve and bottle with herb sprigs. Store for one week before using.

Fruit vinegar

You will need 450g (1lb) raspberries and blackberries, plus extra for bottling, 600ml (1 pint) wine vinegar.

1 Break up fruit with back of spoon and add vinegar. Cover and leave to stand 3 days, stirring now and then.

2 Strain through a muslin-lined sieve and bottle with extra fruits. Store for two weeks before using.

Spiced vinegar

Perfect for pickling.

You will need 500ml (18fl oz) malt vinegar, 1 tbsp mace, 1 tbsp allspice berries, 1 tbsp cloves, 18cm (7in) cinnamon stick, 6 peppercorns, 4 dried red chillies, 1 small bay leaf.

1 Put all the ingredients in a pan and bring to the boil. Remove from the heat, cover and leave to infuse for about 2 hours.

2 Strain the vinegar through a muslin-lined sieve to remove the herbs and spices.

3 Pour the vinegar into sterilised bottles or jars and seal tightly. The vinegar can be used straight away or stored until required.

Making flavoured sugar and salt

Sugar or salt flavoured with spices or aromatics is a great way to add instant flavour to sweet or savoury dishes. They can be stored almost indefinitely in an airtight container in a dry place.

Flavoured sugars

Perfect for using in cakes, biscuits and desserts.

1 Cinnamon sugar Mix 1 tbsp ground cinnamon with 200g (7oz) caster sugar.

2 Citrus sugar Mix 200g (7oz) caster sugar with 1 tbsp finely chopped orange, lemon or lime zest and store in an airtight container. Cover and leave to stand for a few days before use.

3 Lavender sugar Mix 200g (7oz) caster sugar with 2 tbsp dried lavender flowers. Cover and leave to stand for one week before use.

4 Vanilla sugar Put a whole vanilla pod in an airtight container and pour in caster sugar to cover. Cover and leave to stand for at least one week before use.

Flavoured salt

1 Chilli salt Grind 2 tbsp dried chilli flakes to a coarse powder and mix with 4–6 tbsp fine salt.

2 Herb salt Grind 2 tbsp dried herbs to a coarse powder and mix with 4–6 tbsp fine salt.

3 Spicy salt Roast 2 tbsp whole spices (see page 429) and leave to cool, then grind to a fine powder in a mortar or spice grinder. Mix with 4–6 tbsp fine salt.

Variations

- **Spices**: black or white peppercorns, cardamom, coriander, cumin, fennel seeds, fenugreek, mustard seeds.
- **Herbs**: chervil, mixed herbs, marjoram, oregano, parsley, rosemary, sage, tarragon, thyme.

19 FREEZING AND DRYING

Keeping a well-stocked freezer can be a real boon to the home cook. This chapter provides invaluable advice on how to freeze everything from liquids such as stocks, soups and stews to solid foods such as meat, fish, poultry, fruit and vegetables. There are also essential hints on labelling and packing your freezer and safe storage times so you know how long you can keep food for. However, freezing isn't the only way to preserve foods and there are also techniques showing you how to dry fruits, vegetables and herbs, plus tips on reconstituting them for future use.

Freezing stocks, sauces and stews

Stocks, stews, sauces and soups can be frozen for up to four months. Liquid-based dishes are among the most straightforward to freeze. Make sure that the containers are not overfilled and that they are well seale

Freezing in tubs

1 Line a plastic container with a freezer bag and pour the food into the bag to leave a space of 2.5cm (1in) at the top to allow the food to expand as it freezes.

2 Cover tightly and freeze as quickly as possible. Once the food is frozen, you may remove from the container and store in the bag. Alternatively, store in the container.

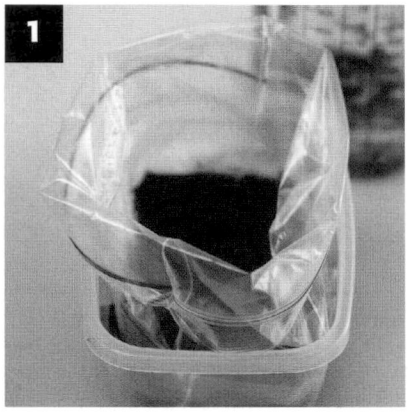

Freezing tips

- Use only suitable, food-approved containers with tight-fitting lids.
- Never put hot or warm food in the freezer.
- Leave space at the top of the container; food expands when frozen.

Freezing stock

Frozen stock is very useful in the kitchen, but it can use up a lot of freezer space. Save valuable space in the freezer by concentrating the stock before freezing it. To use, simply reconstitute it to its full volume by adding water.

1 Concentrating the stock Put the clarified, degreased stock (see page 35) in a clean pan and bring to the boil. Bubble to reduce it to about 25 per cent of its volume.

2 Pour the stock into plastic containers, filling to leave a space of 2.5cm (1in) at the top.

3 Put the lid on tightly and freeze as quickly as possible.

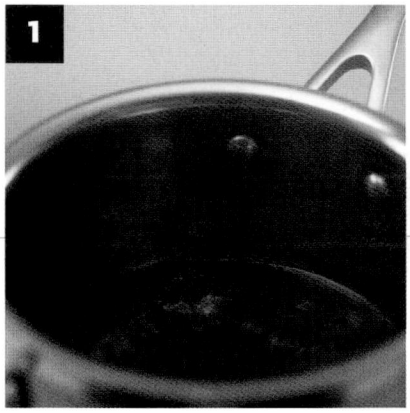

Frozen stock cubes

1 Freeze the reduced stock in an ice cube tray, then put the frozen cubes in a sealable tub. You can take out as many cubes as you need and re-seal the tub. If the cubes have a build-up of ice on the surface, just wash it off under the cold tap before adding the cube to the dish.

Freezing fruit

Fruit can be frozen for up to six months. Although freezing affects the texture, it preserves the flavour wonderfully and the thawed fruit is perfect for use in cooking, purées, smoothies and fruit salads.

Sugaring

Most fruits can be frozen without cooking, but when defrosted they will soften because of cell damage from ice crystals. To minimise that damage, freeze fruit pieces dusted with sugar or in syrup. Because of the extra sugar, you should use this method only with fruit that you are planning to use in a sweet dish.

1 Wash the fruit gently and dry thoroughly on clean teatowels or kitchen paper. Prepare as required, then place on a baking sheet or shallow roasting tin, spacing them well apart.

2 Sprinkle on enough caster sugar to give all the pieces of fruit a generous, even coating.

3 Freeze until solid, then quickly transfer to a sealable container and return to the freezer.

Perfect freezing

- Sugaring is best for sliced or halved stone fruits, and berries (except raspberries).
- Freezing in syrup is suitable for every type of fruit except bananas, which should be frozen in their skins and then used in cakes and muffins.

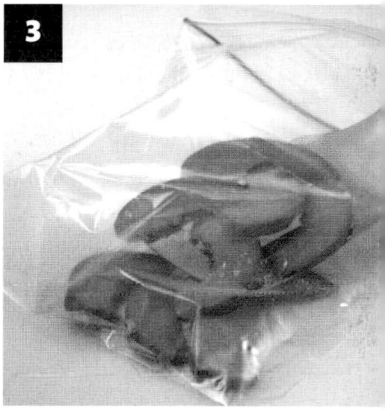

Freezing in syrup

You will need 175g (6oz) sugar per 600ml (1 pint) of water.

1 Dissolve the sugar in the water over a low heat. Bring to the boil and boil for 2 minutes, then cool.

2 Wash and dry the fruit, and cut it up as needed. Put in a sealable container and pour the syrup over to cover. If any fruit protrudes, place a piece of greaseproof paper on top and press down, then freeze.

Storage

- Always label containers with contents and date.
- Keep track of what you have in the freezer so that you never keep food for too long.
- Store containers with the oldest items towards the front of the freezer.

Freezing vegetables

Vegetables can be frozen for up to six months. Most must be cooked or part-cooked by blanching before freezing to reduce the activity of enzymes that would affect nutritional value and quality.

Blanching in water

1 Wash and prepare the vegetables and cut them into bite-sized pieces as appropriate.

2 Bring a pan of water to the boil using at least 6 litres (10½ pints salted water per 450g (1lb) of vegetables. Have ready a large bowl of iced water.

3 Put the vegetables in the boiling water, bring quickly back to the boil, and cook as shown in the table below. They should be hot all the way through and slightly tender, but not fully cooked.

4 Lift out with a slotted spoon and plunge into the iced water.

5 Dry thoroughly on kitchen paper and pack into containers. Freeze.

In season

Freeze vegetables when they're in season. They're cheap, in abundance and at their very best so it makes sense to preserve them now. If you grow your own – even better! Freeze them when they're freshly picked and their flavour is at its very best.

Blanching in steam

Ideal for most vegetables, especially those that might get waterlogged if cooked in water.

1 Wash and prepare the vegetables. Have ready a bowl of iced water.

2 Steam the vegetables for the time shown in the table, right. They should be hot all the way through and slightly tender, but not fully cooked. Plunge into the iced water. Dry, pack into containers and freeze.

Blanching times

Times given are for blanching in boiling water. For blanching in steam add 2–4 minutes. Test regularly to avoid overcooking.

Vegetable	Preparation	Blanching time
Asparagus	stalk ends removed	2–4 minutes
Broad beans	shelled	2–3 minutes
Broccoli	woody stalks removed	3–5 minutes
Brussels sprouts	trimmed at the base	3–5 minutes
Cauliflower	broken into florets	3–5 minutes
French beans	topped and tailed	2–3 minutes
Runner beans	strings removed, sliced	2–3 minutes
Sweetcorn	whole ears, husked	4–6 minutes

Freezing meat, poultry and fish

These all follow essentially similar procedures and principles. The most crucial point is to keep air out and avoiding 'freezer burn'. Follow the freezing times given below to ensure the food quality remains good.

Freezing in bags

1 Put the food in the bag, keeping it as flat as possible.

2 Squeeze all the air out so that the bag fits snugly around the food.

3 Tie the bag securely and freeze as quickly as possible.

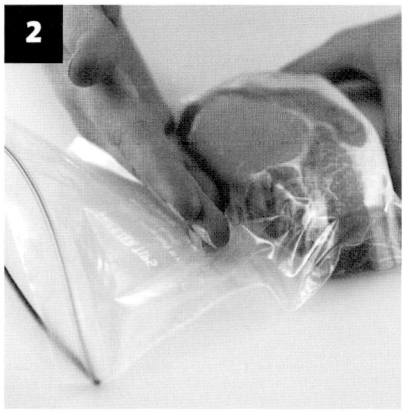

Freezing tips

- Squeeze out all the air to avoid 'freezer burn'.
- Divide individual pieces of food such as steaks or burgers with two sheets of waxed paper.
- Keep flat items, such as fish fillets, as flat as possible.

Tray freezing

1 Pieces of food can be frozen separately, then bagged together so you can use one piece at a time.

2 Put the pieces on a baking sheet, making sure that they don't touch each other. Freeze until solid.

3 Quickly transfer to a freezer bag, squeeze out the air and seal. Return to the freezer.

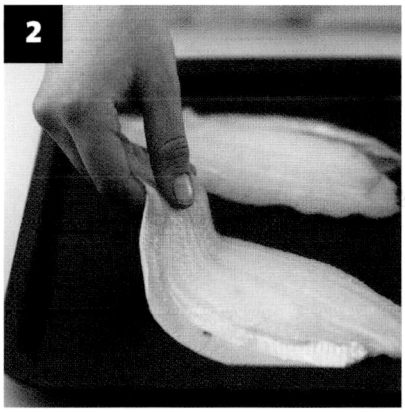

Maximum freezing times

Meat	Maximum time
Mince (any meat)	3 months
Bacon	1 month
Sausages	1 month
Steak	6 months
Chops	4 months
Joints, lean	10 months
Joints, fatty	4 months
Offal	3 months
Cooked meat	3 months

Poultry	Maximum time
Poultry, whole	1 year
Poultry, pieces	9 months

Fish	Maximum time
White fish (such as cod, haddock, plaice)	6 months
Oily fish (such as herring, mackerel)	2 months
Cooked fish	4 months
Smoked fish	2 months
Shellfish	3 months

Drying fruit, vegetables and herbs

Herbs can be frozen for up to three months. It is a good way to preserve fresh summer herbs for use later in the year. Herbs are also great for drying, as are other foods, including fruit, mushrooms and tomatoes.

Drying fruit

You can dry fruit in the oven or in the open air if the weather is hot and dry. An electric dehydrator is very efficient but only useful if you're going to dry fruit regularly.

1 Prepare the fruit for drying (see right). Preheat the oven to its lowest possible setting.

2 Put in the fruit and leave the door ajar. Dry the fruit until it has lost 90 per cent of its weight. This can take up to 24 hours for large fruit, or 6–8 hours for slices.

3 Leave the fruit to cool, then pack into containers about two-thirds full and loosely cover. Leave for another seven days, shaking the container every day to distribute the remaining moisture evenly. Pack into airtight containers and keep for a maximum of 12 months.

Preparing fruit for drying

Enzymes in fruit cause it to discolour once cut. You can slow their activity by soaking the fruit in a bath of acidulated water. Squeeze the juice from 6–8 lemons and mix with an equal quantity of water, or stir 1 tsp citric acid (available in Asian and health-food shops) into 1 litre (1¾ pints) water; or make an ascorbic acid solution by crushing 4 x 500mg tablets of unflavoured vitamin C per 1 litre (1¾ pints) water.

Wash the fruit and prepare; apples, pineapples and bananas should be sliced about 5mm (¼in) thick, stone fruits halved and stoned, cherries stoned. Soak the fruit for 10 minutes, then drain on racks before drying.

Drying mushrooms

1 Put the unwashed mushrooms on a flat wire rack.

2 Dry in a warm, well-ventilated place for 1–2 days, turning now and then.

3 When the mushrooms are dry, store in an airtight container for up to one year. To reconstitute, soak in warm water for 10–20 minutes until soft all over. Clean well before use.

Drying tomatoes

1 Halve the tomatoes lengthways and remove the cores and seeds. Sprinkle with salt and place, cut side down, on a wire rack. Leave to drain for 30 minutes.

2 Preheat the oven to its lowest setting. Dry the tomatoes for 10–12 hours until wrinkled and leathery. Store for up to six months in an airtight container

Rich flavour

- Use plum or Roma tomatoes for the best results, as these have thick skin and a lower percentage of seed and jelly to flesh.
- Choose red, ripe summer tomatoes with a good flavour.

Drying herbs

1 To air-dry fresh herbs, tie them in small bunches and hang in a warm, well-ventilated place until dry.

2 To bag-dry herbs, tie the herbs in small bunches and cut holes in several brown paper bags. Put each bunch in a bag, leaf side down, and tie string around the stems. Hang in a warm, well-ventilated place until dry.

Bag drying

The following herbs are all prone to developing mould, so are best dried in a paper bag. Never try to dry them in a plastic bag.

- Basil
- Lemon balm
- Mint
- Tarragon

Herb ice cubes

Unlike drying, freezing preserves the flavour of herbs perfectly. However, it does affect their texture, which makes them suitable for cooking only, rather than garnishing. One of the easiest ways to freeze herbs is to freeze them in ice cubes. Simply add them to food and as it cooks, the ice cube will melt, releasing the herbs.

1 Wash the herbs, pat dry and chop finely. Put about 1 tsp in each compartment of an ice cube tray, then fill with water and freeze.

2 Pop the cubes out of the tray and put in plastic bags. Squeeze out the air, seal, label and return to the freezer. Use within three months.

20

MICROWAVES

Although invaluable for thawing and reheating, microwaves are also fabulous for cooking certain foods and dishes. This chapter shows you how to make the most of your microwave oven with easy-to-follow step-by-step techniques for all the basics including thawing, heating and cooking vegetables, fish and poultry, plus tips on safety, getting to know your microwave and understanding how it works. There is also a short collection of basic recipes including scrambled eggs, porridge, quick cheese sauce, jam and syrup sponge pudding.

Using a microwave

One of the most useful innovations in cooking, the microwave oven is also one of the most under-utilised. When you know how to use it fully, it can transform your life in the kitchen.

How it works

Microwave ovens work by pulsing energy waves through the food, causing the molecules in it to change position rapidly and bump into each other, which generates heat. Because the energy penetrates only a couple of centimetres or so inside the food, microwaved food must rest before it is served to allow the hot areas to cook the colder ones, or thaw the frozen areas.

Getting to know your microwave

Microwave ovens are not all the same. Some 'combination' ovens have a grill and an ordinary convection oven built in so that you can cook using both types of energy, either singly or together. Even those that are purely microwave ovens have different power levels. A maximum level of 800–900 watts is common, but many others go up to 1,000 watts and some go as high as 1,500 watts. Generally speaking, the higher the wattage the faster the oven will work, but the internal dimensions also affect the speed of energy transfer. These variables make it difficult to give precise timings for thawing, reheating or cooking. Manufacturers try to help with programmes for certain tasks – thawing, cooking certain dishes, and so on. These should be used for guidance only. The best way to learn how to use your oven is through your experience.

Thawing

It is very difficult to thaw something completely without heating it so much that cooking begins. Planning ahead – even by 30 minutes – gives you enough time to allow the resting period to complete defrosting. To ensure the best results, don't defrost on full power but use a medium-high setting to start, then reduce to a medium setting.

1 To defrost a steak, unwrap the steak and place on a plate. Microwave for 1 minute at 600 watts and 1 minute at 300 watts.

2 Feel the steak to see whether it is getting warm. If it is, let it rest for a few minutes, then turn it over. Defrost for 1 minute at 300 watts.

3 If it seems nearly defrosted, let it rest at room temperature for 30–60 minutes to defrost completely.

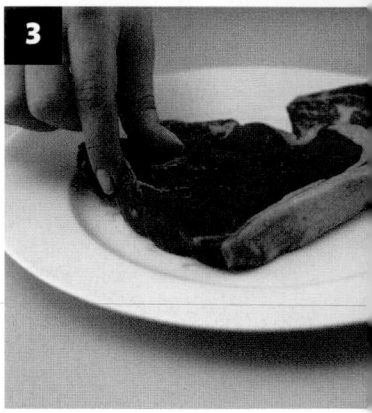

Reheating

When reheating, allow time for the food to rest before serving.

1 For example, when reheating 1 litre (1¾ pints) soup, microwave at 900 watts for 2 minutes, then stir. (Do not overfill, to avoid the risk of splashing as it heats.)

2 Heat for 1 minute more at full power. Stir the soup again and microwave at full power for 1 minute more, or until bubbling.

Safety

- Microwaves are safe as long as they are in good working order.
- Check food is heated through.
- Stir at least once while cooking and allow to rest for a few minutes before serving.
- A heat of 88°C, kept up for a few minutes, will make food safe to eat.

Cooking in the microwave

The microwave oven is not suitable for all types of cooking but it excels at cooking certain types of dishes, particularly anything that cooks well in a steamer. Here are a few examples.

Vegetables

1 Cut vegetables into bite-sized pieces and put in a microwave-proof bowl. Add a splash of water, season and cover with clingfilm. Cook at full power for 2 minutes. Toss, re-cover and cook for 2 minutes more.

2 Continue in 2-minute bursts until cooked al dente. Towards the end of cooking, switch to 1-minute bursts.

Great veg

- Don't cook too large a volume of vegetables in a single dish – no more than 12.5cm (5in) deep.
- Use a cooking bowl that holds the vegetables comfortably – this will make tossing easier.

Fish

Whole fish can be microwaved but chunks or fillets are easier.

1 Arrange the fish in a deep, flat-based dish. Season. Cover with clingfilm, and cook at full power for 2 minutes. Check and continue cooking in 2-minute bursts until just done. Towards the end of cooking, switch to 1-minute bursts. Rest for 2–3 minutes before serving.

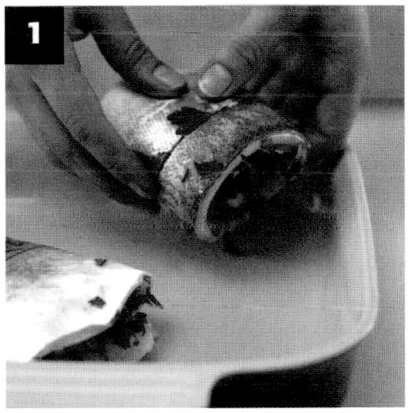

Perfect fish

- Use fillets of flat fish, rolled up (with seasonings inside) for more uniform cooking.
- Use a dish deep enough to hold the pieces without letting them protrude above the rim. Arrange them about the rim of the dish, for even cooking.

Poultry

1 Cut the chicken into even, bite-sized pieces and marinate (see page 117) or coat with sauce. Cover with clingfilm or a plate, and cook at full power for 2 minutes.

2 Stir thoroughly and continue cooking in 2-minute bursts until just done. Towards the end of cooking, switch to 1-minute bursts. Leave to rest for 2–3 minutes before serving.

Top poultry

- Use skinless pieces cut to a maximum thickness of 2.5cm (1in). Coat with oil or marinade to prevent them drying out.
- Don't cook more than 450g (1lb) of chicken at a time.

Scrambled eggs

1 Put eggs, milk and butter in a bowl and beat well.

2 Cook at full power for 1 minute (the mixture should be just starting to set about the edges), then beat again.

3 Cook again at full power for 2–3 more minutes, stirring every 30 seconds, until the eggs are cooked the way you like them.

Porridge

1 Following the guidelines for quantities on the packet, put the oats and milk in a serving bowl.

2 Microwave at full power for 4–5 minutes, stirring frequently.

3 Leave the porridge to rest for a couple of minutes before serving.

Quick cheese sauce

To make about 300ml (½ pint) sauce, you will need 300ml (½ pint) milk, 25g (1oz) butter, 25g (1oz) flour, 50g (2oz) Cheddar cheese, grated, ½ tsp mustard, salt and ground black pepper.

1 Whisk the milk, butter and flour in a jug. (The butter won't mix in properly, but don't worry.) Heat at full power for 2 minutes.

2 Remove from the microwave, whisk, then cook for 2 minutes more and whisk again. The sauce should be thick and smooth.

3 Season well with salt and pepper, add the cheese and mustard and stir until melted.

Melting chocolate

1 Break the chocolate into pieces and put in a bowl.

2 Microwave at full power for 1 minute. Stir, then cook again for 30 seconds at a time until the chocolate is smooth and melted.

Jam

To make 900g (2lb), you will need 700g (1lb 9oz) sugar, 700g (1lb 9oz) prepared fruit, the juice of 2 lemons.

1 Put all the ingredients in a 2 litre (3½ pint) microwave-proof bowl and mix well. Cook at full power for 12–16 minutes, stirring once or twice, then test for setting (see box, right). Leave to stand for 5 minutes before potting (see page 405).

Setting point

- This jam has a soft set and is best served after two to three days.
- Use a thermometer (it should be 110°C) or put a little jam on a chilled plate for a couple of minutes (it should wrinkle when you run your finger through it).

Syrup sponge pudding

To serve four, you will need 50g (2oz) softened butter, 50g (2oz) caster sugar, 1 egg, 125g (4oz) self-raising flour, the zest of 1 lemon, 3–4 tbsp milk, 2 tbsp golden syrup.

1 Put the butter, sugar, egg, flour and lemon zest in a bowl and beat together until smooth and creamy, then stir in the milk to give a dropping consistency.

2 Put the syrup in a greased 600ml (1 pint) pudding basin. Spoon in the pudding mixture and microwave at full power for 5–7 minutes until a skewer inserted in the middle comes out clean.

3 Leave the pudding to stand for about 5 minutes, then carefully turn out on to a plate and serve with custard or thick cream.

Health and nutrition

A diet that is healthy, varied and tasty should be everyone's aim. A sound diet, combined with regular exercise, will help you to keep healthy and full of energy, even with the demands of a modern hectic lifestyle. Diet can not only affect weight, but mental well-being too. A balanced diet is the answer, but what exactly does that mean?

Food gives us energy – in the form of calories – which is burnt up naturally with everyday living, but if we consume more calories than the body can use, even with increased exercise, excess calories are stored in the body as fat and the result is weight gain.

A basic understanding of food values will help you towards a healthy diet. It is important to eat as wide a variety of foods as possible, taking care not to over-eat, while cutting down to some extent on our intake of saturated fats. To maintain a healthy body, everyone needs protein, vitamins, minerals, fibre, carbohydrate and a little fat.

Protein is made up of smaller units called amino acids, which are an important part of every cell in the body and therefore necessary for healthy skin, teeth, internal organs and other tissues. The body can manufacture some of these amino acids itself, but the 'essential amino acids' must be derived from food. Animal protein and soya protein contain almost all of these and are regarded as 'complete'.

The best sources of protein are meat, poultry, fish, eggs, dairy products such as yogurt, milk and cheese, and soya products. Other vegetable proteins are lacking in one or more of the essential amino acids. However, this need not necessarily be a problem for vegetarians (see page 449).

Vitamins are vital for a variety of body processes and a deficiency will result in illness. The fat-soluble vitamins A, D, E and K – as their name suggests – are largely derived from foods which contain fat, though the body acquires most of its vitamin D from the action of sunlight on the skin. These vitamins are stored in the liver. Water-soluble vitamins B and C cannot be stored by the body so a regular intake through the diet is important.

Minerals are needed in minute quantities to maintain a healthy body. Iron, calcium and zinc are especially important. A deficiency of iron will lead to anaemia. Meat and leafy green vegetables are good sources of iron, and the absorption of this mineral is greatly increased if some vitamin C rich food – even a glass of orange juice – is consumed at the same meal.

Carbohydrates provide the body with the most readily accessible form of energy. Carbohydrates in the form of sugars are found in fruit, milk and sugar; starch carbohydrates are familiar in cereals, pasta, rice, potatoes, bread and pulses. In a healthy diet, starch carbohydrates supply a higher proportion of energy than fats or sugar carbohydrates.

Fat is important in small quantities in a healthy diet, for heat, energy and to aid the absorption of fat-soluble vitamins A and D, which are present in fatty foods. All fats are made up of smaller units, called fatty acids. There are three types: saturated, monosaturated and polyunsaturated fatty acids, which occur in different proportions in foods. Saturated fatty acids are linked to higher blood cholesterol, which can lead to heart disease.

Saturated fats are mainly found in dairy products, especially butter and cream, as well as in meat and poultry; monosaturated fats are present in olive oil; and polyunsaturated fats are found in vegetable oils extracted from nuts, beans and seeds. Oily fish, such as mackerel, sardines and herring, are high in unsaturated fat as well as essential fatty acids which are very important for good health.

Fibre can't really be classified as a nutrient, but it is necessary for the proper functioning of the digestive system. Fibre abounds in unrefined cereals, wholegrain breads, the skins of fruit and vegetables and, of course, bran-related products. If you start the day with a wholegrain cereal and eat plenty of fresh fruit and vegetables, you will easily have enough fibre in your diet.

Salt contains minerals, but should be added to food in moderation; remember that convenience and processed foods are often high in salt so always check the nutritional information provided on food packaging. You should aim to consume no more than a total of 6g salt a day.

Water is essential to life because it is the main constituent of all cells, but it is all too easily overlooked. most of us do not drink nearly enough water. Ideally, we should consume at least 1.5 litres (2½ pints) every day. In hot weather, or if you are very active, you should drink more than this.

Balancing your diet

Eating a variety of foods is essential to ensure that your body receives all the nutrients it needs, but a balanced intake is also important. Supplements should not be necessary, except when there are excessive losses of certain nutrients – due to pregnancy, illness or infirmity, or a poor diet. Your diet should be nutritionally sound provided that you eat some foods from each of the following food categories every day:

- Cereals and grains – bread, pasta, rice and breakfast cereals – for energy, fibre, B vitamins, calcium and iron.
- Fruit and vegetables – excellent sources of vitamins, especially C, A (in the form of beta-carotene), and minerals, notably iron and calcium. Fruit and vegetables are also good sources of antioxidants, which boost the immune system and may help to provide some protection from certain forms of cancer and other diseases. It is recommended that you eat at least five portions of fruit and vegetable every day. (A portion is equivalent to 80g fresh, frozen or canned fruit or vegetables; 150ml fruit juice; 1 heaped tbsp dried fruit. Juice and dried fruit may only count as one portion per day, no matter how much you eat.)
- Meat, poultry and fish – for those valuable amino acids that make up protein, plus energy and iron. Unless you are vegetarian, eat a little red meat once or twice a week, balanced with chicken or turkey and fish throughout the week (not necessarily every day). Try to eat oily fish, such as sardines, mackerel or fresh tuna, once a week, as these are very good sources of omega-3 fatty acids.
- Pulses, nuts and seeds – for protein, energy, fibre, calcium, iron and zinc.
- Dairy products – valuable sources of protein, energy, calcium, minerals, vitamins D and B_{12}.
- Water – at least five glasses a day, including fruit juices, milk etc., will help flush out impurities in the system and balance water loss at night. This does not include the intake of tea and coffee, both of which have a diuretic effect (encouraging the body to lose water) and should therefore be consumed in moderation.

Convenience foods

It is all too easy to rely on ready-meals, popping them into the microwave at a minute's notice, but a meal quickly prepared and cooked from fresh ingredients is likely to have a better nutritional balance. Chilled ready-meals are acceptable from time to time, but do try to serve them with freshly cooked vegetables or a salad – and follow with fresh fruit if possible. Always try to have ingredients in the refrigerator or storecupboard that can be made into a healthy meal in a matter of minutes. This way you are less likely to resort to less healthy convenience foods.

A vegetarian diet

A vegetarian diet is one that excludes meat, poultry and fish. Many vegetarians also avoid other animal products, such as gelatine, animal fats such as lard and suet, and animal rennet in non-vegetarian cheeses. However, the majority of vegetarians do eat dairy produce, including milk, vegetarian cheeses and free-range eggs. Vegans follow a more restrictive diet, which also excludes all dairy products, eggs, and even foods such honey because it is produced by bees.

Provided a wide range of foods is eaten, a vegetarian diet is unlikely to be lacking nutritionally, but variety is important to ensure a good intake of protein. Vegetable proteins are lacking in one or more of the essential amino acids, but by eating certain foods together, this problem is overcome. For example, you can obtain complete protein by combining cereals with milk or other dairy products; pulses with rice or pasta; pulses or nuts with dairy produce; and nuts with grains. This tends to happen naturally in most vegetarian meals – for example serving pasta with a cheese sauce or a lentil or chickpea curry with rice.

A vegan diet can be deficient in vitamin B_{12}, which is only present in animal and dairy foods. To make up for this, fortified breakfast cereals, yeast extract and/or soya milk should be consumed. Soya products are particularly valuable sources of protein, energy, calcium, minerals, vitamin B_{12}, vitamin D and beneficial omega-3 fatty acids.

Food storage and hygiene

Storing food properly and preparing food in a hygienic way is important to ensure that food remains as nutritious and flavourful as possible, and to reduce the risk of food poisoning. When you are preparing food, always follow these important guidelines:

- Wash your hands thoroughly before handling food and again between handling different types of food, such as raw and cooked meat and poultry. If you have any cuts or grazes on your hands, be sure to keep them covered with a waterproof plaster.
- Wash down work surfaces regularly with a mild detergent solution or multi-surface cleaner.
- Use a dishwasher if available. Otherwise, wear rubber gloves for washing-up, so that the water temperature can be hotter than unprotected hands can bear. Change drying-up cloths and cleaning cloths regularly. Note that leaving dishes to drain is more hygienic than drying them with a tea-towel.
- Keep raw and cooked foods separate, especially meat, fish and poultry. Wash kitchen utensils in between preparing raw and cooked foods. Never put cooked or ready-to-eat foods directly on to a surface which has just had raw fish, meat or poultry on it.
- Keep pets out of the kitchen if possible; or make sure they stay away from work surfaces. Never allow animals on to work surfaces.

Shopping

Always choose fresh ingredients in prime condition from stores and markets that have a regular turnover of stock to ensure you buy the freshest produce possible.

To ensure food safety, stick to the following guidelines:

- Make sure items are within their 'best before' or 'use by' date. (Foods with a longer shelf life have a 'best before' date; more perishable items have a 'use by' date.)
- When supermarket shopping, pack frozen and chilled items in an insulated cool bag at the check-out and put them into the freezer or refrigerator as soon as you get home.
- During warm weather in particular, buy perishable foods just before you return home. After you pack items at the supermarket check-out, sort them according to where you will store them when you get home – the refrigerator, freezer, storecupboard, vegetable, rack, fruit bowl etc. This will make unpacking easier – and quicker.

The storecupboard

Having a storecupboard well stocked with the basic essentials will save repeated visits to the shops to pick up missing items. Although storecupboard ingredients will generally last a long time, correct storage is important.

The following guidelines apply:

- Always check packaging for storage advice – even with familiar foods because storage requirements may change if additives, sugar or salt have been reduced.
- Check storecupboard foods for their 'use by' date and do not use them if the date has passed.
- Keep all food cupboards scrupulously clean and make sure food containers and packets are properly sealed.
- Once opened, treat canned foods as though fresh. Always transfer the contents to a clean container, cover and keep in the refrigerator. Similarly, jars, sauce bottles and cartons should be kept chilled after opening. (Check the label for safe storage times after opening.)
- Transfer dry goods such as sugar, rice and pasta to moisture-proof containers. When supplies are used up, wash the container well and thoroughly dry before refilling with new supplies.
- Store oils in a dark cupboard away from any heat source as heat and light can make them turn rancid and affect their colour. For the same reason, buy olive oil in dark green bottles.
- Store vinegars in a cool place; they can turn bad in a warm environment.
- Store dried herbs, spices and flavourings in a cool, dark cupboard or in dark jars. Buy in small quantities as their flavour will not last indefinitely.
- Store flours and sugars in airtight containers.

Refrigerator storage

Fresh food needs to be kept in the cool temperature of the refrigerator to keep it in good condition and discourage the growth of harmful bacteria. Store day-to-day perishable items, such as opened jams and jellies, mayonnaise and bottled sauces, in the refrigerator along with eggs and dairy products, fruit juices, bacon, fresh and cooked meat (on separate shelves), and salads and vegetables (except potatoes which don't suit being stored in the cold).

A refrigerator should be kept at an operating temperature of 4–5°C. It is worth investing in a refrigerator thermometer to ensure the correct temperature is maintained.

To ensure your refrigerator is functioning effectively for safe food storage, follow these guidelines:

- Store cooked and raw foods on separate shelves to avoid bacterial cross-contamination, putting cooked foods on the top shelf. Ensure that all items are well wrapped.
- Never put hot food into the refrigerator as this will cause the internal temperature of the refrigerator to rise.
- Avoid overfilling as this restricts the circulation of air and prevents the appliance from working properly.
- It can take some time for the refrigerator to return to the correct operating temperature once the door has been opened, so don't leave it open any longer than is necessary.
- Clean the refrigerator regularly, using a specially formulated germicidal 'refrigerator cleaners'. Alternatively, use a weak solution of bicarbonate of soda: 1 tbsp to 1 litre (1¾ pints) water.
- If your refrigerator doesn't have an automatic defrost facility, defrost regularly.

Maximum refrigerator storage times

For pre-packed foods, always adhere to the 'use-by' date on the packet. For other foods the following storage times should apply, providing the food is in prime condition when it goes into the refrigerator and that your refrigerator is in good working order:

Vegetables and Fruit	
salad leaves	2–3 days
green vegetables	3–4 days
soft fruit	1–2 days
hard and stone fruit	3–7 days
Dairy Food	
milk	4–5 days
cheese, soft	2–3 days
cheese, hard	1 week
eggs	1 week
Fish	
fish	1 day
shellfish	1 day
Raw Meat	
joints	3 days
poultry	2 days
game	2 days
raw sliced meat	2 days
minced meat	1 day
offal	1 day
sausages	3 days
bacon	7 days
Cooked Meat	
joints	3 days
casseroles/stews	2 days
pies	2 days
sliced meat	2 days
ham	2 days
ham, vacuum-packed	1–2 weeks

(or according to the instructions on the packet)

Glossary of cookery terms

Acidulated water Water to which lemon juice or vinegar has been added in which fruit or vegetables, such as pears or Jerusalem artichokes, are immersed to prevent discolouration.

Al dente Italian term commonly used to describe food, especially pasta and vegetables, which are cooked until tender but still firm to the bite.

Antipasto Italian selection of cold meats, fish, salads etc., served as a starter.

Au gratin Describes a dish that has been coated with sauce, sprinkled with breadcrumbs or cheese and browned under the grill or in the oven. Low-sided gratin dishes are used.

Bain-marie Literally, a water bath, used to keep foods, such as delicate custards and sauces, at a constant low temperature during cooking. On the hob a double saucepan or bowl over a pan of simmering water is used; for oven cooking, the baking dish(es) is placed in a roasting tin containing enough hot water to come halfway up the sides.

Baking blind Pre-baking a pastry case before filling. The pastry case is lined with greaseproof paper and weighted down with dried beans or ceramic baking beans.

Baking powder A raising agent consisting of an acid, usually cream of tartar and an alkali, such as bicarbonate of soda, which react to produce carbon dioxide. This expands during baking and makes cakes and breads rise.

Bard To cover the breast of game birds or poultry, or lean meat with fat to prevent the meat from drying out during roasting.

Baste To spoon the juices and melted fat over meat, poultry, game or vegetables during roasting to keep them moist. The term is also used to describe spooning over a marinade.

Beat To incorporate air into an ingredient or mixture by agitating it vigorously with a spoon, fork, whisk or electric mixer. The technique is also used to soften ingredients.

Béchamel Classic French white sauce, used as the basis for other sauces and savoury dishes.

Beurre manié Equal parts of flour and butter kneaded together to make a paste. Used to thicken soups, stews and casseroles. It is whisked into the hot liquid a little at a time at the end of cooking.

Bind To mix beaten egg or other liquid into a dry mixture to hold it together.

Blanch To immerse food briefly in fast-boiling water to loosen skins, such as peaches or tomatoes, or to remove bitterness, or to destroy enzymes and preserve the colour, flavour and texture of vegetables (especially prior to freezing).

Bone To remove the bones from meat, poultry, game or fish, so that it can be stuffed or simply rolled before cooking.

Bottle To preserve fruit, jams, pickles or other preserves in sterile glass jars.

Bouquet garni Small bunch of herbs – usually a mixture of parsley stems, thyme and a bay leaf – tied in muslin and used to flavour stocks, soups and stews.

Braise To cook meat, poultry, game or vegetables slowly in a small amount of liquid in a pan or casserole with a tight-fitting lid. The food is usually first browned in oil or fat.

Brochette Food cooked on a skewer.

Brûlée A French term, literally meaning 'burnt' used to refer to a dish with a crisp coating of caramelised sugar.

Butterfly To split a food, such as a large prawn or poussin, almost in half and open out flat, so that it will cook more quickly.

Calorie Strictly a kilocalorie, this is used in dietetics to measure the energy value of foods.

Canapé Small appetiser, served with drinks.

Candying Method of preserving fruit or peel by impregnating with sugar.

Caramelise To heat sugar or sugar syrup slowly until it is brown in colour; ie forms a caramel.

Carbonade Rich stew or braise of meat, which includes beer.

Casserole A dish with a tight-fitting lid used for slow-cooking meat, poultry and vegetables, now used to describe food cooked in this way.

Charcuterie French term for cooked pork products, including hams, sausages and terrines.

Chill To cool food in the fridge.

Chine To sever the rib bones from the backbone, close to the spine. This is done to meat joints, such as loin of pork or lamb, to make them easier to carve into chops after cooking.

Clarify To remove sediment or impurities from a liquid. Stock is clarified by heating with egg white, while butter is clarified by melting and skimming. Butter that has been clarified will withstand a higher frying temperature.

To clarify butter heat until melted and all bubbling stops. Take off the heat and let stand until the sediment has sunk to the bottom, then gently pour off the fat, straining it through muslin to remove sediment.

Compote Fresh or dried fruit stewed in sugar syrup. Served hot or cold.

Concassé Diced fresh ingredient, used as a garnish. The term is most often applied to skinned, deseeded tomatoes.

Coulis A smooth fruit or vegetable purée, thinned if necessary to a pouring consistency.

Court bouillon Aromatic cooking liquid containing wine, vinegar or lemon juice, used for poaching delicate fish, poultry or vegetables.

Consistency Term used to describe the texture of a mixture, eg firm, dropping or soft.

Cream To beat together fat and sugar until the mixture is pale and fluffy, and resembles whipped cream in texture and colour. The method is used in cakes and puddings which contain a high proportion of fat and require the incorporation of a lot of air.

Crêpe French term for a pancake.

Crimp To decorate the edge of a pie, tart or shortbread by pinching it at regular intervals to give a fluted effect.

Croquette Seasoned mixture of cooked potato and fish, meat, poultry or vegetables shaped into a small roll, coated with egg and breadcrumbs and shallow-fried.

Croûte Circle or other shaped piece of fried bread, typically used as a base for serving small game birds.

Croûtons Small pieces of fried or toasted bread, served with soups and salads.

Crudités Raw vegetables, usually cut into slices or sticks, typically served with a dipping sauce as an appetiser.

Crystallise To preserve fruit in sugar syrup.

Curdle To cause sauces or creamed mixtures to separate once the egg is added, usually by overheating or over-beating.

Cure To preserve fish, meat or poultry by smoking, drying or salting.

Daube Braising meat and vegetables with stock, often with wine and herbs added.

Deglaze To heat stock, wine or other liquid with the cooking juices left in the pan after roasting or sautéeing, scraping and stirring vigorously to dissolve the sediment on the bottom of the pan.

Dégorge To draw out moisture from a food, eg salting aubergines to remove bitter juices.

Dice To cut food into small cubes.

Draw To remove the entrails from poultry or game.

Dredge To sprinkle food generously with flour, sugar, icing sugar etc.

Dress To pluck, draw and truss poultry or game. The term is also used to describe tossing a salad in vinaigrette or other dressing.

Dry To preserve food, such as fruit, pasta and pulses by dehydration.

Dust To sprinkle lightly with flour, cornflour, icing sugar etc.

Emulsion A mixture of two liquids, which do not dissolve into one another, such as oil and vinegar. Vigorous shaking or heating will emulsify them, as for a vinaigrette.

En croûte Term used to describe food that is wrapped in pastry before cooking.

En papillote Term used to describe food that is baked in a greaseproof paper or baking parchment parcel and served from the paper.

Enzyme Organic substance in food that causes chemical changes. Enzymes are a complex group. Their action is usually halted during cooking.

Escalope Thin slice of meat, such as pork, veal or turkey, from the top of the leg, usually pan-fried.

Extract Concentrated flavouring, which is used in small quantities, eg yeast extract, vanilla extract.

Ferment Chemical change deliberately or accidentally brought about by fermenting agents, such as yeast or bacteria. Fermentation is utilised for making bread, yogurt, beer and wine.

Fillet Term used to describe boned breasts of birds, boned sides of fish, and the undercut of a loin of beef, lamb, pork or veal.

Flake To separate food, such as cooked fish, into natural pieces.

Flambé Flavouring a dish with alcohol, usually brandy or rum, which is then ignited so that the actual alcohol content is burned off.

Folding in Method of combining a whisked or creamed mixture with other ingredients by cutting and folding so that it retains its lightness. A large metal spoon or plastic-bladed spatula is used.

Frosting To coat leaves and flowers with a fine layer of sugar to use as a decoration. Also an American term for icing cakes.

Fry To cook food in hot fat or oil. There are various methods: shallow-frying in a little fat in a shallow pan; deep-frying where the food is totally immersed in oil; dry-frying in which fatty foods are cooked in a non-stick pan without extra fat; see also Stir-frying.

Galette Cooked savoury or sweet mixture shaped into a round.

Garnish A decoration, usually edible, such as parsley or lemon, which is used to enhance the appearance of a savoury dish.

Glaze A glossy coating given to sweet and savoury dishes to improve their appearance and sometimes flavour. Ingredients for glazes include beaten egg, egg white, milk and syrup.

Gluten A protein constituent of grains, such as wheat and rye, which develops when the flour is missed with water to give the dough elasticity.

Grate To shred hard food, such as cheese and carrots, with a grater or food processor attachment.

Griddle A flat, heavy, metal plate used on the hob for cooking scones or for searing savoury ingredients.

Grind To reduce foods such as coffee beans, nuts and whole spices to small particles using a food mill, pestle and mortar, electric grinder or food processor.

Gut To clean out the entrails from fish.

Hang To suspend meat or game in a cool, dry place for a number of days to tenderise the flesh and develop flavour.

Hull To remove the stalk and calyx from soft fruits, such as strawberries.

Infuse To immerse flavourings, such as aromatic vegetables, herbs, spices and vanilla, in a liquid to impart flavour. Usually the infused liquid is brought to the boil, then left to stand for a while.

Julienne Fine 'matchstick' strips of vegetables or citrus zest, sometimes used as a garnish.

Knead To work dough by pummelling with the heel of the hand.

Knock back To knead a yeast dough for a second time after rising, to ensure an even texture.

Lard To insert small strips of fat or streaky bacon into the flesh of game birds and dry meat before cooking. A special larding needle is used.

Liaison A thickening or binding agent based on a combination of ingredients, such as flour and water, or oil and egg.

Macerate To soften and flavour raw or dried foods by soaking in a liquid, eg soaking fruit in alcohol.

Mandolin A flat wooden or metal frame with adjustable cutting blades for slicing vegetables.

Marinate To soak raw meat, poultry or game – usually in a mixture of oil, wine, vinegar and flavourings – to soften and impart flavour. The mixture, which is known as a marinade, may also be used to baste the food during cooking.

Medallion Small round piece of meat, usually beef or veal.

Mince To cut food into very fine pieces, using a mincer, food processor or knife.

Mocha Term which has come to mean a blend of chocolate and coffee.

Parboil To boil a vegetable or other food for part of its cooking time before finishing it by another method.

Pare To finely peel the skin or zest from vegetables or fruit.

Pâte A savoury mixture of finely chopped or minced meat, fish and/or vegetables, usually served as a starter with bread or toast.

Patty tin Tray of cup-shaped moulds for cooking small cakes and deep tartlets. Also called a bun tin.

Pectin A naturally occurring substance found in most varieties of fruit and some vegetables, which is necessary for setting jams and jellies. Commercial pectin and sugar with pectin are also available for preserve-making.

Pickle To preserve meat or vegetables in brine or vinegar.

Pith The bitter white skin under the thin zest of citrus fruit.

Pluck To remove the feathers from poultry and game birds.

Poach To cook food gently in liquid at simmering point; the surface should be just trembling.

Pot roast To cook meat in a covered pan with some fat and a little liquid.

Prove To leave bread dough to rise (usually for a second time) after shaping.

Purée To pound, sieve or liquidise vegetables, fish or fruit to a smooth pulp. Purées often form the basis for soups and sauces.

Reduce To fast-boil stock or other liquid in an uncovered pan to evaporate water and concentrate the flavour.

Refresh To cool hot vegetables very quickly by plunging into ice-cold water or holding under cold running water in order to stop the cooking process and preserve the colour.

Render To melt fat slowly to a liquid, either by heating meat trimmings, or to release the fat from fatty meat, such as duck or goose, during roasting.

Rennet An animal-derived enzyme used to coagulate milk in cheese-making. A vegetarian alternative is available.

Roast To cook meat by dry heat in the oven.

Roulade Soufflé or sponge mixture rolled around a savoury or sweet filling.

Roux A mixture of equal quantities of butter (or other fat) and flour cooked together to form the basis of many sauces.

Rub-in Method of incorporating fat into flour by rubbing between the fingertips, used when a short texture is required. Used for pastry, cakes, scones and biscuits.

Salsa Piquant sauce made from chopped fresh vegetables and sometimes fruit.

Sauté To cook food in a small quantity of fat over a high heat, shaking the pan constantly – usually in a sauté pan (a frying pan with straight sides and a wide base).

Scald To pour boiling water over food to clean it, or loosen skin, eg tomatoes. Also used to describe heating milk to just below boiling point.

Score To cut parallel lines in the surface of food, such as fish (or the fat layer on meat), to improve its appearance or help it cook more quickly.

Sear To brown meat quickly in a little hot fat before grilling or roasting.

Seasoned flour Flour mixed with a little salt and pepper, used for dusting meat, fish etc., before frying.

Shred To grate cheese or slice vegetables into very fine pieces or strips.

Sieve To press food through a perforated sieve to obtain a smooth texture.

Sift To shake dry ingredients through a sieve to remove lumps.

Simmer To keep a liquid just below boiling point.

Skim To remove froth, scum or fat from the surface of stock, gravy, stews, jam etc. Use either a skimmer, a spoon or kitchen paper.

Smoke To cure meat, poultry and fish by exposure to wood smoke.

Souse To pickle food, especially fish, in vinegar flavoured with spices.

Steam To cook food in steam, usually in a steamer over rapidly boiling water.

Steep To immerse food in warm or cold liquid to soften it, and sometimes to draw out strong flavours.

Sterilise To destroy bacteria in foods by heating.

Stew To cook food, such as tougher cuts of meat, in flavoured liquid which is kept at simmering point.

Stir-fry To cook small even-sized pieces of food rapidly in a little fat, tossing constantly over a high heat, usually in a wok.

Suet Hard fat of animal origin used in pastry and steamed puddings. A vegetarian alternative is readily available.

Sugar syrup A concentrated solution of sugar in water used to poach fruit and make sorbets, granitas, fruit juices etc.

Sweat To cook chopped or sliced vegetables in a little fat without liquid in a covered pan over a low heat to soften.

Tepid The term used to describe temperature at approximately blood heat, ie 37°C (98.7°F).

Thermometer, Sugar/Fat Used for accurately checking the temperature of boiling sugar syrups, and fat for deep-frying respectively. Dual purpose thermometers are obtainable.

Truss To tie or skewer poultry or game into shape prior to roasting.

Unleavened Flat bread, such as pitta, made without a raising agent.

Vanilla sugar Sugar in which a vanilla pod has been stored to impart its flavour.

Whipping (whisking) Beating air rapidly into a mixture either with a manual or electric whisk. Whipping usually refers to cream.

Zest The thin coloured outer layer of citrus fruit, which can be removed in fine strips with a zester.

Index

A

all-in-one cherry cakes 325
all-in-one peanut cookies 332
almond paste
  covering a cake with 331
  marzipan 331
  sweet cherry bread 315
almonds
  almond and orange torte 349
  almond cookies 341
  almond toffee meringues 381
  chocolate amaretti tart 362
  coconut macaroons 335
  decadent chocolate cake 363
  kugelhopf 316
amaretti biscuits
  chocolate amaretti tart 362
American-style plum cobbler 233
anchovy butter 23
apples 206
  apple and blueberry cake 350
  apple madeleines 345
  apple sauce 22
  apples with butterscotch sauce 385
  baked apple and lemon tartlets 297
  cranberry and apple jelly 418
  goose with roasted apples 133
  rustic blackberry and apple pie 229
artichoke hearts 172
  chicken and artichoke pie 290
  pork with artichokes and beans 154
artichokes, globe 172
asparagus 172
  asparagus with lemon dressing 194
  freezing 436
  salmon and asparagus pie 66
aubergines 178
  aubergine and lentil curry 256
  braised lamb shanks 160
  fillet of beef with Roquefort sauce 165
  Greek lamb and feta layer 158
  mushroom and aubergine tian 202
avocados 178
  avocado salsa 24
  mixed leaf salad 191
  smoked salmon parcels 90

B

bacon
  freezing 437
  mussel and potato stew 100
  quick and easy carbonara 267
  see also gammon; ham
bakeware 14
baking
  bread 301
  eggs 55
  fish 81
  fruit 216
  ham 146
  polenta 242
baking blind 280
baking trays 14
baklava 283
balsamic dressing 25
bananas
  banana and butterscotch loaf 352
  banana and pecan muffins 328
  instant banana ice cream 394
  sticky banoffee pies 382
banoffee pies 382
barbecue sauce 425
barbecued figs with Marsala 231
barbecued marinated poussins 127
barding, beef 136
barley 240
basil
  pesto 21
batters 61
  coating fried fish 80
beans 243
  chicken with chorizo and beans 255
  mushroom and bean hotpot 253
  one-pot spicy beef 163
  pork with artichokes and beans 154
  simple bean salad 252
  spicy pork and bean stew 254
  spring vegetable broth 44
  sprouting beans 243
béarnaise sauce 20
béchamel sauce 19
beef
  braised beef 164
  chilli beef noodle salad 272
  chilli Bolognese 268
  fillet of beef with Roquefort sauce 165
  one-pot spicy beef 163
  preparation 136–9
  roasting 151
  steak sandwich 309
  sweet chilli beef stir-fry 162
beetroot 182
berries 209
  berry millefeuilles 293
  see also raspberries, strawberries etc
beurre manié, thickening soups 38
binding sauce 19
biscuits
  all-in-one peanut cookies 332
  almond cookies 341
  chocolate and hazelnut biscotti 344
  chocolate chip cookies 336
  chocolate refrigerator roll 334
  coconut macaroons 335
  cranberry biscuits 340
  creamed choc-oat cookies 332
  decorating and filling 338–9
  gingerbread house 342
  melted ginger biscuits 335
  rolled vanilla biscuits 333
  troubleshooting 339
  Viennese fingers 336
black olive bread 311
blackberries
  fruit vinegar 430
  rustic blackberry and apple pie 229
blanching
  nuts 218
  vegetables 436
blenders 15
  puréeing fruit 217
  puréeing soups 36
blue cheese
  blue cheese dressing 25
  fillet of beef with Roquefort sauce 165
blueberries
  apple and blueberry cake 350
boiling
  chestnuts 220
  eggs 53
  vegetables 183
Bolognese, chilli 268
bombes
  cranberry Christmas bombe 399
  ice cream bombes 389
boning
  beef 136
  fish 76
  leg of lamb 140
  poultry 109
bottled fruits 410
bowls 11–12

braising
fish 82
meat and game 149
vegetables 187
brandy
brandied peaches 410
brandy butter 29
caramelised orange trifle 383
spiced clementines in brandy 419
bread 299–319
black olive bread 311
bread sauce 19
brown loaf 303
chocolate-chunk bread pudding 364
enriched breads 305
focaccia 307
garlic bruschetta 308
mixed grain loaf 302
salt and pepper rolls 310
savoury pudding 68
shaping loaves 301
soda bread 304
sourdough 303
spicy griddled flatbread 304
steak sandwich 309
Tuscan bread salad 309
walnut and garlic bread 312
warm cornbread 313
white farmhouse loaf 300
see also teabreads
bread machines 15, 302
breadcrumbs 308
thickening soups 38
broad beans 174
freezing 436
broccoli 180
freezing 436
quick chicken stir-fry 120
sweet chilli beef stir-fry 162
turkey and broccoli stir-fry 129
brown loaf 303
brownie, the ultimate chocolate 347
bruschetta, garlic 308
Brussels sprouts
freezing 436
sprouts and pancetta 197
bulgur wheat 240
roasted tomato bulgur salad 251
buns, choux 282
butter
brandy butter 29
flavoured butters 23
butter beans
chicken with chorizo and beans 255
buttercream icing 330
butterflying
leg of lamb 140
prawns 83
buttermilk
warm cornbread 313
butternut squash
foil-baked fish 98
roasted root vegetable salad 193
roasting 189
butterscotch
apples with butterscotch sauce 385
banana and butterscotch loaf 352
butterscotch sauce 27
buying food 448
fish 89
shellfish 85

C

cabbage 180
see also red cabbage
cake tins 14
cakes 321–53
all-in-one cherry cakes 325
almond and orange torte 349
apple and blueberry cake 350
apple madeleines 345
chilled chocolate biscuit cake 367
chocolate and cherry gâteau 360
chocolate cherry roll 327
decadent chocolate cake 363
fruity tea cake 326
Italian ice cream cake 400
lime drizzle loaf 348
lining tins 322–3
marbled cake 326
sponges 324–5
sticky ginger ring 353
the ultimate chocolate brownie 347
vanilla cupcakes 328
see also traybakes
Camembert and tomato tarts 284
cannellini beans
spicy pork and bean stew 254
spring vegetable broth 44
cannelloni, mixed mushroom 270
capers, chicken with wine and 124
caramel 372
apples with butterscotch sauce 385
banana and butterscotch loaf 352
butterscotch sauce 27
caramel custard squares 379
caramelised orange tart 294
caramelised orange trifle 383
caramelised pineapple 377
easy pear and toffee tarte tatin 296
mixed nut praline 374
strawberry brûlée 378
carbohydrates 446
carbonara, quick and easy 267
carrots
carrot tray bake 251
lemon and orange carrots 196
roasted root vegetable salad 193
winter coleslaw 190
carving
chicken 113
meat 150–1
casseroles and stews
braised beef 164
braised lamb shanks 160
chicken 116
chicken with chorizo and beans 255
equipment 14
freezing 434
lamb, prune and almond tagine 159
mushroom and bean hotpot 253
mussel and potato stew 100
one-pot spicy beef 163
rabbit casserole with prunes 167
Spanish fish stew 105
spicy pork and bean stew 254
see also curries
cast iron pans 13, 14
cauliflower 180
cauliflower soup 47
freezing 436
mixed dill pickle 424
mustard relish 414
twice-baked soufflés 67
celery 173
cereals 447
champagne
mango gratin with sabayon 71
chargrilling peppers 177
cheese
blue cheese dressing 25
Camembert and tomato tarts 284
cheese sauce 19, 444
cheesy polenta with tomato sauce 249
chicken and artichoke pie 290
fillet of beef with Roquefort sauce 165
garlic cheese pizza 319
Greek lamb and feta layer 158
Mediterranean kebabs 195
Parmesan crisps 46
pesto 21
roasted stuffed peppers 203
savoury pudding 68
soufflé 57
spinach and cheese lasagne 271
stuffed chicken breasts 123
tuna melt pizza 318
twice-baked soufflés 67
see also goat's cheese; mascarpone

cheesecakes
chilled cheesecake 329
lemon cheesecake 329
toffee cheesecake 380
cherries
all-in-one cherry cakes 325
chocolate amaretti tart 362
chocolate and cherry gâteau 360
chocolate cherry roll 327
Italian ice cream cake 400
pitting 208
cherries, glacé
sweet cherry bread 315
chestnuts 220
sprouts and pancetta 197
chicken
carving 113
chicken and artichoke pie 290
chicken with chorizo and beans 255
chicken with wine and capers 124
cooking 112–17
grilled chicken with mango salsa 122
Mediterranean chicken 125
in microwave ovens 443
Moroccan spiced chicken kebabs 119
orange and chicken salad 118
paella 238
quick chicken stir-fry 120
simple chicken wrap 308
simple roast chicken 112
spiced chicken pilau 246
sticky chicken thighs 121
stock 34
stuffed chicken breasts 123
tarragon chicken with fennel 126
chickpeas
chickpea curry 257
roasted root vegetable salad 193
winter coleslaw 190
chilled chocolate biscuit cake 367
chillies 177
chilli beef noodle salad 272
chilli Bolognese 268
chilli onions with goat's cheese 201
chilli salt 431
chilli sauce 413
fusilli with chilli and tomatoes 264
sweet chilli beef stir-fry 162
chips 186
fish and chips 101
chocolate 355–69
banana and butterscotch loaf 352
buttercream icing 330
chilled chocolate biscuit cake 367
chocolate amaretti tart 362
chocolate and cherry gâteau 360
chocolate and hazelnut biscotti 344
chocolate cherry roll 327
chocolate chip cookies 336
chocolate-chunk bread pudding 364
chocolate refrigerator roll 334
chocolate sauce 27, 359
cookies and cream fudge 376
creamed choc-oat cookies 332
decadent chocolate cake 363
decorating biscuits 339
decorations 356–9
filling biscuits 338
ganache 359
hot chocolate 369
ice cream 388
iced raspberry soufflés 401
Italian ice cream cake 400
marbled cake 326
melting 27, 356, 445
nutty chocolate truffles 368
nutty fudge shortbread 343
sweet mocha bread 314
the ultimate chocolate brownie 347
Viennese fingers 336
warm chocolate fondant 365
white chocolate mousse 366
white chocolate mousse cake 361
chopping boards 10
chops
freezing 437
stuffing pork chops 144
chorizo sausage
chicken with chorizo and beans 255
potato and chorizo tortilla 56
choux pastry 282
chutneys
plum chutney 412, 420
rhubarb and ginger chutney 421
tomato chutney 412
cinnamon
cinnamon and nutmeg ice cream 396
cinnamon custard tart 291
cinnamon pancakes 69
cinnamon sugar 431
citrus fruits 207
buttercream icing 330
citrus sugar 431
see also lemon, oranges etc
clams 86
clementines
spiced clementines in brandy 419
coatings, for fried fish 80
cobbler, American-style plum 233
coconut 221
coconut macaroons 335
lime drizzle loaf 348
coconut milk 221
cauliflower soup 47
cod
oven-poached cod with herbs 99
coddling eggs 53
coffee
ice cream 388
sweet mocha bread 314
coleslaw, winter 190
coloured sauces, decorative effects 31
condensed milk
dulce de leche 373
confectionery
caramel custard squares 379
cookies and cream fudge 376
nutty chocolate truffles 368
toffee 373
vanilla fudge 374
convenience foods 447
cookies see biscuits
cookies and cream fudge 376
coriander
coriander pesto 21
salmon and coriander kedgeree 244
corn on the cob 173
sweetcorn relish 422
cornbread, warm 313
cornflour, thickening soups 38
coulis, raspberry 29
courgettes 179
couscous 240
herb couscous 152
summer couscous 250
crab 84
crab cakes with mayonnaise 93
crackling 151
cranberries
cranberry and apple jelly 418
cranberry and lemon stuffing 113
cranberry biscuits 340
cranberry Christmas bombe 399
cranberry sauce 22
crispy duck salad 131
pear and cranberry strudel 292
crayfish 83
cream
pavlova 60
soup garnishes 39
thickening soups 38
cream filling, for biscuits 338
creamed sponges 324
crisps
Parmesan crisps 46
vegetable crisps 186
croûtons 39
crumble, rhubarb and pear 232

cucumber
gazpacho with tortilla chips 40
cumin-spiced gammon 155
cupcakes, vanilla 328
cups, measuring 11
currants
preparation 209
see also redcurrants
curries
aubergine and lentil curry 256
chickpea curry 257
salmon laksa curry 273
Thai green shellfish curry 104
Thai noodles with prawns 274
Thai vegetable curry 200
custard
baked orange custard 70
berry millefeuilles 293
caramelised orange trifle 383
cinnamon and nutmeg ice cream 396
cinnamon custard tart 291
vanilla custard 26
cuttlefish 88

D

dairy products 447
storing 449
see also cheese, milk etc
damson cheese 409
dates
carrot tray bake 251
decadent chocolate cake 363
decorations
for biscuits 338–9
caramel 372
chocolate 356–9
sauces as 30–1
for soups 39
spun sugar 375
deep-frying
fish 80
fruit 215
potatoes 186
poultry 115
vegetables 186
degreasing stocks 35
dicing vegetables 182
diet 446–7
dill
mixed dill pickle 424
dill salmon 95
dip, spiced pear 224
dishes, baking 14
drinks
hot chocolate 369
smoothies 217
drizzling sauce 31
drop scones 61
drunken pears 230
drying
fruit 438
herbs 439
mushrooms 438
tomatoes 439
duck
crispy duck salad 131
marinated duck with prunes 132
dulce de leche 373
easy pear and toffee tarte tatin 296
filling biscuits 338
sticky banoffee pies 382
toffee cheesecake 380

E

eggs 51–73
baked orange custard 70
batters 61
cooking techniques 53–5
creamy baked eggs 63
herb and lemon soup 43
mango gratin with sabayon 71
meringues 58–60, 72–3
mixed mushroom frittata 64
omelettes 56
piperade 62
preparation 52
quick and easy carbonara 267
salmon and asparagus pie 66
savoury pudding 68
scrambled eggs 444
soufflés 57, 67
spiced egg pilau 245
thickening soups 38
vanilla custard 26
warm lentil and egg salad 65
elderflower and fruit jelly 225
electrical equipment 15
enriched breads 305
equipment 10–15
escalopes, poultry 111
exotic fruits 210–11
exotic fruit salad 222
see also mangoes, pineapple etc

F

farmhouse loaf 300
fats 446
bread-making 300
feathering sauces 30
fennel 173
tarragon chicken with fennel 126
feta cheese
Greek lamb and feta layer 158
fibre 446
figs 213
barbecued figs with Marsala 231
fruity tea cake 326
sweet and sour figs 423
filleting fish 76, 77
filo pastry 283
fish 75–105, 447
buying 89
cooking techniques 78–82
fish and chips 101
freezing 437
in microwave ovens 443
preparation 76–7
Spanish fish stew 105
stock 35
storing 449
see also cod, salmon etc
flageolet beans
pork with artichokes and beans 154
simple bean salad 252
flake test, preserves 405
flapjacks, sticky ginger 346
flatbread, spicy griddled 304
flour, bread-making 300
focaccia 307
foil-baked fish 98
food processors 15
making pastry 278
fool, lemon and passion fruit 226
freezing
fruit 435
meat, poultry and fish 437
stocks, sauces and stews 434
thawing food in a microwave oven 442
vegetables 436
French beans, freezing 436
French dressing 25
frittata, mixed mushroom 64
frozen yogurt sorbet 395
fruit 205–33, 447
bottled fruits 410
chocolate-dipped 359
cooking 214–16
drying 438
exotic fruit salad 222
freezing 435
frozen yogurt sorbet 395
fruit cheeses 409
fruit curds 409
fruit kebabs with spiced pear dip 224
fruit vinegar 430
ice cream 388
jams 406

mixed berry jelly 408
pavlova 60
pectin content 406
preparation 206–13
preserves 403–10
sauces 22
smoothies and purées 217
storing 449
summer jam 406
see also apples, strawberries etc
fruit cakes
fruity tea cake 326
testing 326
fruity rice pudding 248
frying see deep-frying; pan-frying; stir-frying
frying pans 13
fudge
cookies and cream fudge 376
nutty fudge shortbread 343
vanilla fudge 374
fusilli with chilli and tomatoes 264

G

game 135
cooking 148–9
game birds 107
see also rabbit
gammon
cumin-spiced gammon 155
ginger and honey-glazed ham 156
see also bacon; ham
ganache 359
garlic 171
garlic bruschetta 308
garlic butter 23
garlic cheese pizza 319
garlic dressing 25
walnut and garlic bread 312
garnishes see decorations
gateau, chocolate and cherry 360
gazpacho with tortilla chips 40
Genoese sponge 325
ginger
almond cookies 341
ginger and honey-glazed ham 156
gingerbread house 342
melted ginger biscuits 335
rhubarb and ginger chutney 421
spicy ginger ice cream 392
sticky ginger flapjacks 346
sticky ginger ring 353
globe artichokes 172
see also artichoke hearts
goat's cheese
chilli onions with goat's cheese 201
goat's cheese parcels 286
mixed mushroom cannelloni 270
mushroom and aubergine tian 202
goose with roasted apples 133
gooseberries 212
grains 240–1, 447
granitas 391
grapes 213
elderflower and fruit jelly 225
gratins
mango gratin with sabayon 71
summer gratin 228
gravy
rich red wine gravy 18
white wine gravy 18
Greek lamb and feta layer 158
green beans
pasta with pesto and beans 265
griddling
meat and game 148
vegetables 188
grilling
chicken 115
fish 82
fruit 216
meat and game 148
polenta 242
vegetables 188
grinding spices 429
guard of honour, lamb 142
guineafowl with prunes 128

H

haddock
foil-baked fish 98
see also smoked haddock
ham 146
ginger and honey-glazed ham 156
leek and ham galette 289
savoury pudding 68
stuffed chicken breasts 123
see also bacon; gammon
hand mixers 15
hare 147
hazelnuts
apples with butterscotch sauce 385
chocolate and hazelnut biscotti 344
nutty chocolate truffles 368
nutty fudge shortbread 343
toasted hazelnut meringue cake 73
health, nutrition 446–7
herbs
chopping 428
drying 439
herb and lemon soup 43
herb butter 23
herb dressing 25
herb salt 431
herb vinegar 430
ice cubes 439
soup garnishes 39
washing 428
see also basil, dill etc
hobs 13
hollandaise sauce 20
hot and sour soup 45
hot chocolate 369
hygiene 448
poultry 108
preserves 404

I

ice cream 388–90
bombes 389
chocolate ice cream 388
cinnamon and nutmeg ice cream 396
coffee ice cream 388
cranberry Christmas bombe 399
fruit ice cream 388
instant banana ice cream 394
Italian ice cream cake 400
mango ice cream terrine 398
nougat ice cream 393
pistachio parfait 390
rippling and marbling 389
spicy ginger ice cream 392
vanilla ice cream 388
ice cream makers 15
ice cubes
herb 439
stock 434
iced lemon meringue 397
iced raspberry soufflés 401
icing
biscuits 338
buttercream 330
easiest icing 331
iron pans 13, 14
Italian ice cream cake 400
Italian meatballs 153

J

jams and jellies
cranberry and apple jelly 418
in microwave ovens 443
mixed berry jelly 408
pectin 406
strawberry and redcurrant jam 416
summer jam 406
jars, for preserves 404, 405
jellies see jams and jellies

jelly, elderflower and fruit 225
jointing
  hare and rabbit 147
  poultry 110
joints, freezing 437
jug blenders, puréeing soups 36
jugs, measuring 11

K

kebabs
  fruit kebabs with spiced pear dip 224
  Mediterranean kebabs 195
  Moroccan spiced chicken kebabs 119
  seafood and lime kebabs 91
kedgeree, salmon and coriander 244
ketchup, tomato 415
knives 10
kugelhopf 316
kumquats
  spiced clementines in brandy 419

L

labelling preserves 404
lamb
  braised lamb shanks 160
  carving leg of lamb 150
  Greek lamb and feta layer 158
  lamb, prune and almond tagine 159
  lamb with orange and mint 157
  preparation 140–2
  roast lamb with orange 161
  roasting 151
langoustines 83
larding beef 137
lasagne, spinach and cheese 271
lavender sugar 431
leaves, chocolate 357
leeks 171
  leek and ham galette 289
  vichyssoise with spinach cream 41
lemon
  asparagus with lemon dressing 194
  baked apple and lemon tartlets 297
  herb and lemon soup 43
  iced lemon meringue 397
  lemon and orange carrots 196
  lemon and passion fruit fool 226
  lemon cheesecake 329
  lemon curd 409
  prawn and lemon risotto 247
lentils 243
  aubergine and lentil curry 256
  squash, lentil and prawn soup 49
  warm lentil and egg salad 65
lettuce
  mixed leaf salad 191
lime drizzle loaf 348
loaf tins 14
  lining 323
loaves see bread
lobsters 85
loin, pork 145
long-grain rice, cooking 236

M

macadamia nuts
  chocolate chip cookies 336
macaroons, coconut 335
mackerel, peppered 103
madeleines, apple 345
mallets, tenderising steak 139
mandolins 11, 182
mangetouts
  hot and sour soup 45
  sweet chilli beef stir-fry 162
mangoes 210
  grilled chicken with mango salsa 122
  mango gratin with sabayon 71
  mango ice cream terrine 398
marbled cake 326
marbling ice cream 389
marinades
  for fish 78
  for meat 147
  for poultry 117
marinated olives 413
marmalade
  quick marmalade 417
  savoury marmalade 288
  Seville orange marmalade 407
Marsala, barbecued figs with 231
marzipan 331
  covering a cake with 331
mascarpone
  caramelised orange trifle 383
  cinnamon and nutmeg ice cream 396
  rum mascarpone 28
  toasted hazelnut meringue cake 73
mayonnaise 23
  crab cakes with mayonnaise 93
measuring equipment 11
meat 135–67, 447
  cooking 148–9
  freezing 437
  marinades 147
  roasting 150–1
  stock 34
  storing 449
  see also beef, lamb etc
meatballs, Italian 153
medallions, pork 144
Mediterranean chicken 125
Mediterranean kebabs 195
melon 212
  exotic fruit salad 222
melting chocolate 356, 445
meringues 58–60
  almond toffee meringues 381
  baked raspberry meringue pie 72
  iced lemon meringue 397
  pavlova 60
  toasted hazelnut meringue cake 73
mezzalunas 11
microwaves 441–5
milk
  fruity rice pudding 248
  hot chocolate 369
millefeuilles, berry 293
mince, freezing 437
mincing meat 139
minerals 446
mixed grain loaf 302
mixers 15
mixing bowls 11–12
mocha bread 314
monkfish
  seafood and lime kebabs 91
Moroccan spiced chicken kebabs 119
moulds, chocolate 358
mouli-légumes
  puréeing fruit 217
  puréeing soups 36
mousses
  quick salmon mousse 92
  white chocolate mousse 366
  white chocolate mousse cake 361
muesli bars 337
muffin tins 14
muffins, banana and pecan 328
mushrooms 175
  drying 438
  mixed mushroom cannelloni 270
  mixed mushroom frittata 64
  mushroom and aubergine tian 202
  mushroom and bean hotpot 253
  mushroom baskets 285
  prawn and lemon risotto 247
  roasted stuffed peppers 203
  shallot and mushroom sauce 18
  warm lentil and egg salad 65
mussels 86
  mussel and potato stew 100
  paella 238
mustard relish 414

N

nectarines
  marinated summer fruit 381
  spiced nectarines 223
noisettes of lamb 142
noodles
  chilli beef noodle salad 272
  cooking Asian-style noodles 263
  pork and noodle stir-fry 275
  quick chicken stir-fry 120
  Thai noodles with prawns 274
nori seaweed
  classic sushi rolls 239
nougat ice cream 393
nutrition 446–7
nuts 447
  mixed nut praline 374
  nutty chocolate truffles 368
  nutty fudge shortbread 343
  nutty toffee 373
  preparation 218–21
  spiced nuts 219
  see also almonds, walnuts etc

O

oats
  creamed choc-oat cookies 332
  muesli bars 337
  porridge 444
  sticky ginger flapjacks 346
octopus 89
offal, freezing 437
okra 175
olives
  black olive bread 311
  marinated olives 413
omelette, classic 56
one-pot spicy beef 163
onions 170
  chilli onions with goat's cheese 201
  onion sauce 19
  pickled onions 411
  savoury marmalade 288
oranges
  almond and orange torte 349
  baked orange custard 70
  caramelised orange tart 294
  caramelised orange trifle 383
  lamb with orange and mint 157
  lemon and orange carrots 196
  orange and bay turkey crown 130
  orange and chicken salad 118
  quick marmalade 417
  roast lamb with orange 161
  Seville orange marmalade 407
  simple orange sorbet 391
  winter coleslaw 190
oysters 87

P

paella 238
pak choi
  stir-fried prawns with cabbage 97
  tuna with coriander rice 94
pan-frying
  chicken 114
  eggs 55
  fish 79
  fruit 215
  meat and game 149
pancakes 61
  cinnamon pancakes 69
pancetta, sprouts and 197
panettone pudding 317
pans 13
papaya 211
  exotic fruit salad 222
parfait, pistachio 390
Parma ham
  stuffed chicken breasts 123
Parmesan crisps 46
parsley
  parsley sauce 19
  salsa verde 24
parsnips 181
  parsnip soup with cheese crisps 46
passion fruit 211
  lemon and passion fruit fool 226
pasta 259–75
  chilli Bolognese 268
  cooking 262
  fusilli with chilli and tomatoes 264
  herb and lemon soup 43
  making 260–1
  mixed mushroom cannelloni 270
  pasta with pesto and beans 265
  penne with smoked salmon 266
  quick and easy carbonara 267
  ravioli 261
  spinach and cheese lasagne 271
  stuffed pasta shells 269
pasta machines 260
pastries
  baklava 283
  berry millefeuilles 293
  goat's cheese parcels 286
  pear and cranberry strudel 292
  salmon, dill and potato pastries 287
  see also pies; tarts
pastry 277–97
  choux 282
  filling and topping 330–1
  filo 283
  puff 279
  rough puff 279
  shortcrust 278
  sweet shortcrust 278
pavlova 60
peaches
  brandied peaches 410
  peeling 208
  summer gratin 228
peanut butter
  all-in-one peanut cookies 332
pearl barley 240
pears 206
  drunken pears 230
  easy pear and toffee tarte tatin 296
  fruit kebabs with spiced pear dip 224
  pear and cranberry strudel 292
  rhubarb and pear crumble 232
peas 174
  pea and watercress soup 42
  smoked fish pie 102
pecan nuts
  banana and butterscotch loaf 352
  banana and pecan muffins 328
  the ultimate chocolate brownie 347
pectin 406
peeling vegetables 181
penne with smoked salmon 266
peppered mackerel 103
peppers 177
  lamb with orange and mint 157
  Mediterranean chicken 125
  one-pot spicy beef 163
  piperade 62
  roasted stuffed peppers 203
  Spanish fish stew 105
  sweet chilli beef stir-fry 162
  warm lentil and egg salad 65
pesto 21
  pasta with pesto and beans 265
pickles
  mixed dill pickle 424
  pickled onions 411
  sweet and sour figs 423
pie tins 14
pies 280–1
  baked raspberry meringue pie 72
  chicken and artichoke pie 290
  leek and ham galette 289
  plum and cardamom pie 295
  rustic blackberry and apple pie 229
  salmon and asparagus pie 66
  smoked fish pie 102
  see also pastries

pilau
spiced chicken pilau 246
spiced egg pilau 245
pineapple 210
caramelised pineapple 377
exotic fruit salad 222
pinenuts
baklava 283
pesto 21
piperade 62
piping
chocolate 358
sauces 31
pistachio nuts
baklava 283
Italian ice cream cake 400
pistachio parfait 390
pizzas 306
garlic cheese pizza 319
tuna melt pizza 318
plaice
fish and chips 101
plums
American-style plum cobbler 233
plum and cardamom pie 295
plum chutney 412, 420
poaching
eggs 54
fish 78
fruit 214
poultry 117
polenta 242
cheesy polenta with tomato sauce 249
warm cornbread 313
polypropylene chopping boards 10
pomegranate 211
pork
carving 151
Italian meatballs 153
pork and noodle stir-fry 275
pork in red wine sauce 152
pork with artichokes and beans 154
preparation 143–5
roasting 151
spicy pork and bean stew 254
porridge 444
pot barley 240
pot-roasting
meat and game 149
poultry 116
potatoes
chips 186
crushing 184
fish and chips 101
frying 186
mashing 184
mussel and potato stew 100
pea and watercress soup 42
potato and chorizo tortilla 56
roasting 189
salmon, dill and potato pastries 287
smoked fish pie 102
vichyssoise with spinach cream 41
pots and pans 13–14
potting preserves 405
poultry 107–33, 447
cooking 112–17
freezing 437
in microwave ovens 443
preparation 108–11
see also chicken, duck etc
poussins, barbecued marinated 127
praline, mixed nut 374
prawns 83
prawn and lemon risotto 247
seafood and lime kebabs 91
squash, lentil and prawn soup 49
stir-fried prawns with cabbage 97
Thai green shellfish curry 104
Thai noodles with prawns 274
preserves 403–25
bottled fruits 410
chutneys 412
fruit curds and cheeses 409
jams 406
jellies 408
marmalade 407
pickles 411
potting 405
preparing jars 404
refrigerator preserves 413
relishes 414
sauces 415
testing for a set 405
protein 446
prunes
fruity tea cake 326
guineafowl with prunes 128
lamb, prune and almond tagine 159
marinated duck with prunes 132
rabbit casserole with prunes 167
sticky ginger ring 353
puff pastry 279
pulses 447
purées
fruit 217
soups 36, 37

Q

quinces 206
quinoa 241

R

rabbit 147
rabbit casserole with prunes 167
rack of lamb 141
raisins
all-in-one peanut cookies 332
kugelhopf 316
raspberries
baked raspberry meringue pie 72
cranberry Christmas bombe 399
elderflower and fruit jelly 225
fruit vinegar 430
iced lemon meringue 397
iced raspberry soufflés 401
marinated summer fruit 381
raspberry coulis 29
ravioli 261
ready-meals 447
red cabbage
marinated duck with prunes 132
winter coleslaw 190
red wine gravy 18
redcurrants
strawberry and redcurrant jam 416
sugared redcurrants 399
refrigerator preserves 413
refrigerators 449
reheating food, in a microwave oven 442
relishes
mustard relish 414
sweetcorn relish 422
rhubarb
rhubarb and ginger chutney 421
rhubarb and pear crumble 232
rice 236–9
fruity rice pudding 248
paella 238
prawn and lemon risotto 247
risotto 237
salmon and coriander kedgeree 244
spiced chicken pilau 246
spiced egg pilau 245
spinach and rice soup 48
sushi 239
tuna with coriander rice 94
rice noodles 263
rich red wine gravy 18
rippling
ice cream 389
sauces 31
risotto 237
prawn and lemon risotto 247
roasting
chestnuts 220
chicken 112

fish 81
meat 150–1
spices 429
vegetables 189
roasting tins 14
rocket pesto 21
rolls 301
salt and pepper rolls 310
root vegetables 181
rough puff pastry 279
roulades
chocolate cherry roll 327
rum
rum mascarpone 28
rum sabayon 28
runner beans 174
freezing 436
rustic blackberry and apple pie 229

S

sabayon
mango gratin with sabayon 71
rum sabayon 28
safety
hygiene 448
microwave ovens 442
poultry 108
preserves 404
salad dressings 25
salads
chilli beef noodle salad 272
crispy duck salad 131
mixed leaf salad 191
orange and chicken salad 118
roasted root vegetable salad 193
roasted tomato bulgur salad 251
simple bean salad 252
summer vegetable salad 192
Tuscan bread salad 309
warm lentil and egg salad 65
winter coleslaw 190
salmon
dill salmon 95
quick salmon mousse 92
salmon and asparagus pie 66
salmon, dill and potato pastries 287
salmon laksa curry 273
see also smoked salmon
salsas
avocado 24
mango 122
salsa verde 24
salt 446
bread-making 300
flavoured salt 431
salt and pepper rolls 310
sandwich, steak 309
saucepans 13
saucer test, preserves 405
sauces 17–31
apple 22
béarnaise 20
béchamel 19
brandy butter 29
bread 19
butterscotch 27
caramel 372
cheese 19, 444
chilli 413
chocolate 27, 359
cranberry 22
decorative effects 30–1
dulce de leche 373
freezing 434
hollandaise 20
onion 19
parsley 19
pesto 21
raspberry coulis 29
rich red wine gravy 18
rum mascarpone 28
rum sabayon 28
shallot and mushroom 18
thick binding 19
tomato 21, 153, 415
tomato ketchup 415
ultimate barbecue sauce 425
white sauce 19
white wine gravy 18
sausages
chicken with chorizo and beans 255
freezing 437
potato and chorizo tortilla 56
roasted venison sausages 166
stuffed pasta shells 269
sauté pans 13
sautéing vegetables 185
savoury pudding 68
savoury sauces 18–21
scales 11
scallops 87
smoked salmon parcels 90
Thai green shellfish curry 104
scones 305
Scotch barley 240
scrambled eggs 54, 444
seafood and lime kebabs 91
searing fish 79
seasoning beef 138
seaweed
classic sushi rolls 239
seeds 447
separating eggs 52
Seville orange marmalade 407
shallots 170
braised lamb shanks 160
shallot and mushroom sauce 18
sharpening knives 10
shellfish and fish 75–105
buying 85
see also crab, prawns etc
shiitake mushrooms 175
shopping 448
shortbread, nutty fudge 343
shortcrust pastry 278
sieves, puréeing soups 36
silicone bakeware 14
skinning
chicken fillets 111
fish 77
smoked fish pie 102
smoked haddock
simple smoked haddock 96
smoked fish pie 102
smoked salmon
classic sushi rolls 239
penne with smoked salmon 266
salmon and coriander kedgeree 244
smoked salmon parcels 90
smoothies 217
soda bread 304
sorbets
frozen yogurt sorbet 395
simple orange sorbet 391
soufflés 57
cheese soufflé 57
iced raspberry soufflés 401
twice-baked soufflé 67
soups 36–49
cauliflower soup 47
chunky soups 37
garnishes 39
gazpacho with tortilla chips 40
herb and lemon soup 43
hot and sour soup 45
parsnip soup with cheese crisps 46
pea and watercress soup 42
puréeing 36, 37
spinach and rice soup 48
spring vegetable broth 44
squash, lentil and prawn soup 49
thickening 38
vichyssoise with spinach cream 41
sourdough 303
spaghetti
chilli Bolognese 268
Spanish fish stew 105
spatchcocking poultry 109

spatulas 12
spiced chicken pilau 246
spiced clementines in brandy 419
spiced egg pilau 245
spiced nectarines 223
spiced nuts 219
spiced vinegar 430
spices
  preparation 429
  roasting 429
  see also cinnamon; cumin
spicy ginger ice cream 392
spicy griddled flatbread 304
spicy pork and bean stew 254
spicy salt 431
spinach
  foil-baked fish 98
  goat's cheese parcels 286
  spinach and cheese lasagne 271
  spinach and rice soup 48
  spinach with tomatoes 198
  vichyssoise with spinach cream 41
sponge cakes
  creamed sponges 324
  testing 324
  whisked Genoese sponge 325
sponge pudding, syrup 443
spoons 12
  measuring spoons 11
spring vegetable broth 44
sprouting beans 243
sprouts and pancetta 197
spun sugar 375
squash 179
  foil-baked fish 98
  roasted root vegetable salad 193
  roasting 189
  squash, lentil and prawn soup 49
squid 88
steak
  freezing 437
  steak sandwich 309
  tenderising 139
steaming
  blanching vegetables 436
  fish 78
  poultry 117
  vegetables 183
sterilising jars 404, 405
stewing
  fruit 214
  vegetables 187
  see also casseroles and stews
stick blenders, puréeing soups 36
sticky banoffee pies 382
sticky ginger flapjacks 346
sticky ginger ring 353
sticky toffee puddings 384
stir-frying
  chicken 114
  fish 80
  meat and game 148
  vegetables 185
stocks 33–5
  chicken 34
  concentrating 434
  degreasing 35
  fish 35
  freezing 434
  frozen stock cubes 434
  meat 34
  vegetable 34
stone fruits, preparation 208
storecupboards 448
storing food 448–9
  see also freezing; preserves
strawberries
  berry millefeuilles 293
  hulling 209
  strawberry and redcurrant jam 416
  strawberry brûlée 378
  strawberry compote 227
  summer gratin 228
strudel, pear and cranberry 292
stuffings
  cranberry and lemon 113
  stuffing pork chops 144
sugar 371–85
  dulce de leche 373
  flavoured sugars 431
  freezing fruit 435
  spun sugar 375
  sugar syrup 375
  see also caramel; toffee
sultanas
  apples with butterscotch sauce 385
  carrot tray bake 251
  lemon cheesecake 329
summer couscous 250
summer gratin 228
summer jam 406
summer vegetable salad 192
sushi 239
sweet and sour figs 423
sweet cherry bread 315
sweet mocha bread 314
sweet sauces 26–9
sweet shortcrust pastry 278
sweetcorn 173
  freezing 436
  sweetcorn relish 422
Swiss roll tins, lining 323
syrup
  freezing fruit 435
  sugar syrup 375
  syrup sponge pudding 443

T

tagine, lamb, prune and almond 159
tagliatelle
  quick and easy carbonara 267
tarragon chicken with fennel 126
tarts 280
  baked apple and lemon tartlets 297
  Camembert and tomato tarts 284
  caramelised orange tart 294
  chocolate amaretti tart 362
  cinnamon custard tart 291
  easy pear and toffee tarte tatin 296
  mushroom baskets 285
  winter roasted vegetable tart 288
  see also pastries; pies
teabreads
  banana and butterscotch loaf 352
  kugelhopf 316
  sweet cherry bread 315
  sweet mocha bread 314
tempura, mixed vegetable 199
tenderising steak 139
tenderloin, pork 143
terrine, mango ice cream 398
Thai green shellfish curry 104
Thai noodles with prawns 274
Thai vegetable curry 200
thawing, in microwaves 442
thermometers, testing preserves 405
thickening soups 38
tins 14
  lining cake tins 322–3
  lining with pastry 280
toffee 373
  almond toffee meringues 381
  easy pear and toffee tarte tatin 296
  filling biscuits 338
  sticky banoffee pies 382
  sticky toffee puddings 384
  toffee cheesecake 380
tomatoes 176
  braised lamb shanks 160
  Camembert and tomato tarts 284
  cheesy polenta with tomato sauce 249
  chilli Bolognese 268
  creamy baked eggs 63
  drying 439
  fusilli with chilli and tomatoes 264
  gazpacho with tortilla chips 40
  Greek lamb and feta layer 158
  mushroom and bean hotpot 253

one-pot spicy beef 163
piperade 62
roasted tomato bulgur salad 251
simple tomato sauce 21
spicy pork and bean stew 254
spinach with tomatoes 198
sun-dried tomato pesto 21
tomato chutney 412
tomato ketchup 415
tomato sauce 153, 415
the ultimate barbecue sauce 425
tongs 12
tortilla, potato and chorizo 56
tortilla chips, gazpacho with 40
tortillas
simple chicken wrap 308
traybakes 337
carrot tray bake 251
muesli bars 337
nutty fudge shortbread 343
see also cakes
trifle, caramelised orange 383
trimming meat 137–8
truffles, nutty chocolate 368
trussing poultry 108
tuna
tuna melt pizza 318
tuna with coriander rice 94
turkey
hot and sour soup 45
orange and bay turkey crown 130
turkey and broccoli stir-fry 129
Tuscan bread salad 309
tying joints 138

U

ultimate barbecue sauce 425
ultimate chocolate brownie 347
utensils 10–12

V

vanilla
rolled vanilla biscuits 333
vanilla cupcakes 328
vanilla custard 26
vanilla fudge 374
vanilla ice cream 388
vanilla sugar 431
vegan diet 447
vegetables 169–203, 447
cooking 183–9
crisps 186
freezing 436
Mediterranean kebabs 195
in microwave ovens 443
mixed dill pickle 424
mixed vegetable tempura 199
mushroom and aubergine tian 202
mustard relish 414
peeling 181
pork and noodle stir-fry 275
preparation 170–82
simple vegetable soup 36
spring vegetable broth 44
stock 34
storing 449
summer couscous 250
Thai vegetable curry 200
winter roasted vegetable tart 288
see also salads and potatoes, tomatoes etc
vegetarian diet 447
venison sausages, roasted 166
vichyssoise with spinach cream 41
Viennese fingers 336
vinegars
fruit vinegar 430
herb vinegar 430
spiced vinegar 430
vitamins 446

W

wafers, chocolate 357
walnuts
chocolate-chunk bread pudding 364
nutty fudge shortbread 343
walnut and garlic bread 312
water, drinking 446, 447
watercress
mixed leaf salad 191
pea and watercress soup 42
wheat grain 241
wheat noodles 263
whisked Genoese sponge 325
whisking eggs 52
white chocolate mousse 366
white chocolate mousse cake 361
white farmhouse loaf 300
white sauce 19
white wine gravy 18
wild rice
hot and sour soup 45
wine
barbecued figs with Marsala 231
drunken pears 230
pork in red wine sauce 152
rich red wine gravy 18
white wine gravy 18
winter coleslaw 190
winter roasted vegetable tart 288
wooden chopping boards 10
wrap, simple chicken 308

Y

yeast, bread-making 300
yogurt
frozen yogurt sorbet 395
Greek lamb and feta layer 158
lemon and passion fruit fool 226
strawberry brûlée 378

Z

zesting citrus fruits 207